Arranging Grief

SEXUAL CULTURES: New Directions from the Center for Lesbian and Gay Studies
General Editors: José Esteban Muñoz and Ann Pellegrini

Times Square Red, Times Square Blue
Samuel R. Delany

Private Affairs: Critical Ventures in the Culture of Social Relations
Phillip Brian Harper

In Your Face: 9 Sexual Studies
Mandy Merck

Tropics of Desire: Interventions from Queer Latino America
José Quiroga

Murdering Masculinities: Fantasies of Gender and Violence in the American Crime Novel
Greg Forter

Our Monica, Ourselves: The Clinton Affair and the National Interest
Edited by Lauren Berlant and Lisa Duggan

Black Gay Man: Essays
Robert Reid-Pharr   *Foreword by Samuel R. Delany*

Passing: Identity and Interpretation in Sexuality, Race, and Religion
Edited by María Carla Sánchez and Linda Schlossberg

The Explanation for Everything: Essays on Sexual Subjectivity
Paul Morrison

The Queerest Art: Essays on Lesbian and Gay Theater
Edited by Alisa Solomon and Framji Minwalla

Queer Globalizations: Citizenship and the Afterlife of Colonialism
Edited by Arnaldo Cruz-Malavé and Martin F. Manalansan IV

Queer Latinidad: Identity Practices, Discursive Spaces
Juana María Rodríguez

Love the Sin: Sexual Regulation and the Limits of Religious Tolerance
Janet R. Jakobsen and Ann Pellegrini

Boricua Pop: Puerto Ricans and the Latinization of American Culture
Frances Negrón-Muntaner

Manning the Race: Reforming Black Men in the Jim Crow Era
Marlon B. Ross

Why I Hate Abercrombie & Fitch: Essays on Race and Sexuality
Dwight A. McBride

In a Queer Time and Place: Transgender Bodies, Subcultural Lives
Judith Halberstam

God Hates Fags: The Rhetorics of Religious Violence
Michael Cobb

Once You Go Black: Choice, Desire, and the Black American Intellectual
Robert Reid-Pharr

The Latino Body: Crisis Identities in American Literary and Cultural Memory
Lázaro Lima

Arranging Grief: Sacred Time and the Body in Nineteenth-Century America
Dana Luciano

Dana Luciano

Arranging Grief

Sacred Time and the Body in
Nineteenth-Century America

NEW YORK UNIVERSITY PRESS   New York and London

NEW YORK UNIVERSITY PRESS
New York and London
www.nyupress.org

Library of Congress Cataloging-in-Publication Data
Luciano, Dana.
Arranging grief : sacred time and the body in nineteenth-century
America / Dana Luciano.
p. cm.
Includes bibliographical references and index.
ISBN-13: 978-0-8147-5222-7 (cloth : acid-free paper)
ISBN-10: 0-8147-5222-5 (cloth : acid-free paper)
ISBN-13: 978-0-8147-5223-4 (pbk. : acid-free paper)
ISBN-10: 0-8147-5223-3 (pbk. : acid-free paper)
1. American literature—19th century—History and criticism. 2. Grief
in literature. 3. Time in literature. 4. Sentimentalism in literature.
5. Grief—Philosophy. 6. Grief—Political aspects.   I. Title.
PS217.G75L83 2007
810.9'353—dc22   2007018424

for Jenn

Contents

Acknowledgments

For a long time now, I've looked forward to this ritual of looking backward; of the many pleasures that writing this book generated, the opportunity to reflect on my good fortune in having known so many wise, generous, and warm people is matchless. To begin with, I thank Ellen Rooney, Neil Lazarus, and the late Roger Henkle for their early inspiration and encouragement while I was at Brown; without them, I'd likely be doing something else right now. At Cornell, outstanding teachers such as Lois Brown, Debra Fried, Biddy Martin, Shirley Samuels, Mark Seltzer, and Michael Warner provided models of engaged scholarship and pedagogy that I hope, one day, to live up to. Lauren Berlant taught me more than I can even now realize; her passion, dedication, and brilliance continue to remind me why I went into this field in the first place. My fellow graduate students inspired me, challenged me, and helped keep me (mostly) sane during the long Ithaca winters; particular thanks to Katherine Biers, Pete Coviello, Jody Greene, Michael Hames-García, Trevor Hope, Chris Nealon, Amy Ongiri, Bethany Schneider, Pam Thurschwell, and the many habitués of the House of Joy.

At Hamilton College, the mentorship and guidance offered by Nathaniel Strout, Catherine Gunther Kodat, Lydia Hammesly, and Margie Thickstun made all the difference during my first years as a new professor. My wonderful colleagues, including Danielle DeMuth, Shoshana Keller, Kyoko Omori, Kirk Pillow, Kamila Shamsie, Jodi Shorb, Mitchell Stevens, Ram Subramanian, and Steve Yao, made leaving Clinton a great difficulty. I especially want to thank Nancy Sorkin Rabinowitz and Peter Rabinowitz; I can't imagine two better colleagues, more generous neighbors, and more steadfast friends. At Georgetown, I am indebted to Gay Cima, Pamela Fox, Lori Merish, and Penn Szittya for their mentorship and to Jennifer Natalya Fink, Leona Fisher,

Patrick O'Malley, Ricardo Ortíz, Kathy Temple, and Kelly Wickham-Crowley for their fellowship and good counsel. Thanks also to Carole Sargent for her wise advice and to Raymond Tolentino for crucial research assistance. Financial support for this project was provided by Georgetown University, Hamilton College, and the Tanner Humanities Center at the University of Utah, for which I am very grateful. The wonderful staff at the American Antiquarian Society helped greatly with the early research on this book. Thanks to the *Arizona Quarterly*, Ashgate Press, and the *Western Humanities Review* for permission to reprint those parts of the manuscript that they have previously published. At New York University Press, I thank Eric Zinner, Ann Pellegrini, and José Muñoz for their enthusiasm for and guidance on this project, and Emily Park for her dedicated support.

For readings and conversations that helped immeasurably as I worked through the ideas in this book, many thanks to Katherine Biers, Erica Bsumek, Christopher Castiglia, Vincent Cheng, Katie Coles, Glenn Hendler, Catherine Gunther Kodat, Barry Maxwell, Vincent Odamtten, Nancy Sorkin Rabinowitz, Peter Rabinowitz, Maeera Schreiber, Kathryn Bond Stockton, Pamela Thurschwell, Barry Weller, and my anonymous press and journal readers. Rob Hardies's willingness to talk through matters of faith and history has been, well, a godsend. Enormous appreciation is due to Elizabeth Freeman for her incredible intellectual and professional generosity and sharp editorial advice, as well as to Chris Nealon for his thoughtful readings and skilled reshapings of vital sections of the project. Pete Coviello's critical acuity is matched only by his *joie de vivre,* and I am fortunate to have both in my life. And for forms of support more difficult to localize, but no less valuable over the years, I especially want to thank Micah Altman, J. D. Biersdorfer, Dave Cutler, Jody Greene, Jenny Nelson, Kathryn Pope, and Henry Rubin; you guys rule.

To my family—my mother, Maureen; my brother, Paul; my father, Paul; his wife, Bernadette; my sister, Lia; my aunt, Marie; and my in-laws, June and Howard—many, many, many hugs of gratitude. My grandparents, Lillian Mancuso Luciano and Peter Luciano, both died as I was writing this book; somewhere within the enormous sadness that left behind is the wish that they could have seen it. To Jennifer Sturm, for her unwavering supportiveness, her infinite patience with this project, her cool-headed crisis management skills, and her sense of humor—and also for making my life better than I ever thought it could be—a million thank-yous, with all my love.

Introduction

Tracking the Tear

Most everyone who lived through the Seventies in the United States can recollect the image of the solitary crying Indian from the Keep America Beautiful public-service announcement that debuted on Earth Day in 1971. In the sixty-second spot, the lonely figure, played by longtime screen Indian "Iron Eyes" Cody, silently articulates a call to mourn the loss of the natural order. As he paddles a canoe through a stream and disembarks to stride across the landscape, the camera's lens captures the debris of modern life—industrial pollution and consumer waste—that mars this idyllic picture. Underscoring the untimeliness of this image, a disembodied male announcer intones, "Some people have a deep and abiding respect for the natural beauty that was once this country. . . . And some people don't." The violent history condensed behind this contrast is suggested in the image track, as the word "don't" coincides with the Indian's arrival at the side of a busy highway, where a white hand tosses a bag of trash from the window of a speeding car. As the bag bursts open at the Indian's feet, the camera zooms in to reveal the effect of this confrontation with the waste of a hurried modernity: a single tear slowly making its way down his solemn face, while the voice-over urges Americans to change this state of affairs.

The conviction that attention to feeling can alter the flow of time marks this PSA as an instance of a distinctively modern affective chronometry: the deployment of the feeling body as the index of a temporality apart from the linear paradigm of "progress."[1] In the slow movement of the Indian's tear, the PSA at once traces an overlooked history and opens another possibility, as it cries out to the "Americans" who inhabit this present to work together toward a different future. The tear, in effect, *recollects* the movements of the human heart that underlie and authorize post-Enlightenment conceptions of the social bond, demanding a change in the pace of history. This conceptualization of human time according to the foundational truth of emotional

1

attachment alters the body's status as a time-piece, rendering it the measure less of mortality than of memory. The corporeal response to the affective residue of the vanished past in the present tense, what we know as grief, permits the feeling body, and particularly the mournful body, to assess the ongoing significance of the past in a culture speeding ever more rapidly toward the attainment of its historical "destiny."

The emotional environment in which the Keep America Beautiful PSA does its work has a long and rich history, involving decisive transformations in both the status of the feeling body and the order of time. By the nineteenth century, grief had become something to be cherished rather than shunned. No longer simply a sign of disobedience to the divine will, the pain of grief was now the body's spontaneous and natural testimony to the importance of interpersonal attachment; indeed, its persistence helped keep alive attachment even in the absence of the beloved object. Time, on the other hand, was not so easy to retain. The radical reorganization that we understand as the advent of modernity constructed a new vision of time as linear, ordered, progressive, and teleological.[2] Nineteenth-century developments in historiography supported this sense of time's essential productivity by dispersing it over the past, devising accounts of humanity's movement through time that stressed the rise of civilizations and the growth of knowledge.[3] Yet exhilarating as this forward-moving vision of humanity's development might seem, it was nevertheless accompanied by no little anxiety about the way the new time-consciousness might situate the human as time's prey, the expiatory sacrifice of modernity.[4] The pronounced nineteenth-century attention to grief and mourning, I contend, responds to anxiety over the new shape of time by insisting that emotional attachment had its own pace—a slower and essentially nonlinear relation to the value of human existence that defended it against the increasingly rapid pace of progress by providing avenues of return to the sacred truths that both preceded and exceeded history as such. Grief constituted one of the body's ways of acknowledging the objective status of linear time, which generated its occasions; yet the enticements associated with what nineteenth-century mourning manuals referred to as the "luxury of grief" in this period offered, if not a way of stopping time, a means of altering the shape and textures of its flow. Grief's pain, then, appeared as tolerable, even as desirable, in the face of a new order of time frequently described as mechanical and impersonal, precisely because the time of grief—the slow time of deep feeling—could be experienced (and thus embraced) as personal, human, intimate.

This is the pivot around which *Arranging Grief* turns: the kinds of time to which mournfulness offered access. The cultural plotting of grief in nineteenth-century America furnishes a distinctive insight into the nineteenth-century temporal imaginary, since grief at once underwrote the social arrangements that supported its standard chronologies and sponsored other ways of advancing history. Accordingly, this book examines the regulatory arrangements (social, religious, familial, and psychological) that worked to keep grief faithful to both the sacred time of origins and the recognized ends of mourning. Yet it emphasizes, as well, the tensions that permitted grief to sketch out alterations to those arrangements—tensions that, as I show, accumulated around the newly diachronic status of "nature" and the multiple temporalities consequently assigned to the body.

The expanding cultural significance of grief in the West from the eighteenth century onward links it to what Michel Foucault identifies, at the end of the first volume of the *History of Sexuality,* as the fundamentally historical shift announcing the arrival of modernity: the supplementation of the traditionally "reductive" power of death by the productive power he associates with the maximization of "life."[5] This development tends, however, to be obscured by the chronology of decline plotted in the thanato-historiography put forth by the Ariès school. The French historian Phillipe Ariès describes the newly marked attentiveness to mourning in this period as a transformative stage in the centuries-long *displacement* of death from the center of communal life to the margins of modern social consciousness. He asserts that the embrace of mourning that emerged in the eighteenth century and dominated the nineteenth was a decisive stage in this displacement, as it moved the consciousness of death from the self to the other: "Henceforth . . . the death which is feared is no longer so much the death of the self as the death of another, *la mort de toi,* thy death."[6] As the penultimate stage in the displacement of death, nineteenth-century mournfulness prepares the way, in this account, for the era of "denied" or forbidden death that begins with the twentieth century.[7] Yet although Ariès's recognition of the new emphasis on the other's death in the nineteenth century has been profoundly important for scholarship on the culture of sentiment, his reading of the part played by the emergent culture of mourning in the modern *denial* of death, compounded with the sermonic tone of much of this work, recalls Foucault's description of the repressive hypothesis.[8] For Foucault, the insistence on reading the history of modernity through the lens of repression—on arguing, in effect, that the "progress" of modernity has entailed the loss of a healthier and more honest prior relationship to matters of the body—tends to replicate, rather than to expose, modern technologies of power/knowledge. From this perspective, we can recognize the way the displacement/denial account itself echoes the melancholy longing that characterized the nineteenth-century embrace of mourning; indeed, even in the nineteenth century, consolation literature depicted mourning as a deeply meaningful practice that was vulnerable to erasure by the advancement of history, prefiguring the story that twentieth-century historiographers would tell about the displacement of death by modernity. Much Americanist work that remains faithful to Ariès's grand narrative of thanato-history has further reduced the complexity of nineteenth-century mourning practices by minimizing its examination of cultural approaches to bereavement outside that of the Anglo-American middle class—an omission that prevents attention to the way "othered" forms of bereavement (particularly those ascribed to Native and African Americans) were positioned as "abnormalities" that structured nineteenth-century notions of normative mourning.[9] In this sense, the displacement/denial account is more a symptom than an explanation of modern mourning.[10]

Scholars influenced by Foucauldian thought have challenged the tendency to classify examples of nineteenth-century mourning culture as mere moments in a larger history of decline. This reframing, exemplified in historical work such as Karen Halttunen's important study of the role that bereavement etiquette played in the elaboration of American middle-class identity, attends more closely to the profound productivity of mourning. The social rituals surrounding mourning, as Halttunen shows, provided the middle-class subject with an opportunity to display both an emotionally sensitive interior and a suitably restrained disposition.[11] Insofar as those qualities generate a sense of middle-class belonging, careful management of grief becomes, in effect, the affective component of the Protestant work ethic: an ability to marshal the energies of the body in a way that demonstrates one's worthiness.[12] For this reason, grief could not be squandered; it must, rather, be judiciously circulated and, at the same time, carefully treasured up. The requirement of self-restraint did not, however, mean that the genteel mourner was to abandon sorrow for the dead. She was, instead, expected to engage in continued spells of weeping and sighing, though only in private. The need to maintain this image of self-governed sensitivity also meant that grief itself could not be quickly surrendered: rather, it would *remain*, becoming what Edgar Allan Poe describes as "that sorrow which the living love to cherish for the dead."[13] The cherishing of sorrow differed markedly from the Puritan ethic that dominated American mourning until the mid-eighteenth century. That system, as Mitchell Breitwieser writes, encouraged a "manly constancy or Christian stoicism that measures grief, that is, confines or delimits grief to a defined interval and a well-bounded area in the terrain of resolve."[14] This does not mean, as Breitwieser explains, that mourning was forbidden, but that the "constant" Christian sought "immediately to measure mourning" and, by knowing in advance what the experience would be and mean, to subdue all untoward and dangerous indulgence in feeling—"womanish . . . wayling and shricking"—while adhering as closely as possible to precept.[15] The tenderness toward prolonged sorrow that was not only permitted but positively encouraged in the nineteenth century might seem, at first glance, simply a de-repressive move, a loosening of restraint on "natural" feeling. Yet the contrast in the two styles may be more precisely understood as emerging from differing valuations of the "nature" to which grief was linked. Whereas the Puritan assessment of nature placed it, as Breitwieser observes, "beyond the pale," the site of the chaos opposed to the uprightness of the elect, the comprehension of nature that informed the nineteenth-century culture of mourning was, rather, temporal: "nature" indexed an Enlightenment account of (positive) origins, overlaid by a Romantic nostalgia for a receding past. The preservation of sorrow permitted the subject to maintain a constant connection to these profoundly humanizing moments in time.

Exceptional Times

These transformations in the conception of nature—not only from malevolence to benevolence but also from space to time—help to point us toward the nineteenth-century apprehension of the grieving body as an instrument of affective time-keeping. But to understand how feeling helped the modernizing West clock its own progress, we must first trace some contemporary developments in the history of time. Most histories of the modernization of time track this process through the development and social installation of the machinery that emerged to support it: the standardized clocks, railroad schedules, and other means of measurement and order that bespoke time as objectively given, concrete, measurable, orderly, and ultimately productive.[16] The development of what E. P. Thompson refers to as time-orientation, which, following Weber, he links to the rise of capitalism, was supplemented by the discipline of history, which dispersed the growing insistence on time's essential productivity over the past, crafting accounts of humanity's movement through time that stressed the rise of civilizations and the growth of knowledge, and thus allowing for the collection and distribution of the gains enabled by this newly rational time-sense.[17] *Arranging Grief,* however, concerns itself with an alternate mechanism for the collection of time: the feeling body. As an index of the depth of feeling, grief was aligned with a sensibility that sought to provide time with a "human" dimension, one that would be collective rather than productive, repetitive rather than linear, reflective rather than forward-moving. As a newly rational and predominantly linear understanding of time came to dominate the West, the time of feeling, deliberately aligned with the authority of the spiritual and natural worlds, was embraced as a mode of compensation for, and, to some extent, of resistance to, the perceived mechanization of society.[18]

We can begin to comprehend the stakes of this resistance by considering Michael O'Malley's assessment, in his study *Keeping Watch: A History of American Time,* of the 1840s Sabbatarian movement. Sabbatarians sought to protect Sundays, by law, from the encroachments of industry. As O'Malley points out, the Sabbatarians were not wholly opposed to the profit-oriented rationalization of time; they simply "hoped, by setting Sundays aside from the industrial hue and cry, to prevent industrial time from overcoming the 'natural time' of the soul."[19] In effect, then, the Sabbatarian movement sought not to eradicate but to balance the new rationalization of time by making space within the week for continued fidelity to the forms of temporal authority it posited as *prior* to the modern order of things: nature's time and God's time.[20] The nineteenth century's elaborate arrangements of grief point us toward a time-space comparable to the Sabbath—one *set aside* for the renewal of foundational priorities, one that operated to conserve the affective dimension of the human. Grief's time moved, like Sundays, at a different pace from ordinary time: it was slower, more capacious, almost spatialized, enabling contradictory feelings (pain and pleasure) to be indulged at once and without traumatic contradiction. Just as Sundays were kept apart as a time of religious devotion, the time of grief perpetuated a devotion to the natural affections, opening the heart to the preservation of ties essential to maintaining an affirmative humanness. If grief was something that people "love[d] to cherish," that was because they had come to cherish, even to sacralize, love itself. The "natural" consequence of the newly exalted human capacity for interpersonal attachment, grief recalled, through the pain of loss, the timeless truths that supported and stabilized the historical development of a humanity founded in fellow-feeling. Love, in this sense, was not only chronologically prior to grief—since one did not mourn what one did not first love—but also ontologically prior to the nineteenth-century subject, located at and as its origin. In this light, the altered flow of time experienced by the mourner could be (and, I argue, was) understood as a version of sacred time, the regenerative mode that transcended ordinary time in a ritual revisiting of origins.[21]

The sense of the sacred to which I here refer should not be tied exclusively (in fact, not even primarily) to religion. On the contrary, as Talal Asad asserts, "there is nothing essentially religious, nor any universal essence that defines 'sacred language' or 'sacred experience.' "[22] The term "sacred" historically designates "individual things, persons, and occasions that were set apart and entitled to veneration," but there has been no singular mode of setting-apart or style of worship that characterizes its diverse uses.[23] Asad observes, in fact, that the consolidation of the sacred by anthropologists and theologians into a concept that registered an essentially transcendent force linked to a universalized notion of religious experience did not take place until the late nineteenth century, a development that, he speculates, may be linked to the European world's construction of Enlightenment against and through its encounters with non-European others. (A similar spatiotemporal confrontation, as I will show in this study, marks the middle-class embrace of grief in this period.) What I am outlining as grief's affiliation with sacred time does not, then, designate a belief that registers solely in the realm of religion. Rather, grief was positioned as connecting to conceptions of origins that ranged from a Romantic cosmogony, emphasizing the perpetual reassurance of a benevolent nature, to monumental nationalism, lauding the venerated and everlasting principles on behalf of which nations are founded, to familial and individual narratives that celebrated the affections as testimony to an originary human bondedness or, alternately, appealed to the fantasmatic before-time of the infantile. Origin, here, is not a synonym for beginning; whereas the latter precipitates something into the flow of time, the former rises above linear time and can be ritually perpetuated through it but never dissolved into it.[24] The cultural embrace of grief that I consider in this study spanned these varying accounts of origin, bringing them into alignment—though not, as I will show, always rendering them fully compatible. Countering Foucault's sweeping assertion that "time . . .

was detached from the sacred in the nineteenth century," then, I am proposing not simply that this detachment must be understood as taking place gradually and unevenly but also that it may more usefully be understood as a proliferation of modes of "sacred time," many of which we have come to locate within ostensibly secular frameworks.[25]

At the same time, it is also important not to omit the part played by Christianity in a mourning culture whose appeal, Halttunen notes, was increasingly genteel and self-consciously Euro-American. Grief, effect and sign of a human nature that was to be respected, even venerated, for its capacity to form deep bonds to others, was additionally depicted as an element of a divine plan that, when read and engaged properly, would turn the subject (and, in some deployments, the nation) toward redemption. That turn involved a redirection and partial retemporalization of attachment, supplanting the memory of past connection with assurance of a future reunion. The ability of nineteenth-century American mourning culture to integrate the visions of origins cited above in a single, socially stabilizing formation depended, in large part, on this redirection, which constructed a homology between the eternal present of sacred time and the Christian afterlife while insisting that the former must be embraced only as the means to the latter—and hence, that anything that might tend to counter the individual's progress toward future reward must be rejected. The conjunction of religious, national, affective-natural, and familial-sentimental formations of the sacred under the sign of enlightened Christian civilization was both a powerful configuration and a volatile one; although by the early nineteenth century, grief was accepted as the effect of a human nature that was generally valorized rather than despised, the precise role of emotion and experience in faith, along with disagreements over the temporality of conversion, remained live questions, at the center of theological debate and doctrinal difference. Works intended for the new mass market for consolation literature could, nevertheless, present themselves as addressed to all Christians across denominational and regional differences. Part of that capacity comes from what Tracy Fessenden recognizes as the ability of the adjective "Christian" "to indicate the specific concerns of [the white middle] class," even though Christianity was by no means limited to that class.[26] This configuration of "Christian," that is, stood in for those that understood themselves as the leaders and guardians of the nation's steady progress toward a spiritual and social future, even while it posed its appeal as universal. Though Christianity is not *essentially* characterized by either an embrace of directed, linear-progressive time or the maintenance of a particular social hierarchy, the latter was, in the nineteenth century, distinctly dependent on an ability to affirm, across denominational and doctrinal divisions, degrees of fidelity to the former.[27]

It is this assumption of directedness, and the resultant power to direct, that underlies what Asad identifies as the prophetic language that characterizes American political culture, which predicates the promise of freedom on a definition of the human that inscribes an exclusionary origin: those from whom the founders morally distinguish and narratively separate themselves, particularly the English tyrant, Amerindian pagan, and African slave. This exclusion, Asad comments, permits the nation to present a concept of the fully human, who is guaranteed freedom, without ideological self-contradiction: what we can grasp as the posited inhumanity of the tyrant, prehumanity of the Indian, and subhumanity of the slave permitted their exclusion from this category. (Asad does not address gender in his analysis, though, as we will see, gender further complicates this narrative by introducing temporal divisions within registers of the human.) Crucially, the foundational exclusions Asad identifies are based on distinct temporal configurations: inhumanness may change over time and become humanized—a possibility on which liberal-sentimental culture wagered the whole of its political potency—but the pre- and subhuman remain in permanent suspension before or below the community of free citizens. The issue here, moreover, is not one of the specifically religious origin of this national fantasy; Asad observes that nations founded on the notion of natural rights nevertheless also manage to maintain dehumanizing exclusions insofar as they base their notion of sacred life on an abstract or presocial conceptualization of "the human."[28] Rather, as we can conclude, the possibility of directedness, of cumulative movement through time synchronous with the dominant timeframe of a given social and historical context, is tied not simply to inclusion within the space of community but, more precisely, to the temporal force associated with conceptions of origin.

Asad's reflections help point the way toward a consideration of what, extending the temporal dimension of Foucault's argument in *The History of Sexuality*, I call chronobiopolitics, or the sexual arrangement of the time of life. Before outlining this configuration, however, I want to briefly address Giorgio Agamben's highly suggestive, but problematic, reconsideration of biopolitics by way of the "state of exception"—that which is included in politics by virtue of its categorical exclusion.[29] Agamben's exploration of the sacred—which he posits as originally a juridical, not religious, category—returns to Classical thought via the figure of the *homo sacer,* who may be killed with impunity but may not be used in rituals of sacrifice, and whom Agamben links with bare life. This mode of life—which is not directly continuous with "nature" but, rather, founds the social by virtue of being thrown back from it in a suspension of the law—is the life, he charges, with which biopolitics is concerned, and hence all politics is biopolitical. Agamben positions his analysis as a "correction or completion" of Foucault's emphasis, in the first volume of the *History of Sexuality,* on the emergence of biopolitics as specifically a technology of modernity; what is distinct about modernity for Agamben, rather, is that we have all become, in some sense, sacred: "modern democracy does not abolish sacred life but rather shatters it and disseminates it into every individual body, making it into what is at stake in political conflict."[30] This provocative argument has, however, the effect of suspending time both within and around Agamben's account of the state of exception, so that it is difficult to discern how one might begin to specify the historically selective narrativization of multiple exceptions through varying accounts of origin, such as those in Asad's discussion of the American context.[31] Foucault, conversely, facilitates a more precise assessment, in part by asserting that biopolitics, as the corporeal regulation of populations, is fundamentally connected with but not identical to an anatomo-politics concerned with the arrangement and productivity of the human body; both technologies are conjoined in the deployment of sexuality under the rubric of a biopower that operates to "invest life through and through."[32] The framework Foucault begins to develop in this volume identifies biopower as a *spatiotemporal* phenomenon; it incorporates the production of "life" according to a number of temporalities, some of which are contained within given narratives of directedness and reproduction while others diffuse themselves across the social field in less predictable ways.[33] The human body, in this light, cannot be temporalized in relation to (its) death alone; rather, it becomes implicated in a proliferation of temporalities dominated by, but not limited to, the linear, accumulative time of development, the cyclical time of domestic life, the sacred timelessness of the originary bond and of the eternal reward toward which the faithful subject progressed; or, beyond these norms, the wayward time of perversity, the nonprogressive time of pure sensation, et cetera. These were ordered, on the national level, through a dual appeal to stability and progress, though the nationally conceived mapping of time could also give way to a selectively transnational sense of modernity, a sense of synchronicity across borders, as manifested in appeals to refined Euro-American sensibilities or certain articulations of "Christian" (against, say, the heathen or primitive).[34]

Both these appeals, as we will see in chapter 1, were central to the middle-class language of mourning. Indeed, the sustained cultural attention devoted to grief in this period formed a crucial part of the diachronic deployment of life over time that came to dominate discourses of sexuality—indicating that feeling is not simply *analogous* to what Foucault identifies as sexuality but constitutes a crucial dimension of the *dispositif* of sexuality itself: the modern intensification of the body, its energies, and its meanings. As Foucault points out, the deployment of sexuality does not encompass only those behaviors and typologies we can grasp as "obviously" sex-related; it addresses, rather, the forms taken by "power in its grip on bodies and their materiality, their forces, energies, sensations and pleasures."[35] The coupling of the feeling body to history through the incitement to grief is, I argue, precisely the sort of linkage that the historian of sexuality who understands the category of "sex" as speculative rather than given ought to pursue; after all, that coupling constituted a remarkably productive development, insofar as it supplied a source of knowledge about the subject that both shaped the understanding of "natural" relations between self and others and provided a means of sorting different sectors of the population in terms of emotional behavior. Grief, then, is not merely "like" sex, or linked to sexuality only at the level of the unconscious—it is central to the historical apparatus of sexuality. Of course, Foucault himself was not free of the habit of privileging more "obvious" forms of sex in the study of sexuality. In the first volume of *The History of Sexuality,* in the course of outlining the development of bourgeois anatomo-politics as historically prior to the institution of biopolitics, Foucault comments that the proliferation, in the late eighteenth century, of writings on hygiene, childrearing, and longevity "attest[s] to the correlation of this concern with the body and sex to a type of 'racism' "—a budding "dynamic racism" that, he observes, must wait another century before its full development.[36] This brief chronology of eugenicism might have been more effectively calibrated if the geographic (colonial sites served, as Ann Laura Stoler documents, as early laboratories for these strategies)[37] and the conceptual terrain had been more carefully considered; the notion of "full development" here seems to privilege the adoption of reprosexual policing as state practice as the telos of this narrative despite Foucault's insistence that the state does not center power and that "sex" as we know it does not center sexuality. A different analysis might have been produced had Foucault incorporated other addresses to the body within this chronology. Julie Ellison's tracking of the eighteenth-century emergence of a racially conscious culture of sensibility, for instance, indicates that what we would now call "emotional" life should be comprehended within the framework of bodily hygiene, since the discourse of the passions does not draw boundaries between feeling and other dispositions of the body.[38] A more capacious understanding of the lifeworlds of the body might, in turn, have altered the overly linear historical framework that this gloss on dynamic racism projects—one that, as postcolonial critics have insisted, unduly limits Foucault's comprehension of racism as a historical phenomenon.[39]

The contemporaneous operations of anatomo- and biopolitics are, I propose, already visible in the rhetorical framework developed by middle-class mourning culture in the early nineteenth century. While condolence literature pointed to the transhistorical universality of grief to evoke the "common bonds of humanity," contemporary standards for bereavement also mapped the population along a timeline that excluded the chronically or insufficiently mournful (categories of waywardness that retained significantly raced and gendered associations) from the progressive projects of nation-building and global regeneration. So, for instance, the moderated sensibility that was assigned to the middle-class white family coupled a lingering attachment to the dead with disciplined Christian devotion to future reunion in order to project its form across time, linking past, present, and future under the rubric of familial affection. In contrast, what we earlier saw as the "prehumanity" of the Indian and "subhumanity" of the black slave were preserved within the emotional and spiritual "primitiveness" indexed by Native and African American mourning, untimely behaviors that, unlike the alterations in time that allowed the proper mourner to recollect origins, were associated with a lack of historical force and excepted from chronologies of directedness.

Sacred Wounds

In a recent study of the force of feeling, Philip Fisher proposes that subjective distinctions in time are wholly generated by passionate experience. The passions, he asserts, *are* the structure of time as it enters our own lives; they create a "temporal landscape" out of an otherwise homogeneous time both by distinguishing in content between past, present, and future (Fisher insists, for instance, that one cannot "fear the past . . . or feel anger or shame about what is in the future") and by marking off intervals of duration.[40] The fading of intense grief, for instance, constructs the difference between the immediate past and the more distant past of memory, while the active presence of hope distinguishes between the imminent future and the more "abstract" terrain of the imagination.[41] This common-sense description of the subjective experience of time still retains an essentially linear construction which makes it difficult to comprehend slippages in feeling that defy this timeline; to say that one cannot fear the past would, seemingly, be to disregard the premises of most Gothic literature, to say nothing of psychoanalysis, both of which play on the instability of the boundary between immediacy and memory in ways that also question the separability of past, present, and future as such. Fisher addresses this problem in his consideration of the Freudian economy of mourning, which contains Freud's earliest articulation of the concept of griefwork. This concept, Fisher observes, underscores the fact that "we do not simply wait for the passions to fade of their own accord" but, rather, construct the narrative forms in which they may be dispersed.[42]

Freudian narratives of mourning, I would argue, provide a certain resonant insight not only into the disciplinarity of mourning but also into the corporeal dispositions of time in the nineteenth century. As I earlier observed, while middle-class consolation literature continued, in this period, to posit God's authority as regulating and limiting the possibilities of the temporal, emphasizing the need to prepare oneself for death, it also incorporated the newer cultural appeal to the naturalness of feeling by promising eternal reunion with one's loved ones as compensation for the divinely authorized pain of loss in time. Love was thus tied to the careful self-monitoring needed to assure the celestial completion of the beloved circle; and indeed, Christian consolation literature specified precisely the modes of engaging grief that sustained this possibility and those modes—self-absorbed, superstitious, or overly sensational—that negated it. The time-discipline exerted in this religiously oriented specification of blessed and sinful, enlightened and heathen, engagements with grief finds an echo in Freud's early theorization of mourning as an end-directed process. Contrary to those assessments of nineteenth-century mourning culture that discount Freudian theory as anachronistic to the socio-sentimental ritualization of mourning in this period, I maintain that an examination of the evolution of Freud's thinking on grief and mourning can illuminate the temporal implications of affect in this historical period by precipitating the temporal ambivalences of the nineteenth-century appeal to grief.[43] Michael Moon points out that Freud's initial theorization of mourning, in the 1917 essay "Mourning and Melancholia," corresponds in its general outlines to the insistence on moderating grief and submitting to the discipline of loss visible in nineteenth-century consolation literature, a discipline that the earlier body of writing represented as a necessary means of preserving the order of the civilized, Christian subject.[44] Freud, however, replaced consolation literature's insistence on spiritual redemption against sinful waywardness with the contrast between psychically healthy mourning and the pathological condition of melancholia, which appeared as a refusal of the temporalizing work of mourning; the normal mourner was able to withdraw his psychic investments in the lost object and reattach them to the world of the living, whereas in the melancholic, this process was arrested, resulting in an ongoing psychic split.

The Freudian theory of mourning initially articulates itself, according to Tammy Clewell, as "a process geared toward restoring a certain economy of the subject"—an economy that, as I show in the first chapter of this study, is fundamentally directed and time-minded, based on the maximization of the subject's earthly and spiritual productivity.[45] Yet Freud's secular-scientific account differs from nineteenth-century consolation literature in one significant respect: its avoidance of any divinely authorized theory of timelessness as a compensatory prop for the losses sustained in time. Freud represents the submission to time's passage that orders the normal mourning process as mandated not by God's commands or the promise of heaven but by a *collective agreement* about the nature of time—what he terms the "reality principle," which forces the subject to acknowledge loss in the external world even if the psyche resists it; this resistance, which nineteenth-century consolation writing identified with the "longings of nature," emerges, in Freud's account, from the fundamental atemporality of the unconscious—an atemporality without the stabilizing timelessness of origin.[46] The Freudian account of the mourning subject, when considered alongside other post-Enlightenment accounts of human sociality, demonstrates that, in the absence of assurances about divine authorization or nature's benevolence, the persistent return of the grief-stricken subject to the memory of the lost beloved becomes visible as an attachment to attachment *as such*. "Mourning and Melancholia" thus maintains in altered form the conviction that mourning should work to remove any obstacles to the forward-moving flow of time, at once distancing the modern conception of the human from any necessary dependence on the divine and preserving as a psychosocial imperative the end-directed capacity for self-discipline that Christian consolation literature mobilized through the promise of heaven.

Freudian thought furnishes a further insight into the complex temporal functioning of grief in this period by underscoring the way that grief both animated and exceeded the temporal discipline of mourning. Despite Freud's faith in the regenerative capacity of the normal psyche—its self-restoring ability to successfully complete mourning, locating a substitute-object for its affective energies—he remained puzzled by the tendency of grief to *linger* even in putatively "normal" cases of mourning. In the short 1916 essay "On Transience," for instance, Freud confesses himself perplexed by some friends' refusal of his rationalization of loss in contrast to their devastated response to the ongoing war.[47] When his friends fail to be consoled by his insistence that the inevitability of loss in linear time raises the value of transient objects, he hypothesizes that "some powerful emotional factor was at work which was disturbing their judgment," a factor he later identifies as a resistance to the pain involved in mourning's working-through of loss.[48] He adds, however, that he does not know why mourning should be so painful and can "only see that libido clings to its objects and will not renounce those that are lost even when a substitute lies ready at hand."[49] The desire to understand the ongoing emotional pain associated with frustrated attachment eventually led Freud to revise his understanding of melancholia's relation to mourning. Beginning with *The Ego and the Id*, melancholia appears not simply as an effect of the temporally wayward subject's relation to grief but also as the foundational condition of subjectivity itself, insofar as Freud now hypothesizes the ego as the precipitate of early melancholic attachments.[50] *The Ego and the Id* thus dissolves—or, more accurately, displaces —the temporal distinction between mourning as a linear process of restoration and melancholia as the pathological refusal of time's discipline featured in the earlier work, insofar as the melancholic basis of the ego offers Freud a way to explain the seemingly interminable pain of ordinary grief. Since an atemporal attachment to others resides at the very origin of the subject, the *abandonment* of that attachment suggested in the earlier image of serial substitution now appears to be contradictory to human nature. As Clewell points out, Freud implies that the cherishing of attachments to lost objects is effectively what makes us human: "Although we know that after . . . a loss the acute state of mourning will subside, we also know we shall remain inconsolable and will never find a substitute. No matter what may fill the gap, even if it be filled completely, it nevertheless remains something else. And actually, *this is how it should be*. It is the only way of perpetuating that love which we do not want to relinquish."[51] This transformation in Freud's thinking about loss has been represented by Clewell and others as his evolution from a late-Victorian to a fully modern thinker.[52] I would propose, in contrast, that Freud's belated understanding of the persistence of grief as "how it should be" marks a point where his thinking *catches up to* the nineteenth century, as it recalls that century's pronounced embrace of retained grief. In this light, Freud's fundamental "difference" from the tenets of nineteenth-century consolation literature—his refusal to posit heaven as a compensatory time-space for the "perpetuation" of those attachments—appears rather as an alternate *realization* of the possibilities of time as glimpsed through the sustained cultural attention to loss in this period.

The "something else" that persists in this gap manifests most provocatively when critics follow through the temporal implications of Freud's thinking about the durations of grief, rather than succumbing to the temptation to categorize instances of mourning as normative or pathological. This mode of engagement is exemplified in Breitwieser's insightful book-length reading of Mary Rowlandson's 1682 account of her captivity among Algonquian Indians during King Philip's War. Breitwieser connects the ability of Rowlandson's narrative to break with the representational norms of her culture, despite its official fidelity to church and state (the narrative, intended to support the colonists' interpretation of the conflict, is titled *The Sovereignty and Goodness of God, Together with the Faithfulness of His Promises Displayed*), to its composition during what was, for Rowlandson, a prolonged and still-incomplete process of mourning—a period Breitwieser, following Rowlandson's own language, avoids classing as pathological and instead identifies as an "afflicted time"—a time idiosyncratic and intrinsic, "dissevered from public time, governed by eccentric and private accelerations and retardations that she shared with no one," and thus one that could permit a radically atypical perspective on her social world.[53] My own study extends this framework in another direction, considering how nineteenth-century engagements with the corporeal sociality of grief might produce alternate perspectives on time, perspectives that not only challenge the content of official histories but also reimagine the arrangements of time upon which those histories are constructed and reproduced: rendering time, in effect, as "something else" even in its most familiar manifestations.

Freud's disconsolate perpetuation of love for the dead and Rowlandson's insistent attachment to her ruined world both exemplify the importance of attending to anachrony in any would-be historical inquiry. By anachrony, I do not simply mean expanding our understanding of what counts as historically "relevant." I might well justify my inclusion of the early twentieth-century analyst and the late seventeenth-century chronicler in a nineteenth-century study on the basis of such an expanded conception of relevance; even as the Freudian subject may, as Moon and others have argued, be understood as a version of the nineteenth-century sentimental subject, Rowlandson's own account seems, for all its fidelity to contemporary convention, oddly anticipatory, producing, at times, moments that read to Breitwieser like something out of Melville or Dickens.[54] But my intention is not, ultimately, to exonerate these particular references from the charge of anachronism while otherwise keeping faith with the boundaries that charge seeks to enforce. Instead, I am interested in the uses of anachrony and other modes of untimely presence as means of multiplying the futures of the past. If the construction of anachronistic space has historically operated within modernity, as Anne McClintock charges, as a means of domination, anachrony nevertheless also presents an opportunity to refigure the very terrain of the historical.[55] In this sense, this study draws upon and participates in a recent intensification of the temporal in American literary and cultural studies. That development—visible in such works as Wai Chee Dimock's innovative study *Through Other Continents*, which, dilating upon the presence of anachronism in Emerson, James, and other "American" writers, revises the spatiotemporal coordinates of American literary history itself, rejecting the narrowing chronology of the nation in favor of a planetary frame[56]—is guided by a desire to determine how the way we chart time delimits the kinds of relations we imagine across social space;[57] for if, as Peter Osborne contends, all politics is centrally concerned with "struggles over the experience of time," then the temporal work of culture, as the locus of production of "different senses of time and possibility" (and hence of different relations to history and futurity) demands particularly close attention.[58] Until recently, however, most critical work on the cultural politics of time neglected to question configurations of the corporeal, to think through the temporalities of social belonging by interrogating how sexual and familial arrangements determine the human over time.[59] My focus on grief in this study is, accordingly, directed toward developing an understanding of how the movements of life under the *dispositif* of sexuality might transfigure these forms of relatedness by emphasizing the way the affectionate body is, by its very "nature," subject to anachrony. Grief, as I have been arguing, provides particularly fertile terrain for tracing such temporal disjunctions by virtue of its connection to multiple framings of sacred time. The modern embrace of grief at once signals and perpetuates visions of the subject as founded on a *rift* in time, as maintaining an attachment to sacred time that it knows to come too late. The persistence of that rift—whether imagined as an investment in irrecoverable origins, a deathless attachment to a past love, an insistence on the ultimately irreparable status of the ruptured bond, and/or a cherishing of the pain that maintains it as such—establishes the feeling body as a potential site of historiographic and temporal interventions. The deeply embodied nature of those interventions, moreover, intensifies their ethical dimension, underscoring the interconnections between the way we think about social forms such as nation or culture and the way we assess the temporality of particular life forms. In this light, the asynchronic traces that haunt narrative dispositions of the grieving body in nineteenth-century American literature not only bring the conventions ordering which forms of life *count* as such into sharp relief but also enable particular arrangements of grief to propose forms of connection in and across time that fall outside or athwart the confines of both recognized history and familial generationality.

The tendency to depict the rift in the grieving subject as a *wound*, however, complicates the political/temporal leverage of many of these proposals. This propensity is particularly marked in sentimental culture; in light of recent work in this field, in fact, it can even be said to constitute sentimentality as such. Sentimentality and wounding are conceptually linked in Roland Barthes's work on the *punctum* in photography; Barthes, as Marianne Noble points out in her study of sentimental masochism, declares that his interest in the photograph is "sentimental" insofar as he wants to explore it as a wound, something that uses feeling to open its critical engagements.[60] Significantly, Barthes's analysis of the photograph thinks through its incorporation of a temporal alterity, the trace of another time that it inscribes, in relation to what he calls the punctum, the "beyond" within the photograph that acts on the body.[61] In this light, "sentimental" does not simply indicate a noteworthy intensity or deplorable excess of feeling (depending on one's taste) but, more particularly, a way of using deployments of mixed feeling (pleasure and pain) to negotiate problems in time.[62] This dual focus on the bodily and formal processes constituting the sentimental distinguishes much recent work on the nineteenth-century American culture of sentiment.[63] A recent assessment by Mary Louise Kete, for instance, goes so far as to characterize sentimentality as a type of mourning, one that seeks consolation by means of restoration. For Kete, sentimentality's "signal concerns"— "*lost* homes, *lost* families, and *broken* bonds"—are tied to its attempt to speak across space and time by developing tropes that *restore* continuity, by diminishing the distance between individuals, and by "bridg[ing] the gap between temporality and eternity."[64] Noble, similarly, proposes that wounds do more than inspire sympathy in sentimental fiction; in Stowe's *Uncle Tom's Cabin,* she argues, wounding opens what we might comprehend as an ecstatic temporality, at once erotic and religious, working as "[metonym] for God's full presence" and as a "form of sexual transcendence."[65]

Sentimentality's inclination toward eternity and transcendence, however, troubles critics seeking to understand the way the appeal of the wound operated in and on historical time. This line of critique is pursued by Lauren Berlant, who expands the terrain of sentimentality, affirming that in a culture lacking a viably rational political public sphere, manifestations of a liberal-sentimental consciousness take the place of public culture. That consciousness similarly seeks to privilege an idealized wholeness—not only in the maintenance of the homes, families, and bonds it projects as eternal but more fundamentally in the wish that "identity categories . . . be ontological, dead to history," preserved against change.[66] The unconflicted identities treasured in liberal-sentimental consciousness are imagined, crucially, both as *prior* to extant social formations and as *private,* bound up with highly normative domestic-familial configurations. This sacralizing of a domesticated wholeness points, according to Berlant, toward an intimate affinity between sentimental culture and the market it officially deplores as a threat to that wholeness, so that the circulation and consumption of images of woundedness comes to operate, in effect, as a cure for wounding. The weakness of the sentimental political imaginary is not simply its historical alignment with commodity culture but more specifically the temporality in which the "cure" is effected; sentimentality, Berlant asserts, "seeks out monumental time, the sphere of dreaming and memory, and translates its idealities into an imaginary realm where agency is somehow unconstrained by the normative connections of the real." Sentimentality's sacred time, in this view, attempts not to transform but to transcend history, using feeling to mimic the fulfillment promised by eternity.[67]

Berlant's account of sentimental culture's appeal to commodified moments of sublime suffering, exemplified in her reading of the persistent attraction to the scene of Eliza's crossing of the Ohio River in *Uncle Tom's Cabin,* foregrounds a combination of the sentimental and the sensational that occupies a different temporality than my discussion of grief has thus far evoked. "Sensation" signals a mode of intensified embodiment in which all times but the present fall away—a condition simultaneously desired, in its recollection of the infantile state, and feared, in its negation of social agency; as a case in point, it was, as we will see in chapter 1, a condition projected onto the black body as justification for slavery. The affective mode I have been examining in relation to grief, however, (dis)organizes time differently. In grief, the sensory body does not rise out of time so much as fall behind it; everything but the past fades away and yet, at the same time, remains—a consequence of the irreversibility of time upon which the experience of grief is predicated, since if one could live wholly within the past toward which grief inclines, grief itself would dissipate. Hence, although both wish away historical time, the slow time of lingering grief does so with a sense of its inescapability, whereas sensation makes a fetish of the moment. These two temporal modes come together, as I demonstrate in the first three chapters of this study, in the widespread nineteenth-century attachment to mourning the prehistorical and the infantile, an attachment that amounts to a sentimentalization of primal sensation. This nostalgic devotion to the life of the body before (linear) time constitutes a key feature of strategies of affective incitement, manifested most clearly in domestic-sentimental culture's accommodation-through-negation of the time of the market but also, as both Berlant and Elizabeth Maddock Dillon have shown, in liberal politics generally.[68] Yet this sort of suspension toward originary or eternal timelessness is not the only way in which grief can intervene in the temporal imaginary of nineteenth-century America. Rather, as I will show, grief may also be deployed innovatively through and against the traumatized time of the sentimental, gesturing not toward an originary wholeness but toward the necessary reinvention of forms of connection and belonging. Such possibilities emerge when the homology posited between the sacred time of origins, the time before linear-historical time, and the eternal glory of the posthistorical and posttemporal, is strained by the persistence of asynchronic traces affixed to embodiment, which can work to desacralize or detraumatize the arrangements upon which the official chronologies of sentimental culture depend.[69] From this perspective, the "nature" to which the life of the body is linked becomes not the *origin* of a conservatively conceived culture but what Elizabeth Grosz suggestively describes as "the endless generation of problems for culture"—the insistence of which, as she asserts, may lead to "human, or cultural, innovation and ingenuity, self-overcoming, and the creation of the new."[70]

Touching Moments

Arranging Grief draws upon an archive of writings circulated in the United States from the 1820s through the 1860s, a period that saw both an increased proliferation of modes of retaining grief and significant transformations in national consciousness, religion, and the cultural status of the capitalist market.[71] Examining a range of sources addressing—or, perhaps more accurately, caressing—grief, including mourning manuals, sermons, and memorial tracts, novels and short fiction, poetry, speeches, and memoirs, I pursue a mode of close reading that is at once historically and temporally attentive. The tendency of the grief-marked text to dwell within the sensuality of deep feeling requires consideration of the distinct textures of particular texts as they rearrange the dominant chronobiopolitical dispositions of the historical moments in which they were produced.[72] My attention to texture and detail is intended to address the complexity of how these texts *make time appear,* an assessment that is particularly crucial insofar as the grief-work incited in these texts often signifies at a self-conscious distance from the "official" materials of history.[73] What I seek in these readings, then, is to demonstrate how close attention to the ripples in time that mark nineteenth-century writing about grief might help to move American cultural criticism not only to a more precise understanding of the history of time but also toward ways that history might be remade. For as Foucault asserts (and as queer critique, in particular, has usefully demonstrated) the point of historically grounded inquiry is not to provide us with insight into the past "as it really was" but to provide the attentive reader with models of variability that might illuminate and animate critical practices across time.[74] And it is, finally, in this register that my interest in the temporal play authorized by grief is intended to resonate: as a critical examination of both its historicity and its ongoing potential to alter the course of time, opening slippages that manifest not only as outright resistance to or critique of historical norms but also as subtler alterations enabling minute, enlivening variations in the becoming of the human subject and the perpetuation of its histories.

    Arranging Grief is divided into two interdependent sections. The first section highlights the relations between time and feeling within early-nineteenth-century appeals to grief as a way of conserving the human, focusing on the cultural arrangement of sorrow around figures identified as prepolitical or prenational: the lamented child, the romanticized Indian, and the sentimentalized mother. In the second section, I examine the explicit extension of the "private matter" of the grieving body to the social and political terrain of the American present tense around the questions of slavery and war.

Chapter 1 develops a political archaeology of grief that highlights the complex textures of time in nineteenth-century consolation literature, centering on accounts of child loss. Although the Christian orientation of this body of work urged a fundamentally conservative deployment of the alternate temporalities accessed through grief, insisting on the need to prevent sorrow over the past from diminishing earthly productivity and preventing one's access to eternal reward, its evocative attention to the pleasures of grief complicates these orderly arrangements, positing prolonged sorrow in an unstable and potentially disruptive relation to histories both public and private. Chapter 2 pursues the question of sacred time into the realm of sound, focusing on the sustained attention, in the early American novel, to the "music" of the Indian voice, which it tuned to the key of lament. This literary attraction to the sonorousness of the Indian voice, a noteworthy aspect of historical romances by James Fenimore Cooper and Catharine Maria Sedgwick, at once demonstrates a narrative intention to bury its temporal alterity, as the ineffable grain of the presocial and prenational body, and the novelistic desire to resurrect it as the echo of an as-yet-unrealized plenitude associated with corporeal memory. Chapter 3 traces the contours of middle-class sentimental domesticity, examining the sacralizing of the affectionate mother in antebellum sentimental culture and that culture's corresponding nostalgia for childhood as a form of sacred time. The failure of the mother to fully conform to this (pre)temporal positioning unsettles its generative frameworks, as I show by interrogating the way maternal melancholy marks two 1850s domestic-sentimental orphan novels, Susan Warner's enormously popular *The Wide, Wide World* and Harriet Wilson's complex response to the genre, *Our Nig*. In both these novels, the figure of the not-quite-dead mother accrues anachronistic meanings that reanimate sentimental desire while opening powerful critiques of middle-class visions of domestic order.

Beginning with chapter 4, I focus on how grief operated in writing that confronted the national public with the immediate time-pressures of slavery and war, challenging chronologies of national belonging by means of the instability resulting from confrontations between the sexuality of the citizen-subject and familial and monumental rubrics of Americanness. Contending that slavery itself, which we can comprehend, in light of Hortense Spillers's work, as an institutionalized form of sexual violence perpetuated through race, constituted an ongoing interruption to the mutually imbricated time-lines of family and nation, I examine antislavery and Civil War–era writers who sought to animate that interruption in the present tense. Chapter 4 centers on the way selected antislavery writers sought to rework the senti-mental deployment of universalized feeling as a counter to the slave sys-tem. Expanding the temporal implications of recent critical work on the pol-itics of sentiment, I consider the sentimental reading of grief as an appeal to the timeless familial values underwriting the social fabric—exemplified in Stowe's *Uncle Tom's Cabin*—against three writers—Frederick Douglass, Her-man Melville, and Frances E. W. Harper—whose work I characterize as coun-termonumental, in that it resists reduction to the nationalist manifestation of sacred time exhibited in the monument. The chapter examines in turn Douglass's insistence on the time of the "now," the alternate relation to the present opened in Harper's revision of sentimental simultaneity into a poli-tics of contemporaneousness, and finally Melville's formal emphasis on the disruptiveness of the archaic. Chapter 5 describes the consolidation of affec-tive nationality in the Civil War period. Focusing on representative mourn-fulness as facilitating a mode of passionate national belonging, I show how the national rituals of mourning for the assassinated president Lincoln high-lighted his capacity for grief, indexing a peculiarly American attachment to historical trauma as a sacralized, regenerative time-space to which ordinary citizens ritually return in order to affectively reorient themselves toward the redemptive promise of the future. I close the chapter by analyzing Elizabeth Keckley's use of this monumental arrangement of national trauma in her memoir of an ex-slave's life in the White House, noting that Keckley's mem-oir ultimately reveals the incapacity of affective nationality to comprehend the institutionalized reproduction of sexual violence at the core of the slave system, returning us to the consideration of the problematic temporality of the body in sentimental culture with which the book's first section con-cluded. And finally, in a brief coda, I extend the questions of contemporary memorial practice that closed chapters 4 and 5, addressing the problematic persistence of our profound cultural faith in the productivity of mourning, audible, notably, in the proliferation of calls for effective memory work around events such as 9/11. The ongoing appeal to mourning as a means of social consolidation, I argue, should draw our attention to the need to develop ways of thinking that avoid merely embracing alternative temporalities as the means of humanity's salvation and, instead, attempt a desacralizing reworking of grief's times—resisting the tendency to consider grief as always exceptional but instead positing its very *ordinariness* as a ground of political action.

Moments More Concentrated than Hours

Grief and the Textures of Time

"I cannot be serious!" John Adams announced in a March 2, 1816, letter to Thomas Jefferson. "I am about to write You, the most frivolous letter, you ever read."[1] Inspired by recollections of his remarkable era prompted by Baron von Grimm's *Correspondance Litteraire, Philosophique et Critique*, Adams wondered whether his friend Jefferson, given the chance, would choose to live his entire life over again, just as he had experienced it the first time. In Jefferson's April 6 reply, which he proclaimed a "full match" for Adams's frivolity, the third president of the United States assured its second that he would gladly relive his own life.[2] Declaring himself in sympathy with Adams's belief in benevolence, Jefferson represented the possibility of repetition as a source of no little satisfaction. He contrasted his optimistic and "sanguine" embrace of Adams's proposal to the negativity of those who would forgo the opportunity to relive their lives; these he scorned as pessimists, possessing "gloomy and hypocondriac [*sic*] minds, inhabitants of diseased bodies, disgusted with the present, and despairing of the future."[3] But the lighthearted tone marking the two statesmen's playful indulgence of this temporal fantasy vanished as the question of grief entered into the dialogue. An acknowledgment that sorrow came even to the optimistic prompted Jefferson to interrogate the moral purpose of pain:

> I have often wondered for what good end the sensations of Grief could be intended. All our other passions, within proper bounds, have an useful object. And the perfection of the moral character is, not in a Stoical apathy, so hypocritically vaunted, and so unjustly too, because impossible, but in a just equilibrium of all the passions. I wish the pathologists then would tell us what is the use of grief in the economy, and of what good it is the cause, proximate or remote.[4]

Adams's response to his friend's question, in a letter dated May 6, 1816, followed Jefferson in abandoning the playful tone of previous missives to pursue the serious matter of grief. Adams theorized that grief signaled a "mechanical and inseparable" connection between pleasure and pain, so that the disruption of any continuity of pleasure—whether the death of a loved one or the failure of a business—must inevitably produce the pain we experience as grief.[5] But this pain, in his view, was fundamentally productive. Insofar as it tempered the love for pleasure, discouraged excesses of "Imagination and Avarice," and "compelled [mourners] to reflect on the Vanity of human Wishes and Expectations," grief taught both resignation and virtue. Observing that all portraits of great men revealed "Furrows . . . ploughed in the Countenance, by Grief," Adams proposed that the most effective legislators and judges were those who had been disciplined by sorrow.[6] The mournful were best suited to governance, perhaps, because grief itself served a governing function in the ex-president's assessment; he argued that it "compels [men] to arrouse their Reason, to assert its Empire over their Passions[,] Propensities and Prejudices."[7] Yet even as he saw grief working to abet reason by "sharpen[ing] the Understanding," he also maintained that it "softens the heart," supplementing that rationality with a well-managed capacity for feeling.[8] Grief, that is, taught not only discipline but also *sympathy*; balancing reason with emotion, it produced both citizens and subjects. For Adams, then, the role grief played in the "just equilibrium" of the passions Jefferson idealized was that of maintaining the balance.

We can glimpse, in this epistolary conversation, the key terms organizing grief's cultural significance at the beginning of the nineteenth century. The emergence of the subject immediately reigns in the imaginative play associated with the dream of reliving a revolutionary life, indicating that grief emphasized the limits posed by time, summoning the specter of loss and, with it, time's irreversibility. Kept within these limits, however, grief possessed a significant degree of social productivity. Adams and Jefferson's discussion suggests that as a "natural" impulse, the body's automatic response to the vicissitudes of time as they took the form of loss, grief could provide both the sympathetic responsiveness and the impetus to self-governance that shaped the model American. For Adams, a lifetime of concentration on grief's discipline perfected the moral, legislative, and economic capacities that protected against transience, "elevat[ing] [men] to a Superiority over all human Events."[9] Proper reckoning with the affective fallout of time as it collided with human bodies and souls would, in this view, enable the self-governed subject to rise above the debris, providing a measure of control not only over the body and its desires but also over time itself. But whereas Adams stressed the moral effect of grief, highlighting it as an opportunity for the exercise of the will, Jefferson's comments emphasized, in contrast, the involuntary physiological aspect of feeling. His humoral typography of emotion depicted the self-control Adams commended as accessible only to the emotionally well-balanced, or "sanguine"; others, in his assessment, were constitutionally unable to maintain this kind of equilibrium. Typifying grief in this unhealthy form as "hypochondria," a term used interchangeably with "melancholia" in eighteenth-century physiology, Jefferson suggested, in effect, that the feeling body might have not just a mind but a time of its own, defying the ordering of the will.[10]

The correspondence between the two ex-presidents heralds the emergence of grief in the nineteenth century as a means not simply of tempering but also of *temporalizing* the body and its feelings. The attention given to grief signaled a historically new emphasis on affection and sympathy as natural phenomena demonstrating the inherent sociality of the human animal, the idea that, as Jefferson wrote to another friend, "nature hath implanted in our breasts a love of others, a sense of duty to them, a moral instinct, in short, which prompts us irresistibly to feel and to succor their distresses."[11] Yet the passionate dimension of human existence, Jefferson insisted, had its "proper place" in private life, outside the spheres of commerce and politics. This arrangement calls our attention not only to the spatial plotting but also to the distinct *timing* of private life as it occasioned a restorative return to this originary impulse.[12] The nature to which Jefferson refers here is a temporal principle, referring not, as Ernst Cassirer explains, to "the existence of things but the origin and foundation of truths."[13] Human emotion represented, in this vision, the instinctive swelling of the divine spirit within the human subject—the "social dispositions" that proved, as Jefferson had written, that "[t]he Creator . . . intended man for a social animal."[14]

If grief, as I show in this book, came to occupy a place of epistemological privilege in this essentially narrative organization of the body and its uses, this is because the story grief tells effectively corresponds to this arrangement of the sociotemporal value of feeling. Extending further in its temporal implications than states like content or elation, grief, as John Adams's account suggests, narrates the corrosion of attachment by time. Referencing the natural longing for connection that served as the foundation of human community, grief both appears as the inescapable condition of life in linear time, which inevitably severed some of those foundational bonds, and furnishes the impetus for memory to reconnect to the form of truth they represented. Grief thus provided an opportunity for the nineteenth-century subject to revisit the scene of human origins—experiencing, in the pain of its negation, the innate desire for bondedness to others that underscored the nurturant disposition of the natural world. The emotional aftermath of loss established human attachment as a foundational principle in a world in which traditional temporal frameworks were undergoing a radical transformation, beginning to shift toward a model of "history" as ordered, linear, and teleological. Given the dependence of modern nationalism upon this model of history, the former presidents' willingness to submit to the disciplinarity of linear time by marking their engagement with the willed fantasy of reversal as idle play is unsurprising.[15] Yet if the unquestioned dominance of linear time circumscribed as self-evidently "frivolous" a conversation about voluntary temporal repetition, the turn to grief as a means of both forswearing and continuing the discussion of alternate temporalities suggests that grief's involuntary nature, coupled with its affiliation with the regenerative mode associated with private life, nevertheless held open the possibility of compensatory temporal forms—forms that offered ways of conserving the pleasures associated with the refusal of linearity without appearing to negate historicity as such.

In this chapter, I will begin assessing grief's centrality to what Michel Foucault terms the deployment of sexuality: the intensification of the body, its uses, and its effects in modernity. Considering texts drawn from early and mid-nineteenth-century mourning culture, ranging from sermons and eulogies to consolation manuals and mourner's handbooks to discussions of the new rural cemeteries, I demonstrate how the play of grief in nineteenth-century culture can illuminate the historical relationship between time and the body. Though the archive of the chapter is deliberately diffuse, in order to enable a general overview of chronobiopolitical deployments of grief, I have incorporated a particular focus on materials dealing with the death of children. This emphasis on child loss is motivated both by the fact that the death of a dependent child appears, as Karen Sánchez-Eppler points out, an "almost purely emotional event," and hence one that offers particular insight into what constitutes an emotional event as such, and by the popular conviction that the untimely death of the child, though a common occurrence, is a disruption of the natural order of things.[16] Child loss tellingly consolidates the affective and temporal energies of nineteenth-century consolation culture, providing a site where the longings of "nature" met the future-directedness of the "soul." As the poem "On Seeing a Deceased Infant" expressed it, "The spirit hath an earthly part / That weeps when earthly pleasure flies, / And heaven would scorn the frozen heart / That melts not when the infant dies."[17] The first half of the chapter assesses the balance that middle-class mourning culture sought to establish between the earthly and heavenly directions of the spirit. For as the verses cited here indicate, grief in this period came to be justified as a natural and hence laudable expression of the human spirit. Moreover, despite the limited duration of the official mourning period, sorrow over the dead was expected to *linger*. I examine both the sacralized spaces set aside, in the early nineteenth century, for the indulgence of retained grief and the way consolation literature framed the contradictory temporal pull of the mournful moment, which slowed or suspended ordinary time in its yearning after sensual continuities. Middle-class mourning culture's limitation of the exceptional temporalities associated with grief, its insistence on drawing the mourner's potentially asynchronic attachments back toward the future-directedness of the civilized Christian, also supported cultural and biological accounts of racial and sexual difference in bereavement norms that constructed Native and African Americans as emotionally out of sync with the Anglo-American populace. Yet the widespread cultural appeal of grief, as I show, also offered reform-minded writers such as Harriet Beecher Stowe and William Apess a means of contesting the exclusionary time of national life by publicizing the grief it authored. Finally, the chapter closes with a consideration of the way the politicized time imagined in reform movements was distinguished from the prepolitical temporality associated with personal feeling. Examining grief's appeal to love as the foundation of human relations, I uncover the asynchronic traces buried within consolation literature's normalization of time through the structures of domestic privacy. These asynchronic traces point us, I suggest, to the temporally uncertain status of the "love" indexed by grief.

Time's Change: The Production of the Human

The view that Adams outlines of loss as an occasion for self-discipline characterized the Puritan way of death, which insisted that the event of loss should orient survivors toward the pending moment of divine judgment. In the Puritan framework, death bespoke temporality in opposition to eternity; that is, it uncovered its "truth" as *transience*, emphasizing the fleetingness of human life by pointing insistently toward its end. Time, in this worldview, belonged to God alone, whose authority transcended it altogether; temporality was thus but the earthly shadow of the timeless truth of the divine, and indulgence in grief constituted a denial of this truth.[18] The nineteenth-century understanding of mourning, in contrast, was marked by a historically new insistence that the proper response to death was an *emotional* one —a painful longing to return to a wholeness located in the past. The duration of this pain testified both to the value of what had been lost and to the sensitivity of the mourner, who recognized that value and responded appropriately, with intense suffering. Grief thus came to be valorized not simply as an impetus to self-chastisement but also as an emotional *event,* a feeling worth having for its own sake. By the eighteenth century, American sermons had begun to move away from the traditional disapproval of mournfulness as defiance of God's will, using Biblical texts to argue that sorrow on the death of a loved one was to be expected. As a natural response, the sermons insisted, grieving could not be sinful, since sin was an act of the will. Nineteenth-century mourning culture expanded the corporeal dimension of this insistence on the naturalness of grief, representing deep, and deeply embodied, feelings of sorrow as not only an instinctive but also, crucially, a *healthy* response to loss, insofar as they signaled the mourner's engagement with the affective dimension of human existence. Condolence literature spoke frequently of the "burning tears and aching sighs" of the bereaved, strong expressions that emerged from the "earthly part" of the spirit.[19] These bodily emissions of the earthly were no longer rejected outright as false attachments to the temporal world, signs of a wayward preference for the flesh; instead, if kept within certain bounds, they were embraced as expected, sincere, and appropriate tokens of human love. In 1828, for instance, the Congregationalist minister Jacob Scales reassured his New Hampshire congregation that the Bible did indeed permit weeping over the dead, because it was *natural*. Tears, he asserted, were "an expression of sensibility. . . . Dear friends, removed from our sight . . . may naturally open the channel for a flood of tears. . . . There is a 'time to mourn,' and the stoick [*sic*], who forbids humanity to speak her native language, can scarcely deserve our love, or invite our envy."[20] Scales's coupling of the oft-cited passage from Ecclesiastes and the allusion to humanity's "native" language—the language of the heart, as articulated in the speech of tears—demonstrates the extent to which a view of the essential *benevolence* of the natural, and of the feeling body as part of that redeemed nature, now informed even cautionary approaches to emotion. The "time to mourn," in this configuration, is also the time of a return to this originary source, the time to speak the naturalness of feeling. The painful pleasure of bereavement—what mourning manuals referred to as "the luxury of grief"—was valued not just because it indexed the strength of interpersonal ties but, more fundamentally, because it verified an arrangement of time that underscored the foundational truths of human nature; indeed, as Scales suggests, those who refused to embrace truth, who insisted on suppressing feeling, were not only not admirable but actually unlovable.

The new emphasis on emotion reflected the expanded influence of feeling on faith. As the relationships American Christian denominations formed with the divine became ever more organized around love above fear, the doctrine of the vile flesh in need of regeneration gave way to a conception of spiritual grace as inherent in the human condition, and a growing emphasis was placed on human action rather than divine election as the way to salvation.[21] This change is markedly visible in nineteenth-century consolation writing; for whether religiously affiliated writers sought to limit or to expand upon the authority of "nature," the cultural centrality of grief itself demonstrates that they could no longer afford to ignore it. The new embrace of grief signaled its redefinition as an exemplary emotion, at once the evidence of and a way to activate this originary grace. Grief was still seen as an impetus to good behavior, demonstrating a desire for celestial reunion with the departed, but the self-control it occasioned flowed naturally from a spontaneous outpouring of feeling for the departed rather than conscious and fearful preparation for the moment of one's own death. Grief, as outlined in the literature, served as the motivating impulse for the labor of love powering the mode of affective production that would come to be known as griefwork. As the Reverend P. H. Fowler explained in an 1856 sermon,

> The feelings center the thoughts on the lamented ones, and much is recalled in connection with them, that had passed entirely from us. The heart fondly dwells on the review, and one thing is suggested after another, until a multitude of particulars are remembered, of which no note before appeared. And the influence of the example which memory thus brings before us is greatly energized. *Enkindled affection* gives it increased effect.[22]

In the Presbyterian minister's protopsychological understanding of the mourning process, the interaction of attachment and memory creates an "energized" image of the departed with significant power over the bereaved. Through the emotion-driven psychic labor of the mourner, an affectively vitalized past could find a place in the present. Accordingly, the burgeoning field of nineteenth-century consolation literature—mourner's handbooks, etiquette guides, consolatory poetry, printed sermons, et cetera—took upon itself the dual task of soliciting the feelings "naturally" associated with loss and of shaping and regulating their social productivity.

The psychological account of mourning offered by Fowler differs significantly from the set of social rituals established in and as "mourning" in this period. Formal mourning conventions—the draping of the house of the bereaved in black; the wearing of "widow's weeds," mourning bands, and veils; limitations on communications; and the suspension of ordinary social activities—furnished a temporary physical demarcation that served to distinguish the time-space of recent loss from that of everyday life. The conventions of mourning both distanced the recently bereaved from ordinary living and narrativized this liminal period, arranging it over time toward an anticipated endpoint.[23] The mourning period thus recognized and ordered a period of subjective disorder. But although the formal mourning period came to a prescribed end, the mourner's lingering feelings of grief were not required to vanish; indeed, they were understood as antiteleological. Though the traumatic, time-stopping pain of recent loss was expected to diminish, lingering grief, as Washington Irving's Romantic persona, Geoffrey Crayon, observed in a sketch of rural funerals, was treasured as a sign of continuing connection to the departed:

> The sorrow for the dead is the only sorrow from which we refuse to be divorced. Every other wound we seek to heal, every other affliction to forget; but this wound we consider it a duty to keep open, this affliction we cherish and brood over in solitude. . . . the love which survives the tomb is one of the noblest attributes of the soul. If it has its woes, it has likewise its delights; and when the overwhelming burst of grief is calmed into the gentle tear of recollection, when the sudden anguish and the convulsive agony over the present ruins of all that we most loved is softened away into pensive meditation on all that it was in the days of its loveliness, who would root out such a sorrow from the heart?[24]

The marital relation invoked in this passage positions grief as the subject's *better half*; its preservation signified not simply the worthiness of the departed but, more fundamentally, the value of human attachment. The insistence that the truly feeling person never abandoned the receptivity to sorrow associated with the memory of the departed, but sought, instead, to keep the wounds of time open in grief, reworked the "convulsive agony" of recent loss, which swallowed all meaning in trauma, into a "cherished" vision of the temporal capaciousness of privacy, which enabled the conservation of both the past times associated with the dead and the originary truth of humanity's bondedness.

The picturesque rural world that Irving's Crayon, in contrast to the bustle of the city, romanticized as holding fast to this "truer" emotional connection found material form in new locations for memorial: social spaces set aside for the indulgence of grief, which provided a refuge from the anxieties over acceleration that accompanied the nineteenth-century emphasis on progress. These new locations, arranged to accentuate their distance from the bustle of public life, permitted the mourner to focus attention on the continuities associated with the regenerativity of the human spirit. Most noteworthy among these was the "rural" cemetery, introduced to the States by Mount Auburn in Cambridge, which opened in 1831, and Brooklyn's Green-Wood, launched in 1838. Though the rural cemetery was developed largely as a sanitary response to urban overcrowding, the design of the new memorial parks—located in picturesque, out-of-the-way settings, traversed by winding roads and decorated by trees intended to shade the grounds and provide some measure of privacy for mourners—revealed a change in the cultural framing of bereavement.[25] Within the "dying-of-death" framework developed by the Ariès school, this change is generally understood as a spatial removal of death from everyday life; the relocation of the burial ground from the churchyard, at the center of civic existence, to the out-of-the-way rural cemetery reveals, in these accounts, its displacement of the dead from the eyes of the living.[26] Contemporary commentators, however, emphasized the alternate *temporal* implications of these bucolic locations, highlighting the way they suited the disposition of grief. The dead, they argued, should be interred outside the city center because this location served the mourner best. The setting of the rural cemetery—in the country but within view of the city—matched the alternate perspectives on time opened in the subject by feeling. The rural cemetery's spatial arrangements suggested the distinctly expansive temporality they effectively condensed: situated beyond the city, where time was hemmed in by the many demands placed upon it by a modernizing culture, the rural cemetery permitted the modern subject to view, so to speak, its horizon. Joseph Story's dedicatory speech at the opening of Mount Auburn underscores the necessity of this way of seeing time. Story, the Supreme Court justice who would, a decade later, write the majority opinion in *United States v. Amistad,* emphasized the new cemetery's location at the "borders of two worlds," permitting access to future-oriented "dreams of hope and ambition" and past-directed "melancholy meditations."[27] The contrast visible from this spatiotemporal border appears, in Story's speech, as the most significant achievement of the new cemetery, since it combined both perspectives into a vision of "profound wisdom," an all-encompassing view of the time of humanity. Departing from the Puritan vision of mortality as an end to temporality, however, the rural cemetery movement's Romantically derived aesthetic emphasized the persistence of the human spirit, highlighting the redemption made possible by attending to nature. Jacob Bigelow, one of Mount Auburn's founders, justified the rural cemetery as best befitted to this type of mortuary pedagogy:

> The monuments of Mount Auburn mark an earthly sepulchre; but the spot itself, with its abundant and impressive beauties is, as it were, the inscribed Monument of Nature to the neverfading greatness of the supreme Judge of both quick and dead—the invincible Arbiter of our fate, both here and hereafter. Heathen must be that heart which does not worship the Almighty amidst these consecrated frames. . . . The history of mankind in all ages, shows that the human heart clings to the grave of its disappointed wishes . . . [and] seeks consolation in rearing emblems and monuments, and in collecting images of beauty over the disappearing relics of humanity. This can be fitly done, not in the tumultuous and harassing din of cities . . . but amidst the quiet verdure of the field, under the broad and cheerful light of heaven, where the harmonious and ever-changing face of nature reminds us, by its resuscitating influences, that to die is but to live again.[28]

Illustrating the transhistorical universality of human attachment, which cannot easily reconcile itself to the losses sustained in linear time, Bigelow holds that the natural urge to grieve is best satisfied away from the "din" of the modern city, which only underscores the heartbreaking passage of time, and within the natural setting, whose reassuringly "harmonious" repetitive rhythms are stabilized by the "broad and cheerful light of heaven." Bigelow thus accounts for the design of the new cemeteries by aligning three extralinear modes—the "clinging" of lingering grief, the cyclical regenerativity of nature, and the "neverfading greatness" of the Almighty—against the pain of loss.

Another version of this redemptive arrangement of grief as extralinear continuity was established in the domestic confines of the middle-class household, where memorial art and other tokens of familial bereavement intertwined themselves with middle-class décor.[29] The temporal dimension of these homely arrangements is suggested in Thomas Baldwin Thayer's observation that "[i]n every home there is an enshrined memory, a sacred relic, a ring, a lock of shining hair, a broken plaything, a book, a picture, something sacredly kept and guarded, which speaks of death, which tells as plainly as words, of some one long since gone."[30] Meant to underscore the universality of bereavement, Thayer's comment also suggests how sentimental artifacts consecrated the home, allowing domestic shrines to function as in-house supplements to the gravesite. Memorial relics became increasingly regular features of the home space, as homemade objects (commemorative samplers and handwoven hair jewelry) were supplemented by mass-produced, personalizable inducements to memory that incorporated the dead within the affective present tense of the family.[31] These staples of middle-class domestic culture offered material forms for the preservation of the past, indexing the way that grief's openness to recollection conserved the "human" apart from the ever more rapid pace of a self-consciously modernizing society.[32] Maintaining the memory of the dead within the home—a site associated with the origin of interpersonal bonds in the form of the affectionate family and hence celebrated by an increasingly domestic culture for giving the human its value—ameliorated the sense of loss that might attend a strictly linear view of time by preserving a sense of cyclical continuity. The regenerativity of the family, in this sense, offers another example of the continuity established through the appeal to "nature" in nineteenth-century mourning culture; its stable, repetitive rhythms, articulating on the small scale as the methodical sequences of domestic life and on the large scale as the reproductive/generational cycles suturing the family to history, made space within time for the consolidation and preservation of the timeless truths revealed by the "naturalness" of the human.

This insistence on continuity suggests a more nuanced understanding of nineteenth-century constructions of publicity and privacy as designating not social spaces per se but temporal *structures*—linear (public) or extralinear (private) time—associated with distinct modes of production. Whereas the linear time of public life corresponded to an insistence on time's gainfulness, figured as invention, creativity, or progress, the largely cyclical time of private life made space, as we have seen, for the reproduction of that which was understood to be *always already given* about the human—the foundational affective dispositions on which the post-Enlightenment conception of the social depended. And as the cycles of privacy made space for a periodic return to human origins, the public emphasis on progress kept the private moving forward, organized not around mere *return* but around *renewal.* In this sense, the "arrow" of linear/public time pulled the inclusive circles of repetitive/private time forward, permitting the retention of affective ties to the past without allowing them to overtake the future-directedness of the present.[33] This necessity was underscored, as we will see in the next section, by the historical/temporal tutelage provided in nineteenth-century consolation literature, which solicited "natural" feeling for the dead while organizing the feeling body and the moments that authorized its conservation of time in relation to the "completeness" of a posthumous future whose insistent immanence would always counterbalance the (regressive) heart-tuggings of emotion.

Conservation and Consolation: Textures of Attachment

Grief's ability to serve as a lynchpin between public and private temporalities was predicated on its perception as the subjective shadow of an objective truth about time. While loss, which set grief into motion, demonstrated that external time was linear and irreversible, the pain of grief spoke, in essence, to duration, the psychological *experience* of time.[34] Nineteenth-century consolation literature dramatized grief's duration as a time apart, a deeply personal, and yet widely known, relation to the passage of the moment. In a world increasingly constructed around change, the connections forged in grief's lingering preserved some measure of continuity, precisely through its affiliation with extralinear temporal modes. The altered relation to time that characterizes the emotional world of the mourner is repeatedly invoked in Nehemiah Adams's 1859 tract *Catharine.* Following on the success of the Congregationalist minister's popular *Agnes and the Key of Her Little Coffin* (1857), *Catharine* was written, like the earlier book, from the perspective of a bereaved father, mourning his nineteen-year-old daughter's death from consumption. It presents itself, accordingly, as offering sympathetic fellowship to the mourner, rather than authoritative instruction. Interestingly, however, it is precisely the *waning* of sympathetic consolation in the lived world of the mourner, and thus the widening of a gap between interior and exterior time, that occasions the text. Adams opens by insisting that it is not recent but *remembered* loss that troubles most, associated as it is with an emotional isolation whose pace is radically distinct from the ordinary experience of time:

> the greatest suffering at the death of a friend does not occur immediately upon the event. It comes when the world have forgotten that you have cause to weep; for when the eyes are dry, the heart is often bleeding. There are hours,—no, they are more concentrated than hours,—there are moments, when the thought of a lost and loved one, who has perished out of your family circle, suspends all interest in every thing else; when the memory of the departed floats over you like a wandering perfume, and recollections come in throngs with it, flooding the soul with grief. The name, of necessity or accidentally spoken, sets all your soul ajar; and your sense of loss, utter loss, for all time, brings more sorrow with it by far than the parting scene.[35]

Adams's description of such compressed moments highlights their alluring nature; despite the pain of the mourner's "suffering," the seductiveness of sorrow is amply demonstrated in his comparison of memory to "wandering perfume" and his emphasis on the soul-opening brought about by the sound of the departed's name. This intermingling of the pain of grief with sensory traces evoking the material presence of the lost beloved accounts for the mourner's desire to dwell within such moments, spots of time outside the ordinary sequence of daily life, as compensation for the ineradicability of loss. Grief appears, here, as a pleasurable pain, as it both measures, in its anguish, the depth of the loss and recalls the bliss of connection. Adams extends this reflection on the mixed nature of grief in his meditation on a precious relic of his daughter's childhood, a guitar that he taught her to play during her illness:

> We kept [the guitar] in its case in my study; and sometimes, on coming home, and feeling in the mood of it, I wished to handle it, and instead of unlocking the case to see if the instrument were there, I would knock upon it; and straightway what turbulence of harmonies rang from all the strings. Now, it is so with every thing connected with her memory; every

> thing associated with her, even though outwardly sombre and dreary, like those black cases for musical instruments, being appealed to, or accidentally encountered, sings of her still, with a troubled and a pathetic, pleasing music.[36]

The complex emotional/temporal texture assigned to grief in this comparison resonates through Adams's use of the musical metaphor. The melancholy of mixed feelings, the "pathetic, pleasing" nature of the memory-songs emanating from things connected with the lost child, is linked to the experience of sorrow over the dead, an experience that obeys its own temporal rules, through music, a figure for duration.[37] The ability of music, in this passage, to "mean" beyond the denotative and grammatical limits of language, to "sing still" of the lost child, responds to the mourner's impossible desire to reproduce the experience of encountering the departed by offering a displaced sense-memory that both amplifies and faintly compensates for the palpable feeling of absence suffered by the mourner.

Catharine's meditation on the temporality of lingering grief aligns its engaging seductiveness with a *retrospective* opening of the subject: it sets the soul "ajar" but permits only "recollections" to enter. But although the desire for such moments is understood as both "innocent" and "natural," the book itself is dedicated to advancing the search for the departed forward in time, reframing the mourner's quest according to a celestial calendar:

> Sometimes we feel as though we were sailing away from our departed friends, leaving them behind us. Not so; we are sailing towards them; they went forward, and we are nearer to them now than yesterday; and the night is far spent; the day is at hand.[38]

Catharine's insistence on regulating the regressive pull of the mournful moment reorients the Christian mourner toward the memory of the future. Grief, Adams insisted, should not work toward "bringing [the departed] back, in our thoughts, to our dwellings" but rather should push the mourner "forward . . . to their dwelling," toward the eternal reunion that stood as the telos of the redeemed life.[39]

Though not always as consistently focused on conversion as the work of Adams, nineteenth-century American consolation literature generally held to the timeframe outlined in *Catharine*. Mourner's handbooks, formerly composed entirely of religious discourses on the necessity of preparation for the afterlife, now became mixtures of works deemed consolatory, incorporating poetry, extracts from fiction, and letters of condolence alongside Biblical texts and sermons. These collections represented themselves, implicitly or explicitly, as productions of mourners just like the reader, whose experience guaranteed that the writings therein contained would have a salutary effect.[40] Such works both solicited intense feeling and, importantly, warned against allowing the temporality of lingering grief to congeal into *lagging*— to move backward, against the requirements of life and the telos of the Christian subject.[41] They underscored the need for any subject who wanted a future to forswear the asynchronicity of "repining," allowing grief to prevent a return to ordinary time, by associating such behaviors with a mode of pastness that was not timeless but simply archaic: the heathen or savage past.[42] An insistence on keeping this past in its place—refusing to allow it to permeate and pervert the present—infused contemporary discussions of the aesthetics of memorial. Although the rural-cemetery movement understood itself, as I observed in the preceding section, as constructing the kinds of nonlinear time-spaces appropriate to the regenerative work of mourning, commentators also insisted that care should be taken, within these spaces, to avoid the "melancholy" motifs redolent of a past better left abandoned. An 1825 mourner's manual authored by a Unitarian minister reminded the reader that "the cypress shade, night and darkness were fit objects and images to be connected with death, among those who 'sat in the region and shadow of death'—who mourned as having no hope. But Christians are forbidden to mourn as they did."[43] It was not only church-affiliated writers who emphasized this timeframe, however. The identity of proper mourning with progress was also foregrounded by an anonymous writer in the *North American Review*, who, in a discussion of the new rural cemeteries, chastised mourners who chose for the graves of their departed obelisks and other icons of ancient Egypt. Declaring that this imagery was "anterior to civilization" and thus could not be considered beautiful, the writer went on to argue that

> Egyptian architecture reminds us of the religion which called it into being—the most degraded and revolting paganism that ever existed. It is the architecture of embalmed cats and deified crocodiles: solid, stupendous, and time-defying, we allow; but associated in our minds with all that is disgusting and absurd in superstition. Now, there is certainly no place . . . where it is more desirable that our religion should be present

39

> to the mind, than the cemetery, which must be regarded either as the
> end of all things—the last, melancholy, hopeless resort of perishing hu-
> manity . . . or, on the other hand, as the gateway to a glorious immortal-
> ity—the passage to a brighter world.[44]

In this aesthetic vision, memorial is meaningless, mere "superstition," if it
fails to articulate the present as linked to the Christian vision of eternity—a
link that articulated the superiority of the nineteenth century to the primitive past. The spiritual impoverishment of that past is suggested by its pur-
ported attachment to the materiality of *thingified* bodies, apart from the
sanctifying spirit that might redeem them. The pagan worship of lowly life-
forms suggests, for this writer, the desire for preservation of the body at the
cost of the soul, a conflict articulated in the insistence that only two possible
readings could be given to the space of death: it would reflect either termination or continuity, either the inescapable acting-out of a "melancholy"
connection to the past or the prelude to the "brighter" future that connoted,
at once, the promise of heaven and, implicitly, the teleological vision of hu-
mankind's progress from degradation to enlightenment.

The distinction between past- and future-directedness enforced in these
articulations of the aesthetics of memorial presses the alternate temporalities engaged in moments of intensive mourning into correspondence with a
binary division imposed by the linear model of time. Civilization and Christianity both pointed toward the future, whereas the "perishing" debris of
the physical body, apart from these, could speak only of the past.[45] This correspondence applied limits to the sensory qualities that could properly be
engaged in the slowed time of the mourner; the lack of "beauty" ascribed to
certain relics of prehistory is aligned with a lack of the redemptive hope associated with faith, rendering them pathetic but not pleasing. Unlike the
sentimental music of Catharine's guitar, then, things that could not transcend their thingly nature were not permitted to serve as props for the
painful pleasure of recollection, for such prompts promised only regressive
associations, failing to manage the asynchronous pull of a human "nature"
posited in and through the affective and sensory capacities of the body by
displacing its desires onto a longing for the future. The aesthetics of mourning developed in nineteenth-century consolation culture sought, in other
words, to temper the appeal to nature by developing and encouraging only
those continuities that bespoke a vision at once Christian and civilized, enabling historical as well as spiritual transcendence. The division between re-

demptive and nonredemptive relics imposed in this vision worked to assure that the sacred truths to which grief appealed would not be profaned by mere archaism.

The Biopolitics of Feeling: Culture, Race, and National Subjects

As we have seen thus far, the coupling of the feeling body to time enacted in the nineteenth-century appeal to grief—figured in Irving's *Sketch-Book of Geoffrey Crayon* as a *marriage* between the self and its noblest feelings, the "sorrow from which we refuse to be divorced"—was remarkably productive. It supplied a source of knowledge about the human subject that shaped the understanding of "natural" relations between self and others while providing a means of distinguishing between mourners in terms of emotional behavior. This latter process forms part of what Michel Foucault, in *The History of Sexuality, Volume 1,* calls "biopolitics," or the corporeal management of populations.[46] The validation of emotion and the emphasis on the dynamics of fellow-feeling that characterized even theologically conservative nineteenth-century consolation tracts demonstrate the increased emphasis on the body in the culture of mourning and its connection, through grief, to alternate temporalities. The dynamics of consolation extended the effects of the rift in time opened in the subject by loss, moving it both outward to link feeling to all "humanity" and backward to reconstruct human history itself as the repository of sacred exchanges of feeling. The preface to the popular compendium *The Mourner's Book,* for instance, justifies its collection of various accounts of grief and mourning by representing it thus:

> It is soothing and grateful to [the mourner] to have the mourner of other times and distant lands breathe forth their sorrows in the language which his own feelings are prompting him to utter. Heart speaks to heart, and a common sorrow unites him in strong bonds of brotherhood with all of his race, who have mourned like himself.[47]

Consolation literature's relation to the mourner-reader was predicated on this self-presentation as a timeless storehouse of fellow-feeling, couched in the language of the intimate exchange. Positing itself as the reader's contemporary, it depicted its guidance as a horizontal act of sympathy—demonstrated in *The Mourner's Book*'s vision of a common affective language and in

Adams's authorial situation of himself as a bereft father—instead of a linear imposition of authority on the mourner.

The transpersonal connectedness of sympathy was evoked as a means of restoring the regenerative capacity of human nature. Sympathy, valorized as the foundational principle of the self-regulating society insofar as it revealed the "moral instinct" that, as Jefferson insisted, authorized humans to "feel and to succor . . . distresses," was formally installed as social convention—indeed, as social *obligation*—in the culture of mourning.[48] Consolation literature's insistence on the naturalness of sympathy appears in its tendency to ornament its texts with the prelinguistic speech of affect, the corporeal speech-acts of humanity's "native language." Its contention that tears, sighs, and signifying silences spoke more truthfully than "mere" words established a standard of sincerity that acknowledged the body as the site of *collective* return to the foundational truth of the human. Accentuating the intersubjective production of the natural, consolation literature insisted that "the tear of sympathy not only refreshes the heart on which it drops, but it elevates and beautifies the nature of him from whom it springs."[49] The affective speech of sympathy posited consolation as a means of correcting the isolated and potentially wayward temporality of the mourner; the sympathetic exchange would return the bereaved to the present tense of the community.

But while they actively solicited the corporeal speech of affect, consolation manuals also strictly demarcated appropriate bounds for the expression of grief and sympathy. Middle-class mourners were pressured to conform to a strict set of behavioral rules, discouraged from extreme displays of emotion and from refusing condolence calls; condolers were likewise warned to refrain from encouraging the bereaved to indulge extensively in longing for the past and implored, instead, to remind the mourner of the consolations of faith. These rules defended against behaviors that were not only unseemly but, importantly, *untimely*; since sympathy created a conduit that shared the sensations of the body, both parties were required to exert a degree of self-regulation in order to prevent the transmission of disorder. Condolence culture, accordingly, organized its representations of the feeling body in order to limit the possibility of perverse effects. Nineteenth-century mourners were urged, as Karen Halttunen observes, to "assume an air of quietly controlled grief"; consolation literature reminded them of this directive, arguing that the irreversibility of linear time mandated compliance: "We should be calm, humble, and discharge every duty. Excessive grief will do no good—the event has occurred—the departed cannot be recalled."[50] In its insistence on accepting the facticity of the "event," its assertion that emotion could not alter the linear course of time, nineteenth-century consolation literature sought to prevent human nature from arresting progress, offering the timeless future in exchange for the seductiveness of the past.

In this sense, consolation literature's insistence on the priority of the future served historical as well as spiritual purposes. The failure to be comforted by the promise of heaven called into question the very basis of one's civilized status; as Jacob Bigelow contends in his reflection on the consolations of nature quoted earlier, this failure branded one as "heathen," out of step with the spiritual norms embraced by the churchgoing American. The heathen, emblem of precivility, was surpassed in history by the Christian, who alone was guaranteed a future both in and out of time. Consolation culture's repeated evocation of the specter of such failures suggested the temporal as well as spiritual rewards to be gained by dedicating oneself to its vision of the order of time. Nehemiah Adams's popular book *Agnes and the Key of Her Little Coffin* (first published in 1857), which, like *Catharine*, deployed the shared sorrow of child-loss as a means of spiritual instruction, contains a particularly revealing instance of this type of dedication. Moved by his desire to console other bereaved parents, *Agnes*'s narrator encounters Mr. Burke, a drover, a "stout, coarse-looking man" whose heathen behavior excites some alarm.[51] Refusing to mute his sorrow in company, Burke instead wails aloud and beats his head against the wall, motivating the narrator to compare the man to "one of his own bullocks, drawn by a rope and windlass to the slaughter."[52] After the narrator and his wife succeed in converting the drover to Christianity, however, he exchanges his hopeless sorrow for the consolation of commercial life, becoming a successful merchant and a member of his church choir. Halttunen cites this incident as evidence of the class-based cultural work of consolation, arguing that it demonstrates mourning's use as an antecedent to "bourgeois respectability"; she comments wryly, "Affliction had brought to this once coarse and lowly man not only a new heart and a new countenance but a new job and a new suit of clothes."[53] It is worth emphasizing, however, that what purchases both the new body and the new social standing of the drover in Adams's account is not affliction per se but his eventual submission to the temporal dictates of Christian mourning—his newfound ability to use grief as a means of recalling the spiritual necessity of self-management in time, so that, in addition to becoming "tenfold more of a man than he was before," the former drover has "changed his prospects for eternity."[54] Consolation literature thus embraced precisely the ordering of time that grounds the Protestant work ethic: the belief that time belongs to God and that humans bear the responsibility of "improving" upon it by deferring to the future.[55] Even as the moral authority of the faith rested on its ability to promise an eventual transcendence of time itself, then, Christianity also operated in this period to underwrite the material, scientific, and political dimensions of earthly progress; it appeared, in effect, as both a sign of the times, an index of the progressive advancement of civilization over savagery, and an answer to time, the ultimate solution to the trials faced by those who lived under its tyranny.[56] The class-marked civility that distinguished the self-understanding of these exhortations to productive mourning was thus also conceived as a Euro- and specifically Anglo-American formation, an extension of the circumatlantic culture of sensibility whose roots Julie Ellison traces.[57] Indeed, although the transhistorical conversation between "hearts" that consolation literature offered was in theory boundless, such works tended to draw a culturally distinctive picture of how, precisely, this body of work imagined "all of his race, who have mourned like himself." The occasional touching spectacle of "primitive" faith was included among their typical selection of Biblical tracts and works by British and Anglo-American authors as testimony to the human universality of grief, but on the whole, these works' ordering of the middle-class white interior came to depend not only on the anxious self-monitoring detailed by Halttunen but also on the contrast between proper, Christian mourning and disorderly modes of bereavement, which were, notably, associated with the Indian and the black slave. This contrast transposed onto the national scale the wounds of time appealed to in the nineteenth-century incitement to grief, tying racial difference—variously conceived as cultural and as biological—to chronologies of cultural affective development that linked the temporal perversity of blacks and Indians, revealed in their wayward feelings, to their failure to signify in the annals of national history.

The persistent white fascination with Native American mourning practices offers an early example of this self-conscious contrast. Early colonists ascribed the ferocity and lengthiness of Native American mourning rituals to the spiritual incompleteness of the unredeemed heathen. In the 1643 *Key into the Language of America,* for example, Roger Williams details the extreme length and solemnity of Indian "bewailing" of the dead; this description resonates against his earlier observation that "Death [is] the King of Terrours to all naturall men: and though the Natives hold the Soule to live ever, yet not holding a Resurrection, they die, and mourn without Hope."[58] Williams's depiction of heathen mourning as the response of the "naturall" man— which is to say, the unconverted man—continued to resound in nineteenth-century consolation literature, visible, for instance, in the skepticism of the aforementioned Congregationalist ministers that human nature alone, un-tutored by Biblical knowledge, might be capable of providing a spiritually satisfactory reaction to loss. Yet as a redemptive emphasis on passion and emotion came, over the course of the eighteenth and early nineteenth centuries, to play a greater part in the self-understanding of the Anglo-American, an affirmation of continuity between "natural" and civilized modes of mourning developed, supplementing the early Christian suspicion of the "bewailing" rituals practiced by Native Americans with an approbation of the fundamentally human dimension of interpersonal attachment they revealed. In his *Notes on the State of Virginia,* for instance, Thomas Jefferson resists Buffon's hypothesis of the degeneracy of life in the Americas by positing an essential physical, mental, and emotional resemblance between whites and Native Americans; the latter, he argues, possess not only physical and intellectual strength but also powerful affections: "his friendships are strong and faithful to the utmost extremity. . . . his sensibility is keen, even the warriors weeping most bitterly on the loss of their children, though in general they endeavour to appear superior to human events."[59] The contention that Native Americans' response to loss reveals not their dissimilarity but their basic similarity to whites in an "earlier" stage of civilization also appears in Jonathan Carver's 1784 *Three Years' Travel through the Interior of North America,* which recounts the story of an Indian couple who engage in conventional Native American rites of mourning the loss of their four-year-old son—bewailing and self-mutilation—with "such uncommon rigour" as to kill the father. At this point, Carver reports, the now dually bereaved mother abruptly ceases to mourn and appears "cheerful and resigned."[60] Astonished, Carver inquires of the woman why she has ceased to bewail her losses and learns that she believes her husband managed, by grieving himself to death, to join their child in the "country of spirits" and care for him. Instead of faulting the Indians for "uncivilized" mourning practices, Carver lauds the woman's simultaneous expression of a deeply human affection for her child and stoical resignation to her fate as a widow: "Expressions so replete with unaffected tenderness, and sentiments that would have done honor to a Roman matron, made an impression on my mind greatly in favor of the people to whom they belonged, and tended not a little to counteract the prejudices I had entertained . . . of Indian insensibility and want of parental affection."[61] Carver's tender admiration of the woman is further confirmed by observing her nightly repetition of a "plaintive melancholy song" at her family's burial site, which demonstrates to him, despite her diurnal stoicism, that "some particles of that reluctance to be separated from a beloved relation, which is implanted either by nature or custom in every human heart, still lurked in hers."[62] The point of Carver's inclusion of this tale is not simply to exhibit the strange "savagery" of Indian mourning customs to whites but to use them as a means of both identifying with and historicizing the Indian, accomplishing the latter through his comparison of the Indian woman's socially mandated stoicism to that of the Roman matron, which forges a connection to the Revolutionary account of the democratic state's origins, and the former on the basis of the universal insight offered by grief into the composition of the human heart. In this view, Indian mourning practices revealed both a temporal difference from whites, accounted for by the historically distinct pace of development in Native and Euro-American cultures, and a glimpse at the timeless truth of feeling that both founded and continued to shape human social interaction.

As appeals to affection became more firmly intertwined in the nineteenth century with the familial nature of "nature" itself, the lack of national futurity assigned to Native American culture, lauded as an illustration of prehistoric human "nature," became, ironically, *more* pronounced. The Anglo-American appeal to the universality of nature was tempered, that is, by the oft-cited insistence on the Indian incapacity for civilization, an insistence that offered justification for the spatial distancing of Native American populations from the scene of American progress.[63] This conviction marked nineteenth-century ethnographic representations of Native American religion as itself temporally perverse, incapable of the kind of spiritual ordering of the passions we earlier saw in Christian consolation literature.[64] In the work of the ethnolinguist Henry Rowe Schoolcraft, for instance, the character of the Native American afterlife explained the Indian's putative disinterest in progress:

> [The Indian] believes a future state to be one of rewards, and restitutions, and not of punishments. The Indian idea of paradise is the idea of the orientals. It consists of sensualities, not spiritualities. He expects the scene to furnish him ease and plenty. Ease and plenty make the Indian's happiness here, and his heaven is but a bright transcript of his earth.[65]

The Indian idea of the afterlife, Schoolcraft contended, neutralized any desire for earthly self-improvement, the gradual attainment of temporal mastery that would permit the realization of heaven as a promised future, rather than a fuller instantiation of the present, disabling precisely the kind of spiritual/temporal pedagogy that Christian consolation literature sought to enact. The problem with Native American religion, in this account, is that its essentially quantitative distinction between the material and spiritual worlds—the vision of heaven as "but a bright transcript" of earth—promotes a vision of sensual continuity that fails to make a significant difference in time.

Schoolcraft's writing outlines how the Native American preference for continuing the "natural" rhythms of life, lacking the spiritual means of connecting itself to American "progress," was seen by whites as collapsing in upon itself in time.[66] But although the Indian lacked a future in national-historical time, the timeless quality of the natural world that he bespoke was Romantically conserved in the image of the noble savage, the cherished symbol of the harmonious state of nature, lamentably vanishing into the past at the onset of civilization. Thus, if Indians could not mourn properly according to the Anglo-American ideal, they could still be properly mourned by whites, whose accounts of the nation increasingly sacralized the figure of the Indian, aligning it with the immemorial time of the prenational past, and thus extended the interior attachments of the white subject to embrace a cultural as well as a familial history.[67] The linear model of progress embraced by the new nation, however, made no room for the material repetition of this past; once transcended, precivility could only return, within the time-space of the nation, as memory: the prized image of a distant origin. The (Anglo-) American sacralization of the Indian, in this sense, posited an absolute distinction in space to regularize the distribution of time: the life-world of the Indian, exterior to the new nation's modes of ordering, could only be incorporated into its historical timeline through its construction as permanently anterior, the cultural memory-trace of a (transcended) other way of living, cherished for the natural plenitude it commemorated but incapable of survival in a civilized era.[68]

Anglo-American attention to the Indian relationship to death and mourning in this period supplants a posited corporeal continuity, a similarity of basic human feeling, with an insistence on the cultural dissimilarity revealed by religious difference. Within the contemporaneous ascription of an affective time-lag to African Americans, however, we can observe the "nature" of racial difference moving directly into the space of the (black) body itself, which came to be understood as signifying a mode of temporal recalcitrance less cultural than biological. Cultural models of temporal difference informed early colonists' view of the otherness of the slave; for instance, African American funerary practices, drawn from West African religious traditions, were dismissed by white observers as "primitive" and unruly, and commentators reported with dismay that even slaves who had been converted to Christianity were subjected after death to these "Heathenish rites" by fellow slaves whose fidelity to traditions out of step with American norms appeared undiminished.[69] Yet late-eighteenth- and nineteenth-century accounts of African American difference came increasingly to stress not cultural or religious affiliation but embodiment as the origin of African American asynchronicity. An account of the untimely body informed, as we have seen, Thomas Jefferson's epistolary dismissal of the melancholy subject as unfitted for democratic leadership; for Jefferson, a melancholy nature directed the subject's gaze too insistently toward the past, preventing the optimism necessary for a correctly progressive disposition.[70] In *Notes on the State of Virginia,* Jefferson developed a complementary account of the untimely body in his insistence on the unfitness of African Americans for citizenship. In a comparison that departed from the essential similarity he posited between Europeans and Native Americans, Jefferson implied that the difference of the black body was a matter of time. Arguing that that their superior bravery and ardency emerged from a "want of forethought" and an amorous eagerness that lacked the "tender delicate mixture of sentiment and sensation" proper to whites, he conceived the black body as cognitively and emotionally childlike, observing, "Their griefs are transient. Those numberless afflictions, which render it doubtful whether heaven has given life to us in mercy or in wrath, are less felt, and sooner forgotten with them. In general, their existence appears to participate more of sensation than reflection."[71] The "want of forethought" that Jefferson ascribed to blacks was thus compounded by a want of hindsight, an insufficient relationship to loss, particularly damning for a thinker so attached to the naturalness of the human bond. The transience of black grief in his account underscored the paucity of the moral basis for self-control: the inability to abstract oneself from the immediacy of sensation, a condition whose pathology also surfaced in his denigration of the gloomy "hypocondriac." If the melancholy body suffered from an excess of the past, the black body, for Jefferson, was physiologically suspended in the present, unable to develop the capacity for "reflection" that permitted the subject to orient himself in time and, accordingly, consigned to a permanently infantile existence. Proponents of slavery embraced such models of the black body's biological asynchronicity to argue for the natural authority of the institution; the sensational and infantile nature of the black body, they insisted, justified its location within the "peculiar institution," which now began to depict itself in domestic terms. In such accounts, the slaveholding household was represented, in effect, as doing "service" to the nation by creating a time-space for the containment of the African American body, which it separated from the progressive and self-managing time of public life and tied, instead, to the repetitive rhythms of labor.

The permanent suspension of the infantilized black body within a white-managed holding system represents an effacement of the problem slavery posed within the accepted temporal frame of liberal subjectivity. Elizabeth Maddock Dillon's recent assessment of liberalism as a narrative that "begins in privacy and moves forward into public agency" illuminates the way this account of the civil subject posits privacy as prepolitical—yet "privacy," she stresses, is a *retrospective* formation dependent on the mode of publicity toward which it is understood to lead.[72] Liberalism's narrative orders the division we earlier saw established between publicity and privacy, where the latter was set aside for (re)producing the givenness of the human: we can say, in this light, that the time-scheme of liberalism reproduces privacy as constitutively prior to—as the *natural ground of*—political agency. Slavery, as Dillon observes, presents a problem for liberalism's distinction between the affective space of the family and the rational space of the public sphere, insofar as the temporality of the slave counts, within this narrative, as not pre- but *a*political: the slave is suspended within the narrative of liberalism but, because he or she is not understood to participate in the propulsion of the civil subject forward toward publicity, falls out of sync with its narrative organization—an effect that threatens to reveal the fictive nature of privacy itself as the ground of liberal political identity.[73] Dillon proposes that a critical understanding of this location reveals the way "slaves become a particularly *sacred* form of property insofar as they sustain a connection between whiteness, property ownership, and political subjectivity."[74] The sacralizing of the slave-as-property follows the form I have earlier identified with the sacralizing of the Indian as, in effect, constructing a kind of property that can be understood as national "heritage": it creates an exceptional loop whereby a selected population is expended from the progress of a national history that yet depends on this exception, and this dependence itself requires the designation of these narratives of national agency as sacred, unable to be touched without profanation—which is to say, without revealing their status as foundational *fictions*. Dillon's analysis thus helps to clarify how the pathologizing of African and Native American timeways supported the narrative construction of democratic subjectivity as both a micropolitical account of individual agency and a macropolitical account of national progress; the expulsion of the Indian lifeworld to the margins of the nation reflected its deliberate location as prenational, a temporality generative of Americanness but incompatible with its modern organization, while the asynchronic suspension of the black slave within the "householding" system of slavery constituted a mode of internalized containment designed to mask the potential contradiction between liberal ideology and national practice.[75]

Yet the same exceptional temporality that served to contain both black and Indian agency could return, from some perspectives, as a wound: a perpetually unresolved contradiction in time that threatened its steady progression. Jefferson, for example, despite his dismissal of black grief as reflecting a natural corporeal inferiority, understood slavery as an essentially *temporal* inconsistency within the history of the Americas, as its implicit negation of natural rights undermined the very foundation of the democratic nation.[76] Jefferson's perception of the instability generated by the institution of slavery registers the damage as an effect of two unresolved accounts of nature: as at once a principle of origin that generates the nation and a corporeal iteration that maintains a set of inclinations. In what follows, I will examine how nineteenth-century American reformers situated this wound itself as a means of regenerating time.

Retaining Grief, Changing Futures

Refusing Jefferson's distinction between black sensation and white reflective emotion, sentimental opponents of slavery appealed to popular accounts of the universality of grief in order to underscore an essential similarity between the distress of the black slave and the feelings of bereaved whites. Harriet Beecher Stowe's monumental deployment of the sentimental strategy in *Uncle Tom's Cabin* makes this equation explicitly, as her narrator repeatedly aligns the pain experienced by slaves in response to the familial separations mandated by the slave trade with the sorrow of white parents grieving the demise of children. Such appeals to grief, and particularly to the peculiar emotional temporality associated with child-loss, work, as Karen Sánchez-Eppler observes, to keep the social meaning of deeply private feeling, represented as the ongoing woundedness of the mournful subject, "importantly open."[77] This openness is reflected in Stowe's conviction that the lingering sorrow associated with the dead—the very cherishing of the wounds of time that Crayon depicted as a cultural duty—could, despite both religious and rational-political attempts to limit the direction of its significance, still be appealed to as a means of reordering the social body. In Stowe's novel, indeed, that appeal refounds the nation itself as a collection of familially oriented subjects seeking a millennial and fundamentally maternal regeneration of damaged national time. An example of the novel's logic of affective pedagogy comes in the reader's introduction to the Ohian family of Senator Bird, shortly before the fugitive slave-mother Eliza seeks that family's assistance in escaping North to protect her son Harry, who has been sold by their master to a slave-trader.[78] When Eliza, after her perilous crossing of the Ohio River, arrives at the Bird home, the scene of familial grief that she inspires functions to correct public indifference, altering the Senator's conviction that he represents and therefore cannot contravene the "rational" decisions of the nation. Crucially, what this incident models is not simply the reformation of social space through the sentimental appeal to grief but also the systematic inversion of the liberal hierarchy of public and private *time* championed in the opening pages of the chapter by Senator Bird, who voted for the Fugitive Slave Act because, as he tells his wife, "public interests" require "private feeling" to be set aside (144). Indeed, the chapter's very title, "In which it appears that a Senator is but a man," condenses the narrative shape that this temporal inversion will take; it both predicts the chapter's arrest of the indifferent forward movement of national time through a return to the slowed time of private feeling and frames this arrest as a process of *rehumanization*: the affective becoming-man of a public figure. Eliza accomplishes this transformation by asking Mrs. Bird (who, she notices, is dressed in mourning) if she has ever lost a child and, upon receiving a pained affirmative response, sharing the story of her own two traumatizing child-losses as a means of accounting for her desperate desire to save Harry; by the time she is through, the Senator, who weeps over the story along with his family, has become thoroughly committed to her cause. The attentive reader will also recall that Eliza's canny ability to reset the pace of the scene in the Bird household comes as the result of her own instruction in grief, told in the novel's second chapter, "The Mother." It is in this chapter that the reader first learns of the deaths of Eliza's two children and learns, significantly, that she "mourned [them] with a grief so intense as to call for gentle remonstrance from her mistress, who sought, with maternal anxiety, to direct her naturally passionate feelings within the bounds of reason and religion" (57). The excessive grief to which Eliza is subjected by her "passionate" nature both recalls and inverts the model of the untimely black body outlined in Jefferson's vision of its sensational imbalance; here, Eliza is marked not by transient but intransigent grief. But maternality, for Stowe, is naturally allied to religion, and hence the "reflective" capacity that Jefferson insists the black body lacks is amply provided, in Stowe's narrative, through repeated applications of the cyclical/maternal principle: first Eliza is taken in hand by Mrs. Shelby, her motherly white mistress, and after she is recalled to "reason and religion," her wounds are seemingly cured by the birth of Harry, when "every bleeding tie and throbbing nerve, once more entwined with that little life, seemed to become sound and healthful" (57). The hesitant language of this passage sets the stage for the immanent reopening of that wound when Harry is sold, yet instead of collapsing into grief, she launches a heroic campaign to save Harry, using every tool at her disposal, including her cunning engagement with the Birds' visible wounds. Eliza's story not only succeeds in winning the Bird family to her side—the Senator, despite his previous championing of the law, agrees to take the mother and child to a stop on the Underground Railroad—but also reopens, against the commercial rationalization of time championed by the Senator, the natural time of affection, showing how the cherishing of grief makes space for the restorative feeling-in-common of sympathy. After the success of Eliza's appeal, the narrator pauses to explore the mood of the moment, describing Mrs. Bird's emotions upon gathering up some clothes of her dead son Henry to aid in Harry's escape:

> There are in this world blessed souls, whose sorrows all spring up into joys for others; whose earthly hopes, laid in the grave with many tears, are the seed from which spring healing flowers and balm for the desolate and the distressed. Among such was the delicate woman who sits there by the lamp, dropping slow tears, while she prepares the memorials of her own lost one for the outcast wanderer. (154)

The "slow tears" emphasized in this passage, which recall both those wept for Eliza's dead children and the many others shed in the past on behalf of

Henry, model the affective creation of a cross-racial, cross-class connection between dead and living children through the medium of mourning. The mother's tears function, here, to make space in time, nourishing the regenerativity of hope, the restoration of futurity through the cyclical action of the natural. The fluidity that tears confer upon time is limited, however, both by the slowness proper to the productive cherishing of grief (in fact, it is crucial to this passage that Mrs. Bird's tears are *not* hysterical; they do not disrupt, but actually augment, her ability to get things done) and by the monumentality associated with the sacred figure of the child: for although Harry and Henry may be different children, as the *sign* of the beloved child they signify an identity beyond their particularity in time and space. This identity assures a modicum of continuity between past and present that complements the regenerative work of sympathy as it operates across boundaries of class and race, softening the potential temporal disruption of social change into the (natural) variability of the everchanging-sameness at the heart of the affective/social bond.

The mode of negotiating occluded national wounds through personal grief that Stowe employed in *Uncle Tom's Cabin* has been critiqued, as we saw in the introduction to this study, for its tendency to perpetuate an effectively traumatized national public, one trained to mistake collective participation in the temporal suspension peculiar to moments of intensified feeling for political action.[79] To the extent that Stowe's novel does so, I would suggest, part of the problem lies in the tendency to dissolve distinctive pasts into an affirmatively universalized present. The affective equivalence established between the past-tense loss of Henry due to natural causes and the threatened loss of Harry by means of political ones reveals the extent to which Stowe's insistence on the universality of feeling leads her to efface causes as she equates effects—an approach that meets its limits when, as Glenn Hendler warns, "any significant cultural or experiential difference between the subject and object" of sympathy returns.[80] Another mode of engaging retained grief is foregrounded in the deliberately partial deployment that characterizes the Methodist minister and Pequot activist William Apess's *Eulogy on King Philip*, an address delivered (and later printed) in Boston in 1836, which both rewrites American history in terms of the prolonged grief of the Indian population (Apess, notably, calls for all people of color to don mourning clothes on both the Fourth of July and the anniversary of the Plymouth Rock landing) and refuses to universalize that grief by extending to whites the invitation to sympathetically identify with it.

Apess's eulogy for Metacom, the Wampanoag sachem who led a confederation of tribes in the seventeenth-century uprising against the New England settlers known as King Philip's War, subtly inverts the temporal strategy of conventional eulogy, which functions as a means of regularizing the passage of time.[81] The stages of formal eulogy seek to overcome the rupture occasioned by the death of an individual, establishing an ordered distance between past and present while positing a compensatory timelessness—the promise of eternity or, in secular-nationalist eulogy, the "reward" of monumental lastingness—that makes losses in time bearable. Although the *Eulogy on King Philip* follows this conventional structure, it also suggests that its temporal operations are far from innocent, tying them to the drive to displace the Indian, in time and in space, from American national history. Recent critical assessments of the *Eulogy* have emphasized Apess's audacious (though by no means unprecedented) equation of Metacom, viewed by the Puritans as an enemy of the state, with the figure of George Washington as American national founding father.[82] The *Eulogy*'s deft engagement with the temporal implications of grief in this period, however, moves beyond this challenge to the *content* of national narrative and into an assessment of the very *forms* that, as we have seen, underlie the temporality of liberalism. Writing in 1836, Apess had to contend with two divergent white American stories of "King Philip": one that located the Wampanoag rebel spatially outside the nation as an enemy and another that, drawing on the sacralized figure of the noble savage, enfolded him within national tradition, but only by situating the Indian as anterior to the modern nation—the very temporal division that authorized the emergent removal policies against which Apess posited his claim for full Native American citizenship. In this light, the most significant temporal intervention of the *Eulogy* is not its promotion of Philip to the status of monumental icon, with a legacy rivaling that of "the immortal Washington [who] lives endeared and engraven on the hearts of every white American, never to be forgotten in time," but instead its depiction of contemporary Native Americans as "those few remaining descendants [of Philip] who now remain as the monument of the cruelty of those who came to improve our race and correct our errors."[83]

These two images (which appear in the *Eulogy* within the same complex sentence) generate a tension between two affectively coded forms of temporal extension—the temporal transcendence of the founder-hero and the retained grief of his descendants, testimony to monumental cruelty—which is not sentimentally resolved into a unifying appeal to transtemporal feeling.

Instead, Apess keeps the grief of the Native American in view, maintaining its legitimacy without directly inviting his white audience to participate in it. At a crucial point, the *Eulogy* invokes the mechanisms of sympathy by appealing to the emotional/temporal problem of child-loss as a means of bridging the gap between the seventeenth and nineteenth centuries: "O white woman! What would you think if some foreign nation, unknown to you, should come and carry away from you three lovely children. . . . What would you think of them?"[84] This interjection predicts a later moment, near the close of the *Eulogy,* in which Apess recalls Jefferson by assuring his audience that Indians love and mourn their children as much as do whites. Yet Apess's emphasis in the earlier direct address invokes the grief imputed to the bereft (Indian) parent to demand not fellow-feeling but critical thought from the white addressee, a demand that preserves history along with feeling. Refusing the conventions of sympathetic consolation, the *Eulogy* explicitly reserves the invocation to grief for those *not* present, whom Apess apostrophizes in a passage shortly afterward: "O savage, where art thou, to weep over the Christian's crimes?"[85] The absence of the mournful savage underscores the *Eulogy*'s active resistance to the sentimental fantasy that shared grief might itself serve as some kind of consolation for the damage of national history. Whites in the audience are, instead, invited to "blush, while the son of the forest drops a tear."[86] Apess's emphasis on these differing responses, weeping and blushing, establishes a distinction between the temporalities corresponding to grief and shame; shame, in effect, signals a present-tense loss of innocence, the affective immediacy that marks the severing of the liberal subject from the conviction of his or her own innocence, without offering the attachments invoked in the incitement to grief as a compensatory temporal prop for that self-division.[87]

The *Eulogy*'s refusal to solicit shared sympathy via the spectacle of child-loss thus echoes on an affective level its historical critique of the nation. Its resistance to sentimentality and the displacement of its opening appeal to the Revolutionary founding fathers by the cruelty emphasized in its review of the seventeenth-century Indian wars—the narration of which also affords Apess occasion to denounce the institution of slavery, whose advocates he assesses as "worse than . . . beast[s]"[88]—alike expose the violence that underlies the nation's favored accounts of itself. This resistance continues through the address's concluding appeal to the commonality of affective feeling and political desire between whites and Indians; while Apess replicates, in this appeal, the concluding move of conventional eulogy, which works to bring together survivors as a community of the consoled, he also refuses the complete dissolution of history in the moment of that coming-together. Observing that he has some "dear, good friends" among whites, he nevertheless insists that the perpetuation of past violence in present treatment prevents him from trusting them completely; similarly, he insists that the missionary drive to conversion be preceded by transformative legal action that will enable Indians to be in sync with the nation as "citizens," not merely as Christians.[89] Apess's ambivalent engagement with the universality of feeling in the *Eulogy* in part reflects his Methodist training, which combined the doctrines of universal salvation and prevenient grace—the prior status of divine love—with an insistence on perseverance, the need to maintain salvation through action; as Barry O'Connell observes, however, the *Eulogy* reflects his abandonment of the conviction that the invocation of Christian fellowship might effect change in the political or material status of Native Americans.[90] The *Eulogy*'s appeal to the grief of the Indian thus refuses both the affective dissolution of sympathy and the deferral to divine judgment in order to outline a different temporality for the progress of the nation: one that requires neither a sense of common origins nor faith in full affective simultaneity in order to generate a collective future in time.

Although Apess's strategic engagement with consolation's forms varies from Stowe's insistence on the equitability of feeling across histories, both writers maintain the conviction that the strategic display of persistent affective wounds may effect change in the nation's future. And yet paradoxically, although both writers explicitly associate personal feeling and national politics, each also understands both feeling and family to be originally and properly prepolitical: natural formations that may be affected by (radically misguided) public policies and that may, in turn, be appealed to in order to correct those policies, but without any inherent politics or histories of their own. In the next and final section of this chapter, accordingly, I want to return to the putatively apolitical genre of consolation literature in order to further interrogate the temporal implications of the nature it posited.

Timing the Interior: Grief's Archaeologies

In the preceding section, we saw the emergence of a divided temporality associated with the notion of "nature," which signified both as foundational, the prehistoric and therefore timeless principle of social origins, and as a repetitive corporeal manifestation moving through historical time. These two temporal principles combine to characterize the imagined realm that Dillon identifies, within the narrative construction of liberalism, as the paradigmatic space of the prepolitical: the domestically oriented middle-class private sphere, which reproduces the (white) liberal subject, generationally, across time as well as projecting him forward into public agency. Consolidating the affectional and bioreproductive dimensions of the human under the sign of the family, domesticity also functions to set these dimensions apart from political life by affixing them to another time, rendering, as Dillon explains, both sexual and racial difference as "mute truth[s] of the physical world rather than . . . political assertion[s] subject to negotiation among contracting individuals."[91] Nineteenth-century appeals to grief ceaselessly solicited the corporeal speech that underlay these "mute truths"—the feelings of the diachronically conceived embodied subject, who suffers losses in time and responds with feeling, as "nature" demands—but solicited them as outside and prior to the (historical) realm of politics as such. And although politics was indeed, as we have seen, understood to create grief in history, it was not understood to generate grief as such: that generation came from "nature" alone.

At this juncture, then, I want to return to the question of grief's prepolitical status in consolation literature, examining in some detail a contemporary representation of the emotional eventfulness of loss. This depiction, the poem "The Little Shroud," centers on the feelings produced by the loss of a child, filtered through its "natural" complement, the figure of the mother. First published in 1822 in the London-based *Literary Gazette,* the poem, authored by the British poet L.E.L. (Letitia Landon), was reprinted in several midcentury American mourning manuals. Its inclusion within a study of American mourning culture is motivated both by its circulation in the United States and, more particularly, by the way it illustrates what we earlier saw as that culture's connection to a genteel sensibility that constructed itself self-consciously as Euro- and particularly Anglo-American.[92] The migration of the poem from the *Literary Gazette,* a journal devoted to literary culture, whose poetry section featured regular contributions from L.E.L., to the pages of American mourner's handbooks demonstrates the way that consolation literature posited itself as a cross-cultural and transtemporal collection of intensive moments—those moments in which, as the preface to *The Mourner's Book* (which reprinted "The Little Shroud") put it, "Heart speaks to heart, and a common sorrow unites [the mourner] in strong bonds of brotherhood with all of his race, who have mourned like himself."[93]

Centered, as its title implies, on the loss of a child, "The Little Shroud" reveals the foundational status of mourning motherhood, which combined, in one figure, the divided temporality of "nature" we observed earlier, in relation to this ideal of affective brotherhood. As mothers, women suggested at once a cultural location, the home, and a corporeal disposition, the nurturance of life-giving, which could reproduce itself across time through their natural and harmonious coexistence in a single figure. The historically new association of the privacy I earlier identified as linked to the reproduction of the human with a maternally nurtured domesticity marks the time of the mother as differing from both the antenational (but extrapolitical) immemorial time symbolized by the lamented figure of the Indian and the incorporated apolitical asynchronicity imputed to the sensationally unsentimental black slave. In effect, the affectionate (white) mother is, as Dillon points out, paradigmatically prepolitical, both inaugurating and reproducing, for each successive generation, the foundational affective dispositions on which the continued progress of the democratic nation would depend.[94] This domestication of privacy in the figure of the mother at once generates and depends on a distinctive balance of time, which we may begin to trace with reference to Julia Kristeva's influential essay "Women's Time." Citing the three temporal modes we have thus far observed to interact within nineteenth-century accounts of the progress of the human—the linear time of progress, the cyclical time of regeneration, and the timelessness of sacred truth—Kristeva observes that these modes have historically taken gendered forms in Western cultures; she associates linear time, "time as project, teleology, linear and prospective unfolding," with the masculine, and repetition and timelessness with the feminine.[95] Outlining the duality of feminine time, she observes,

> On the one hand, there are cycles, gestation, the eternal recurrence of a biological rhythm which conforms to that of nature and imposes a temporality whose stereotyping may shock, but whose regularity and unison with what is experienced as extrasubjective time, cosmic time, occasions vertiginous visions and unnameable *jouissance.* On the other hand, and perhaps as a consequence, there is the massive presence of a monumental temporality, without cleavage or escape, which has so little to do with linear time (which passes) that the very word "temporality" hardly fits.[96]

Though Kristeva traces the repetitive structure of women's time back to the time of the reproductive body, whose essential "conformity" to nature here appears as timeless, she also suggests that these two types of time have become feminized only insofar as woman "is thought of as necessarily maternal."[97] In this sense, this affinity is most usefully understood not as an *essential* assertion of women's conformity to nature but as an identification of a particular chronobiopolitical location of women in relation to "nature"— the view of motherhood (not simply reproduction) as the temporal destiny of the female body. Motherhood, here, constitutes the maintenance of the human's humanness, emblematizing at once the cyclical rhythms of nature and a repository of the timeless truth of affection that stabilizes the race's travel toward the future.

Insofar as motherhood becomes, here, an ideological rather than a biological function, the ideal manifestation of motherhood was reserved for those whose offspring counted as subjects with recognized futures; hence, as Hortense Spillers has shown, in a system in which the possession of normatively gendered attributes was reserved for whites, black female bodies, for instance, reproduced but did not gain the status of "mother."[98] Sentimental appeals like Stowe's, as we have seen, sought to extend the recognition of that status to those whom custom excluded, such as the slave-mother Eliza. But Eliza's example also points us to the way that the temporal (re)productivity of this arrangement manifests in the mother's grieving over lost children, which served at once to poignantly underscore the instinctive nurturant tendencies ascribed to the female body and to emphasize the way mothers' "natural" affective openness returned, in mourning, as a problem to be managed.[99] This problem—the challenge of preserving the affective predispositions exemplified by grief while preventing grief from turning time back on itself—was, as we have seen, central to nineteenth-century norms of mourning, and the mother's unique place in time, as both foundational and iterative, leads to the particularly troubling potential for temporal perversity enfolded in her disposition. Stowe's novel implicitly affiliates Eliza's naturally passionate nature with her race—and yet, at the same time, the novel insists that *all* good mothers are naturally passionate, though the best ones learn to manage these passions well. In much the same way, condolence literature insisted that all mourners and all mothers in particular needed to manage their grief through attentive self-discipline, modulation of expressions of sorrow, faithful dedication to Christian tenets, and a return, after a brief, respectful interval, to the rhythms of everyday domestic routine—the very bounds of "reason and religion" that Mrs. Shelby seeks to impress upon Eliza. Mourning mothers' indulgence in unbounded grief intensified this temporal misbehavior into a form of abuse, since, as they were warned, it could harm their surviving children, throwing their future (and accordingly, the future of the nation) into disarray. Excessive attachments to the dead were seen, in this light, to strike at the foundation of the social order through the specter of the neglected child, who appears as the negative form of that memory of the future that consolation culture insisted must outweigh the regressive potential of the "heart."[100]

The mother's emotional relationship to the child thus emerges in the nineteenth century as an affective/temporal configuration of monumental significance; it becomes the primary means of stabilizing "progress" by extending an essential *identity* between past and present into the future.[101] This principle of temporal regulation is dramatically outlined in "The Little Shroud," which narrates the need for emotional control as an effect of emotional attachment itself. Landon's poem recounts the story of a mother who, after burying the last of her children, weeps so intensely by her dead son's grave that he returns and begs her to stop. I quote it here in its entirety:

> She put him on a snow-white shroud,
> A chaplet on his head;
> And gathered early primroses
> To scatter o'er the dead
>
> She laid him in his little grave,
> 'Twas hard to lay him there
> When spring was putting forth its flowers,
> And everything was fair.
>
> She had lost many children—now
> The last of them was gone,
> And day and night she sat and wept
> Beside the funeral stone.
>
> One midnight, while her constant tears
> Were falling with the dew,
> She heard a voice, and lo! her child
> Stood by her, weeping too!

His shroud was damp, his face was white,
He said, "I cannot sleep,
Your tears have made my shroud so wet,
Oh, mother, do not weep!"

Oh, love is strong! . . . the mother's heart
Was filled with tender fears,
Oh, love is strong! . . . and for her child,
Her grief restrained its tears.

One eve a light shone round her bed,
And there she saw him stand.
Her infant in his little shroud,
A taper in his hand.

"Lo! mother, see my shroud is dry,
And I can sleep once more!"
And beautiful the parting smile
The little infant wore!

And down within the silent grave
He laid his weary head,
And soon the early violets,
Grew o'er his grassy bed.

The mother went her household ways
Again she knelt in prayer,
And only asked of heaven its aid
Her heavy lot to bear.[102]

"The Little Shroud" depicts the refusal to limit indulgence in sorrow over the lost past as denying a future to both the living and the dead. Although the mother's prolonged mourning succeeds in temporarily restoring her child to her sight, his distress indicates that this restoration is a disruption of the natural order of things. Intense grief thus appears in the poem as resistance to the flow of time, defiance of both divine law and the logic of generational succession appealed to in the family, where even dead children must be cared for properly in order to be assured a suitable future. For even the death of her *last* child, in the poem, does not free the mother from the continued obligation to be maternal; the same care required to allow the living child to move on *in* time, developing into a healthy adult, is demanded to enable the dead child to move on *from* time, passing into eternal "sleep." The mother's affective overflow must thus be corrected by a return to its place of origin—an appeal, on the part of the child, to the very love from which her grief emerges. Once the mother's "grief restrain[s] its tears," temporal order is regained; the child is able to "sleep," accessing eternity, while the violets growing over his grave signal the regeneration of spring, a renewal that allows the mother, as the child's earthly counterpart, to reenter everyday time, resuming her cyclical "household ways." Love for the child thus appears as a sacred reminder of the primacy of the future, keeping the mother's feelings in order so that time can continue moving forward.

The story told in "The Little Shroud" suggests the reproductive/generational orientation at the heart of what we can recognize as a sexual politics of time in the nineteenth century—a politics that both proliferated the temporal and chronological meanings of the body and insisted that grief's minor, extralinear time-spaces fall in line with a future-directed mandate. In this configuration, love for the child takes on the stabilizing function aligned with the monumental in Kristeva's depiction of "women's time," protecting cyclical repetition from temporal collapse; this split between the cyclical and the monumental is arranged diachronically to enforce the necessity of progression, of moving on from the suspension of time within traumatized mourning. For the mother, "moving on" signifies a return to the repetitive rhythms of the home, maintained as the time-space of human generation even in the absence of living children. The necessity of proper mourning for the child thus conserves the prepolitical timing of motherhood; doubling the domestic work that makes possible the development of the living child in time, it ensures the reproduction of the generative space that grounds the temporality of the liberal subject.

From one perspective—the one illuminated by the critical trajectory that my consideration of the affective ordering of time in nineteenth-century consolation literature has thus far followed—this doubling speaks to the gentle insistence of mourning culture on compliance with its modes of ordering. The moralizing effect of Landon's poem, in which the mother's mourning resonates as the individual playing-out of a general truth about time, befitted it for its circulation in the context of consolation literature, which reinforced this connection by reproducing the mother herself as an

instructive example to readers, who were encouraged to emulate her un-
selfish self-control regardless of their own social/familial positioning. In this
sense, the poem reads as extending the temporally normalizing work of the
culture of mourning into the interior of the bereft subject, reproducing the
didactic insistence of writers like Nehemiah Adams on limiting the asynchronic pull of grief-stricken moments. Yet I want to call attention, as well,
to how "The Little Shroud" illuminates and amplifies the pull of such moments even as it ostensibly insists on the necessity of surrendering them
—how its dilation on the painful pleasure of longing intimates that the
sticky textures of attachment might tug against authoritative arrangements
of time, pointing toward the buried traces of resistance that consolation
worked to cover over.

A recognition of the primarily psychological, rather than religious, depiction of the mourning process in the poem will help to open this interrogation. The narrative development of correct bereavement behavior organizing "The Little Shroud" corresponds not only to the psychological assessment of mourning process we earlier saw suggested by Fowler but also to the
more developed account later put forward by Freud, in which the mournful
subject is gradually enabled to relinquish attachments to a lost object by the
painful psychic labor—the grief-work—that produces a sufficient memory-
image of that object (in the poem, the parting image of the child's smile) allowing the subject to resume ordinary life in time.[103] This prevision is less
striking, however, if we recall not only that the affective subject to which
sentimental condolence culture addressed itself appears, in retrospect, as
what Glenn Hendler rightly terms an "early form of the psychoanalytic subject" but also that Freud's account of normative mourning was grafted directly onto the very conventionality of the narrative repeatedly outlined in
and through consolation writing: what we call "normal" mourning, Freud
observes, might also strike us as pathological were it not so familiar to us.[104]
The mechanisms for that familiarization—and concurrent *familialization,*
along the lines of domestic privacy—reveal themselves in the disciplinary
narrative traced within "The Little Shroud." Yet this regulatory story is not
the only one told within the poem. For even as its conclusion reinstates the
bereaved mother in the time of the living, repairing the rupture effected
by traumatizing loss and bringing the mourning process to its prescribed
end, the poem's melancholy excesses point to another reading of the temporal dynamics of grief: the resistance of the complex textures of time traced
around attachment to the ordering of narrative. That resistance emerges in

the poem's poignant imagery: for example, in the opening stanza's tracing of the mother's loving arrangement of the child's dead body and in the pained contrast, detailed in the second stanza, between the generative movements of nature and the gesture of surrendering the child's body through burial, echoed in the reference to her vigil beside the unresponsive "funeral stone" and the parallel between her "constant tears" and the "dew." These moments work, through their attention to detail, to evoke precisely the exhaustive search of human nature for the material presence of the lost beloved we earlier saw in Nehemiah Adams's writing, slowing the poem's move toward the mother's final abandonment of the search posited near its close. The concentration of moments in "The Little Shroud" at once underscores and delays the impact of the need to relinquish the search for the lost child, pointing us toward the way the aesthetic appeal of the poem founds itself precisely upon the reader's assumption of an ambivalence toward this necessity.

A similar ambivalence, I would suggest, surfaces in the poem's structure, as the overall narrative flow of its movement from the child's burial to the mother's achievement of "closure" is not simply suspended but also abridged by moments of irregular repetition. Here, we must recall not only the back-and-forth temporal movement of the seventh and eighth lines ("She had lost many children—now / The last of them was gone"), which recollects, in the wake of the burial, the mother's multiple experience of loss as it affects her response to the child's death, but also the duality of the adverb "again" as it modifies the closing image of the mother kneeling to pray for divine support in bearing the burden of bereftness. "Again," in this line, suggests both resumption, a return to practices abandoned during deepest mourning, and repetition, an activity that must be iterated in time in order to assure its success. The implicit connection, here, between repeated loss and repeated prayer seems to serve a spiritually didactic purpose, the need for faith to "correct" the longings of human nature, a necessity that consolation literature enforced in part by promising a compensatory reunion with the lost beloved in heaven. Significantly, however, the poem itself promises no such reunion. The dual return of the dead child suggests a posthumous existence, but the child returns, as his speech makes clear, to demand *release* from the earthly sign of that existence, requesting that his mother relinquish him to the "sleep" of the grave without prophesizing any compensatory exchange. This request recalls, moreover, the utter abandonment of the mother emphasized in the backward turn of the seventh line; without that compensatory promise, she seems to have no future as a mother in *or* out of time. And here, we might note that the account of mourning offered by the poem differs from Freud's early analysis, in "Mourning and Melancholia," in one significant respect: the availability of a substitute-object in everyday time to which the ego can reattach itself, confirming the successful conclusion of the mourning process. Indeed, in its refusal to posit a substitute-object for the mother's affections, the poem strikingly predicts Freud's later recognition that mourning is effectively endless: that "we shall remain inconsolable and will never find a substitute" for the lost beloved, an observation that Freud connected to the human desire to *perpetuate* love rather than relinquish it.[105] At the close of "The Little Shroud," the "beautiful" memory-image of the child alone is finally insufficient to prevent a recurrence of the mother's hopeless mourning; her "burden" can only be supported by the regular repetition of prayer, substituting regular incursions of divine assistance for the stabilizing presence of the child himself. This conclusion, as I suggested earlier, seems to echo the insistence in tracts like Adams's *Catharine* that human affection must remain supplementary to God's authority; in Adams's view, the longing for the dead should always point survivors "onward and upward." Yet in "The Little Shroud," the balance of authority is effectively reversed; divine aid becomes merely supplementary to the primacy of "love" itself. The power of love is appealed to, in the poem, in the repeated interjection, "Oh, love is strong!" which recurs twice in the sixth stanza, immediately following the child's first return. The apostrophe's ambiguous address, here, both echoes the child's appeal to the mother in the preceding line ("Oh, mother . . .") and diffuses it—not precisely "turning away" from the primary addressee but amplifying the appeal of the assertion across space and time—an amplification that both requires and displaces the supplementary assistance of prayer at the end of the poem.[106] For in suggesting that the mother's love for the child, the very cause of her grief, is also, in the absence of posttemporal compensation, the only means of "restraining" that grief's excesses, the poem posits love alone as that compensation—posits, that is, love as *its own* compensation. Prayer's secondary status, in this sense, reveals the poem's assessment of emotional attachment as not the effect but a cause of the divine spirit; we might see praying itself, in this light, as an activity that permits the mother a periodic reacquaintance with her "heavy lot," the painful weight of the absence that stands, at the end of the poem, as the only remaining link to the child's presence.

The temporal logic of the "The Little Shroud," in short, both reproduces and significantly reverses the authoritative coordinates of Christian consolation culture, in a move that posits the conservation of its future-directedness in the guise of an ongoing familiality (and specifically maternality) as the condition of possibility for a covert continuation of the pleasures of asynchronic attachment. In this light, what I earlier identified as a largely psychological, rather than religious, depiction of the mourning process takes over the spiritual-temporal discipline we saw in earlier sections almost without skipping a beat. That "almost," however, is crucial. For if the poem points us to the way that the authority of "love," in the nineteenth century, came not simply to supplement but eventually to begin supplanting that of "God" (the displacement that constitutes what Foucault nominates as the emergence of sexuality) and demonstrates, further, the way that the perpetuation of the human's humanness intertwined itself with the maintenance of gendered familial positions that understood the very "nature" of their affections to mandate continued subservience to the needs of a future whose promise took the sacrosanct form of the child, that should still not distract us from the way the poem's melancholy repetitions expose the occluded forms of time's division. That is to say, the appeal to "love" as a means of stabilizing the temporal relations between self and other—between the mother and the child—is significant not simply because it is historically new but also because, read against itself as the repetition invites, it threatens to undermine its own temporally stabilizing function. We might recall, here, Kristeva's suggestion that the dual temporalities of repetition and timelessness, both of which are assigned to woman as a consequence of her conception as maternal, are interrelated and perhaps mutually supporting—each occasions but also limits the other. The limitless potential of "love" here—a love that threatens, in its return as grief, to undo the mother—is finally brought under control by its (re)direction toward the child, in the recollection of the timeless "nature" of maternal affection that transforms her endless vigil into ordinary domestic rhythms, a recollection that orders the mother's continuing subjection to this positioning in time.[107] But as I have suggested, the poem directs this affective intensity toward the image of a "future" *recognizable* as a necessary fiction—for at the close of the poem, as a result of the mother's love, no child remains to her, save in the burden of his absence. In this light, we can grasp the problem of love itself at the exposed foundation of the poem—an exposure that returns us to Sánchez-Eppler's suggestion that the appeal to grief functioned in nineteenth-century sentimental culture to keep the social meanings of an affective subjectivity (meanings that,

I would add, are always temporally elaborated) conceived as foundationally wounded importantly *open*. Although the close of the poem may order the mourner in time, it does not terminate the pull of the wound at its center —the ongoing mode of *lamentation* invoked in that repeated, melancholy "oh"—and hence does not finally close down what the future of love may become.

I would not argue that readers of "The Little Shroud" necessarily followed the poem's melancholy exposure of the fictive nature of affective/reproductive time in precisely the way that Apess's audience, for instance, might follow the logic of the direct challenge "Oh, white woman! . . . what would you think of them?" What I am proposing, rather, is that they could *sense* it, in a manner similar to the operation of the sensory force Adams associates with intensive moments of grieving. This potentially profane pleasure appears, in Adams's tract, as a possible distraction from the religiously mandated necessity of deferring completion—the arrival of the perfect "bliss" that the subject is always awaiting—onto the (posttemporal) future; in "The Little Shroud," we see how that distraction threatens to overwhelm the "natural" affectionate structures that govern domestic privacy with an abundance of love. But it is precisely the attraction of such distractions, I am arguing, that pulled readers toward the "history" of their own feelings in literary appeals to grief—a history that perpetually invited but never precisely coincided with the temporal discipline of consolation culture. Understood in this way, the melancholy and abundant pleasures promised in reading, writing, and speaking grief in nineteenth-century print culture can be seen to trace an archaeology of the subject's interiority which highlights the buried question at the heart of consolation culture: the always-uncertain relation of "love" to time.

The economy of grief, as cultural historians remind us, had become big business in antebellum America. The sale of consolation tracts and mourner's handbooks like the ones I have been describing, the marketing of rural cemetery plots and markers, and the mass production of memorial artifacts— what Esther Schor christens the "calm commerce of condolence"—effectively established the time-apart associated with lingering grief as a prevision of what would come to be known as leisure time.[108] In this sense, it provided both a point of entry for regularized narratives of self and nation and, crucially, a space where work on both self and nation might be accomplished. For that reason, it remains crucial to consider the pull of grief within and against history as such—a pull that, as I have outlined here, both placed mourning at the center of sentimental reformist challenges to national narratives and generated a number of less conventional but still palpable moments in which wholly familiar forms of time were rendered partly unrecognizable to themselves. The variable intensity of these moments, as they surface in the nineteenth-century literary insistence on caressing grief, will be my focus in the chapters that follow.

2

Evocations

The Romance of Indian Lament

In the final scene of *The Pioneers* (1823), the first novel in James Fenimore Cooper's Leatherstocking series, the white frontiersman Natty Bumppo visits the grave of his longtime companion, the Mohican sachem Chingachgook. Gazing at the images decorating the stone—a pipe and a tomahawk—Natty grudgingly admits that the carving is not bad, although it was likely done by someone "who never seed 'ither of the things."[1] But Natty, having spent his life in the woods, is illiterate, and so Oliver Effingham, the genteel grandson of the English officer who lies buried beside Chingachgook, must read the inscription aloud to him. The grave's poor transliteration of the spoken Delaware language leads Effingham (who, having shared a hut with Chingachgook for several months, might be expected to know better) to mangle both his tribal and given names; Natty, listening, protests the erroneous writing, insisting, "The name should be set down right, for an Indian's name has always some meaning in it."[2] As Effingham reaches the end of the epitaph, however, Natty finally finds something on the stone he can endorse:

> " 'He was the last of his people who continued to inhabit this country; and it may be said of him that his faults were those of an Indian, and his virtues those of a man.' "
>
> "You never said truer word, Mr. Oliver; ah's me! if you had knowed him as I did, in his prime . . . you'd have said all that, and more too."[3]

Natty's insistence that there is "more" to Chingachgook than the words on the stone can say sets the mournful work of recollection against the amnesia of official history. This opposition is linked, in the scene, to the inferiority of writing itself, which is incapable of accurately conveying the essence of Indian oral culture; indeed, the stone's flawed inscription of the Indian past reproduces itself in the incorrect speech of the young American Effingham, who consults its writing in place of his own memory, as if the amnesia inherent in monumental history has already begun to infect him.[4] Yet Effingham's mistake also serves to remind the reader that if speech, compared with writing, is capable of expressing "all that, and more," it is also as evanescent as the "smokes . . . from the Delaware camps" that Natty remembers adorning the surrounding hills; unlike the writing on the grave, it expires along with the speaker.[5] For the other truth Natty hears in Oliver's recital is the declaration that Chingachgook was the *last* of his people to live in the region. His objections to the monument's lapses in accuracy thus underscore the absence of the Indian voice that, supplanted by the ring of settlers' hammers and their writing on the stone, will never again be heard—a fatalistic conclusion reinforced in Natty's own melancholy sigh, "ah's me!"

This evocative sigh, gesturing toward those virtues now present only to Natty's memory, recalls the untimely dilemma associated with his preference for voice over writing: the alignment of voice's presence with an "authentic" experience of temporality, one that writing can never fully convey, versus the desire for (self) preservation in history, which the ephemerality of voice cannot guarantee. The true sound of the Indian voice resonates, in this passage, as belonging to another time, the time before the establishment of the nation opened the continent to "progress," when meaning resided not only in speech but also, as Natty's insistent correction of Effingham's reading suggests, in *sonorousness*.[6] This sense of sound as particularly active in the Indian voice pushes the temporal dilemma that Natty articulates still farther back in time, until it brushes up against the radically extralinear time associated with the sonic origins of speech—a time in which meaning is understood to be conveyed by the immediate intuition of feeling rather than the accumulation of significance enabled by language. This conception of the sonic connectedness enabled by voice speaks to the synchronization of the human according to currents of sympathetic feeling that could draw distinct individuals together in space and time, but it provides no diachronic principle for the perpetuation of that affective connection—hence Natty's sense of melancholy.

In this chapter, I examine the way the romance of the Vanishing American—the popular nineteenth-century story of the lamentable-yet-inevitable disappearance of the Indian in the presence of civilization—managed the temporal dilemma evoked in Natty's sigh. Considering the fascination with the *sound* of Indian speech as the aural trace of another time that marks early-nineteenth-century Anglo-American writing about Indians, I argue that this writing works to consolidate a "heritage" for the young nation by imagining a diachronic mode of transmission for the evocative time of the voice: the affective connectedness of the family, whose future-directed generativity, as we saw in the preceding chapter, was embraced as a means of navigating the gap between extralinear immediacy and the new insistence on the fundamentally linear order of historical time. The sacred affections of the family sentimentalized the sensational appeal of Indian orality, transposing the prehistorical and prenational time of the Indian to the prepolitical time of the Anglo-American private sphere and revising the *anteriority* of that voice in terms of the foundational positioning of human *interiority*. At the same time, the romance of the Vanishing American worked to revive and order the time of the voice by projecting its anachronistic potential onto Indians.[7] Indian orality, converted from the "terrible noise" heard by early colonists to a harmonious dialogue with nature, was nevertheless understood as incompatible with a progressive historical era.[8] As I will show, however, the "vanishing" narrative permitted the citizens of the new nation to retain certain aspects of this fantasy of primal sonic vitality as a means of enlivening emergent sexual arrangements. The ability of voice to signal both interiority and anteriority, that is, structured the spatiotemporal fantasy that would come to characterize middle-class domesticity, which also posited its affective interiors as coming *before* the historical time of public life.[9]

The indirect status of voice in written texts—its appearance, of necessity, as an evocation—places a particular pressure on my analysis of the history of voice's exceptional status; accordingly, I want to pause here to sketch in some detail the trajectory of my argument in this chapter, as it seeks to uncover and retain the ephemerality of voice in the service of literary analysis.[10] I begin by exploring how the sound of the voice has been sacralized in modernity. Considering accounts of the history of language from the eighteenth through the twentieth centuries, I show how the voice has been aligned with an extralinear and prehistoric temporality radically distinct from the linear/accumulative ordering enabled by language and, especially, by writing. I contend that historical romances of the 1820s positioned the Indian voice in order to produce a distinctly American (re)telling of this story about time. This self-consciously transitional positioning was made possible by the historical romance's coincidence with what I identify as the "time of mourning Indians," a temporality that evokes both the asynchronic traces that contemporary white auditors heard in Native American oral bereavement rituals and the historical moment in which their accounts emerged—a moment that saw the deliberate transposition of the Indian to the past tense in the American historical imagination, a cultural "policy" that, as a number of commentators have shown, aided in the legitimation of federal removal policies. This transposition, I suggest, fixed the resonance of the Indian voice within a minor key; the "melancholy" echo of this voice, that is, bespoke civilized man's rueful "recognition" of the fact that time could not go backward, a conviction that was rearticulated in the ethnographic distinction between Indian and white time, which insisted that the fundamental distinction between savagery and civilization was the ability to make a difference in (and with) time, a task it claimed the politically melancholic Indian could not manage.[11]

Both of the novels I discuss participate in this process of articulating the Indian voice as a kind of heritage for the contemporary American reader, positioning that voice within the register of affection/sexuality, although, as I show, they arrange its temporal legacy according to divergent sexual politics. Cooper's *The Last of the Mohicans: A Narrative of the Year 1757* (1826) works through the evocative citation of voice that closed the preceding Leatherstocking novel. *The Last of the Mohicans,* set in a mid-eighteenth-century American wilderness conceived as transitional, maps the chronotopic significance of that prenational wilderness through sound. Yet the novel insists that the vitalizing memories inspired by imaginative contact with the Indian voice—memories that work to supplement the historical exhaustion of European patriarchal authority—must be continually scrutinized for lingering traces of a temporal duplicity it associates with (and abjects as) femininity, one that marks the voices of both forward-thinking women and strangely "backward" men in the narrative. Catharine Maria Sedgwick's *Hope Leslie; or, Early Times in the Massachusetts* (1827) reads as a deliberate response to Cooper's positioning of the feminine. In Sedgwick's historical romance, set in the seventeenth century, the attempt to reclaim the voice of the Indian woman helps inspire a "humanizing" correction to the abuses associated with patriarchally ordered social and sexual systems. Yet the radical rethinking of political time provoked by this correction is, as I show, partly limited by the novel's insistent appeal to the maternal as a principle of reordering.

Histories of the Voice: Sacred Displacements

The temporal dilemma encoded in Natty's evocative appeal to voice at the end of *The Pioneers* reflects, as we have seen, an anxiety about the authority of "human" bonds in a modernizing era. The pioneer's dismay at the displacement of the continent's most natural sounds by the noise of civilization's progress can, in this light, be seen to transpose a by-now-familiar debate about modernity's increasing displacement of the voice by language and, especially, by writing. Natty's melancholy reflects his recognition of the way the writing on Chingachgook's grave (writing he himself cannot decipher) marks the inscription of a national history that not only makes no room for the future of the Indian but also fixes the "pioneering" contribution of his own generation of whites as about to end.[12] But it is this very melancholy, I argue, that establishes the temporality of voice as *ephemeral*, precisely by linking it to a particular notion of *vitality*. I am proposing, that is, that the lament for the natural authority of the voice—for the immanent loss of a temporal difference understood as foundational—corresponds to a chronobiopolitical formation that we might understand as the sacralization of voice, one that provides the putatively ephemeral voice with a certain *duration* through its association with the extralinear and extrahistorical time that grounds the human's progress through history.

This location of the voice appears, as Giorgio Agamben points out, in Aristotle's *Politics*, where voice as the sign of feeling, of "pain and pleasure," is what man has in common with all other animals; language, in contrast, permits moral reflection—it distinguishes man and therefore becomes the foundation of political existence, bios, the directed quest for the good.[13] Agamben contends that from the classical era onward, voice has been aligned with bare life, the realm of sensation and feeling, against the affiliation of language, politics, and directed life; hence, voice is both excluded from rational political life and aporetically retained through the retroformation of the exceptional loop that Agamben identifies with the *homo sacer*. In light of this distinction between life and direction, we may note the chronobiopolitical dimension of the distinction in *time* between the continuous rhythms of bare life and the directed and progressive orientation of politics —a distinction that, as I have suggested, characterizes modernity's temporal ambivalence, as it seeks to "conserve" the rhythms of affective life beneath (and before) the dominance of the linear mode of time.[14] Voice, then, is understood not simply as outside linear time but in a significant sense as a recollection of (sacred) origins. Yet it is, I would stress, the very immediacy and ephemerality allotted to voice that allows it to signify in this manner. For while the conventional insistence on voice's vitality suggests its link to the ostensibly contradictory temporalities assigned to the body, as both the index of a forward-moving, developmental principle, or "growth," and the locus of a regenerative "nature," its ephemerality allowed it to escape full coincidence with either the linear-accumulative or the cyclical-repetitive mode; instead, it stabilized both of them through its fugitive gesture toward "timeless" concerns. Voice's citation of both linear and cyclical modes points us toward an understanding of the way modernity sutures such exceptional temporalities to progress in the form of a loop, the very form that accounts for the fascinating status of voice as viewed from the perspective of language and writing. The multivalence of the loop is suggested in its appearance as the circular manifestation of linearity; as Margot Bouman points out, as form, the loop both "binds and separates, and refuses a singular shape."[15] As a temporal structure, the loop articulates at once a (cyclical) return to origins and the *impossibility* of return in linear time. What Agamben terms the "aporetic" appeal of the state of exception thus becomes visible within the modern subject's distinctive preoccupation with the nature of time, a preoccupation that linked fascination with the voice to its positioning as *anterior* to the linguistic order. Voice, that is, becomes sacralized insofar as it can be *prioritized,* resounding as (the memory of) an idealized exception to time's inexorable linearity.

The critical tendency to pit voice *against* language and writing, I would suggest, exemplifies the way voice is romanced in modernity. An explicit connection between voice and the sacred appears, for example, in Walter J. Ong's influential work on orality and literacy. Ong insists on voice's capacity for interpersonal attachment; he argues, for instance, that since "the spoken word proceeds from the human interior and manifests human beings to one another as conscious interiors, as persons, the spoken word forms human beings into close-knit groups."[16] Ong ties speech's "interiorizing force" to "the sacral, . . . the ultimate concerns of existence," arguing that as the "manifestation of presence," voice carries "permanent religious possibilities."[17] The explicitly Christian framework of Ong's analysis narrates the replacement of speech by writing as the history of "a certain silencing of God, . . . prepared for by the silencing of man's life-world."[18] Ong positions his work on orality as a phenomenological response to the textual emphasis of poststructuralist literary criticism; yet the spiritual underpinnings of his embrace of the world of voice reveal, as Jonathan Sterne points out, its coincidence with the ontotheological prioritization of presence critiqued by Derrida.[19] Following Sterne, I want to call attention specifically to the *sono*-centrism that manifests in the sacred time of Ong's phonocentrism—the belief, that is, that sound's ability to bring one into time with others precedes speech's ability to produce a sense of being in time with oneself. For it is the voice's relation to the world of sound that endows it, in Ong's reading, with this vitality. Ong maintains that "voice is alive because sound is alive"; as an ephemeral phenomenon, he argues, sound manifests the real existence of time in its interaction with the universe.[20] As Sterne observes, however, insofar as this temporal account can be given of any process, Ong's particularized embrace of the liveness of *sound* engages in a "very selective form of nominalism."[21]

Ong's appeal to the sonic liveness of voice, apart from other bodily processes, to tell this story about sacred time thus follows, despite its ostensibly phenomenological basis, the general outlines of the modern narration of voice as indexing a division in the human relation to linear time, one that both concedes and resists its status as an inescapable objective reality. In this account, the time of the speaking voice is always already divided against itself: on the one hand, submitting to the ordering effect of language and, on the other, clinging to an extralinear mode of relation to the natural world that is associated both with materiality and with feeling. And although Ong, a Jesuit, explicitly links his early thinking to a Christian worldview, we can also see a similar account of the voice emerging, in modernity, in self-consciously secular accounts of the "natural" history of feeling. One such account emerges in the proto-Romantic history of language offered by Rousseau, which links the birth of the human voice to the materialization of the passions, corporeal "needs" that are moral, rather than merely physical.[22] The earliest vocal sounds, those inarticulate "exclamations, . . . cries and groans" that emerge "naturally" from the body, work, for Rousseau, to overcome the primary separation enforced by the drive for physical survival: "All the passions tend to bring people back together again, but the necessity of seeking a livelihood forces them apart. It is neither hunger nor thirst but love, hatred, pity, anger, which drew from them the first words. . . . [F]or moving a young heart, or repelling an unjust aggressor, nature dictates accents, cries, lamentations."[23] Significantly, in this passage, the earliest emergence of voice, which will evolve forward in time toward language, is already a regressive movement, intended to bring people "back together *again,*" toward an originary connection that is located prior to the separations of the physical body. The sonorous voice, in this sense, narrates what Derrida aptly identifies as the delayed origin of the human in the body: a foundational belatedness that suggests why the first specifiable direction ascribed by Rousseau to the tonal voice is that of *lamentation*.[24] A similar structure marks psychoanalytic accounts of the infantile relation to voice as a "blanket" of sound enveloping the body, in effect a sonic extension of primal continuity with the maternal body; the tactility of the sonorous voice pulls the infant forward in time, toward language, but this quasi-corporeal contact also resounds as the echo of a primary connectedness that can be recollected, but never reproduced, in linear time.[25] Overlapping the transition in the context of the sonorous voice's appeal to feeling, in these complementary analytic frameworks, from primal to familial (and especially maternal) attachment, is the citation of the sound of the voice as indexing a *lost* moment in time: the bridge between the atemporality of the purely physical and the linear orientation of the civilized individual. In both models, the voice uses the material of the body to redeem the body from pure materiality. Its inspiration, we might say, sets the body in motion toward the achievement of a humanity that is then willed to be foundational. In this light, the temporality of sound—its extralinear immediacy—emerges as the retrospective echo of the progressive accumulation of meaning made possible by language, an asynchronicity that is synchronized by means of a formation we can recognize not only as sexual (in the Foucauldian sense) but specifically as chronobiopolitical: the sacralization of voice perpetuates a link between the sonic and the sacred outside the time of history.

Recent works in American cultural studies document the way the modern insistence on the vitality of voice, as glimpsed in the aforementioned accounts, resonated through post-Revolutionary America. Indeed, an implicit connection between voice and corporeality underlies Christopher Looby's alignment of the American enchantment with voice in the Revolutionary period and the desire for a "visceral" nationality. Because "voice embodied a certain legitimating charisma that print could not," Looby asserts, it connoted "the more passionately attached, quasi-somatically experienced nation for which many Americans longed" in the absence of hereditary models of governance.[26] But although Looby maintains that attachments to voice are not necessarily "nostalgic," his own location of voice as a *charismatic* alternative to the disembodied authority of print itself predicts the temporalizing strategy that emerged in this period to govern voice's attractions: the representation of the sonorous voice as a means of recollecting the body's natural, presocial attachment to others.[27] And crucially, the divided temporality of this recollection increasingly resonated against *race* as an emergent chronology of human development. By the late eighteenth century, as Michael Warner observes, as the capacity for letters became the norm for white citizens, structural and legal limitations on literacy for Native Americans and for black slaves established race as "one of the social meanings of the difference between writing and speech."[28] This structural distinction took temporal form as the unruly noise of the nonliterate was romanticized into the "natural" speech of the *pre*literate. The oral and aural world of the Indian, in particular, signified as not simply exterior but, as we saw in the preceding chapter, as ineradicably *anterior* to the future-projected historical time of the new nation. Whites depicted the Indian relation to the "liveness" of the world of sound as revealing a distinctly primitive disposition; Richard Cullen Rath points out, for instance, that the tendency among northeastern Native American tribes to interpret thunder as the *act* of a mystical being was represented by white colonists as an Indian belief in thunder as the *voice* of (a) god, precisely the conception favored by earlier generations of European settlers and gradually abandoned as irrational.[29] Anglo-Americans' projection of their own past "soundways" onto the Native American population thus constructed the relationship between the two groups as a developmental difference: Indians were, essentially, less evolved versions of whites, a temporal gap that enabled them to serve as civilization's sonic past. The value of this difference, however, varied in response to competing historical valuations of temporal alterity. The "animistic" approach to thunder, for instance, could signify as mere superstition, antithetical to the redeemed Christian worldview, a "backward" belief that should be corrected through conversion. For the Romantically inclined writer, however, it could also bespeak an enduring (and endearing) attachment to the animation of nature: an articulation of the sacred that was not contradictory but supplementary to Christianity as a locus of authority.

This latter articulation is particularly resonant in the mode of acoustic mirroring that characterized nineteenth-century ethnolinguistic celebrations of the *eventfulness* of Indian language.[30] In these accounts, the eloquence of Indian speech was attributed to both its natural simplicity and its affective immediacy: Indians, they insisted, avoided the burdensome rhetorical rules of the civilized world and spoke straight from, and to, the heart.[31] An enchantment with this idea permeates Peter Duponceau's praise of the Delaware language in an 1819 letter to John Heckewelder:

> To me it would appear that the perfection of language consists in being able to express much in a few words; to raise at once in the mind by a

few magic sounds whole masses of thoughts which strike by a kind of instantaneous intuition. . . . such, I should think, were I disposed to indulge in fanciful theories, must have been the language first taught to mankind by the great author of all perfection.[32]

Duponceau's chronology locates the "natural" eloquence of the Indian as an index of the interface between the human and the divine. The effect of Indian languages is linked, in his view, to their sonic immediacy: the replacement of complex passages of grammar and rhetoric by a "few magic sounds," whose resonance initiates a vision of an Edenic lifeworld organized according to an intuited simultaneity. This hypothesized origin is not less attractive to Duponceau for its acknowledged "fancifulness"; indeed, the intertwining of memory with fantasy here seems to form part of the very appeal of thinking through sound.[33]

The same intertwining marked the emergence of the historical romance in America. As Warner observes, the eighteenth-century American novel seems caught between a sense that literature should serve as an exemplary public instrument and the tendency of novel-reading in particular to encourage private fantasy—a tension that, he notes, underlies the common critical perception of all American novels before Cooper as oddly anomalous, insofar as they fail to correspond to the liberal aesthetic that informs that very critical history.[34] With the emergence of the historical romance (particularly as exemplified by Cooper), however, the novel begins to comprehend nationalism as a kind of possession rather than an aspect of a republican public sphere, enabling it to suture a common national history to the familial frameworks of private life. Indeed, what we can see in these novels is a fundamental division between private and public, between the human interior and the national exterior, in terms of *time*: the latter would be ordered, cumulative, and progressive, whereas the former would allow imaginative return to the timeless truth of affective attachment. The early-nineteenth-century historical romance, we might say, both facilitated a modern perspective on time and provided the supplementary enchantments that made it livable—enchantments that are visible, or rather audible, in the romance's emphasis on voice, music, and sound, whose alternate modes of ordering combine with the narrative drive to arrange its sympathetic appeal to affection at a suitable distance from the developmental time of the nation.

The voice becomes, in this sense, not simply a *substitute* for exterior structures of hereditary authority but a *transposition* of those structures into the body's interior, as the sign of the fundamental humanity articulated in feeling. And the voice of the Indian, whose sonorous quality positively fascinated the early American romance, seemed to furnish particularly effective material for that transmission, since its palpably antenational resonance could be recuperated in the rhetoric of a distinctly American heritage that served to authorize and legitimate love for the nation as a natural extension of love for the family. Ventriloquizing the Indian voice, in this sense, served as a particularly efficacious mode of what Philip Deloria terms "playing Indian," the ritualized taking-on of Indianness by whites in order to (re)found American identity, insofar as this voice-play helped order the spatiotemporal relations between national and what came to be "personal" life.[35] But taking on the Indian voice was a risky form of play because it also registered as a taking-*in*, something felt through the body. Accordingly, while the early American historical novel vitalized and sacralized the story of American origins by infusing its narratives with the authenticating intensity of the Indian voice, it also sought to defend against the return of the primitive by insisting on the melancholy orientation that secured the Indian to the past. As it naturalized the story of Indian "vanishing" into history, then, the novel also worked to perpetuate the human resonance of Indian sounds in what we can recognize as a distinctly minor key.[36]

The Time of Mourning Indians

The nineteenth-century insistence on reading temporal difference across a register of sameness resonated through accounts of Native American mourning rituals. As we saw in the previous chapter, Roger Williams's 1643 *Key into the Language of America* contains an early commentary on the depth of Indian grief and the intensity of ritual "bewailing," which he ascribed to their hopelessness in the absence of Christianity's promise of resurrection.[37] By the second half of the eighteenth century, however, Anglo-American commentary on Indian bewailing rituals had begun to hear in them a more hopeful resonance, which they identified as a primitive articulation of human affective connectedness. We can see this interpretation in Samuel Kirkland's 1764 description of his response to an Oneida bewailing ritual. Kirkland, a Protestant missionary, could not yet fully understand the language of the chant, but he nevertheless intuited something about its meaning by attending to the sound of the voice:

when they left the house and were carrying the [corpse] to the grave-
yard they sung the most mournful ditte [sic] I ever heard. A small number of them seemed to keep the time and rise and fall pretty much
together, others halloed & some screamed & yelled like dogs. It produced a variety of feelings in my breast, finally a tender pity and compassion toward them prevailed considering their ignorance and superstition.[38]

Kirkland's mixed reaction to hearing this lament stresses his humanistic recognition of the grief it conveys while maintaining his self-positioning as distant from its savage, even animalistic, form. His admission that the chant
produces "a variety of feelings in my breast" acknowledges the profound affective power of its sensory appeal, as he does not need to comprehend its
language to characterize its mournful primacy. Yet the insistence on "finally" reducing those feelings to "pity and compassion" for the Oneidas'
"ignorance and superstition" demonstrates that he, too, uses the chant to
"keep time." His reasoned ordering of the affective tumult that the Oneida
chant provokes, that is, shows how the interpretation of cultural difference
as temporal distance could simultaneously provide a kind of emotional pro-
phylaxis for whites, distancing them from the sensory immediacy of the vitalized Indian voice, and channel such events into self-confirming circuits,
cherishing them as evidence of white sophistication. Kirkland's diary entry
thus signals the eighteenth-century development of a specifically Anglo-
American culture of sensibility, which used the spectacle of the dying Indian
to balance what Julie Ellison identifies as a transcultural "practice of mobile
connection" with a reassuring chronology that confirmed its own sympathetic transcendence of that plight.[39]

While Christian missionaries' depictions of Indian "primitivism" and
"superstition" embraced the revelation of a common, if underdeveloped,
core of humanity as a sign that Indians were capable of instruction and conversion, secular ethnographers such as Henry Rowe Schoolcraft saw in this
religious retemporalization of Native American cultures the destruction of
Indianness as such, which they understood as distinctively asynchronous.[40]
Schoolcraft detected within Indian oral culture a relation to the past that
made them resistant to change. In a study of Indian storytelling, he observed that the nostalgic cast of these stories revealed a fundamentally an-
tiprogressive culture:

> There is, it is true, a spirit of reminiscence apparent [in Indian tales] which pleases itself in allusions to the past; they speak of a sort of golden age, when all things were better with them than they now are; when they had better laws and leaders; when crimes were more properly punished; when their language was spoken with greater purity, and their manners were freer from barbarism. But all this seems to flit through the Indian mind as a dream, and furnishes him rather the source of a pleasing secret retrospection than any spring to present and future exertions. He pines away as one that is fallen, and despairs to rise. He does not seem to open his eyes on the prospect of civilization and mental exaltation held up before him, as one to whom the scene is new or attractive.[41]

Schoolcraft's characteristic condemnation of the perversity of this temporal orientation—the indulgence of the past as a secret "pleasure," rather than a means of propelling oneself toward the future—also exposes it as the root of the Indian's persistent primitivism: "With a people who look back to some ancient and indefinite period in their history as an age of glory, an adherence to primitive manners and customs naturally occupies the place of virtue."[42] The obdurate Indian attachment to pastness indicates, for Schoolcraft, a widespread cultural melancholia—a refusal to let go of the lost past, which results in an inability to move on in time. From this perspective, the Indian substitution of primitivism for "virtue" suggests an inability to grasp the bifurcated and mutually conditioning rhythms of (linear) public and (cyclical) private time in the modern world.

The fatally melancholic Indian "attachment" to the past conveyed in views such as Schoolcraft's also resounded as a reminder of the necessity of separating the (public) time of progress from the private time of feeling—a reminder, that is, to embrace melancholy as a means of defending against melancholia. Juliana Schiesari has persuasively argued that the modern subject's embrace of melancholy as a mode of illumination was predicated on the borrowing of certain characteristics from a designated other whose self-splitting appeared, in contrast, as an inherent and nonilluminating "nature."[43] And insofar as a properly divided ambivalence about the pace of progress characterized the "reflective" civilized subject in the nineteenth century, the Indian provided an ideal "other" for American melancholy. Indeed, as Lucy Maddox comments, the term itself was a favored one among

nineteenth-century whites writing on the "fate" of the Indian precisely because it served, at once, to obscure the agency behind Indian "vanishing"
and to demonstrate the civilized man's capacity for feeling—a capacity that
could, as she observes, easily coexist with the drive for imperial expansion.[44]
The progressive substitution of Indian melancholia, the ultimately fatal embrace of the past, by white melancholy, the reflective look backward that enabled one to continue moving forward, thus bespoke, to whites, their own
more sophisticated comprehension of the "true" nature of time's passage,
which might be regretted but could not be arrested, for it was itself a law of
nature. Three years before the address that praised Mount Auburn Cemetery's inspirational location on a spatiotemporal border, Joseph Story delivered a lecture on New England history that embraced this account of American time: "By a law of nature, [Indians] seem destined to a slow, sure exclusion. Everywhere, at the approach of the white man, they fade away. We
hear the rustling of their footsteps. . . . They pass mournfully by us, and they
return no more."[45] The melancholy tale of the Vanishing American as told
from the perspective of civilization invested the Indian with a distinctly Romantic aura—a combination of (affective) nearness and (historical) distance
that resonated most suggestively against voice, because voice, unlike the
naturalistic but unredeemed faith that marked "primitive" religion, might
be embraced across time without disrupting the progress of the civilized,
precisely because of its ephemerality. The deployment of Indian voice as a
temporal bridge, however, projected onto its tones a distinctively melancholy resonance, an intuition of its own diminishing status in the vicinity of
the white ear. In this way, the Anglo-American attraction to the sonorous
voice of the Indian as the echo of an ineradicable temporal transition between the natural and the civilized worlds positions a melancholia at the
heart of its mourning for the Indian that legitimated, again and again, white
indulgence in the Romantic time of lament. It is to the most lasting example
of this novelistic indulgence—James Fenimore Cooper's *The Last of the Mohicans*—that I will now turn.

Nature's Forgotten Harmony: *The Last of the Mohicans*

The phonocentricity that marked Natty Bumppo's last appearance in *The Pioneers* returns upon the character's first appearance in the next novel of the
series, *The Last of the Mohicans* (1826), in the context of an argument be-

tween the scout and Chingachgook about the legitimacy of the white presence on the American continent—an argument that Natty's attachment to voice, ironically, sets him up to lose. Chingachgook, ritualistically offering Natty the chance to defend his position, asks for the "tale told by your fathers" about the first centuries of Indian-white contact, but Natty can only admit that he does not know it: "my people have many ways of which, as an honest man, I can't approve. It is one of their customs to write in books what they have done and seen, instead of telling them in their villages, where the lie can be given to the face of a cowardly boaster, and the brave soldier can call on his comrades to witness for the truth of his words" (31). This idealization of orality ostensibly faults writing for its alienation from the face-to-face community that validates the truth of the past; yet this separation is most problematic for Natty, as he subsequently reveals, precisely because it distances *him* from (white) history. By virtue of the Delaware oral tradition, Chingachgook can claim the tribal past as part of his own experience, an ability he takes full advantage of in the pages that follow, whereas Natty, as an illiterate white, lacks sufficient historical knowledge to compete; as he observes, "a [white] man who is too conscientious to misspend his days among the women, in learning the names of the black marks, may never hear of the deeds of his fathers, nor feel a pride in striving to outdo them" (31).

Natty's idealization of historical storytelling maps his phonocentrism onto a protonationalist vision of progress stimulated by masculine crosstemporal competition. In his vision, sons are not simply the passive recipients of the past but the generational *agents* of history, as they turn their admiration for the fathers into an attempt to surpass them. Natty's vision of orality is already historical in the modern sense, insofar as it supplants the traditional vision of the oral world as a stable but largely static social system with a belief in progress as dependent upon the play of difference across time. Indeed, Natty's understanding of the admiring-yet-competitive relation of fathers to sons is much closer to the generational/reproductive narrative codified in psychoanalysis as Oedipality than to traditional models of patriarchy.[46] There is, of course, nothing in Natty's progressive vision that automatically precludes the emergence of written historiography; indeed, from a progress-driven perspective, writing can appear as a historical *improvement* on speech—the sons surpassing the fathers—insofar as it extends the reach of history past the compass of the spoken voice. What troubles

Natty, rather, is writing's lack of vitality, its failure to connect to living, responding beings, which threatens the ability to take the kind of visceral pride in the past that he aligns with the forward movement of his nation.[47]

Despite Natty's disdain for the "black marks," the second novel in the Leatherstocking series is, on the whole, less interested in combating the falseness of writing as such than in ordering the sonorous origin that both authorizes and troubles the fundamentally historical vision Natty bespeaks —an origin that at once appears as the basis of the voice's power and as a sonic *simultaneity* that signals the radical alterity of the (Indian) past. Cooper's novel, that is, turns backward in time in order to retrospectively organize the sound of the past toward the future that can recognize it as an inspiration. This desire for (American) history accounts, as recent scholarly analyses of the racial politics of language in Cooper's writing have proposed, for his embrace of an essentially Rousseauvian romance of language in his attention to the oral world of the Indian.[48] I would like to further this line of inquiry by emphasizing *The Last of the Mohicans*'s negotiation of the primarily *temporal* dilemma that emerges from its attention to the status of the voice as it resists assimilation to the linear-historical order of things. The novel's sacralizing of Indian voice can only be achieved, finally, through an appeal to the "natural" origins of a national history that relies upon both the temporal division between nature and culture and the narrative of generational reproduction that governs the emergent logic of heterosexuality. *The Last of the Mohicans* thus engages in an energetic campaign to inherit the vitality of the Indian voice while looping its asynchronic reverberations to the prepolitical duality of women's time.[49]

Cooper's meticulous attention to sound in the novel evokes a wilderness world in which writing appears—on the rare occasions that it appears at all —in order to bring news of its own incapacity.[50] Contrasting the writing that governs the settlements, sound is the wilderness's means of self-preservation; Natty proclaims that he has "listened to all the sounds of the woods for thirty years, as a man will listen, whose life and death depend on the quickness of his ears" (62). Life in the novel often *does* depend on the ears of Natty and the Mohicans, as they must repeatedly defend and rescue a party of settlement whites (composed of Cora and Alice Munro, the daughters of the colonel in command of the English forces at the fort; their American-born military guide, Major Duncan Heyward; and David Gamut, a New England psalmodist who joins the party at Alice's invitation) from their Huron enemy, Magua, who attaches himself to the group. After the band of woodsmen executes a particularly timely rescue of the whites, Heyward wonders how the men saw them captured; Natty responds, significantly, that they *heard* it, adding, "An Indian yell is plain language to men who have passed their days in the woods" (120). The novel even suggests that for Indians, wordless sounds are preferable to language, the knowledge of which is limited by tribal experience; when Natty insists on disposing of the carcass of David Gamut's horse lest it become food for wolves and betray their location to an Iroquois war party, he explains that, "though the Delaware tongue is the same as a book to the Iroquois," being Indian, they are nevertheless "quick enough at understanding the reason of a wolf's howl" (51). This ability to read even animal sounds accurately marks the Indian attunement to the forest as less oral than *aural*: oriented to sound rather than speech per se, possessing an intuitive continuity with the wilderness that, Natty claims, enables the Indian to grasp "the nature of the woods . . . by instinct" (34).

Natty marvels that Chingachgook can understand even "white sounds" better than he as a white man can; however, he is not entirely right, for even the aural abilities of the Indians have limits (35). When the party, on the run from Magua, hears a mysterious cry, the baffled woodsmen can only conclude that its origin must be supernatural. After some moments of suspense, however, Heyward, drawing on his military experience, recognizes the noise as the wail of a wounded horse, a sound foreign to the American forest. Heyward's solitary ability to "read" this cry demonstrates that the sounds of the wilderness are also time-bound; its residents can only interpret noises of which they have had direct experience. The military man's limited but crucial contribution to the auditory experience of the party marks the American forest as a sonic chronotope for this transitional era—a space in which the *longue durée* of nature comes into contact with the new noise of transition that forms part of American history.[51] That new noise includes, crucially, not only the sounds of military history but also the echoes of the settlements, which are projected there along with Alice and Cora, the white women whose displacement into the forest sets the narrative in motion. In an early scene, Alice seeks to demonstrate her own aural attunements, avowing to Heyward her "faith in the tones of the human voice" as an index of moral character (21). (Heyward, however, must explain to her that the "savage" on whom she wishes to test this skill, Magua, marks its—and her—limits, since she will not be able to get him to speak to her in English.) Alice insists on indulging her "keen relish for gentle sounds" (58) even in the forest, inviting the psalmodist David Gamut to join them on their ride for her entertainment. And although Gamut's church music seems oddly out of place in the forest, his inclination to sacred song also provides the narrative with occasion to demonstrate the timeless appeal of domestic affections.[52] This demonstration takes place within the shelter of a hidden cavern, where the party, having gained a momentary respite from danger, improves on the occasion by staging something like an ordinary evening at home in the settlements: dining, drinking, and singing hymns. Even Natty, whose strongest sonic affiliation is to the "speech" of his rifle and who repeatedly derides Gamut's profession as useless, is moved by the tones of a hymn sung in a moment of repose:

> the scout, who had placed his chin in his hand, with an expression of cold indifference, gradually suffered his rigid features to relax until, as verse succeeded verse, he felt his iron nature subdued, while his recollection was carried back to boyhood, when his ears had been accustomed to listen to similar sounds of praise, in the settlements of the colony. His roving eyes began to moisten, and before the hymn was ended, scalding tears rolled out of fountains that had long seemed dry, and followed each other down those cheeks that had oftener felt the storms of heaven, than any testimonials of weakness. (59)

Sacred music here serves as a medium for time travel, undoing the rigidifying effect of experience and allowing even the stoic scout to experience nostalgia for the comforts of home and family as he once heard them articulated in a "civilized" register. As if to underscore the cavern's rearticulation of the sounds of settlement, the sudden eruption within the cave of the horse's mystifying cry, which gives Heyward an occasion to refer to his battle experiences, takes place just as the hymn reaches its final notes. This sonic overlap, gesturing, as it does, toward the military in its appointed position as protector of the settlements, locates the cavern as a fold within the time of the wilderness—a prehistoric inversion through which the history of the white settlers can be inscribed as memory.

But while Natty's sentimentality (re)establishes affective-domestic time as foundational, the timeframe of Chingachgook and Uncas remains outside this fold, as the Mohicans, for whom Christian music possesses no cultural resonance, listen respectfully, but without Natty's display of emotion.[53] The apparent noncontiguity of the two lifeworlds is, however, mitigated by the natural "music" of the Indian voice, whose resonance bridges—or, more accurately, loops across—the gap between civilization and the wilderness. This music first sounds in Chingachgook's voice, when, as he demonstrates his knowledge of the tales of the fathers, his voice drops to the "low, guttural tones, which render his language, as spoken at times, so very musical":

> then, Hawkeye, we were one people, and we were happy. The salt lake gave us its fish, the wood its deer, and the air its birds. We took wives who bore us children; we worshipped the Great Spirit; and we kept the Maquas beyond the sound of our songs of triumph. (33)

This passage demonstrates the association of the musical times of Indian speech with memory, as this Edenic past is one that Chingachgook himself has never directly experienced; the arrival of the Dutch drove his ancestors away from their traditional lands and decimated their numbers years before his own birth. Chingachgook's belatedness in relation to this age of glory makes mourning a way of life for him; in a later scene, as he recounts the story of a long-past victory against the Mohawks, the narrator observes that a "strain of melancholy . . . blended with his triumph, rendering his voice, as usual, soft and musical" (126). The insistent presence, in Chingachgook's speech, of the musical strains that denote a *mournfulness as usual* fixes the Indian voice in relation to the (lost) primal world, a positioning that accounts for the fascination of that voice's melancholy tones to the white reader: it corresponds to the tonal logic that makes the human ear, as the narrator elsewhere observes in the cavern scene, greet "those low, dying chords" that end a hymn by "[devouring them] with such greedy rapture, as if conscious that it is about to lose them" (59). The self-confirming effect of this aural consumption is demonstrated by the way Chingachgook's lament arranges that primal world as always-already domestic, pre-bespeaking, in its successive gestures toward family, spirituality, and defense against enemies, the self-arrangement of the settlements. His memory thus supplies the linear chronology of civilization with a supplementary cyclical dimension that restores the foundational truths of the human, while the insistently melancholy key of his voice-music offers a mode of distancing the "savage" whose face remains steadfastly turned toward his past.

Chingachgook's disinclination to meddle in the time of the settlements is pointedly counteracted by Magua, who is at once the hereditary foe of the Mohicans and the newly historical enemy of the whites. Magua's campaign to capture the Munro sisters results from his desire to avenge a whipping administered under Munro's command as punishment for drunkenness—a punishment that, he insists, he did not deserve, since whites made the "evil" for which they punished him, and that left him with scars that he "must hide, like a squaw, under the painted cloth of the whites" (103). He intends to unman Munro in turn by inflicting a similarly lingering wound on his memory: abducting the Scotsman's eldest daughter and forcing her to marry him. Damaged by his exposure to the liquor that made him, as he insists, "not himself," Magua sees duplicity in all aspects of white culture, particularly their language. In an uncanny repetition of Natty's phonocentric critique of writing, Magua observes, "the pale faces . . . have two words for each thing, while a red skin will make the sound of his voice speak for him" (91). Yet Magua's own speech resounds dually, with the power of voice and with the capacity for self-serving political gain that marks him as a product of the temporal miscegenation impelled by what the narrator terms the "imbecility" of English military leaders in America (13), who introduce Magua not only to alcohol but also to injustice and deception, violating the codes of the natural world. Accordingly, his crafty orations work both sides of this temporal divide, just as his bilingualism and dual tribal affiliation enable him to play both sides during the French and Indian War.[54] Magua's regressive appeal to the sound of the voice undoes the melancholy looping that binds and separates past and present, causing the diachronic distinctions of the civilized world to collapse in upon themselves. His character effectively Gothicizes the savage voice as a traumatizing return that results from the present's improper contact with the past and resounds as a verdict on that present. The sound of the voice, in this (re)turn, occasions not a pleasurable melancholy but pain; just as the "indecency" of Magua's proposal "wound[s]" Cora's ears (105), the shrieking of his war parties "drive[s] the swift currents of Heyward's blood, back from its bounding course into the fountains of his heart" (66). The frightened reversal of the civilized man's blood actualizes the regressive psycholinguistic movement in which language "degenerates" into sound; temporarily obliterating the hearer's reason and agency, the voice, in this deadly manifestation, can help render the hearer's reduction to body permanent. The regression of voice, here, undoes the conventional progression of linear time, looping backward and forward to arrive at a premature end that is also an uncanny repetition of the beginning, turning the euphonic caresses of primary sociality into the carnal clamor of mortality. David Gamut, with his inveterate habit of translating all experience into Biblical terms, precisely identifies this temporal effect as he compares the noise of a battle between the Mohicans and Magua's men to the arrival of the Final Judgment: "sounds of discord have rent my ears, such as might manifest the fullness of time, and that nature had forgotten her harmony" (82).

If Magua's voice resounds in the register of the profane, however, that of Uncas, the son of Chingachgook, restores voice to the sacred. The liveliness of Uncas's voice, in which the "music of the Delawares" has not yet turned to melancholy, awakens in Chingachgook the "playful tones of affection" that he uses only when he believes no whites to be listening:

> It is impossible to describe the music of their language, while thus en-gaged in laughter and endearments, in such a way as to render it intelli-gible to those who have never listened to its melody. The compass of their voices, particularly that of the youth, was wonderful; extending from the deepest bass, to tones that were even feminine in softness. The eyes of the father followed the plastic and ingenious movements of his son with open delight, and he never failed to smile in reply to the other's contagious, but low laughter. While under the influence of these gentle and natural feelings, no trace of ferocity was to be seen in the softened features of the Sagamore. (200)

The "wonderful" power of Uncas's voice here is its ability to soften his mel-ancholy father toward a gentler articulation of his "nature": the humanizing familial affections he failed to manifest in the cavern scene. Indeed, al-though the narrator opens this passage by foregrounding the ephemerality of the Delawares' distinctive vocal "music," which can never be reproduced, only experienced in real time, the passage works to construct a familiar anal-ogy for the reader through this connection to the loving bonds of the fam-ily; Indian voice-music, in this sense, sounds like affective connectedness. But the same "wonderful" vocal capacity that enables Uncas to serve as the sonic sign of timeless human feeling also returns to challenge the historical order of things, as a manifestation recalling the Delaware's sacred past, the pristine time of which Chingachgook speaks to Natty on their first narrative appearance. Near the end of the novel, as Uncas speaks to Tamenund, the aged sage of the Delawares, the sachem, "ben[ding] his head aside, as if to catch the fleeting sounds of some passing melody," wonders in bewilder-ment if he has gone back in time: "Have the winters gone backward! Will summer come again to the children of the Lenape!" (308).[55] Uncas's return does inspire the Delaware to return to the warpath against the Hurons, but this turn back toward their glorious past is indeed "fleeting," as Uncas's death renders them "a nation of mourners" once more (339), and Tamenund, in the novel's final speech, is forced to admit, "the time of the red-men has not yet come again" (350).[56] Even within this episode, however, the inspiring music of Uncas's voice remains enclosed within the Delawares' collective sense of time. That is to say, unlike Magua's radically individualistic temporal perversity, which respects neither tribal distinctions nor the division between civilization and savagery, Uncas's activation of the Delawares' tribal spirit, like his hold on his father's natural affections, poses no direct threat to the whites; instead, his voice resonates across the gap separating the two cultures as an inspiration to analogous national and familial feeling.[57]

Yet the voice of the younger Mohican does convey to the white characters a magnetism outside the bounds of family and tribal tradition, whose controlling contexts they lack. The startling effect of its melodious inflection is described in a passage from the cavern episode, as Uncas attends the Munro sisters at a meal:

> Once or twice he was compelled to speak, . . . [making] use of English, broken and imperfect, but sufficiently intelligible, and which he rendered so mild and musical, by his deep, guttural voice, that it never failed to cause both ladies to look up in admiration and astonishment. (56)

Whatever Uncas has to say in this scene is not significant enough to be worthy of mention; what does signify, here, is the sound of a voice seductive enough to cause an involuntary physical response on the women's part. The effect of Uncas's voice-music recalls the ambivalent relation to the sound of the voice that shadows Western phonocentrism—an ambivalence that, as Mladen Dolar has recently argued, connects to the "dangerous attractive force" of the "voice beyond the words"[58] and particularly to the musical voice, which transcends language to suggest both divinity and degeneration: music, he notes, is said both to "[elevate] the soul" and "[present] carnality at its most insidious since it seems liberated from materiality, . . . the subtlest and most perfidious form of the flesh."[59] Crucially, however, Uncas's voice unsettles, in this scene, because it seems liberated not from the body but from the chronology that organizes it, leaving the settlement whites, to whom its music is wholly new, unsure of which historical frame might best contain it. Indeed, shortly before hearing Uncas speak, they engage in a moment of discord concerning how best to describe the "force" of Uncas's beauty (53). Though Alice admires the young chief "as she would have looked upon some precious relic of the Grecian chisel, to which life had been imparted, by the intervention of a miracle," Heyward, praising Uncas as "a rare and brilliant instance of those natural qualities, in which these peculiar people are said to excel," yet insists that moral virtue is even rarer among savages than Christians; he winds up his minilecture on morality by hoping, on the basis of their "common nature," that Uncas will prove a friend to them. Cora, in turn, takes the last part of Heyward's speech in another direction, embarrassing the group into silence by wondering, "who, that looks at this creature of nature, remembers the shades of his skin!" (53).

Whereas Alice sees Uncas's "perfection of form" as an occasion for neoclassical aesthetic approbation and Heyward seizes on it as a lesson in Christian morality, tempered by a sympathetic gesture toward universal humanity, Cora's embrace of "nature" comes a bit too close to the body. For although she insists that nature should make them forget about skin color, she instead manages to make the others *remember* it—an unintended reversal that gestures not only toward Uncas's skin but also toward their ambivalent relation to her own. Much darker than the "fair" Alice, Cora's skin is described, on her first appearance in the novel, as "not brown, but . . . rather . . . charged with the colour of the rich blood, that appeared ready to burst its bounds" (19). Colonel Munro later accounts for the difference in his daughters' complexions, telling Heyward that his first wife was a woman "whose misfortune it was . . . to be descended, remotely, from that unfortunate class, who are so basely enslaved to administer to the wants of a luxurious people!" (159). This "connexion" is represented by the Scottish colonel as a digressive episode in his own past: though his family was "ancient and honorable" (159), it was not wealthy enough to allow him to marry his first love; instead, he joined the king's service and traveled to the West Indies, where marriage with Cora's mother enriched him and left him, after her death, free to return to Scotland and win the hand of that first love, Alice's mother. The "embarrassment" that pervades this conversation between Munro and Heyward—in which the colonel charges the young southern major with racism on the basis of his romantic preference for the unmixed Alice, while revealing his own discomfort with Cora's "degraded" origin— deflects the men's anxiety over the "base" mercenary roots of empire as they echo through their own family histories onto Cora's insufficiently white body as the lingering sign of their shame.

Though Cora's skin signifies as history to the whites, it appears differently to Uncas, who does not need to "forget" an accumulation of memory alien to his own time. Accordingly, in the aforementioned episode, the narrator observes that the young Mohican attends politely to both sisters, but while he waits on Cora, his "dark eye linger[s] on her rich, speaking countenance" (56). What Uncas hears in the "speech" of Cora's countenance is precisely the sense of vitality encoded in the descriptive passage cited earlier: the suggestion that her body can barely contain itself. Indeed, the attraction that follows this audition may well account for the noteworthy resonance of his voice's music in the cavern scene, as it occurs immediately afterward. The possibility that Uncas keys up the attractiveness of his voice in response to the speech of Cora's body introduces a *difference* in its time: it no longer resounds as simply the sonorous continuity of primary sociality but also suggests the return of the voice's music in the unstable register of desire. As the doubling of the voice into a seductive imitation of its own "natural" music predicts, Uncas will no longer be quite himself after this episode; indeed, Natty later remarks in surprise that the young Mohican has become "as impatient as a man in the settlements" (185). This newly quickened rhythm is associated with an altered chronological framework; the narrator asserts that Uncas's newly awakened "sympathy" for the Munro sisters' familial affection "advanced him probably centuries before the practices of his nation" (115). Lora Romero perceptively identifies this acceleration with the novel's drive to "naturalize" the death of the Indian, arguing that the "unnatural" pace of his desire-inspired development is blamed for the young Mohican's demise; Cooper's novel, she summarizes, deftly "translates fire-power into mother-power."[60]

Romero's account of Uncas's fatal division from himself in time, however, undervalues the temporal duality that the novel assigns to its female characters as well: a division that posits mother-power itself as, at once, a "timeless" function of nature and an effect of history. Cora's imprisonment within this temporal paradox is aptly articulated by Alice, who pronounces Cora "my more than sister, my mother" (115). This articulation of Cora's surplus relation to the present generation itself recalls the sense in which Cora bears a certain responsibility for Alice's birth, insofar as it was her West Indian family's colonial wealth that enabled Munro to marry Alice's mother —a history at once suggested and deflected onto the body in the novel's repeated references to her visibly "rich" blood. In context, however, Alice's speech ascribes Cora's dual position not to her familial inheritance but to her generous willingness to sacrifice herself for her sister's sake.[61] Alice's unwitting depiction of herself as Cora's child also emphasizes the way that the younger Munro sister, suspended between girlhood and womanhood, similarly serves as an index of woman's temporal duality. But Alice, as a child-woman, poses no threat to the civilized order of things. Instead, she occupies a crucial temporal-ideological position as an index of the vulnerable future of the nation: that which must be protected in order to assure the continuity of civilized life. The ingenuous arrangement of Alice's bifurcation in time enables her to serve as an impetus for the characters to seek a return to the future that they have already claimed as their own—the settlements —and, once there, to provide the means of its generational perpetuation, as she is passed on from her historically exhausted Scots father to the young, vital American Heyward, who, after the death of that father, takes over her care by marrying her.

Unlike her younger sister, however, Cora can be sacrificed without disturbing the possibility of the future; in fact, the novel effectively demands that sacrifice, as the doubleness that characterizes the simultaneously historical and affective roots of her maternal relation to Alice (echoed in the way her skin bespeaks both a disavowed history and a "natural" corporeal vitality) remains a troubling "embarrassment" to the whites, making her body a problem in (their) time. The "base" mercenary history that her body bespeaks is thus transformed into the sexual/maternal duplicity that marks her actions in the wake of the cavern episode—a doubling that suggests the temporal conflict between the future-directedness of maternal self-sacrifice and what the narrator terms the *"lingering* emotions of a woman" (109, emphasis added).[62] Cora reveals an "intuitive" awareness of her "power" over Uncas near the end of that episode, using it to entice him away from his stated resolve to defend her to the death against Magua, an action she argues would lessen the possibility of their release from captivity (79). Here, as elsewhere, Cora displays an ability to influence the men attracted to her away from their initial convictions, suggesting that once exposed to her, these men no longer have "but one mind," as Magua insists a chief must (315). (Indeed, even Magua's initial desire for vengeance against Munro becomes complicated by a palpable attraction to Cora, which serves only to magnify his desire to keep her captive.) And in this light, it is significant that these men appear drawn not simply to the "speech" of her blood-charged body but also to the admirable self-possession that resounds both in her manner and in the tones of her voice—a heroic quality that serves, in the logic of the novel, to unsex her, as it is a manner more typical of warriors than women.[63] The self-possession that, in the gendered logic of the novel, properly belongs to men thus works in tandem with Cora's physical attractions to undermine the two warriors' ability to remain in time with their original purposes.

Cora is positioned as a problem in civilized time not only by the shameful history she bespeaks but also by a conflict in the gendered nature of her character: she is simultaneously maternal and female in a way that troubles the yet-patriarchal self-image of the novel's vision of reproductive generationality. Accordingly, she too is made to bear the blame for her own eventual demise. Midway through the novel—between her first and second captivations by Magua—Cora describes herself as fundamentally *melancholy,* an outlook that she describes, characteristically, as an effect of both "experience" and "nature" and that itself predicts her eventual fate, a fate that results directly from her attempt to find common time with the Indian lifeworld.[64] Near the end of the novel, pleading her case in front of Tamenund, the sage of the Delawares, Cora attempts to win Alice's freedom from Magua by first appealing to her father's renowned reputation; when it becomes clear that Tamenund cannot (or refuses to) remember that reputation, she shifts tactics, attempting to win the sage's sympathy: "Like thee and thine, venerable chief . . . the curse of my ancestors has fallen heavily on their child!" (305). A profound "shame" crushes Cora during this speech and Tamenund's reply; since it appears without explanation, it is critically uncertain whether this shame, in the wake of the father's failure, reads as racial or sexual in origin—whether, that is, it attaches to the embarrassment that habitually greets the white characters' remembrance of her ancestry or to the "forwardness" implied in her implicit consent to Magua's proposal.[65] But by this point in the novel, it scarcely matters; the simultaneous invocation of race and sexuality in the specter of interracial union functions primarily to confirm the way that sexuality permeates the white world's racial chronologies—and, crucially, vice versa. For although Cora's plea for Tamenund's mercy fails to move him (he dismisses her attempt to create, through an appeal to the family, a moment of sympathetic *simultaneity* by insisting on the cyclical time of the Indian lifeworld, which shares no common season with whites) the very terms of his refusal unexpectedly revive Cora, who, realizing that he has given her another temporal card to play, summons Uncas forward to deliver the musical speech that makes the sachem believe "the

winters [have] gone backward" (308). Yet it is, ironically, this strategic embrace of Indian time that seals the fates of both Cora and Uncas. For while
Uncas's privileged tribal perspective counteracts Magua's duplicitous appeal
to Delaware history—an advantage the Mohican follows up by successfully
challenging Magua's right to hold Natty, Heyward, and Alice as prisoners—it
also firmly locates Cora's own case within the timeless dictates of tribal law,
which determines that she belongs to Magua.[66] In the end, Uncas can only
seek her restoration through the traditional right of conquest—the very
plan whose fatal failure (re)turns the Delaware nation to mourning.

The Last of the Mohicans's insistence on replacing the natural simultaneity
of the Indian with the linear-historical time of civilization thus articulates,
as well, a story of the *sexual* order of things: an insistence on privileging the
future-directedness of male-ordered reproductive-generational rhythms over
the anachrony that results from the waywardness of (mistaken) desires. This
(pre)determination is apparent in the split-second narrative pacing of the
novel's rescue scenes, which arranges the characteristic rhythms of the doubled temporalities belonging to the three key figures I have been considering
here—Cora, Uncas, and the child-woman Alice—in order to assure the
emergence of the settled future that the novel has already claimed as its own
memory. From a realist perspective, of course, the novel's melodramatic pacing appears excessive, even absurd, a critique best embodied in Mark Twain's
well-known essay on Cooper. Twain charges Cooper's writing with possessing "no order, system, sequence, or result" and therefore no "lifelikeness"
—a critique that connects the realist novelist's semblance of life to a certain respect for the modern order of time.[67] I am suggesting, however, that
Cooper's deliberate manipulation of pacing can rather be understood as an
effort to use sound to *make space in time* so that the (temporal) order that
grounds Twain's understanding of literary realism can itself emerge. In the
proposal scene, for instance, Alice, in the wake of Cora's offer of self-sacrifice, significantly *hesitates*. Torn between a childish (and, the narrator insists,
natural) desire for life and her consciousness of the duties of womanly virtue, she remains silent, suspended in the contradictions of her own temporal figuration; though she does, eventually, decide on the "correct" path,
consenting to die to keep her sister pure, her slowness to speak makes just
enough space in the time of the scene for the Mohicans and Natty to arrive
and effect a last-minute rescue. A notable contrast takes place between the
salvation assigned to this hesitation and Cora's pause in response to Uncas's
voice in the penultimate chapter. When Uncas, just a few paces behind

Magua's party, calls ahead to demand that he "stay," Cora suddenly halts and refuses to go any farther. But her hesitation generates just enough delay for Uncas's fatally ill-timed rescue attempt; the distraction of his arrival contributes to Cora's death and, in turn, his own.[68] The simultaneously momentary and momentous determination of the fates of the trio collectively articulates the emergent timing of civilized life: Alice is preserved in order to become the vehicle for the new nation's generational perpetuation, while Cora and Uncas can exist only as an inspirational memory. True to form, *The Last of the Mohicans* closes with both a wedding and a funeral, rituals intended to mark the distinction between those who have a future in time and those who do not.[69] But although the marriage of Alice and Heyward, noted in the final chapter, is the novel's temporal conduit to the world of its own readers, its limited relation to these "later" developments is suggested in the way the narrator hastens to return from the brief mention of this development to the funeral, the "time . . . which concerns our tale" (348). That funeral, insofar as it effects the transition inaugurating the temporal order of the new nation, must precede the wedding that provides the means of its perpetuation.[70] Yet the chapter's extended attachment to sound, as manifested in the evocative mourning rituals of the Delaware, suggests the novel's tendency, despite its insistence on closure, to linger in the realm of attachment to the primal world of the Indian, creating an unexpected slippage in the temporal order it is devoted to establishing.

The Indian funeral ceremony frames itself as a quest for interpretation; it opens as Tamenund, whose hollowed tones resound as though they are "charged with some prophetic mission," proclaims Uncas's death a divine "judgment" on the tribe whose meaning yet remains unclear (341). The dual memorial ceremony that follows this pronouncement points up a conflict in the correct organization of memory—a conflict whose competing temporal frames are at once raced and gendered. The first proposal surfaces in the funeral chant sung by the Delaware women, a chant whose "thrillingly soft and wailing" sonorosity seems to correspond to the nonlinear time of deep feeling, but which, the narrator insists, nevertheless contains a "regular descant, which, in substance, might have proved to possess a train of consecutive ideas" (342).[71] These ideas, however, take a sudden departure from the ritual praise of Uncas's valor as a warrior, as the singers unexpectedly deploy "remote and subtle images" to arrange a posthumous marriage between Uncas and Cora, a marriage justified, tellingly, by the distinctive temporalities that the novel has already established for the characters: Uncas's attraction to Cora confirms the model of return that he outlined to the Delaware (his "wishes," they assert, "had led him back to a people who dwelt about the graves of his fathers" [343]), while Cora is understood as uniquely suited for the warrior by virtue of her "richer" blood and extraordinary courage, and the singers celebrate her providential delivery from the settlements "to a place where she might find congenial spirits" (343). Yet this bout of musical matchmaking does not go unchallenged; although the Delawares "[listen] like charmed men," Natty, the only white person present who can understand the words, stops listening when the mourners allude to the posthumous coupling, "[shaking] his head like one who knew the error of their simple creed" (344). Most contemporary critics argue that this action signifies Natty's rejection of the interracial match, but the narrator's commentary here is ambiguous. Natty is said to reject their "creed," not their story, and as readers of *The Pioneers* would know, Natty's latent Christianity is just strong enough to make him resist the synchronic Indian idea of the afterlife as a continuation of earthly happiness; accordingly, the mere *fact* of a posthumous coupling, rather than its interracial status, may be what provokes this refusal.[72] Yet while Natty resists subscribing himself to the Indian afterlife, he is also careful to preserve the cultural purity of its time-sense by refusing to allow the other whites to taint the Delawares with Christian beliefs; when Munro gratefully predicts that all present will eventually "assemble around His throne without distinction of sex, or rank, or colour" (347), Natty again shakes his head, insisting that to say so to Indians is tantamount to reversing the natural rhythms of their world, and translates Munro's thanks into more suitable terms.

Natty's final actions in the funeral scene, however, suggest that the roots of his resistance to the lament may be less racial or cultural than *gendered*: a resistance to the feminization of time in a song that wanders away from its expected theme in order to bring the two characters' ostensibly conflicting temporalities into cohesion through marriage. Natty's own desire for life with the Indians—or, rather, with Chingachgook—exceeds any inclination toward marriage, as the narrator suggests when, after the rest of the whites leave the scene on their journey back to the settlements, he describes Natty's return "to the spot where his own sympathies led him, with a force that no ideal bond of union could bestow" (348), in order to plight his troth unto the sachem. Pointing out that he too has "no kin, and I may also say, like you, no people," Natty pledges himself to the last surviving Mohican on the basis of the mutual love for Uncas that binds their memories (349). This coupling on the basis of collective mourning for the dead warrior-child and the (lost) tradition that he represents balances the future-directed time of the reproductive couple whose return to the settlements they have helped to arrange. In this light, Natty's insistence on retrieving Uncas's memory from the "thrillingly soft" voices of the women's lament substitutes his own pairing with Chingachgook as the wilderness's complement to the marriage of Alice and Heyward, demonstrating the way the fantasy of the masculine-homosocial "beautiful friendship" is arranged in nineteenth-century male adventure literature as an antidote to the excesses of femininity, a "remedy" that functions more often to confirm than to undermine the civilized model of generational reproduction.[73]

In this sense, the posthumous pairing that is rejected because it is too primitive can also be understood as too *modern* for the paternally ordered model of repronarrativity that the novel embraces: not simply because it is a coupling arranged by women (rather than an exchange between men) but also because it justifies itself as the pairing of two people who are, despite the nominal opposition of their sexes, more alike than different. Indeed, while the Delaware women pay lip service to the essential distinction between the sexes, their insistence on finding a way to bring Uncas and Cora in time with each other also positions the couple as something approaching equals, an arrangement distinctly audible in their lavish praise of Cora. The feminine perversion of tradition in this romance of a cross-sex simultaneity, which slides indeterminately between homosocial collegiality and a patriarchal heterosexuality arranged according to the transgenerational exchange of child-women, is directly blocked from crossing the culture barrier by Natty, who declines to translate the content of the song to the whites; but the presence of the musically attuned psalmodist David Gamut partly erodes that linguistic barrier through his sensitivity to the sound of the voice. Gamut's brief performance at the funeral seems, at long last, to locate for him a role in which he is neither irrelevant nor dangerous; his ability, as "one who . . . knows the Christian fashions" (346), to sing a hymn over Cora's grave extends to the elder Munro daughter the security of a regular Christian burial, ostensibly correcting the Delaware women's incorporation of her into their imagination of the afterlife. Yet Gamut's "correction" is also, as the novel emphasizes, an *extension* of their emotional lament. During the women's song, he hears neither the "wild sounds" perceived by Heyward and Munro (344) nor the heresy that Natty comprehends; instead, his "soul [is] enthralled" by the sweet tones of their voices. When his own turn to sing comes, his "full, rich voice" responds in kind. Significantly, the lyrics of his hymn are not given—rendered unnecessary not only by the reader's presumed familiarity with the content of Christian sacred music but also because they have already been effectively summarized in the sympathetic response of the Delaware women, who "listened like those who knew the meaning of the strange words, and appeared as if they felt the mingled emotions of sorrow, hope, and resignation, they were intended to convey" (346). Gamut's ability to engage in a musical exchange of sympathies with the Delaware women, finally hearing the appeal of sounds that he had previously rejected as the howling of idolaters, and likewise gaining the affective response that he failed to win from the Mohicans in the cavern scene, establishes a channel of cross-cultural sonic contact that the novel had previously managed to achieve only through analogy, in the description of the "music" of Delaware speech as it resonates against the timeless nature of familial affection.

Gamut's ability, in the funeral scene, to use music to establish contact across cultures—a contact that resonates, here, as a touch across time—resounds against the anachronism that has previously marked the character. Gamut's outdatedness, revealed in his old-fashioned penchant for Biblical allegory and embodied by the "six-and-twentieth edition" of a seventeenth-century Puritan psalmody that he carries with him everywhere (26), functions, up to a point, as comic relief. In light of the novel's ethnographically coded insistence on the spiritual-temporal difference of the Indian, Gamut's fond faith that he can influence the natives with the "holy charm" of Christianity by singing at them appears humorously irrational; the Hurons, as it turns out, believe that he is "gifted with the protecting spirit of madness" (178). But what Alice aptly identifies as "an unfitness between sound and sense" (26–27)—the contrast between the archaic language that marks him as the remnant of a mildly embarrassing moment in America's early history and the pleasingly "full, sweet, and melodious tones" of his voice—works to provide his comic anachrony with a simultaneously attractive and dangerous capacity, most notably when Magua follows the familiar sound of his voice to the Munro sisters amid the "cacophony" of the massacre (179).[74] Gamut's funeral performance seems finally to locate his character in the realm of sentimentality. Significantly, he succeeds with the Delaware women where he failed with their men, apparently confirming Natty's repeated derision of his musical profession as unmanly and his "tooting w'epon" as useless (266).[75] But although Gamut's affiliation with women might suggest the alliance between ministers and mothers that Ann Douglas describes in *The Feminization of American Culture,* something more resounds in his voice during the funeral scene, unsettling the sentimental time of this civilized alliance: a something-more that the novel suggestively attaches both to the Indian women and to the figure of Cora. Gamut's final song is so powerful because, as the narrator observes, his voice is peculiarly impassioned: "Excited by the scene he had just witnessed, and *perhaps influenced by his own secret emotions,* the master of song exceeded his own usual efforts" (346, emphasis added). Here, the narrator's emphasis on Gamut's excitement by Indian lament privileges Gamut's sacred song as the means by which the inspiring spiritual traditions of the Delaware might be transmitted to the settlements. Yet this "excited" contact still resounds, as I earlier observed, within the register of sympathy, at once bringing Gamut's outdated doctrines into harmony with the emergent nineteenth-century embrace of nature's spiritual influence and marking the psalmodist as the medium by which the Indian voice is transposed into the white interior.[76] The narrator's supplementary speculation on Gamut's "secret emotions," however, provides Gamut with a hitherto-unsuspected interiority—an explanation, presumably, for the "unusual fire" that marked the psalmodist's uncharacteristic insistence on joining the war party that was raised to rescue Cora (327)—yet the precise nature of his attachment to Cora remains strangely underspecified.[77] Gamut assures Heyward, on seeking to join their party, that he entertains no designs on the women, insisting that he knows his own mind—something that, he acknowledges, is not easy where women are concerned—and seeks only the fellowship of "good company" (23). The obscure transformation of this early wish for "social communion" (24) into the ultimate mystery of Gamut's "secret emotions" leaves open the question not only of what those emotions might be, precisely, but also of *when,* in the course of the narrative, this influence emerged. Gamut's secret may be assumed to parallel that of that other musically marked male figure, Uncas, who is won over by Cora's exemplary conduct over the course of the story, with its mixture of manly vitality and motherly generosity. Intriguingly, however, Gamut also shadows Magua on both his first and last appearances in the novel; indeed, the effect of his first contact with the Huron, who distracts him from looking at the horses that he has been associating with "Old England" by providing a "new and more powerful subject of admiration" (17), is identified by the narrator as unspecifiable, and it is only after this contact that Gamut pursues the party into the woods, proposing to join them.[78] In this light, the "honest" Gamut's potential attachment to Cora can be seen to move uncertainly between the benevolent, if doomed, affection of Uncas and Magua's drive to undo the white family; that is to say, it is neither Romantic nor Gothic but queerly indeterminate, given neither cause nor direction.[79]

The temporal uncertainty opened by this sonic manifestation of desire in mourning, moreover, unsettles the ability of narrative ordering to lay the past securely to rest; for, significantly, although Gamut returns to the settlements with the whites (presumably to resume his role as the guardian of sacred song, a socially stabilizing function upon which his own doubleness casts a newly uncertain light) he yet remains the only character in the novel whose future trajectory is wholly unspecified. Just as it is not known from whence his attachment to Cora emerges, then, it is also unclear where, in the new nation, that queer attachment may manifest. Through the sound of Gamut's voice, then, the narrative enfolds the potentially radical function of anachrony—for what appears initially as mere *archaism* in this figure is both vitalized by his sympathetic contact with the timeless dimension of the Indian lifeworld and destabilized by an uncertainly erotic attachment to a figure whose (feminine) temporal duplicity he remains capable of somehow reanimating in some other place, at some other time.

This final obscure deployment of the voice's extralinearity emphasizes the difficulty of managing the temporal surplus of the voice in a historical era—for if even the mourning song of a Puritan psalmodist cannot be entirely purged of a disorienting resonance, then the act of mourning the prenational and prepolitical time that voice bespeaks, of appropriating and internalizing its virtuous aspects and laying the remainder to rest, defies completion. Gamut reads, in this light, both with and against the grain of his name, as the lingering aural trace of the novel, incorporating the possibility of deviance into the sacred spaces supporting an ostensibly *settled* model of futurity. The surplus resonance between Gamut's dislocated anachronism and that of women who refuse their "proper" place in time gestures, through the backward turn of a shared mournful inventiveness, toward the possibility of other principles of moving forward: the disarticulation of long-settled narratives in favor of new forms of relationality, forms that seek not to escape but to differently animate the potentiality of the affective arrangements that organize this vision of the American social world. It is to another such instance that we will now turn.

Mourning (as) History in *Hope Leslie*

Catharine Maria Sedgwick's *Hope Leslie; or, Early Times in the Massachusetts,* published a year after *The Last of the Mohicans,* might be said to pick up where Cooper's novel leaves off—with the resistant possibilities opened by the figure of Gamut.[80] But unlike Cooper's insistence that his novel is founded in historical truth, Sedgwick reflects, in her preface to *Hope Leslie,* on the "liberties" she has taken with the past, insisting that the novel is not "in any degree a historical narrative" and that although she has found it "very convenient" to refer to actual historical events and players, her object in doing so was to "illustrate not the history, but the *character* of the times."[81] Sedgwick insists, however, that although she has not been bound by a desire to remain faithful to history, she has endeavored to exclude anything "inconsistent" with the period in which she locates her story. In expanding on this point, she strikes a note that Cooper himself would, intriguingly, later echo, by defending a character whom readers might find unrealistic—the Pequot girl Magawisca. Just as Cooper would later acknowledge that Natty was largely a "poetic" device,[82] Sedgwick contends that any reader unconvinced of Indian "virtue and intellect" by the historical example of Pocahontas should simply remember that as a romance, her narrative is "not confined by the actual, but by the possible" (6). Sedgwick's understanding of history as a font of possibilities demonstrates what Jeffrey Insko has astutely identified as the world-making orientation of her deliberately anachronistic approach to the past, which "disrupt[s] the unidirectional course of history."[83] My consideration of *Hope Leslie* extends Insko's attention to the ironic dimension of the novel's narrative voice, which aligns the temporal doubleness of the female characters with a greater degree of agency than did Cooper's, by examining the novel's reliance on the thrillingly melancholy voice of Magawisca, one of the few survivors of the English settlers' massacre of the Pequot tribe: a reliance that binds together the metaphorical —what Insko terms her position as the novel's "voice of authority"—and the literal—that is to say, the sonic—presence of that voice as the key to the novel's reimagination of historical time. *Hope Leslie*'s noteworthy investment in Magawisca's resonant tones returns the "primal" temporal division of sound to the text-bound historical time of the Puritan settlements, by seizing on Magawisca's melancholy speech as at once figuring the suspension of the obscured past within the present and endowing that suspension with a revolutionizing *liveness* that might enable it to rearticulate the range of contemporary social possibilities.[84]

Magawisca's function as the compellingly musical voice of mourning in the novel is evident from her very name: "Magawisca" is Sedgwick's rendition of the Pequot word for whippoorwill, a bird frequently noted, in Anglo-American literature of the period, for having a pleasantly melancholy note. This sense of the whippoorwill as an instance of the aesthetic pleasures offered by nature contrasts strikingly, however, with the belief that the bird was understood by Native Americans to echo the traumatic history of colonization; understood as a manifestation of the spirits of Indians killed by the English in an early massacre, it was viewed as a bird of ill omen, the harbinger of death.[85] Sedgwick seems deliberately to have aligned this account with the character's own history: Magawisca is herself the survivor of the Puritan massacre of the Pequot tribe, in which her older brother was killed, while she, her mother, and her younger brother Oneco were taken captive by the English soldiers. After her mother's death, since her father, the Pequot sachem Mononotto, remains missing, Governor Winthrop sends the siblings to live with the Fletchers, a frontier Puritan family, as servants. Her appearance at the Fletcher household indeed proves an "ill omen" for the settlers, as it is followed by an ambush by Mononotto, in which several members of the Fletcher family are killed, while the eldest son Everell is taken captive along with Faith Leslie, a ward of Mr. Fletcher.

Tellingly, however, although Mrs. Fletcher initially intuits a threat to her family in the arrival of the Pequot girl, she classifies that threat as not lethal but sexual. Just before she is killed in the ambush, she writes to her husband of her "vague forebodings" of Indian attack (35); the primary purpose of this letter, however, is to persuade her husband to send Everell to England to finish his studies because she is wary of the attachment that he is developing to Magawisca. Mrs. Fletcher insists, in writing, that she imputes no dishonor to the girl; indeed, she lauds her, significantly praising the "natural deep and most sweet melody of her voice," though she hastens to add that she herself is not, like Everell, simply a "charmed bird to" Magawisca, and defends the girl's worthiness by comparing her to Biblical figures (32). Yet this comparison cannot overcome the stepmother's belief that such an inappropriate attachment, formed during youth, might be fatal to one or both of the pair in later life. Mrs. Fletcher's letter both acknowledges and resists the appeal of Magawisca's resonant voice, which has charmed Everell since their first meeting, when the "scream of agony" that she emitted at the sight of a scalp that she (mistakenly) believed to be Mononotto's inspired Everell to attack the Indian who carried it, "losing all other thought in his instinctive sympathy" for her (26). Although the power of Magawisca's voice touches Mrs. Fletcher in a slightly different register—she is less attentive to its capacity to thrill than to the "plaintive . . . tone that touch[es] the heart like a strain of sad music" (24–25)—she, too, responds to its sympathetic appeal; listening to the girl speak, Mrs. Fletcher immediately regrets and attempts to silence expressions of the Puritan disdain for the Indian that she had regarded, seconds before, as "self-evident truth" (24). As a good Christian mother, however, Mrs. Fletcher tempers her sympathy for the Pequot girl with what she understands as a proper concern for the future, a concern that her adolescent stepson abandons in his dual attraction to the sensational and sentimental registers of Magawisca's appeal. That abandonment will have disastrous results. Later in the novel's first volume, Everell passes an evening fascinated by her mournful recital of the massacre of her tribe; though he is familiar with English accounts of this incident, Magawisca's lips impart to the events a "new form and hue" that heats his imagination (53). Although the novel's narrator apparently sympathizes with Magawisca's side of the story, echoing Everell's conviction that her retelling places it in "the hands of truth" (53), the timing of this "recital" is nevertheless suspicious; Everell, while listening, completely forgets that he has been charged with the duty of obtaining information from her on the mysterious behavior of the Indians around the Fletcher home, the same behavior that inspired his stepmother's "vague forebodings." And as the narrator makes clear, Magawisca does possess information about Mononotto that she is conflicted about passing on, torn between her attachment to her family and her desire to protect her new friends. Her fascinating narration thus serves as both a restoration of the "truth" of the past and a timely distraction, which permits Mononotto's vengeance to execute itself the very next day.

Sedgwick's arrangement of the overlapping sensational and sentimental appeal of Magawisca's mournful story—its ability, that is, to articulate both trauma and melancholy—enables it at once to suspend time and to alter its flow, turning official history back on itself. This alteration not only drives forward the plot but, significantly, also creates space for the actualization of counternational and counterfamilial histories into the novel. The retelling of the massacre challenges Puritan histories while permitting Mononotto to regather his family as he avenges the massacre, though he is too late to prevent Magawisca's affections from becoming shared between himself and the Fletchers (a self-division literalized when she interposes her own body between Everell's neck and her father's blade, losing an arm). Significantly, however, in the wake of the blow, the Pequot family is reconstructed along *different* lines, as Magawisca's interruption of the intended exchange (Everell's life in trade for that of Mononotto's eldest son, killed in the massacre) changes her place within it; after receiving the blow meant for Everell, she behaves not as a dutiful daughter but, in effect, as a *son* to Mononotto. While her surviving brother Oneco distracts himself with Faith Leslie, retained by the Pequots as a captive, Magawisca involves herself deeply in her melancholy father's plan to unite the Native American tribes to drive the English from American soil. In this turn of events, then, sexual and national politics are intertwined as the reconfiguration of the family becomes at once the cause and the effect of possible alterations in national history. In this way, the (anachronistic) return of Magawisca's voice in the text-based time of the Puritan settlements resists the containment of the voice's synchronic simultaneity by the complementary prepolitical realms of nature and domesticity that, as arranged in Cooper, allow the progress of history to retain its essentially linear character; instead, voice operates, in this novel, to challenge the very equation of history with progress that drives that linear accumulation.

Yet as Magawisca becomes more deeply intertwined with the counternational claims of the Pequots, the novel moves toward a temporal impasse in its alignment of the sonic power of her voice with the moral "truth" of her speech: for although the simultaneity of the voice can alter one's relation to time, it is not understood to have the power to undo that aspect of the past's progression that remains marked by death.[86] Not coincidentally, this impasse first begins to surface in the episode set in the Boston burial ground where both Monoco (Magawisca's mother) and Alice Leslie (Hope and Faith's mother, and Mr. Fletcher's first love) lie entombed.[87] Magawisca's purpose at this midnight meeting is to arrange an encounter between Hope and her long-lost sister Faith, now adopted into the Pequot tribe and married to Oneco. Hope believes, wrongly, that the meeting is provoked by Magawisca's kindness alone and will effect the restoration of her sister to white society. But Magawisca acts in accordance with the dying wish of the Pequot healer Nelema, who, owing Hope a debt of gratitude, promised to do what she could to help her see her sister. However, Magawisca fails to inform Hope that her compliance with Nelema's wish is intended to empower her father, since Nelema has prophesied on her deathbed that Mononotto will not be able to carry out his plans until after the Leslie sisters have met once more. The difference in pace that characterizes the two women in the grave-yard scene ironically reverses the difference in duration that each allots to the planned reunion. While Hope's feverish impatience markedly contrasts Magawisca's calm conformity to ritual rhythms, Hope assumes that Faith will naturally wish to remain with her, as her only surviving blood kin, but Magawisca predicts (correctly, as it turns out) that Hope will be unable to "retain" her, since her affection for Oneco is too strong. And when Hope worries, for her dead mother's sake, about her sister's alienation from the Christian faith that drew their family to the New World, Magawisca coun-ters this implicit embrace of a developmental model of spiritual truth by of-fering, in the name of her own dead mother, a pantheistic appeal to sacred simultaneity: an insistence that all times are equal from the perspective of the divine. The phrasing of this appeal, significantly, supplements the power of argument with the "deep pathos" with which Magawisca voices her "thrilling" faith, and it is the latter that succeeds in finally "riveting Hope's attention" and allowing Magawisca to quell the white woman's lamentations in order to arrange the meeting (189). Magawisca's ability to use her voice to make space in time, here, recollects the opening moments of the episode, during which Hope, understandably eager to know the Pe-quots' intentions, is nevertheless awed into silence by the sacred chant that Magawisca is performing over her mother's grave, which she at once "recog-nizes as an act of filial devotion" and, moved by the "sweet and varied" mu-sic of Magawisca's voice, imagines as mysteriously spiritual (187). Hope's conviction of the spiritual mystery attached to filial devotion inspires her, if not to abandon her prejudice against Faith's adoption by the Pequots, at least to contemplate the possibility of cross-cultural sisterhood. After Maga-wisca departs, Hope lingers a moment to reflect on this newly realized tie: "Mysteriously have our destinies been interwoven. Our mothers brought from a far distance to rest together here—their children connected in indis-soluble bonds!" (192).

Hope's enchantment by the "mystery" of Magawisca's poetic alignment of the maternal and the divine points us toward the simultaneously radical and conservative dimension of the Pequot woman's revoicing of time in the novel. Magawisca's appeal to sacred bonds as created by love, not blood (she insists, significantly, that Hope will never persuade Faith to return to Boston because "she and my brother are as if one life-chord bound them together"

[191]), articulates a vision of community authorized not by shared biology or history but by shared *time*: ties that spring up from habits formed by (temporal) coincidence. This vision of the temporality of community as *contemporaneousness* is enabled, through her appeal to sacred simultaneity, to cross boundaries of time as well as place. Hope's final reflection, however, moderates the radical temporality of this vision of community by orienting it toward a "destiny" that, if yet mysterious, seems nevertheless preordained —a belief similar to Magawisca's faith in Nelema's prophecy as integral to the success of her father's plans. And although the narrator characterizes both women's behavior in this scene as alike "romantic," their coincidental purposes, as established in this scene, nevertheless resonate with widely divergent visions of the future toward which those destinies impel them —fundamentally nationalist cultural visions that do not contain space for the time of the other. This incompatibility is reflected both in Magawisca's involvement in her father's plan, which leads her to insist that the Indian and the imperialistic white can never coexist, and in Hope's continued belief in the superiority of blood ties and Christianity (strangely, although Protestant, she is relieved to hear that her sister has become a Catholic because she believes "any christian faith [is] better than none," and at the end of the novel she still wishes to shed the "brighter light of Christian revelation" on Magawisca [189, 332]), a nationalistically oriented cultural bias that seemingly confirms Magawisca's skepticism. It follows, then, that only a thorough reimagination of the nature of the nation's future could allow this coincidence of desires to continue. The burial-ground scene's supplementation of (sororal) simultaneity with filial devotion offers the key to the novel's reimagination of that future: it will be accomplished *in the name of the mother*, emphasizing not the patriarchally ordered connection of blood but the originary status of affection as it (re)humanizes the social world.

It is, however, precisely this turn in the temporal basis of community that partly domesticates the dual pitch of Magawisca's voice, taming its thrill and privileging its melancholy, which becomes increasingly audible in the register of the sentimental. And—again not coincidentally—it is during the courtroom scene, Magawisca's most memorable vocal performance, that this register emerges to contain the power of that voice. Captured as she oversees the promised meeting between Hope and Faith, Magawisca is arraigned on charges of conspiracy and brought to trial in Boston; though she is advised by her English supporters that she would do best to speak demurely, as a "maiden," or, as a foreigner, not to speak at all, she instead uses the time granted for her own defense to challenge the historical legitimacy of the trial itself, asserting that, since her tribe has never recognized the colonial administration, she remains outside their laws. When she is asked mockingly where that tribe is now, her voice reproduces, in its moving force, the profoundly melancholic structure on which her autonomy rests:

> "My people! Where are they?" she replied, raising her eyes to heaven, and speaking in a voice that sounded like deep-toned music, after the harsh tones addressed to her,—"my people are gone to the isles of the sweet south-west; to those shores that the bark of an enemy can never touch: think ye that I fear to follow them?"
>
> There was a momentary silence throughout the assembly; all seemed, for an instant, to feel that no human power could touch the spirit of the captive. (287)

Magawisca's reliance on the evocative power of an absence, characteristically, suspends time, stunning into silence an audience that had, moments before, scorned her as a member of a "diabolical race" (284). Her speech transforms her status from subhuman to superhuman, a transformation that serves as a first step in winning the sympathy of the audience. But that sympathy is ultimately won only when Magawisca's speech draws upon the register of sentiment, traveling through the (wounded) body of a woman into an invocation of the mother. At the close of the trial, when the court has determined to delay the trial and return her to prison, she attempts to change its decision by allowing her body to speak for her:

> Advancing to the feet of the Governor, [she] threw back her mantle, and knelt before him. Her mutilated person, unveiled by this action, appealed to the senses of the spectators. Everell involuntarily closed his eyes, and uttered a cry of agony, lost indeed in the murmurs of the crowd. (293)

Once again, what speaks most clearly through Magawisca is an *absence,* the missing arm that all present know she lost in saving Everell's life. Significantly, however, his "involuntary" sympathetic response to the sight of the loss she sustained on his behalf renders the otherwise audacious public speech of an exposed body permissible as an articulation of feminine self-sacrifice—she reveals, that is, not a body but a *wound*. Magawisca follows this sentimental corporeal argument by yet again framing her appeal in terms of a speaking absence. Reminding Governor Winthrop of his promise to her dying mother to treat her children well, she sutures this maternal appeal to the rhetoric of the Revolution by demanding, in that mother's name, either "death or liberty" (293).[88] Here, the novel itself mimes the complex temporal effect of Magawisca's voice by folding time at once backward and forward: Magawisca, significantly, *pre-bespeaks* the rhetoric of the American Revolution, a rhetoric that resounds as historical memory for Sedgwick's readers; yet the courtroom crowd, which knows no comparable history, seems nevertheless to be affected in much the same way, as they immediately begin calling out for liberty.[89] Yet if Magawisca's audience cannot logically be expected to share with Sedgwick's the specifically historical resonance of this speech, the conventional nineteenth-century appeal to the timeless status of human affection authorizes the assumption that they instinctively comprehend the *first* part of her appeal—the one that replaces the memory of the revolutionary fathers with the powerful name of the mother.

In the trial scene, then, we can trace the success of Magawisca's appeal to the audience as predicated on the movement of Magawisca's melancholy evocations from historical to personal loss: a transformation accomplished by means of a direct citation of the body whose heroic wounding is made to resonate in the register of the sacred-maternal. And although this arc has a profound effect on public sentiments, it must nevertheless be remembered that *none* of it makes any difference to the law; for, notably, Magawisca's *first* claim—that the colony itself has no right to exist and therefore no right to judge her—escapes the public's claiming of her cause as their own, leaving her at the mercy of a colonial authority that deems itself both impersonal and absolute. Accordingly, Governor Winthrop, acting in his public capacity, is constrained to return Magawisca to jail, and it is ultimately left up to Hope and Everell to secretly effect her liberation.

The courtroom scene, then, brings the novel to an impasse in its deployment of the temporality of voice, which cannot resolve the doubled nature of the charges against Magawisca. On one level, these charges are false; they are based on fabricated evidence given by the loquacious liar, Sir Philip, whose desire for Magawisca's conviction emerges from a complex of economic, political, and sexual motives. On an abstract national level, however, his charges are true; Magawisca is, indeed, conspiring against the colony, as she affirms in her courtroom speech: "Do you wait for him to prove that I am your enemy? Take my own word—I am your enemy" (292). Magawisca's insistence on the justice of her tribe's prior claim to the land and the incompatibility of the two cultures leaves no room for compromise. Accordingly, the justice of her claim is both acknowledged in and then *forgotten by* the novel as the trial, without means of adjudicating the national question, devolves into a contest of character between the English knight and the Indian "princess." Sir Philip attempts to sway the court by insisting on the diabolism of the Pequot's "savage" nature, describing the mourning chant witnessed by Hope as a perverse satanic ceremony; Magawisca responds by revealing the secrets that the knight has kept from Boston society: his Catholicism, his royalist sympathies, and most importantly, his sexual exploitation of the orphan Rosa, who accompanies him to the colony dressed in boy's clothing and posing as his page.

Although the transformation of charges of national-political heresy into allegations of carnal misconduct in the court scene suggestively highlights the relays between national and sexual violence, it does so at the cost of locating at the level of *character,* and hence *individualizing,* these public and structural concerns. As a rake, a racist, a seducer, an adventurer, a traitor, a liar, and a hypocrite, Sir Philip manages to embody simultaneously all the failings of the political and familial systems that *Hope Leslie* critiques. This embodiment brings into focus the persistence of men's sexual and marital exploitation of women within the patriarchal familial arrangements of the English, a pattern enacted in incidents ranging from Mr. Fletcher's marriage to a woman he does not love after he is prevented, because of his religion, from marrying the one he does, to Everell's obstinate persistence in his engagement to Esther Downing despite his passion for Hope, to Sir Philip's pursuit of Hope on the basis of her fortune, to the violence of a band of pirates who first, finding Hope alone at night, chase and try to rape her and, later, abduct Jennet, mistaking her for Hope, after Sir Philip has purchased their assistance. The narrative effect of this condensation is, however, the absorption of the novel's profound challenge to the patriarchal domination that underlies these events in its quest to halt the behavior of "that bad man" (329).

In the aftermath of the courtroom scene, then, nationalist politics are increasingly displaced by sexual ones, a development that seemingly confirms Magawisca's insistence on the impossibility of justice for the Indian. New Historicist readings of the novel cite this development as confirmation of the novel's essential conformity to the naturalizing tendency of the Anglo-American "Vanishing" narrative, the drive to project onto Indian culture the blame for its own erasure. Yet although Magawisca does indeed recapitulate the nature-bound terms of that narrative in the courtroom scene, the specific context of her metaphors gives them a distinctly historical resonance:

> The white man cometh—the Indian vanisheth. Can we grasp in friendship the hand raised to strike us? Nay; and it matters not whether we fall by the tempest that lays the forest low, or are cut down alone, by the stroke of the axe. (292–93)

Magawisca's emphasis on the violence of the (white) hand of the state denaturalizes the metaphor that follows this image, recalling, in the "tempest that lays the forest low," the massacre that decimated her tribe; her reference to being "cut down alone"—the possible outcome of her trial for treason, and the sentence she now represents as preferable to being sent "back to that dungeon—the grave of the living, feeling, thinking soul" (293), similarly underscores the lack of freedom that determines her "choice" between liberty and death. The novel's final account of the remnants of the Pequot tribe also recalls the threat of violence that motivates their "choice" to go west. Once Magawisca, helped to escape from prison by Hope and Everell, returns to Mononotto, he is "renewed" by his joy, turning away from his fixation on the mournful past: "for a while, he forgot, in the powerful influence of his protector, his old wrongs and sorrows" (339). Magawisca's return, significantly, redoubles the gender transformation that located her as a son by maternalizing her father; in place of his former desire for national vengeance, he is now overcome by anxiety over his family's safety, and takes them west, away from the still-present threat of their Puritan "enemies." In this sense, the novel shifts the characteristic framing of Indian vanishing as an effect of the natural *environment*—it becomes, rather, an effect of familial "nature," as protective love for the family overcomes love for the nation, causing the counternationalist claims of the Pequots to diminish into silence; the narrator closes their tale by observing, "That which remains untold of their story, is lost in the deep, voiceless obscurity of those unknown regions" (339).

Just prior to Magawisca's disappearance into these "voiceless" realms, however, she manages the transfer of the dissonant energies associated with the mixed time of her voice to the three young white women whose fates are intertwined with hers in the narrative. For two of these women, she helps to create historically new possibilities within the arrangements of the family. Undoing Hope's estrangement from Everell, she informs the couple that they no longer need her, as they have each other and will "each be to the other a full stream of happiness" (333). This matchmaking move replaces the fundamentally patriarchal arrangement that characterizes the settlement's Puritan families, in which wives are counted as "dutiful helpmate[s]" (14), with an anachronistically modern heterosexuality composed (much like the Delaware women's posthumous matchmaking) of an alliance between equals. She also inspires the destiny of Esther Downing, Hope's demure Puritan foil, who visits Magawisca daily while she is in prison and who, like Magawisca, ends up renouncing her adolescent affection for Everell in favor of what she believes to be a higher calling: spinsterhood. A self-sufficient woman guided by an unshakable sense of duty, Esther forges a respectable space for the single woman in American national life, demonstrating the "truth . . . that marriage is not essential to the contentment, the dignity, or the happiness of woman" (349–50).[90]

This dual reformation of the boundaries of the family, which improves and expands the possibilities open to (white) women, is, however, troubled by the unexpected resonance between Magawisca's auratic melancholy and Rosa's tangential subplot, for the Catholic orphan's sexual slavery to Sir Philip indexes the limited control women have over their own destinies in a male-dominated social order. That subplot, as we have seen, highlights the abusive effects of relegating the body to the prepolitical time of the private sphere. Rosa, whom Sir Philip has seduced away from a convent, embodies the abjection of the woman whose sexual exploitation is denied even the guise of marriage; her radically dependent condition suggests, as well, an echo of the muted history of slavery that speaks through Cora in Cooper's novel, as Rosa is implicated in Sir Philip's attempts to gain social and financial status without being able to share in his potential gains. Isolated within her dependence on the knight, who does not scruple to conceal from her the violence and greed that he hides from the community and who actually enlists her in his plot to marry Hope, Rosa slowly loses both reason and self-respect. Her neediness, desperation, and hysteria place her in opposition to the self-possessed Pequot woman in every way save two: the melancholy effect of her presence, produced by her constant mourning over her own "lost" state, and the evocative sound of her voice. Though Rosa, in an effort to disguise her sex, rarely speaks in public, the alternately "melancholy" and "thrilling" tones of her enigmatic utterances in her sole conversation with Hope, just prior to the graveyard meeting with Magawisca (167), recall the Indian woman's characteristic inflections. And like Magawisca, whose "mutilated form" is emphasized to the reader by virtue of the cloak she dons to conceal it, the damage done to Rosa's body—her lost virginity—is also continually kept before the reader's eyes by virtue of its concealment in the boy's costume she wears. The wounded energy emanating from Rosa reverses the trajectory taken by Magawisca's voice; the voice of the Catholic girl moves from melancholy to increasingly thrilling articulations, transforming her grief into an all-consuming rage that proves literally explosive. Sinking deeper into the web of Sir Philip's schemes, she finally accompanies him on board the ship of the pirates who have helped him kidnap the house servant Jennet, believing her to be Hope. When he calls on Rosa for assistance in dealing with his captive, however, she shrieks, "It cannot be worse for any of us!" and tosses a lamp into an uncovered barrel of gunpowder, which obliterates the ship, killing all the novel's unredeemable characters at one blow (324).

Rosa's subplot thus indexes the by-now-familiar fantasy of women's rage as having the power to demolish men's sexual abuses simply by manifesting —by being given "voice." This obliterative action logically completes the narrative conversion begun in the courtroom scene, where structural political problems become visible as individual sins and, hence, available for punishment or redemption. And as with the evaporation of Magawisca's powerful voice in the "voiceless" end of the Pequot story, this explosion of dominant/masculine narratives by the diva-auratic performance of embodied female emotion leaves little tangible in its wake—except, that is, for the ripples of time, folded upon itself as a (re)humanizing *echo*, spreading outward from the wreck of the ship. The explosion distracts the members of the colony from news of Magawisca's escape, allowing her time to avoid recapture and saving her life, as though it were exchanged for Rosa's. Rosa herself is posthumously rehabilitated by the sympathy of the survivors: "tears, of humility and pity, were shed over her grave; a fit tribute, from virtuous and tender woman, to a fallen and unhappy sister" (348). The Puritan women's attendance at Rosa's grave layers the nineteenth-century insistence on mourning as a way of making lasting meaning out of grief against the Puritanic insistence that the only difference between the living and the dead was *time*; in this light, the women's tears of humility, as well as pity, emphasize a consciousness of their own vulnerability to the fate that befell the living Rosa.

The humanizing resonance of the explosion also exonerates Hope, whose behavior in the second volume has pushed beyond the limits assigned to the dutiful Christian daughter but whose family and friends are so relieved to learn that she was not killed in the wreck that they overlook her transgressions. Even the state is partly "humanized" in this manner, as Governor Winthrop, prompted by "secret and kind dispositions," decides to overlook Everell and Hope's illegal freeing of Magawisca. Winthrop, however, must conceal this humanity behind what the narrator terms the "melancholy policy" of the colonial administration to actively promote intertribal warfare, which helps Winthrop justify his otherwise unaccountably "human" leniency; he rationalizes that executing the Pequot girl would be counterproductive because it might distract the neighboring tribes from a new war that promises to be devastating to them (341).

The novel's deliberate return to the key of "melancholy" in its description of a state policy that at once shelters Winthrop's (partial) humanity toward Hope and Everell and exposes a certain inhumanity on the part of the colonial administration suggests the limited effect that an affective-familial humanity can have in reforming the practices of the state. Although the humanizing resonance of the shipwreck creates enough space in time for certain characters to escape a punishment that the novel clearly views as unjust, it does not fundamentally alter the death-dealing orientation of state policy. In this sense, the novel implicitly foregrounds the ambivalence of the sacred, as it marks both the incorporation of the "timeless" values that we hold most dear and the abjection of expendable populations that are deemed incompatible with the temporal movements of the social body. Significantly, it is here that the novel's resistance to the naturalization of the "vanishing" narrative becomes most audible; by assigning the adjective "melancholy" not to the putatively objective "fact" of Indian disappearance but to the *willed policy* of the state, the novel's narrator echoes the exposure of this supposed act of nature as an act of state violence that resounds in Magawisca's courtroom speech. (His *deliberate* delay, too, undermines the wish to believe that the "unfortunate" violence of national history has been determined by accidents, a belief that the melodramatic pacing of Cooper's rescues tends, rather, to reify.) In this sense, *Hope Leslie* rechannels the voice that it represents as denied to the Pequots in the "voiceless" western forests, amplifying the resonance of the un(der)told aspects of the "vanishing" story. Sedgwick's redeployment of melancholy thus works to restore the sense of *critical* contemplation of the past that is erased by the pathological manifestation of melancholia as a blind spot, since her rearticulation of a melancholy fate as a melancholy state policy can be understood to reflect forward on her own time as well. Yet this distinctly critical resonance, operating as it does against the dominant Romantic sense of melancholy as opening a split in the nature of time that privileges the sensibilities of the individual while leaving the future-directed movement of the public essentially unchanged, has thus far escaped audition by most readers of her tale, an omission that itself suggests the largely conservative way in which the time of melancholy tends to resonate in the modern era.[91]

The limited change that "humanity" can effect on the fundamental inhumanity of the state is echoed by the ambivalent legacy of Sir Philip, the novel's most "inhuman" character. Sir Philip, whose body is never recovered, remains apart from the process of posthumous rehabilitation and alteration that is opened in the wake of the shipwreck. Indeed, we might read his missing corpse as standing in for the absence of structural transformation that would prevent the future reappearance of characters like him—a possibility glimpsed in the local superstition that Satan has claimed his body as "his lawful spoil," a hypothesis that the narrator warns her more "skeptical" modern readers not to dismiss outright (348). Sir Philip, at the end of the tale, may be numbered among the dead, but the novel suggests that nothing has yet emerged to prevent the abuses that he embodied from recurring in the future that constitutes the present tense of the reader—nothing, that is, apart from the thrilling possibility of a repetition of Rosa's explosive rage in some other register.

We have seen, in this chapter, how the location of voice as anterior to language and writing has designated the voice as sacred, positioning it, both conceptually and historically, as other than the historical time it grounds. My reading of the multivalent temporal resonance of the sonorous voice across the pages of two 1820s historical romances has traced the complex and often contradictory uses to which the voice, as the memory of another (form of) time, has been put in American culture. Voice, as we saw, functions both chronobiopolitically and critically: as both a means of securing the historical self-arrangements of the civilized family and of challenging the forms of dispossession and violence that have accompanied those arrangements in time. *The Last of the Mohicans* and *Hope Leslie,* two novels that share both a preoccupation with the narrative of the Vanishing American and an anxiety over the presence of slavery on the American scene—explicitly cited, in Cooper's novel, in the history of Cora and implicitly invoked, in Sedgwick's, in the story of the displaced orphan Rosa—share, as well, a fascination with voice as a means of addressing the temporal implications of these historical problems. Yet the difficulty of laying the alterity of voice to rest, in Cooper, and of sustaining its asynchronic and interruptive capacity, in Sedgwick, should lead us to recognize the ambivalence of voice as a critical tool—precisely because its evocative ephemerality has historically been tied to a sense of its anteriority, the *prioritized* status that marks its exceptional temporality.

This recognition pertains not only to the implications of the voice in the early-nineteenth-century historical romance but also to the lure of the voice in contemporary cultural studies, visible in the numerous recent appeals to the testimony of the "voice," particularly from the vantage of feminist, ethnic, and cultural studies, as a means of amplifying the resonance of the time-lag that marks American democracy. Drawing on the traditional sense in which "voice," in its appeal to the Western phonocentric imaginary, has conveyed an idea of inclusion in the political process, contemporary feminist citations attempt to actualize this *in*clusion by raising "voice" as a defense against *ex*clusion, leading to its distinctive contemporary resonance as, in Susan Sniader Lanser's phrasing, a "term of identity and power" for the "collectively and personally silenced," those who remain outside the completion of democracy's promises.[92] The affective undertone of the appeal to voice tends to convey a certain wistfulness, suggesting an embrace of the voice as an index of alternative values—a spatialization of difference that, as some feminist critics have asserted, leads to the romancing of voice as a privatization of politics.[93] Along these lines, I would argue that the ethical potentiality of voice is disabled when it is sacralized as the register of an exceptional authenticity, a mode of vital connection outside of and prior to modern civilization—even when it attempts, by virtue of this posited priority, to articulate the barbarity of that civilization. Yet although many contemporary attempts to animate the critical capacity of voice collapse backward into a fundamentally nostalgic longing for its sacred power, this is not the only story about voice that we might hear told in this body of writing. Rather, we might try, as I have sought to do in my exploration of the temporalities indexed by voice, to uncover the alternate modes of comprehending time that it can enable, without affixing those modes to nostalgia. As my reading of *The Last of the Mohicans* and *Hope Leslie* suggests, the romance of the voice fails when what it bespeaks most clearly is the (melancholic) wish to *live within* its other time. What we might attend to, in the uncertain vibrations of the sonorous voice against narrative closure in both novels, is, rather, the possibilities it opens for living our own time differently.

3

Securing Time

Maternal Melancholia and
Sentimental Domesticity

We began to see, in the preceding chapter, the way the new nation's desire for deep pastness, for a collective origin in a time before time, articulated itself alongside and against the problem of arranging familial succession, setting a family form historically organized by bloodline against economic development and political change. Cooper's Colonel Munro, for instance, connects his own marriage to a mixed-race woman to the "unnatural" union between the Scots and the English, a people who are both "foreign" and, most damningly, "trading." The global peregrinations of the mercantile English have not only produced slavery but have also—and to Munro, it seems, more importantly—introduced irregularities into the bloodlines of "ancient and honourable" families.[1] Alexis de Tocqueville examines, in *Democracy in America,* the change in temporality that so troubles Munro. Observing that the long-term stasis of aristocratic families produced a kind of "contemporaneous[ness]" across generations, Tocqueville claims that democracy erodes this temporal familiarity: "Among democratic nations new families are constantly springing up, others are constantly falling away, and all that remain change their condition; the woof of time is every instant broken and the track of generations effaced."[2] The decoupling of bloodlines and hereditary authority gives rise to a socioeconomic mobility that appears, from the perspective of the "ancient" families, as a radical flux, which in turn unsettles relations to time itself. Tocqueville's explication of the sexual politics of time, the comprehension that, as Michael Warner puts it, "[a]s family forms change, temporality changes," is rendered in a language of isolation and loss, contrasting tellingly with the "love" and "respect" that bonds the aristocracy across centuries.[3] *Democracy in America* sums up the affective contours of the new time in this register:

> Thus not only does democracy make every man forget his ancestors, but it hides his descendants and separates his contemporaries from him; it throws him back forever upon himself alone and threatens in the end to confine him entirely within the solitude of his own heart.[4]

A democratic modernity appears, in this passage, as not simply another temporal condition, still less a positive vision of "progress," but a *plight*: what Warner terms a "broken relationship to ancestors and descendants, the reproductive metonyms for the past and posterity," which threatens the individual with perpetual emotional isolation.[5]

The plight of the modern subject, whose relations with time were sundered not only by political but also, as Munro's lament makes clear, by economic changes—the movement and flux that comes with the rise of global trade—was partly ameliorated, in Tocqueville's view, by the laudable domestic arrangements of the Americans. Later in *Democracy in America*, Tocqueville devotes several chapters to the strong familial bonds that American democracy built, reserving particular praise for the "superiority" of American women, who excelled within what they understood to be their natural sphere without seeking to move beyond it, and whom Tocqueville identified as perhaps the chief cause of "the singular prosperity and growing strength of [the American] people."[6] The nation's phenomenal and ongoing progress relative to the time of the "civilized world" was thus imagined as grounded in American women's work within the home, which at once corresponded to a timeless bodily disposition and enjoyed for the first time in history the respect and recognition it deserved. *Democracy in America*'s depiction of the novel arrangements of the democratic private sphere also appeared in many antebellum domestic manuals, which insisted that the new respect accorded to mothers signaled the dawn of a new era for humanity.[7] This paradoxically new timelessness recalls what Mitchell Meltzer identifies as the *oldness* of America's novelty, its status in the European colonial imaginary as a repetition of beginnings, a "pristine realm" unsullied by the debris of a degraded past.[8] As the developing nation moved farther away from the topography of the "pristine realm" (to be replaced, as we have seen, by the fantasy of affective national heritage condensed in the melancholy figure of the vanishing Indian), the image of the American mother, ensconced in the domestic sphere and absorbed in the affairs of the family, also came to suggest a kind of affective heritage, the natural prehistory not of America but of Americans.

Antebellum sentimental-domestic writing based this effect, the home's ability to ground the individual, not simply in women's obedience to a sexual division of labor but above all in the kind of *love* the mother modeled within the domestic sphere. Mother-love served not only to bond the family but also to mitigate the democratic individual's sense of isolation in time. The moralism of right feeling, specifically modeled by sentimental pedagogues as something absorbed from one's elders and, in particular, from one's instinctively loving mother, did more than create a sense of mutual obligation across social space; it also affectively linked generations that would otherwise find themselves with no means of connecting across time. Parents who cared correctly would project love and benevolence, the affective echo of right-feeling predecessors, both outward into the world and forward into the future through the figure of the child. This mode of education would, moreover, furnish the future-bound child with a desirable kind of history: not the centuries-old stasis of a bloodline but the more immediate and yet timeless prehistory of a heart-world, a love out of which it grew and to which it perpetually returned. The figure to which that love was most consistently linked in the nineteenth century was that of the domesticated mother—the source of the humanizing affection that was presented as always already given, residing instinctively within the nature of the true woman, and as the prerequisite for a socially and spiritually productive future. Hence, the tender mother was required, as Lydia Sigourney asserted in the chapter on "Economy" in *Letters to Mothers,* to "secure *time*" for her children—a phrase that resonates both with and across generations.[9] Sigourney uses this phrase in an attempt to persuade mothers, whose duty it is to make "lasting impressions" on young children, to prioritize childrearing above all else, even housework; for Sigourney, it was the middle-class woman's duty to hire all the domestic help she could afford in order to place herself at the center of the child's world, as a kind of emotional ballast against future waywardness. Yet her locution also reveals how the mother makes modernity safe by becoming the kind of anchoring memory that might restore temporal continuity to the potentially isolated democratic "heart." The mother-tended middle-class home thus placed itself of necessity *behind* that future by imagining itself as its foundation. Even that home's all-important distance from the marketplace—a space filled, in the sentimental-domestic imagination, with a promiscuous, unstable, and unpredictable temporality in which the future, dependent on speculation, was always a gamble—came to resonate not simply as spatial elsewhereness but as temporal anteriority: "home" as the site of a *prior* and *truer* mode of existence, the only space for the preservation of values that preceded the modern mercantile (de)valuation of time. Accordingly, time, for sentimental domesticity, was not to be "saved" as much as it was to be *redeemed* from modernity: purged of the multiple taints associated with a market economy (instability, artifice, temporariness, drudgery) and stabilized according to humanity's natural impulses and divine law.

Middle-class domesticity's antipathy to these aspects of the marketplace does not mean, of course, that it eschewed consumption; rather, as Lori Merish has shown, it worked to make capitalism at home by means of an affective logic of interiorization.[10] This introjecting movement depended, in turn, on anteriorization, allying the home's arrangements with the time of origin. Imagined in this way, the middle-class home constructed itself as the only place capable of adequately protecting the figure whose future was most necessary to secure: the child, its sacred investment. The needs of this child increasingly centered the business of the home in the antebellum middle-class imagination, precisely as the child, as Karen Sánchez-Eppler has recently argued, helped center the new status of the family as the "principal moral and social unit of the nation" by means of its emotional labor.[11] The mother-child coupling rhetorically displaced that of husband and wife, declaring the family as neither a sexual nor an economic arrangement but a moral unity.[12] The sentimental home's primary affectionate bond, in this light, existed in a doubled temporality, at once timeless and of necessity transient, insofar as children were both to be cherished and to be raised, and hence to grow away from the mother who remained behind at home.

This doubling accounts for the seeming cultural insistence that, as Carolyn Dever remarks of the nineteenth-century novel, "the *only* good mother is a dead mother."[13] The ejection of the idealized mother-image from the linear time of development, that is, helped transform a dualistic tendency into a complementary temporality, both before *and after* the subject, its immemorial origin and its ultimate goal. This image illuminates, as well, a distinctly nineteenth-century inflection of the "anterior" and spatialized temporal modes that Julia Kristeva describes as historically linked to the conception of (maternal) femininity, repetition and timelessness.[14] Indeed, Kristeva's specification of the mode of maternal-feminine timelessness as *monumental* itself implies the association, historical as well as psychoanalytic, of the mother with the memory of a time of care before the cares associated with the linear, developmental time of the subject; the atemporal bliss of attachment effectively prefigured the earthly prehistory of that fullness that Christianity promises to the faithful as the culmination of life's journey. The ceaseless work of the middle-class woman, in her "natural" guise as the domestic mother, became at once to originate these feelings and to retemporalize their effects by instilling the repetitive cycles of self-regulation within the growing child—a complex and contradictory round of affective labor for which sentimentalists rewarded her by making it eternal.

Antebellum sentimental-domestic fiction's marked investment in developing novelistic virtue out of chronobiopolitical necessity, exhibited in its repeated exploration of loss-as-growth from the perspective of the daughter separated by circumstance or death from the beloved mother, at once confirmed and challenged this time frame, insofar as these novels generally layered the time of the lost mother in yet more complicated ways: in addition to signifying pre- and posttemporal manifestations of timelessness and the regularity of domestic repetition, the mothers in these novels habitually brush up against historical time in a way that makes them seem faintly *dated.* The much-mourned mother, that is, signals at the same time timelessness and anachronism, the latter immanent within intimations or revelations about the mother's prematernal history (which impede her ability to signify as the affective prehistory of the child) and within the difficulties that haunt the daughter's negotiation of generational repetition. In this chapter, then, I consider, against the backdrop of a self-consciously middle-class and sentimental domesticity, both the regulation of time in the fictions of the mother-tended home and the possibilities generated in and through the asynchronic traces retained within such narratives. I will examine in detail two 1850s orphan novels that have themselves attained epoch-defining status: Susan Warner's enormously popular *The Wide, Wide World* (1850) and Harriet E. Wilson's neglected *Our Nig; or, Sketches from the Life of a Free Black* (1859). In each of these novels, the lost and lamented mother appears as anachronistic, possessed by what we might comprehend as a kind of multiple temporality disorder that prevents her from passing into the balanced duality that constitutes the idealized time of the mother. Even as the protagonists' lingering grief invests the novels with a distinctly maternal melancholy, then, the lingering anachrony of their mothers' times, in turn, shadows forth the possibility of reimagining the timing of domestic life.

Maternal Feeling, Home Time, Generational Order

The temporal weave of the distinctly sentimental, middle-class, northern, and white domesticity that marks the work of writers like Sigourney articulated itself not only against the exterior time of the marketplace but also against an image of the misguided and slightly backward time of other household models.[15] Sigourney chided the practical domestic "science" of American housewives whom she saw as stronger on economy than affection —a style of domesticity that, though it remained contemporaneous with their own, the more sentimentally minded writers viewed as a holdover from colonial times. One version of the efficiency-minded domesticity that Sigourney disparages appears in Lydia Maria Child's *The American Frugal Housewife*, a manual explicitly directed at families of modest to middling means, which aligns the home with an economic conservatism intended to shore up the family in an always unpredictable market economy. Child's remarks about the marketplace in the book reflect not a genteel anxiety about the kind of degenerate space it represents but a concern with the kind of time it embodies: speculative, risky, undependable. For that reason, the market economy could not be ignored but must rather be countered by the housewife's habitual saving and precise planning.[16] Child's advice to the housewife to gather up all "the fragments of *time* as well as materials" links domestic temporality to economic accumulation, enabling the mother to secure the family's time against the vicissitudes of the national economy.[17] Not even small children were exempted from this regime of perpetual productivity; Child deplores the custom of allowing children to "romp away their existence" until they hit their teens, a practice that harms both childhood moral development and the "purses and patience of parents."[18] Even a six-year-old, she observes, can be made "useful" in some way; she points out that "it is a great deal better for the boys and girls on a farm to be picking blackberries at six cents a quart than to be wearing out their clothes in useless play."[19]

Child's pragmatic depiction of mothering contrasted notably with that of writers like Sigourney; although the latter also endorsed productivity and habit as important to child development, to them nothing could resound more painfully than to measure out the fleeting, cherished years of childhood at six cents a quart.[20] Consequently, Child's domestic economy was resisted by an emergent group of genteelly identified and Eurocentric sentimentalists, who saw Child's frugality as gender transgression, imploring, as did Sarah Josepha Hale, "Our men are sufficiently money-making. Let us keep our women and children from the contagion as long as possible." Overlooking the distinction between the economic survival strategies of frugal housewifery and the accumulativeness of wealth-seeking, Hale judged Child's manual as worthwhile overall but asserted that the experience of motherhood might have kept Child from writing a book so focused on money and led her instead to privilege "the development of mind and character in those she wished to train to usefulness and virtue."[21] This appeal to a separate-spheres model rendered economic activity at once an inevitability that could not be avoided (boy children, at least, could only be kept away so long) and a kind of illness from which the feminine and infantile must be shielded, as their bodies were made for other economies: the production of mutual affection and care. The genteel sentimental-domestic home thus distanced itself from the marketplace in both space and time, positioning itself apart from and prior to the pathology of the market.[22] The anteriority of the sentimental-domestic sphere was linked to the love of the mother, a love with its own peculiar time, both timeless and perpetually prior. Sigourney asserts, along these lines, that the corporeal sacrifice of the mother founds an affection different from any other kind of love: a love "whose root is in death, whose fruit must be in Eternity."[23] The depth of the future secured by this "deathless" maternal love surpassed the pragmatic planning of the frugal housewife; whereas the latter reasonably sought to save money in order to assure that her children would be provided for until they could earn their own, the former was in for the *really* long haul, all the way to the "perfect bliss of [the child's] immortality."[24] The maternal *longue durée* obtained on earth as well, guiding the chronobiopolitical improvement of the race. Catharine Beecher's 1841 *Treatise on Domestic Economy*, a guide whose meticulous attention to the productive arrangement of domestic space has prompted at least one latter-day critic to read it against Foucault's *Discipline and Punish*,[25] emphasizes the kind of *time* that a home-space so arranged will generate— for notwithstanding the *Treatise*'s everyday practicality, the first priority of the woman who arranges the home, Beecher contends, should be her commitment to the millennial "regeneration of the Earth."[26] Beecher insists that a proper comprehension of the duration of the home, as it extends a "long train of influence" from the mother's body far into the future, affecting the destinies of the destinies of "hundreds . . . from generation to generation," will help the mother to remember that her *first* duty is always to promote the comfort of those under her care.[27] Sigourney makes the same claim in a more ominous key: "If you are thoughtless, or supine, an unborn race will be summoned as witnesses of your neglect."[28] On this view, the mother's ability to gather up time signifies not as economic but as emotional conservation: she facilitates the good of the long-term future by holding fast to the sacred memory of affective origin that she herself signifies.

Insofar as middle-class sentimental domesticity modeled the loving mother in relation to a child who is launched toward a deep future conceived as inspirational horizon (national progress, global regeneration, eternal bliss), it not only surpassed the pragmatic economy of the frugal housewife but bypassed, as well, any direct rhetorical contact with the vicissitudes of the market. The perspective privileged by Sigourney and Beecher demands that the mother prioritize an affectionately shaped task-orientation over the time-orientated labor that would characterize industrial capitalism. Indeed, their rhetoric predicts the terms of E. P. Thompson's later association of the "pre-industrial" conventions that have passed into modern times in the rhythms of women's work in the home; even now, he notes, "the mother of young children has an imperfect sense of time and attends to other human tides."[29] Thompson's identification of the "human tides" of the child *against* the modern regulation of time preserves the opposition-as-anteriority to which the sentimentalists dedicated their affections. Sigourney represents the human tide marking the "sacred first year" not as "imperfect" but as a vision of perfected time: a "dream of bliss," a "season of languor" in which the pure affective connection of the pair deepens.[30] The dream-time of the maternal-filial connection (and particularly the "halcyon period" of breastfeeding, "the highest pleasure, of which woman's nature is capable," which she urges women not to cut short)[31] posits itself as recompense for both "past suffering" and "future toil."[32] This vision of the mother-child dyad as fulfilled time depends, of course, upon both the mother's distance from wage labor and, as much as possible, her freedom from other domestic labor—for, as we saw earlier, this timeless interval can only be secured if the mother offloads non-child-related work onto other bodies. In marked contrast to the middle-class monumentalization of the infantile period, Thompson's essay elaborates the domestic retention of task-oriented time in the lives of working-class women. In the forced conjunction of two simultaneous obligations—agrarian wage labor and home care —associated with different temporal measures, Thompson describes an exhausting contradiction that Mary Collier, the eighteenth-century English washerwoman whose poem "The Woman's Labour" he quotes, identifies as leaving women "hardly ever *time to dream*."[33] The weariness of the working-class mother rematerializes the time that, in Sigourney's monumental vision of the middle-class home, is not simply spatialized but, more specifically, channeled through and absorbed into the loving maternal body whose timeless truth obscures the material distinctions on which she depends. In this way, the mother's corporealized time takes form, as Kristeva reminds us, not in terms of but *against* the linear time of history, naturalizing the economy from which it projects itself as a refuge by erasing the historical difference in modes of production registered in the bone-weary dreamlessness of the working woman and replacing it with a story about the timeless history of a human heart bound for glory.

Sentimental Subjects and Domestic Routines

The time out of time that Sigourney idealizes as the period of mother-child intimacy could only be maintained, as she herself concedes, for a brief interlude, after which it must be supplanted by the child's first lessons in obedience and self-management; these lessons needed to begin early, allowing the child to internalize a productive time-sense before its lack became a problem—before the point at which "the little voyager is liable to be thrown among the eddies of its own passions, and wrecked like the bark-canoe."[34] This emphasis on securing the steady development of the child toward the future complemented the sentimental insistence that that development be founded in love before duty; indeed, in this model, a sense of duty would flow naturally from love, with the child's first accomplishments growing out of a desire to please the mother. This sequencing held even in matters of the spirit; Sigourney laid out the course of a maternally ordered conversion as a seamless progression from the mother's prayers over the baby to the infant's cherishing of love as its religion to later instruction, once it comprehends language, in the tenets of Christianity, which the child would then naturally accept. Maternal affection was held to be the most effective means of launching the subject forward on a *dual* trajectory, bound at once for the progressive and cumulative temporality that saw the education and refinement of the child as a contribution to the growth of race and nation and for the perfected celestial time of the redeemed.

The mother's responsibility to this dually conceived deep future thus mandated both early guidance and a continued abundance of affection. Yet while cycles of domestic duty not founded in deep affection became, from

127

the sentimental perspective, mere drudgery, surplus maternal tenderness was also suspect, as it tended toward the production of children who lacked any drive toward the future—children who valued the pleasure of maternal *presence* above the future-oriented *development* that constituted affectionate childrearing's ostensible end. That immaturity would render them, if not backward, certainly wayward. Mary Ryan points out, along these lines, that in antebellum temperance stories, the mothers of drunkards had often been not absent but overpresent in the life of the child.[35] The "Maternal Love" chapter in *Letters to Mothers* includes one such tale, by means of which Sigourney simultaneously lauds the mother's deathless love and remonstrates the blind indulgence it may provoke.[36] The mother's pleasure in the presence of the child could not set itself against the laws of time by seeking to defer the child's inevitable growth. Sentimental domesticity accordingly endorsed a carefully balanced arrangement of domestic time; the child, beginning in the timelessness of affection, would be led, gradually, through repetitive training and habit, into its own linear, teleological development. This early link between love and training forms the core of Richard Brodhead's Foucauldian assessment of the generalized cultural turn toward "disciplinary intimacy" in nineteenth-century America. Assessing Sigourney's description of intimate pedagogy, Brodhead describes this bourgeois "scheme" as a narrative progression in which "normal family romances" are first intensified, then the child is "center[ed]" emotionally on the parent, and the strategy finally culminates when "the parent known outwardly only as love [is implanted] as an inwardly regulating moral consciousness."[37] Intended to interrupt the assumption that "love" could operate outside authoritative structures, as either an escape from or a reward for obedience to them, Brodhead's analysis remains an influential and productive one. His assessment of disciplinary intimacy, however, tends to minimize the detailed temporalization of bodies in and through the imbrications of love and authority that his analysis posits as near-identical. Concerned to demonstrate this scheme as it emerges to regulate the subject from childhood onward, for instance, Brodhead does not pursue the production of the maternal bodies that this "system" requires—that is, the way that the "needs" of the child exerted a retrospective pressure on the female body that produced maternal affection through and against other possible dispositions of that body. Brodhead simply terms affection "traditionally feminine," but we might rather comprehend the feminization of affection as something accomplished by the new discourse on maternal love, and accomplished in part by refining away the untimely traces that did not cohere with the perfection of this ideal—including the histories of female bodies depicted otherwise and the troublesome corporeal or personal inclinations that threatened to interrupt or inhibit proper childrearing. The exertion of such refinement in the life of the mother began, according to Sigourney, with the need to forswear the desire for any substance whatsoever—intoxicants, food, fashionable clothes, social intercourse, or "agitating passions"—that might either damage the child or induce the mother to cut short the "work" of the "halcyon" breastfeeding period;[38] it continued, through the enfolded time of prospective retrospection, throughout the life of the child, as the mother was urged, as we have seen, to learn to resist giving way to all inappropriate emotions— from the desire to be "supine" to annoyance at the laziness of others—in order always to model the perfect evenness of temper that would be remembered, from the perspective of the future-borne child, as perfect loving constancy. Inappropriate feelings were tied in with inappropriate temporal dispositions—laziness, impatience, overstimulation—that might disrupt the orderly pace of the child's progress and/or produce the wrong kind of memories. Sentimental domesticity thus constructed the times of mother and child as mutually productive; as Sigourney insisted, proper childrearing was necessary precisely because children "are in the end to impress their own semblance onto us."[39]

In addition to omitting the temporal reversibility of sentimental education—the way that this fantasy of the child retrospectively constructs the mother in its own image—Brodhead's analysis, modeled after *Discipline and Punish,* also posits a panoptic near-identity between love and authority. However, Foucault's later articulation of the relation between power and pleasure in *The History of Sexuality* makes a case against the assessment of love *as* authority, pleasure *as* power. Positing these as effectively identical, as many New Historicist readings tend to do, inhibits critical development of the gaps and reversible relations that effect, sustain, and transform the perverse implantation as Foucault describes it, since its "perpetual spirals of power and pleasure" may also index conjunctions that foreground temporal and spatial *non*identity.[40] And crucially, what we might, after Foucault, term the affective implantation of nineteenth-century sentimental culture, as modeled in the account of internalizing parental guidance given earlier, depended upon the necessarily incomplete alteration in temporality that marks the last stage of that process. The effectiveness of the move from outward "love" to inward self-regulation results from the temporal incommensurability between the two—between, that is, the originary time of a "love" that is (as Sigourney extensively details) not simply intense but immediately and abundantly corporeal, the outside-time of primal attachment, and the iterative time of the refined, domesticated interiority that seeks to order the uses of the body. What Brodhead glosses as an intensification of *grief* within the family as a "resource" for psychic regulation also underscores, then, the temporal rift that centers sentimental education: an attachment to a time-less past known only through its loss.[41]

That this beloved past is most signified as infantile time's suspended plenitude is indexed in the sentimental obsession not merely with the care-free days of childhood—a cultural preoccupation so pervasive that, as Karen Sánchez-Eppler has recently demonstrated, even children engaged in it[42]—but specifically with the scene of the infant or child *in contact with* the mother, recalling the primary connectedness of an atemporal anteriority characterized by material continuity rather than linear sequence, the "ma-ternal envelope" of sonic and tactile contact. Sánchez-Eppler locates, in the 1852 diary of a ten-year-old Massachusetts girl, a poem titled "To a Picture of my Mother," in which the speaker dwells upon her desire to be the "babe" depicted sitting on the mother's knee in the portrait (which, Sánchez-Eppler proposes, may be the child's own infant self).[43] The poem's final couplet be-speaks the child's impossible wish to "stem the world" in infantile time.[44] The lament for the lost timelessness of infancy couples itself to a lament for, specifically, the mother's *touch*. The poem's dedication to a picture raises the possibility (though the text itself is unclear on this point) that the mother addressed through her image may herself be dead and that this poem is in-tended specifically as a memorial poem—that the speaker longs for her infancy as the time when the mother was alive. Yet whether the mother is living scarcely matters, as the poem remains, either way, a lament for a time now lost and irrecoverable: the time Kaja Silverman glosses as the "too-early" atemporality of the infantile, viewed from the "too-late" ordered time of the subject.[45] The child's nostalgia for infancy thus suggests precisely what the distinctly elegiac tone that Sigourney employs throughout *Letters to Mothers* recognizes—that mothering and growing up are, in sentimental culture, both akin to an extended process of mourning what counts for the child as the outside-time of origin and for the mother as the "climax of her being." We can see this process at work in a poem by George Bethune, a Northeastern Dutch Reformed minister and editor, titled "To My Mother," in which the speaker elegizes childhood through an extended address to a mother still living.[46] The first turn to the mother opens a phantasmatic return to childhood that culminates in a moment of cessation produced by her touch:

> My mother! Manhood's anxious brow
> And sterner cares have long been mine;
> Yet turn I fondly to thee now,
> As when upon thy bosom's shrine
> My infant griefs were gently hushed to rest,
> And thy low-whispered prayers my slumbers blest.

The speaker's idealization of the sacred maternal breast recalls the sentimental coupling of maternal and divine affection, as the prayers that the mother utters over the sleeping child reflect; such moments indeed approximated corporeal contact with the divine as channeled through the mother. Yet the poem moves to simultaneously animate and disable this fantasy of return through its temporalization in simile:

> I never call that gentle name,
> My mother! but I am again
> E'en as a child; the very same
> That prattled at thy knee; and fain
> Would I forget, in momentary joy,
> That I no more can be thy happy boy;
>
> Thine artless boy, to whom thy smile
> Was sunshine, and thy frown sad night;
> (Though rare that frown, and brief the while
> It veiled from me thy loving light;)
> For well-conned task, ambition's highest bliss
> To win from thy approving lips a kiss.[47]

The time of the child both returns and recedes here, as the speaker struggles to forget the loss that he cannot help but remember—a summation of the poem's mournful attitude toward his now-distant childhood that could just as well describe the developmental course of that childhood itself. In Bethune's poem it is not the mother (who, now widowed and dependent, is invited to seek comfort on the speaker's breast, thus bringing the poem full circle) who is mourned, but childhood and the impossibility of its return. The story of that childhood, however, is prescripted as the process of mourning the mother. Subsequent to the moment of outside-time marked in the sleep of the infant on the mother's breast, each appearance of the child finds him coming closer to an adult experience of time—from the knee-high child's directionless, imitative "prattle," to the brief but painful experiences of discipline in the mother's withheld smile, to the dutiful repetition that culminates in the achievement of the boy's "well-conned task," which brings as its reward another partial and fleeting return of the mother's touch. Bethune's recollection of childhood through the trope of the mother as affective anteriority thus demonstrates the persistence of sentimental woundedness: the perpetual redeployment of the hole in time through which love and grief encounter one another as a means, paradoxically, of movement toward a predestined future.

The doubled nature of that progress, which seems, in sentimental-domestic writing, at once so inevitable and so precarious, is further complicated by gendered variations in the development of the middle-class white subject.[48] Along these lines, we should remember that the passage from Sigourney's *Letters to Mothers* that Brodhead quotes to exemplify his description of the affective implantation appears within a gender-specific discussion, as Sigourney describes *boys'* inherent tendency to rebel against maternal authority. This tendency, she insists, must double the speed with which the mother instills her influence; for the boy child's journey is, for Sigourney, always a journey across spheres and, accordingly, the temporalities associated with them, and the mother who does not act early to complement the impulses of the son's driving nature by molding his conscience will thus arrive too late. The view from the other side of this process, moreover, further complicates Brodhead's assessment of the maternalization of power, since the nostalgia for the touch of the mother may well read, from the perspective of the adult son, as a fantasized projection of autonomy. In this self-consolidating fantasy, the idealized return to the originary, presubjective, and atemporal moment of maternal-child contact, as Eva Cherniavsky stresses, "can only terminate in a recapitulation of the mother's interiorization" by reconstructing the mother, rather than the child, as the dependent figure.[49] Cherniavsky's assertion recalls us to Sigourney's insistence that the child will, in the end, impress his own semblance onto the parent. It is, in fact, precisely this retroversion that closes Bethune's ode to the mother; in the final stanza, he invites his mother, now widowed and dependent, to take shelter on his breast, just as he used to do in hers.

Sigourney, however, narrates the story of the daughter's development rather differently. Her progress to adulthood is understood as both less rapid and less linear; she can seemingly be safely expected to identify with and imitate her mother, rather than breaking away from her early. Sigourney thus insists that a proper domestic existence must be modeled throughout the girl-child's youth, and recommends having daughters accompany their mothers on the round of her daily chores: "Associate her with you. Make her your friend. Purify and perfect your own example for her sake."[50] The lateral pedagogy of mother-daughter connection introduces temporal difference into the affective implantation by means of a spatial distinction: the mother whose image must be interiorized by the boy-child as a tutelary seraph remains consistently in front of the daughter's eyes, lessening, in the course of an ordinary childhood, the distance she will travel from the mother's body: a spatial closeness that also corresponds to a lesser difference in time, as the daughter becomes the mother's "associate" and "friend." The assumption here is that prolonged intimate contact will generate an ongoing imitative drive; the daughter, habituated to accompany the mother on her rounds, will eventually spin off into her own cycle of motherhood. The gendered model of affectionate childrearing thus depends on a particularly sexed vision of nature's temporal inclinations to ensure generational reproduction: boys seek to move beyond the home, whereas women, retained longer within the homespace, will eventually desire marriage and children of their own.

Not all domestic-advice writers—not even sentimentalists—held the imitative model of development as the sole trajectory of daughterly development. Child and Beecher, for instance, both insisted that daughters not be brought up to depend on marriage as their only option, arguing that women should be educated sufficiently to enable them to arrange other livelihoods in the event that they did not marry. This insistence was partly pragmatic and partly ideological: insofar as love alone should, from the perspective of the sentimentalists, arrange the home, the idea of marrying for necessity, an effect of a mercantile economy, must appear particularly repugnant. Consequently, the embrace of love led these writers to some noteworthy innovations on the family form, such as the recommendation, in *The American Women's Home*, that unmarried women who wished to satisfy their "natural" desire to mother couple together to do so; while one woman gained a living (as every woman, the authors observed, should be trained to do), the other would keep house and take in orphans, invalids, and/or "the sinful."[51] But even if the marital model of generational reproduction was not to be considered exclusive, it continued to structure developmental norms. Accordingly, the girl-child was taxed with the seemingly contradictory developmental imperatives of repetition and growth: in order to reproduce maternality effectively, she must move sufficiently forward in time yet neither wander so far as to become wayward nor imperil her destined future by clinging too closely to the mother. Nor would the fantasy of reversal that we saw emerging within the son's nostalgia for the infantile guarantee sufficient distance in time, since the daughter's move to incorporate the mother within the self tended to signify not as mastery but as melancholia: an inability to leave the past behind that could interfere with her ability to dedicate herself entirely to her own children.

The challenge of the daughterly trajectory was embraced by antebellum popular sentimental-domestic fiction, one of whose most cherished subjects was the development of the girl-child. Much of the critical debate around the cultural value of such fictions has centered on their characteristic reliance on maternal mourning as plot device: the necessary, and necessarily traumatizing, loss of the mother serves at once to propel the girl-child in the way she must go and to preserve the mother and the home for which she stands as timeless ideals.[52] Yet the figure of the mother in these works is more irregular than has commonly been considered. She is, in fact, a temporal palimpsest, marked as sentimental origin and yet retaining echoes of the late-eighteenth-century sentimental novel's fallen women, as well as a style of passive feminine dependency that by the mid-nineteenth century had begun, as Nina Baym points out, to appear old-fashioned to middle-class women readers.[53] The simultaneous depiction of the mother as affective origin and anachronism further convolutes the operation of the sentimental wound as we have seen it thus far. Alongside the alignment of the mother with an outside-time that appears unrecoverable, leading at once to the perpetuation of the wound as unsurpassable trauma and to fantasies of (masculine) mastery lived in and as nostalgia for childhood, we can also observe the mother recalling another, less mythified mode of persistence: the extension in time of a form that should already have passed on. Maternal anachrony develops within the mourning of the daughter-protagonist in these novels an additional, melancholic dimension; as long as the mother cannot be made to cohere with a singular meaning, as long as she also signifies historically, she cannot be laid to rest. Hence, the daughter's inability or refusal to properly mourn the mother broaches the possibility of her return in a register other than that of the timeless symbol: as the index of *another* possible history, another measure of social time.

The Ends of the Mother: *The Wide, Wide World*

Susan Warner's *The Wide, Wide World* is one of those novels whose status as event has become as significant as—and perhaps better known than—the story it tells. Following little Ellen Montgomery as she travels from the New York City hotel where she resides with her invalid mother and merchant father, through maternally deprived and rather less congenial living spaces, finally arriving at the home she has come to deserve, Warner's work (which its publisher, George Putnam, purportedly accepted on the advice of his own mother) achieved historically unprecedented sales figures that signaled the novel's ascension to mass-market viability in antebellum America.[54] Jane Tompkins's canonizing analysis assesses the bestselling novel as quite literally a sign of its times; for Tompkins, the novel succeeds because it both parallels and counters the cultural regulation of women's time by "grappl[ing] directly with the emotional experience of its readership, . . . showing how one copes with [powerlessness] hour by hour and minute by minute."[55] It does so, she asserts, by sacralizing domestic, and particularly feminine-maternal, intimacies as time out of the disciplinary daily round, moments of "consummation" that served to manifest the rapture yet to come.[56] And although a number of responses to Tompkins have rightly resisted any automatic separation of maternal tenderness and discipline, it is worth recalling that Tompkins frames maternal intimacy not *outside* extant systems of disciplinary and religious power but *contrapuntal* to them: at once supporting and offsetting them.[57] Indeed, we might say that the present-tense "consummation" of eternity's bliss, by prefiguring this telos, both confirms its necessity and, in effect, disrupts its singularity. Yet Tompkins's suggestive account does not sufficiently acknowledge the extent of feminine/maternal anachrony in *The Wide, Wide World*, nor does she address the novel's ambivalence about it. For while *The Wide, Wide World* sets up a powerfully regulatory developmental schedule by means of a maternal-domestic-Biblical conjunction, it never renders that conjunction fully synchronous; even as it sutures together timeframes held to be necessarily concurrent (specifically, the ends of genteel self-production, Christian salvation, and generational heteronormativity) against the threats of economic instability, materialistic indifference, aristocratic stasis, and the luxury of repining, it remains marked by anachronisms linked to the maternal. Although the sentimental attachment to the mother works to compel both conversion and marriage, it also, paradoxically, undermines both developmental norms as they unfold across the narrative, which retains the trace of a melancholia tied to the impossibility of wholly reconciling its sentimental, spiritual, and reprosexual timeframes. The story does indeed end up setting Ellen on the "straight" path, but the novel itself, we might say, hung up on its relation to the mother, never gets its domestic time-values entirely in order.

In a novel whose first word is "Mamma!" there is never a question, for anyone other than Ellen, that the mother is going to be lost. While the child, in her grief, clutches at the belief that this loss will only be temporary—a chance for her mother, by accompanying Captain Montgomery to Europe, to rest and regain her health—it is made perfectly plain to everyone else, characters and readers alike, that the ailing Mrs. Montgomery will never make it back home.[58] Ellen's willingness to be deceived signals her own extended attachment to the mother, which leaves her hovering uncertainly between precocity, childishness, and outright infantilism. The way that Ellen responds to the news of her mother's impending departure—unleashing a wild burst of grief as she flings herself on her mother's lap—makes her infantile tendencies plain; as the narrator remarks, "For her passions were by nature very strong, and *by education very imperfectly controlled,* and time, 'that rider that breaks youth,' had not as yet tried his hand upon her" (11, emphasis added). Ellen's primitive response to the imminent loss of her mother is not something for which we can wholly blame her; she is, the narrator points out, both emotional by nature and not old enough to know better. Her mother, however, already knows the hand of time—and hence the intermediary clause, which faults Ellen's imperfect education, gestures obliquely in her direction as having thus far failed to perfectly instill the self-control that guides the "passionate voyager." The way in which Mrs. Montgomery eventually manages to subdue Ellen's outburst extends this indirect interrogation. When the sobbing, clinging child responds neither to an appeal to God nor to a genteel request for decorum, Mrs. Montgomery must fall back on her own body, quieting Ellen by mentioning her own ill health: "I am afraid you are going to make me worse, Ellen" (13). The rapid success of this appeal reflects both Ellen's automatic obedience to the mother and the pair's intense corporeal connection—a connection that is accounted rather more ambivalently than most of the novel's critics concede. Accounting for the success of Mrs. Montgomery's appeal, the narrator explains, "Ellen had many faults, but *amidst them all love for her mother was the strongest feeling her heart knew*" (13, emphasis added). The syntax of this sentence, which makes it difficult to tell whether Ellen's filial affection counts as a redemptive exception to her faults or, conversely, as one *among* them, opens a dual account of maternal love: it is both the surest and most effective means of gaining filial obedience *and* a potential hindrance to filial obedience. From the former perspective, Ellen remains perfectly attuned to her mother's regulation; from the latter, Ellen has had too much mother-love and not enough time-discipline. Assessing their initial connection, Brodhead comments that it is less accurate to say that Ellen lives with her mother than "to say that she lives *in* her mother, in the *Umwelt* her mother projects."[59] Yet it might be more accurate still to say that she lives *on* her mother, as that seems to be where she spends much of her time: reveling in the pleasure of a connection, sensory as well as affective, so close that "intimacy" seems scarcely to approach it; she has not, in other words, taken to heart the distinction between the outside-time of undifferentiated corporeal attachment and the interiorized time-sense of the refined, disciplined subject. Lying on her mother's breast, Ellen thinks

> how very, very precious was the heart she could feel beating where her cheek lay—she thought it was greater happiness to lie there than anything else in life could be—she thought she had rather even die so, on her mother's breast, than live long without her in the world. (38)

Ellen remains unable to imagine a life lived as narrative, rather than as immediacy of contact with the maternal body. Love, here, props affection on the body; it manifests in touch and seeks only its own perpetuation. Whereas most critics seemingly assume that the novel itself reproduces Ellen's mournful idealization of this maternal figure, I argue that it exhibits, at the same time, a less idealizing view; Mrs. Montgomery remains, in its pages, subject to numerous moments of wavering, shifting back and forth between a "natural" desire to hold onto the child—which the hyperattached child intuits—and a dutiful recognition that it is time to let her go. (This "recognition" is in fact something to which Mrs. Montgomery has been forced—despite her doctor's urging, she has no intention of accompanying her husband to Europe until he orders her to, at which point she resorts to her Bible to convince herself that it is her spiritual duty.) The maternal "nature" that she cannot entirely subdue creates momentary gaps in her conformity to faith and duty, as her persistent ability to quote texts on the spiritual necessity of submission—"Though we *must* sorrow, we cannot rebel" (12)—is interrupted by equally persistent moments in which, overwhelmed by the promptings of that nature, her grief speaks the corporeal language of feeling. And because she *does* have a better comprehension of time than her daughter, Mrs. Montgomery's grief has an additional edge, since she knows something of the future: that she is not coming back from her trip. The differential time-consciousness of mother and daughter is underscored during a scene in which Mrs. Montgomery, shortly before her departure, takes her daughter shopping to outfit her with the things she needs. In a bookstore, while Ellen goes wild over the multitude of "delicious" books available, demonstrating a susceptibility to both the pull of the moment and the lure of the merchandise, her mother dutifully seeks out the clerk to inquire after the Bible they mean to buy, and then watches as Ellen surrounds herself with Bibles and falls "in love with them all" (29). Balanced on either side of a bookstore counter, mother and daughter experience a simultaneous temporal suspension marked by distinct affective registers: Ellen, aflush with excitement over the multitude of styles, is lost in the moment, having "forgotten there was such a thing as sorrow in the world," but her mother makes up the deficit, moving quickly from joyous observation of her daughter's pleasure to grief over their impending separation, which settles in like a "weight . . . that was nigh to crush her" (30). Pleasure and grief, experienced intensely, both take the subject out of the flow of time; yet pleasure, as Ellen manifests it, responds only to itself, unconscious of past or future, while the mother's deep mournfulness—provoked by the recollection of an imminent future in which this present-tense pleasure will be an irrecoverable past—renders this moment of suspension as a traumatic tear in the fabric of a time she already knows.

This moment of nonidentical mirroring suggests that time both *does and does not* make a difference between mother and daughter—for, broken as Mrs. Montgomery's youth has been by now, her passions remain both strong and imperfectly controlled (although, unlike her daughter, she can regulate their behavior in the marketplace). This ambivalent relation to developmental time is echoed in Mrs. Montgomery's dual characterization of "love." While reading the Bible with her daughter, she maintains that her love for God is greater than her love for Ellen, and yet that makes her maternal feeling "not . . . the less, but the more" (39). Yet on Ellen's last night home, while arranging Ellen's clothes for her departure, Mrs. Montgomery is reluctant to let go of them: "she felt it was love's last act; words might indeed a few times yet come over the ocean on a sheet of paper;—but sight, and hearing, and touch all must have done henceforth for ever" (60). The two passages underscore the duality in the novel's conception of love; the first emphasizes a purified postconversion love that recognizes its affinity to the eternal, but the second recalls the earlier, primal experience of love as propped on the body and timed according to touch. The agonizing displacement of an eternal by a time-bound "love" underscores the difficulty of keeping the two in stable relation—and thus recalls the mother's difficulty in establishing a secure, sufficient difference from the time of her daughter, as she appears, here, not balanced but painfully split.[60] This rupture underscores not only the temporal ambiguity of maternal love but also the novel's fundamentally anachronistic depiction of this mother, who, torn between sentimental and spiritual inclinations, is also situated in an archaic familial position, insofar as her marriage appears governed by law rather than love. As noted earlier, Mrs. Montgomery's spiritual justification of her European journey develops only in the wake of the narrator's revelation that she was forced to the "decision" by the authority of her wholly unsympathetic husband. On the night before Ellen's departure, likewise, the mother must content herself with "love's last act" as touching Ellen's clothes and not Ellen, since her husband has categorically forbidden her to wake the child to tell her that she will have to leave first thing in the morning. Captain Montgomery's rationale is sensible rather than simply sadistic—he wants to avoid having the child exhaust herself by spending the night in "useless grieving" (59)—but it serves to emphasize his disruption of the affectionate time of the home with unfeeling calculations; he literally embodies insensible indifference, as confirmed by the snores that irritate Mrs. Montgomery throughout the night she spends dreading the loss of her child, snores that repeatedly announce "that the only one in the world who ought to have shared and soothed her grief was not capable of doing either" (60). The inauspiciousness of this marital pairing, moreover, insinuates certain questions about their intimate history that are never given a satisfactory answer over the course of the novel. We eventually learn that Mrs. Montgomery was disowned by her elite Scots family for marrying a mercantile Yankee, but never do we discover why she might have made such a choice in the first place. The novel's presentation-through-elision of the mother's unaccounted sexual history serves to remind us that she *has* one; that history, in turn, gives her something in common with the seduced heroines of late-eighteenth-century seduction novels, an earlier mode of literary sentimentality that was borne well past its own historical moment on the current of the literary market and that, as Elizabeth Barnes has argued, haunts the putatively desexualized antebellum domestic novel.[61] Even as the conflict between the spiritual and the sentimental rends Mrs. Montgomery's already ailing body, then, she is rendered further anachronistic by a passé wifely passivity and a whisper of feminine sexual vulnerability that are both incompatible with the timeless fantasy of the maternal.[62]

For this reason, a heroic sacrifice is required before Mrs. Montgomery can bring the timeframes of the mother-daughter relation back into proper alignment—a sacrifice of her own history. Since Captain Montgomery, characteristically, has not given his wife enough money for Ellen's things, the first stop that the mother and child make on their shopping trip is a jeweler, where Mrs. Montgomery sells her own mother's ring to raise funds; she haggles a little but can only get "three-quarters of its real value" (29). The market devaluation of familial feeling is, however, remedied outside the store, where, although Mrs. Montgomery tells Ellen that she can remember her mother without the "trinket," she sheds tears that, the narrator notes, "showed the sacrifice had cost her something" (29). Mrs. Montgomery's painful move from the model of sentimental mourning, the fetishistic propping of memory on a material piece of the past, toward the psychological model, the conversion of the mother into pure memory, creates a more seemly difference in time. For while the scene, obviously, marks the differential value of a mother on the economic and the emotional market, it also underscores the domestic time-value of a mother, which is revealed in the *end* of this economic activity: turning the affective past into the properly productive future by buying Ellen the useful articles—a Bible, a writing desk, and a sewing box—that a middle-class girl-child needs to guide her advancement. Mrs. Montgomery then launches a campaign to make up for lost time, presenting Ellen with materials and occasions for a crash course in spiritual, sexual, and social self-arrangement that serves, as well, to exorcise the specter of the market from her new possessions. In the bookstore scene, Mrs. Montgomery gently transforms Ellen's attachment to the material aspects of books (interestingly, the girl appears invested not only in looking at books but also in smelling and touching them) to an evaluation of their utility, reminding her daughter, each time she chooses a Bible because of some charming feature, that the very quality she finds so attractive will render the object less useful in the long run. (Ellen, of course, ends up choosing a red Bible just like her mother's.) This spiritually authorized tutorial in the necessity of deferred gratification is complemented by a follow-up sentimental session delivered back at home, as Mrs. Montgomery works to transform market value into maternal value, instructing her daughter that the gifts will speak with the voice of the mother, serving "as reminders for you if you are ever tempted to forget my lessons"—specifically, the responsibility of keeping them, and herself, in regular, productive order (37). Mrs. Montgomery further maternalizes the red Bible by inscribing it with two favorite texts and then resting her face on the page as she prays over it. Rescued from the uncertain time of the market—which never directly enters the novel again[63]— Ellen's new things replace Mrs. Montgomery's ring while moving its function forward in generational time; they take on the function of the mother *as memory* in order to reproduce the child properly, projecting her toward the ends she ought to seek.

Mrs. Montgomery's management of these objects deftly gathers together sentimental domesticity's various timeframes (the veneration of affective/ maternal origin, the logic of reproductive generationality, the necessity of spiritual progress toward eternity, and the regularity of genteel self-production) even as it keeps Ellen in good developmental order by recollecting the correct sequencing of an affective/maternal past, a regulated and productive present, and the future toward which she should be moving.[64] The sequencing is rhetorically sealed in the phrase that Mrs. Montgomery chooses as her farewell to Ellen, a prayer that God will bring her to "that home where parting cannot be" (63). Yet the utterance in which this metaphor appears erodes the security of that alignment, as the words, not spoken to Ellen, precisely, but *for* her, demonstrate the limits of the mother. The prayer underscores that although she may instruct her daughter, she cannot, as she has already confessed, convert and regenerate her, and so the necessity of *praying* rather than *promising* insinuates a temporal gap between sentimental and spiritual soteriologies, placing faith in the mother at odds with faith in God.[65]

The anachrony of the maternal-feminine is retained in the next figure to appear in the maternal plotline, Alice Humphreys, an adolescent girl who befriends Ellen after she moves to her paternal aunt Fortune's farmhouse. The daughter of a minister, Alice arrives just in time to save Ellen from utter despair. Her aunt, whom Captain Montgomery describes as a "capital housekeeper," is—unfortunately enough, from the sentimental perspective—precisely that: a woman dedicated to making her farm efficient and prosperous but with no investment in the emotional or intellectual growth of the child whom her half-brother offloads on her. Denied schooling and subjected to an endless round of chores, Ellen finds herself without moral compass or affectionate guidance, suspended in a domesticity predicated on a repetition oriented toward the accumulation of material wealth, so that time, for the child, seems to be passing without progressing. When this state of affairs manifests bodily in a seemingly interminable crying fit, Alice appears and offers Ellen consolation. The two strike up a friendship that does a good deal to ease, though not erase, Ellen's grief, and Alice's tutoring returns Ellen to the path of genteel self-production. But Alice, it turns out, is also marked by anachronism, troubled by an attachment to a past that she cannot quite set in order. She reveals as much when she deliberately turns away from the spectacle of Ellen's joy upon receiving a letter from her mother. When Ellen looks up from the letter to notice Alice sobbing by herself in a chair, the older girl, after a struggle, manages to compose herself and explain, "It is only that I have had a mother once, and have lost her; and you brought back the old time so strongly that I could not command myself" (223). Alice's breakdown in the face of the old time's spectral return implies a sentimental attachment to that past so strong that it interferes with the need to defer her grief, as a good Christian should, onto the hope of the future. Though she claims, when she can finally speak, "It is all past now . . . I would not have her back again. I shall go to her I hope by and by" (224), the melancholic nature of her grief persists, surfacing not only in a marked reluctance to say much about her mother (though she often talks about Ellen's) but also in the tenacity of her sadness over the loss of her brother John, even though he has only removed to divinity school. This last grief, indeed, marks her character so strongly that in her impatience to visit Mrs. Vawse, an elderly Swiss widow who she hopes will provide "a lesson in quiet contentment" (188), Alice brings Ellen up the mountain where the widow lives despite the menace (obvious to everyone else) of an approaching storm; the two get caught in the storm on the way home and blown off course, nearly losing their way in the blinding snow, and both, as a result, fall sick for weeks. Their reunion after this separation furthers the girls' intimacy while, ironically, foreshadowing the eventual arrest of Ellen's progress under Alice's tutelage. At the beginning of a visit from her long-absent

friend—the same visit that later sees Alice's breakdown over her mother—
Ellen, still convalescing, becomes conscious of a painful temporal split:

> "I am too happy," [Ellen] murmured. But she was weeping, and the cur-
> rent of tears seemed to gather force as it flowed. What was little Ellen
> thinking of just then? Oh, those times gone by!—when she had sat just
> so; her head pillowed on another as gentle a breast; kind arms wrapped
> round her, just as now . . . how much the same, and oh! how much not
> the same!—and Ellen knew both. (219)

Ellen's pleasure in Alice's presence reminds her of the mother's absence,
serving at once as a link to and a reminder of Ellen's separation from the
past. The tearfulness prompted by the contrast between past and present,
between "times gone by" and now, indicates that there is, at once, a breach
between the two points in time and, paradoxically, *not enough* space between
them; the difficulty emphasized in the passage is that the corporeal memory
of the mother is *yet too present* for Ellen to be able to comfortably occupy her
own present.

Notably, it is at the end of this scene—after both Ellen and Alice have, in
turn, broken down over their continued attachment to pasts to which they
cannot return—that Alice proposes to Ellen that they become sisters, a proposal she bases on their mutual motherlessness and designs as a relation of
mutual support. The generation of family through melancholia emphasizes
that in the sentimental novel, the family follows from love, rather than the
other way around.[66] Unlike both sides of Ellen's natal family, Alice can perfectly sympathize with Ellen because their experiences match. And yet the
kinship bonds formed in the novel bear the traces of a class-marked corporeal affinity—a sympathy joined to sensibility—that *precedes* experience and
habituation, tying the body to a racialized logic of class in which bodies are
both marked *by* and always-already marked *for* their environments. Alice's
"sweet, silvery" voice and soft touch appeal immediately to Ellen, contrasting with the coarse, homespun Emerson household and recalling the touch
of the mother, so that the child is happy to become physically intimate with
Alice right away, hours before she bothers to learn her name. (In contrast,
when Aunt Fortune, during Ellen's illness, tries to stroke the girl's forehead,
she can feel the difference from her mother even in her fevered state, and
she automatically pulls away. Much later in the story, when Ellen is sent to

live with her aristocratic maternal family, Ellen exhibits the same intuitive tactility: the very first hug she receives from her grandmother thoroughly informs her of the woman's overpossessive nature.) Alice, for her part, praises not only Ellen's good breeding but also her "quick ear" (which seems automatically attuned to prefer the "pleasant" speech of the English to Yankee thickness [173]). And while true gentleness, the novel insists, comes from conversion, a certain degree of gentility seems to be the prerequisite for the construction of kinship bonds. Ellen, who initially shrinks from the Dutch farmer Ned Van Brunt, eventually comes to love him, weep over him, and finally Christianize him, yet when she learns that he is to marry her aunt, she panics, thinking that she can never manage to call him "uncle." The novel thus connects what Noble identifies as Ellen's inclination to a "dangerous sensuality" with the genteel sensibility that, properly ordered, precedes and founds the bonds of affective kin, limiting the democratic mobility of the affections; class-marked bodies seem automatically to find their own "kind" on the basis of an immanent sensibility that always already knows where the potential for cultivation lies.[67]

Yet even the corporeal connection of "true" sympathy in the sororal pairing of Alice and Ellen turns out to be problematic. Alice's maternal melancholia, as we have seen, seemingly leaves her ongoing attachment to the past buried beneath, rather than reconciled with, the dictates of the faith she professes. Accordingly, when Ellen's mother finally *does* die, though Ellen turns automatically to the "sister" who has already experienced such a loss, Alice cannot manage to console her effectively, and the child falls into a deep depression:

> nothing drew her, and nothing could be found to draw her, from her own thoughts. Her interest in every thing seemed to be gone. . . . Appetite failed; her cheek grew colourless; and Alice began to fear that if a stop were not soon put to this gradual sinking it would at last end with her life. But all her efforts were without fruit; and the winter was a sorrowful one not to Ellen alone. (347)

Alice's insufficiency in helping Ellen move through her grief results from the older girl's prolonged silence on the subject of the mother, which locks the two in a melancholic circuit; Ellen never speaks aloud what is constantly on her mind, and Alice "dared not touch upon what the child seemed to avoid so carefully; though Ellen sometimes wept on her bosom, and often sat for hours still and silent with her head in her lap" (348). Alice's shrinking points not simply to timidity but to her own incomplete mourning; both her complete silence on the topic of the mother and the decision to allow Ellen to repine (the narrator notes in passing that the child might actually have done better to mourn her loss at Fortune's farm, where the daily round of hard work would have pulled her out of herself) are mistakes that a genteel Christian woman, versed in contemporary consolation practices, would likely have recognized as such, indicating that aversion, not shyness or ignorance, lies behind her behavior. Hence, the intimate contact between the two girls comes to reproduce only melancholia, as the same maternal loss that once bonded them becomes an untouchable wound that, instead of helping Ellen to mourn, leaves them both suspended in time.

Ellen's mourning brings to a crisis the conflict between two temporal impulses that has marked the novel thus far, a conflict that is resolved only by placing the principle of progressive productivity into masculine hands. Alice's older brother, John, a minister-in-training, is, accordingly, summoned to turn Ellen's maternal melancholia into proper Christian mourning. Unlike Alice, who cheerfully describes herself as "preach[ing] without taking orders," John's ministerial authority displays itself in and *as* the power to order time, as he outlines, step by step, the straight path to the posttemporal future. Indeed, apart from the materialistic Fortune, John is the most productively minded figure in the novel, though he predicates his system not, as Fortune does, on ceaseless labor but on rigorous and systematic balance. Insisting on the need for patience in education, he tells Ellen, "Time is cried out upon as a great thief; it is people's own fault. Use him but well, and you will get from his hand more than he will ever take from you" (481). This devotion to the appropriate uses of time accounts for John's lack of strong attachment to the past; he will, on rare occasion, reminisce, but he consistently refuses to lament, linking "sorrow and sighing" to sinfulness (313). John manages to reverse Ellen's morbid depression in record time—in the space of a single conversation on an afternoon when his sister is out of the house, he does what Alice could not effectuate over weeks, by doing precisely what his sister could not: speaking of the mother, and doing so, moreover, in the present tense. Reminding Ellen, "Haven't you the best reason to believe that all is well with your dear mother?" (349), John rescues her maternal attachment from its unproductive association with an archaic, now-unreachable past, restoring the mother to a perpetual presence that tells, insistently, of a promised future reunion. He follows up by setting Ellen back to her studies (starting with history), scheduling regular exercise, and beginning a reading of Bunyan's *Pilgrim's Progress,* doled out at the rate of an hour per night. The reading of *Pilgrim's Progress* marks the point in the novel where what we may recognize as a narrative Christianity finally predominates. For although, despite its title, Bunyan's allegory dependence on election has prompted critics to question its narrative linearity, the nineteenth-century "Americanization" of even those faiths that remained closest to Calvinism (to which John himself, though his church is never named, is clearly allied) in placing more of an emphasis on human striving enabled the title to resonate in sympathy with an effectively linear view of temporal existence, the conviction that, as the narrator elsewhere comments, "there is no way of getting *over* this life but going through it"[68] (326, emphasis in original). Following Ellen's recovery and return to Fortune's farm, John sends the child her own copy of *Pilgrim's Progress,* one he has thoroughly annotated, and this instructive text becomes her most cherished possession, surpassing even her red Bible, which is not mentioned again in the published version of the novel—a telling conversion in terms of both narrative form and interpretive latitude.

The resolution of Ellen's maternal melancholia in a conversion to the "straight path" is, however, marked by an ambiguous event that returns the novel to the question of maternal anachronism even as it subdues Ellen's own grief. One night during her recovery at the Humphrey household, she opens her red Bible to comfort herself by looking at her mother's writing inside the cover, a practice that is, as the narrator observes, a habitual one, and one that emphasizes her continued desire for contact with the mother's body—even in the metonymic form of "beloved handwriting" (352). This time, however, Ellen is suddenly struck by an observation concerning the content of her mother's inscription, two texts. The first text, "I love them that love me; and they that seek me early shall find Me," enclosing subject and object in a timeless, self-sustaining circuit, may reflect not only Christian faith but also popular depictions of mother-love; indeed, Mrs. Montgomery spoke the phrase aloud to comfort Ellen shortly before writing it down.[69] Yet after penning this text, Mrs. Montgomery had gone on to write another, inscribing "almost unconsciously" words that, the narrator comments, "were not for [Ellen]—what made her write them?" (42). This text reads, "I will be a God to thee, and to thy seed after thee" (42). Describing the progress of generations, an extension of the family's cycle in linear time, ruled over by God's law, the second, quasi-involuntary text can be interpreted as a corrective to the first, recalling the self-enclosed circuit of the mother-child dyad to the memory of the future. Yet it may also be construed as extending the power of the mother over time, amplifying the transgenerational influence that writers like Beecher and Sigourney exalted to the status of near divinity.[70] Though these two readings draw the text in different directions, Ellen manages, here, to find a way to make them cohere, exclaiming that they have both "come true" and, moreover, that her mother "believed they would come true" when she wrote them, and was praying for her all the while (352). Ellen's belated encounter with her mother's prophetic evangelism places herself and her mother at a suitable distance from each other, moderated and enforced by the text's own ordering of generational reproduction, so that she may finally *interiorize* the spirit of the mother:

> There seemed to be a link of communion between her mother and her that was wanting before. The promise, written and believed in by the one, realized and rejoiced in by the other, was a dear something in common, though one had in the mean while removed to heaven, and the other was still a lingerer on the earth. Ellen bound the words upon her heart. (353)

This conversion of "prayer" into "promise" closes the gap that we earlier saw emphasized by the mother's need to pray instead of promising; it provides an answer that establishes the necessary temporal difference between the pair under the guise of this connection. Launched into an inherently indefinite futurity, the promise once fulfilled becomes a contractual measure fixing and defining the period of time between the two moments. Ellen, from this point on, is able, having shifted the maternal bond from (exterior) attachment to interiorized identification, to feel connected to her mother without longing painfully for her physical presence; her lessons in time-discipline, joined to the loving and faithful maternal *spirit* infused into the passage, bind the child's heart to the words by which she now knows herself.

Yet although this sentimentally sublime moment seems to point to Ellen's newfound ability, inspired by John's retemporalization of the mother and his nightly reading of *Pilgrim's Progress*, to combine maternal love, domestic discipline, and faith on her travels along the "straight road," the extent to which it coheres with a dictum of John's is never addressed in the novel. The night before the scene in which Ellen locates her mother through the texts, John has read aloud the *Pilgrim's Progress* chapter in which Christian, reaching the cross, is relieved of his burden and marked by the spirit. John explains this to Ellen as a transformative "change" that makes one different from one's old self (352). When Ellen wonders whether she is changed, John advises her to "carry [her] heart and life to the Bible" and look for one of the "signs and descriptions by which Christians may know themselves" (352). He warns her, however, that if she hopes to test herself in this way, she will "have need to ask for great help," as "the heart is deceitful" in these matters (352). When she opens her Bible and rereads her mother's inscription, Ellen has been praying for the "change" that John describes, and her reading of the maternal covenant effectively transposes John's instructions into the register of the mother, as the "help" Ellen receives is Mrs. Montgomery's and the scene establishes a maternal identification alongside and equivalent to her self-identification as a Christian. Ellen's encounter with this maternal relic thus pushes the extent to which the maternal may substitute for the divine well past the limits of John's theology.[71] Intriguingly, though Ellen confesses to the Humphreys siblings every event, mood, and fleeting thought she experiences, there is never any mention of her reporting the maternal-Biblical bonding episode to either Alice or John. This seeming secrecy about Ellen's re-vision of her maternal/filial history enables the novel at once to bury and to retain the sentimental roots of her spiritual conversion, maintaining its deep faith in the maternal even as it apparently conforms to the more doctrinaire convictions voiced by John.

The melancholic silence that Ellen leaves behind is thus effectively taken up by the novel itself in its relation to the figure of the mother. Ellen's successful internalization of her mother, the "binding" moment that marks, in Brodhead's assessment, the culmination of a disciplinary implantation of affect, transposes what had been a traumatic temporal rift between Ellen's attachment to her mother and her identification with the domesticated model of self-production by locating the maternal not in the outside-time of primal attachment but in a heavenly eternal, while rendering Ellen's own lifespan, as a "lingerer" on earth, as a steady progression toward reunion in the afterlife. But this transposition does not entirely resolve the question of maternal anachronism in the novel, insofar as it ultimately sidesteps the compatibility of the sentimental and the spiritual. Moreover, when Ellen's mother returns to the narrative as an external force, three years after her death, it is an ambiguous intervention, as she (unintentionally) creates a significant disruption in Ellen's "progress." During the intervening years, Alice has succumbed to the same malady that killed Mrs. Montgomery, and Ellen has left her aunt's farm to live with the surviving Humphreys at the parsonage, but when she comes into possession of a letter that Mrs. Montgomery wrote just before her death, she is forced to move once again. In that letter, Mrs. Montgomery announces that she has reconciled with the mother whose ring she sold, and whom Ellen, before receiving the letter, did not even know to be alive. Nevertheless, Mrs. Montgomery reports that the grandmother "longs to have [her] . . . as entirely her own" and rejoices that Ellen will be able to grow up securely in the "old happy home of my childhood" (489). Yet though the Lindsays, Ellen's Scots maternal family, provide both the affection and the material comforts that she had lacked at Fortune's farmhouse, they also prove to be overly possessive, society-minded, antidemocratic, insufficiently Christian, and, most troublingly, unwilling to allow her to maintain connections with the Humphreys. They interfere with the habits that John and Alice taught her, even going so far as to take away Ellen's copy of *Pilgrim's Progress* (which they replace with an expensive watch, indexing their own worldly time-values). Mrs. Montgomery's decision, in this light, appears perfectly natural—she wanted to provide Ellen with both affection and material comfort, neither of which the child enjoyed at her aunt Fortune's—and yet regrettably out of sync with her daughter's life, since she made the arrangement without knowing that Ellen would end up with the Humphreys. The very letter that conveys these instructions itself manifests the mixed feelings that Mrs. Montgomery's action provokes alongside the mixed temporalities to which they are linked. That letter, composed on Mrs. Montgomery's deathbed, has "evidently been written at different times" as the mother's illness periodically overcame her (489). Ellen's response to the letter's delivery, three years after its composition, also spans different times as well as feelings, as she is overcome, the moment she glimpses her mother's "beloved character," with "many feelings; thankfulness, tenderness, joy, and sorrow, past and present" (488). Ellen's last contact with her mother's writing, in her discovery of the maternal covenant inside her red Bible, ostensibly settled her temporal relation to the mother, but that mother's untimely return unsettles it again.

The diffusion of emotion across time provoked by the long-delayed letter may also serve to call our attention to the question of Ellen's own anachronistic condition. From the first scene, when the child regresses from quasi-independence to would-be infantilism in a matter of moments, Ellen's age has been oddly uncertain. John, at one point, identifies her as "twelve or thirteen" to Alice's friend Sophia; when Sophia protests that Alice says Ellen is "only ten or eleven," John replies, "in years—perhaps" (295). Much later, when Ellen is living with her maternal family in Scotland, her aunt and uncle argue over her development, with her aunt insisting that Ellen is excessively childish for her age and her uncle maintaining that she is excessively womanly. Even John, when he visits Scotland in the final published chapter, cannot decide whether Ellen is suddenly "grown" or yet a child; he concludes, enigmatically, that she is "just the same" (562). Ellen's eventual marriage to John, illustrated in a final, unpublished chapter in which the newly-weds return to America, ostensibly resolves the question, but only by coming down on both sides. The residents of the parsonage all exclaim, again, that Ellen is "just the very same" (573) as when she left; yet her marriage and likely pregnancy (intimated in a paleness that she ascribes to lingering sea-sickness and in her father-in-law's whisper, after a long, close embrace, that "something is changed, after all!" [581]) force them to acknowledge time's changes. Ellen's arrival at this imminently maternal matrimonial telos completes the generational cycle by turning the child into a later, more fully realized repetition of her own mother. In this way, she balances the cycle of feminine repetition and—borne forward by the brother/husband's guidance—the American ideology of progress, the upward movement of those who "live right." Yet the unpublished postmarital chapter—in which the long-absent red Bible makes an appearance—also contains a suggestive reminder that the faith to which Ellen was converted retains the touch of the mother, manifested through her continued asynchronic attachment to the sensuality of exteriors and her desire to make that attachment resonate in the register of the sacred.

The final chapter, which was dropped from the published version of the novel—at, it is generally believed, the publisher's request—was, oddly enough, never appended to subsequent nineteenth-century editions, despite the novel's huge success and readers' frequent questions about Ellen's future; it remained unpublished until the Tompkins-edited Feminist Press reprint in 1987, where it appeared as an appendix. Contemporary critics are divided on the reason that the chapter was omitted. Tompkins's edition reports that the publisher felt that the novel was running long, but Tompkins also suggests that Warner felt that the novel's emphasis on the opulence of Ellen's new surroundings conflicted with its emphasis on Christian submission.[72] Susan Williams observes that the chapter's "worldliness" conflicted with the sentimentality that Warner and her publisher had chosen as the novel's most viable market mode, whereas Jana Argersinger contends that it too directly reveals the transgressive desires that Warner sought to mask in Ellen's sweet-tempered submission.[73] All of these readings draw upon the conversations staged in Ellen's study, an upstairs room set apart from the rest of the house and furnished by John before her homecoming, in which she and John spend several pages meditating on the spiritual significance of the aesthetic comparison that John has deliberately arranged there by hanging two paintings side by side. The two paintings are a reproduction of the celebrated "Reading Magdalen," which Ellen greatly admires, praising the gracefulness and "natural abandonment" of the woman's reclining form, and a small painting of the Madonna and child, depicting the pair suspended in the approach to a kiss, coupling the "maternal dignity and love" of the mother with the "perfect heaven of affection" depicted in the child's eye (578). The lesson appears almost embarrassingly obvious: in any contest between a pastless woman with a child and a whore with a book, *of course* the pure mother must win. Surprisingly, however, Ellen transposes this response into another register. When John explains the contrast as a distinction in timeframes—the Magdalen, he asserts, represents "the beauty that fades—the beauty of earth," whereas the Madonna and child is "that which endures" (580)—Ellen resists. Her eyes fixed on the Madonna (which itself, as Argersinger reflects, recalls the Magdalen in the seductive pout of the mother's lips),[74] she points out its material as well as spiritual beauties; refusing to let John get away with dismissing the former in order to exalt the (sacred) truth of the latter, she argues instead that "there is an eternity of the beautiful as well as the true" (579). This provocative establishment of parallel eternities (material/corporeal and moral/spiritual) requires John to do some elaborate reworking in order to make the sentiment doctrinally correct. He accepts Ellen's proposition "with all [his] heart," but only if he can heterosexualize and sequentialize this pair of eternities so that "they are inseparably wedded together, and . . . it is the true that makes the beautiful" (579). Ellen seems to endorse this idea, yet she appends another version of the story, one that returns to the idea of coexistence rather than sequenced generation: "in the utter disarrangement of everything since the Fall, the inward and outward beautiful are not always found together" (579). Ellen's determined preservation of temporal autonomy and duration for the "outward beautiful," a sublimity of bodies and objects, counters John's attempt to establish it as merely ephemeral and/or always consequential, maintaining even within her wifely deference a space where the atemporality of attachment may be preserved without deferral. The possibly pregnant Ellen, in this sense, may also be carrying the anachrony of the mother forward through time.

This dispute over aesthetics returns our attention to the novel's sustained interrogation of the time of the imagination, an attention that surfaces in its repeated commentary on the content, duration, and style of Ellen's reading. Reading is embraced throughout the narrative as a means of self-improvement and spiritual growth, but there is nevertheless something about the relationship that it arranges between time and content that renders the habit not entirely safe. John, as indicated earlier in his subtle substitution of the annotated *Pilgrim's Progress* for the mother's red Bible, prefers Ellen to read only material whose interpretation he may order and limit. That concern extends from the kind of story she is permitted to read to the kind of time she spends reading. He will allow her, on a holiday, to sit for hours entranced by the new copy of Weems's *Life of Washington* that he has given her, but when he finds her, on an ordinary day, consumed by an old copy of *Blackwood's* magazine in which she has lost herself, he demands that she resist the impulse to read any more of the "curious stories" that cause her to forget the time (477). Finally, when, in the last published chapter, he visits her in Scotland, he promises to eventually fulfill her wish to return only if she, in turn, will promise to write him regularly and to "[r]ead no novels" (564). The injunction to avoid novels as part of "keeping a straight line" recalls a comment near the novel's beginning, in which Mrs. Montgomery's doctor, registering, on his patient's body, signs of excitement and exhaustion resulting from the eruption of wild grief that she shared with her traumatized daughter, tells Ellen that she looks as though she has been drinking or "reading some furious kind of a novel" (19).[75] These moments thus disperse across Warner's novel ties between the lost time of reading fiction, moral waywardness, intellectual laxity, and physical disorder—ties made stronger still in the unpublished chapter, as the gorgeous painting of Mary Magdalen, whose physical "abandon" momentarily seduces Ellen, is one that shows her sensually reclining with her attention buried in a book—revealing that what appears as a comparison between a compromised sensuality and a spiritualized sentimentality can also be understood as a concern about the relative merits, across time, of reading and breeding, as two different temporal dispositions of the female body.[76]

The Wide, Wide World's equivocal depiction of reading deeply complicates Brodhead's assessment of novel-reading's role in the affective/maternal power/pleasure nexus of disciplinary intimacy. Brodhead dismisses the "older" view of novels as sexually seductive that is insinuated through John's prohibition.[77] Instead, Brodhead asserts that *The Wide, Wide World* operates in the manner of the mother: creating intimacy with the reader as a means of "transpos[ing] its orderings into the reader's felt understanding through an invisible persuasion."[78] But if the novel does indeed envelop the reader within its own time, any assessment of that time as consistently regulatory in a singular mode projects upon the genre a spatiotemporal homogeneity (much like the idealized constancy of the mother) that is far from exhausting the times of either the genre *or* the figure. *The Wide, Wide World* exhibits, rather, what Wai Chee Dimock describes as the cumulative temporality of the novel, enfolding seductiveness and potential waywardness within its covers.[79] Its time may seek to be regulatory, but it is itself far from perfectly regular in either duration (it varies painstaking, extended narration of single "typical" days with paragraphs enfolding the schedules of months) or affiliation: it enfolds the "outmoded" time of works like *Charlotte Temple* against the timeless truth of the Bunyan allegory; the bliss and claustrophobia of pretemporal connectedness against the purification of posttemporal "truth"; the forward-direction of the ministerial sons against the lingering attachments of the melancholic daughters; the properly reproductive mother against the luxuriating, imaginative sinner. And however much the novel itself might seem to disavow it, the multiple temporalities layered within that accumulation remain open to the particularly intimate, imaginative and sensual, relation to books associated with but not limited to novel-reading. This relation marks Ellen's own behavior as early as the bookstore scene, in which, immediately after opening her nose to the "delicious smell of new books," she succumbs to the "tempting confusion" of the store's seductively disarranged wares and buries herself in a children's storybook (29). Her habit of devouring text persists throughout her development, as, we are told, she will read and reread books until "she had sucked all the sweetness out of" them (335). Though it ostensibly seeks to privilege the time of conversion above the times of the unregenerate body, Warner's novel maintains a melancholic connection to corporeal time—an impasse that, in turn, indexes the quandary that results from the multitemporality of the body in sentimental culture: the insecurity of any ultimate distinction between a morally regulated sentimentality, which properly disperses feeling across time, and an amoral sensationalism that collapses it, causes it to regress, or perhaps places it on some other, wandering, not-yet-known path.

"A Whole New Layer of Time and Experience": *Our Nig*

Harriet E. Wilson's *Our Nig,* which, in marked contrast to Warner's bestseller, received a single print run in 1859, reads as an orphan story in more ways than one. *Our Nig* tracks the history of Frado Smith, a girl who, after the death of her black father, is abandoned by her impoverished white mother, Mag, at the home of the Bellmonts, a middle-class white family, where, at the age of six, she is pressed into service by its matriarch, who beats and oppresses her until finally, upon adulthood, she manages to leave the house only to be beset by illness and corruption. The work sank into obscurity until 1983, when Henry Louis Gates Jr. confirmed the author's identity and classified it as the first novel published in the United States by an African American woman, giving it a foundational status in the African American fictional canon.[80] That status is indexed in the blurb by Alice Walker that adorns the front cover of the modern paperback edition. Walker describes the novel as adding "a whole new layer of time and existence in American life and literature." This archaeological apprehension of time as condensed in layers rather than flowing in lines provides an especially germane image of Wilson's novel, which sediments a number of temporalities within its pages as it positions its protagonist's story in stark opposition to the developmental trajectory structuring sentimental accounts of white middle-class experience.

Our Nig's relation to those accounts has been a key concern within contemporary criticism since Gates, introducing the novel to modern readers, situated Wilson's work in light of recent scholarship on white-authored domestic fiction. Gates accounted an omission of the typical sentimental "respect for mothers" and a departure from the happy ending among the key differences between *Our Nig* and the overplot that Nina Baym condenses from a study of midcentury white women's domestic fiction, arguing that these variations established Wilson as a formal innovator.[81] A number of critics have taken issue with this assessment of the novel's attitude toward Mag, Frado's white mother, but I want to expand this critique toward an interrogation of Gates's retroprojection of an unequivocally respectful attitude toward the maternal in white-authored sentimental-domestic novels.[82] As we have seen, the anachrony attached to the mother complicates, though it does not negate, these novels' projection of affection toward the maternal ideal. Wilson, in this light, does not depart from the white sentimental vision of the mother but rather picks up the anachronistic status of the mother in these fictions and conjoins it to a reading of the asynchronic status of the black domestic servant. Frado's story takes shape out of a life that is, in bourgeois sentimental culture, scarcely accorded the status of narrative form: appearing as not unspeakable but merely uneventful, it is not counted as progression toward the deep future that culture imagines. As the novel subtracts from the sentimental-domestic timeline its "securing" points of narrative orientation (its affective/maternal beginnings and generational/spiritual ends), it leaves their absence explicitly marked, amplifying the anachrony latent within earlier works. That anachrony, in turn, opens *Our Nig*'s exploration of the question of recounting lives that fall under the radar of the overplot without either perpetuating the liberal/sentimental drive toward inclusion or the violent and dehumanizing exclusion from middle-class norms that takes place within the story.

Wilson's interrogation of the narratability of lives like Frado's manifests not only in the novel's refraction of the sentimental mother but also in its preoccupation with the valuation of time. In addition to reopening, through the sexual histories and economic relations that it resists submerging in familial feeling, the question of historically conflicting time-values that we saw in Thompson's consideration of working-class women, Wilson also arranges an elaborate intercultural and transhistorical dialogue on time through the epigraphs appended to each chapter, among which predominate illustrations of narrative emotion (grief, hope, disappointment, nostalgia) or reflections on temporality and transience. The epigraphs to three consecutive chapters are taken from two poems, "Written in the Approach of Death" and "Time, a Poem," by Henry Kirk White (Wilson's only repeat source), a British prodigy who died in 1806 at the age of twenty-one and whose works, including his "Remains" and "Melancholy Hours," were frequently reprinted in both England and the United States; the grim fragment that heads the chapter in which Frado is left with the Bellmonts (ironically titled, "A New Home for Me") comes from Eliza Cook's "The Future," and the final chapter, "The Winding Up of the Matter," opens with a passage from the time-minded book of Ecclesiastes.[83] R. J. Ellis, the literary historian who identified Wilson's source material, observes that the lament for the lost innocence of childhood that characterizes several of these epigraphs was likely selected for its ironic contrast with Frado's living conditions.[84] Although the disparity is clear, I see Wilson's arrangement of this material reaching beyond the obvious contrast toward an ultimately ambivalent assessment of the temporality of emotion itself as it shapes the valuation of life-stories. Juxtaposed with the explicit anachrony of the mother and the atemporality of Frado's life with the Bellmonts, these framing excerpts engage in a sustained reflection on the tendency to equate quality of life with its narratability in familiar forms.

Like *The Wide, Wide World*, *Our Nig* begins by foregrounding the figure of the mother, but here she appears as lost even before she is separated from Frado, rendering the novel's inaugural crisis not the immanent rupturing of the time of attachment but the (prematernal) sexual prehistory that Warner's novel narrates only through suggestive gaps. The always-already-brokenness of affective bonds is stressed in the novel's depiction of "lonely Mag Smith," of whom the narrator reports, emphasizing the past-tense verb, that she "*had* a loving, trusting heart" (5). Mag enters the narrative already friendless and deprived of family, is seduced and abandoned by the genteel young man she had cherished hopes of marrying, loses her place in her social circle, and buries her illegitimate child, all within the first two pages. *Our Nig* thus makes apparent from the first not quite an opposition to but a historical *retiming* of sentimental fiction; beginning where the late-eighteenth-century seduction novel ends, it explicitly exposes the past melancholically suspended within works like Warner's. *Our Nig's* opening incorporation of this generic prehistory thus defers the ability of love-as-maternal-nature to obliterate all other possible dispositions of the female body. This initial move into antebellum domestic fiction's repressed prehistory is followed by a noteworthy reordering of the seduction novel's afterlife. Mag, unlike the seduced girls of those earlier works, inconveniently neglects to die; rather than serving as a monument to innocence betrayed, upon which survivors might re-form sentimental community, she remains above ground and subject to extended castigation. Her survival becomes not an event but an ongoing negotiation. Explaining to Jim, the "kind hearted" black cooper who helps her out, her difficulty in finding enough work to live, Mag observes, "I b'lieve all Singleton wants to see me punished, and feel as if they could tell when I've been punished long enough. It's a long day ahead they'll set it, I reckon" (6, 7). The duration of Mag's sentence is extended indefinitely when she marries Jim, as the two children she has with him indefinitely prolong the social visibility of her sexual transgressions. Mag's status as anachronism reveals not sympathy but *similarity* to be the bodily quality that forms social bonds; the untimely loss of her virginity is described as severing "the great bond of union to her former companions," and her marriage to Jim represents "another bond which held her to her fellows" (5, 9). These ruptures expose the corporeal basis of the social "bond" as a set of regulatory standards rather than the shared veneration of affective foundations, marking the idealized maternal body as not the *source* of but a *type* of social goods that, when marked by sexual contact, remains damaged in a way that forecloses redemption.[85]

Wilson's novel thus sets its attachment to a generic prehistory alongside the occluded relationship of sentimental-domestic ideologies of motherhood to the marketplace, organizing its depiction of mother love, as Julia Stern points out, "according to the principles of market relations."[86] In place of a domesticity that absorbs economic history into the soothing continuity of the affectionate maternal body, in Wilson's novel the market economy determines the value of the mother—and hence of every body. Stern remarks on Mag's tendency to occupy domestic relations in the mode of "business partner" rather than wife and mother.[87] Even Jim, the only kind figure in the Mag chapters, cannily calculates his chances of success before proposing to Mag, reckoning that her diminished value by white standards brings her within his reach, though he himself treats this "white wife" as a "treasure" (11). Jim's death provides yet another opportunity to unmask the trade in domestic fantasy; although the novel's description of his passing, stressing "hope for better days," a desire for celestial reunion, and his "Christian patience" in the face of his illness, echoes the conventional time-values of this characteristically sentimental event, the display is both dramatically abbreviated, occupying a scant handful of sentences, and immediately undercut by the narrator as worth little in economic terms: "these were *all* the legacy of miserable Mag," who, in consequence, returns to her hovel, takes another lover, Seth, and determines, when they remain unable to make ends meet, to abandon Frado and move elsewhere (15, emphasis in original). The simultaneous retention and negation of the hallmarks of sentimental development from this novel, suggested by the minimal duration of the deathbed scene's redemptive effect, is compounded by the insufficiency of maternal mourning as a means of providing its child-protagonist with an improved relation to time. Though Frado's experience in the Bellmont house furnishes grief immeasurable, her desire for relief from the present is never tethered to an idealized past, insofar as Mag's overt anachrony prevents her from dissolving into the status of originary memory. After a particularly violent encounter with the irascible Mrs. Bellmont, Frado laments to James, an elder son who has returned to the Bellmont house for a visit, "Oh, I wish I had my mother back; then I should not be kicked and whipped so" (28). In desiring the mother's return, Frado seeks not tender comfort but protection from abuse, as though she recalls Mag, who was depicted in Frado's youth as a snarling, shouting, swearing presence, as the only conceivable match for Mrs. Bellmont. The omission of sentimental reflection on Mag in the novel reads, for Stern, as a mark of psychological realism. She speculates that Mag's abusive language, in the one speaking scene that she and Frado share, shows that any such recollection would necessarily open "a grief Wilson wants to contain."[88] Alongside this repression, Stern contends, the narrator's retrospective filial wish-fulfillment in an earlier episode, which includes a moment of maternal mournfulness experienced by Mag shortly before she leaves Frado at the Bellmonts, reveals an ongoing desire for the imaginary vision of the nurturing mother. In that episode, Frado, having quarreled with Seth, Mag's lover, wanders away from the family home, leaving Mag in a state of grief and anxious suspense until the child is found. Though it seemingly makes little sense that Mag should grieve over a child she is about to abandon, Stern posits that the novel's narrator, the adult Frado, here creates for herself the idealized fantasy of a caring mother and partly represses the memory of Mag as she was. This explanation accurately captures the retroprojected temporality of sentimental fantasy, but the older, wiser Frado's persistent attachment to the idea of a loving mother nevertheless remains at odds with the account that Stern develops of the novel's critical agency, which depends on a narrative triumph over the seductions of sentimentalized domesticity; indeed, it seems the mother is the one thing this fantasy cannot get over. But it might be more accurate to say, given Stern's insistence that Frado's lament for Mag expresses a general need for "nurture," that what one cannot get over is the *child*: the affectionate mother, in this case, is retained as the indispensable antecedent to the figure of the child who requires nurture in order to grow. When, after the violent episode just noted, Frado runs away, she can imagine no life course to embark upon: "I've got to stay out here and die. I han't got no mother, no home. I wish I was dead" (26). The child's death-wish is not conjoined to a fantasized return to the outside-time of the maternal bond, as was Ellen Montgomery's; it appears, instead, within a lament for the absence of the temporal coordinates that mark the teleological development of the child.[89] Having "no mother, no home" in a culture that posits both as the humanizing prehistory of the subject amounts to a reduction to the status of "bare life," the negated foundation of the social.[90]

Frado's positioning by Mrs. Bellmont in terms of a specifically racialized mode of bare life, one marked by the severing of domestic repetition from self-production, both recalls and significantly alters Mag's punishment at the hands of the town. For whereas Mag's own lack of mother and home is understood by all—whether condemningly or sympathetically—as a story of loss, of having fallen away from the life trajectory projected for her, Frado, in contrast, is read by the Bellmonts as always-already asynchronic. When Frado is first left at her household, Mrs. Bellmont remarks, "I don't mind the nigger in the child. I should like a dozen better than one" (16). The "nigger" Mrs. Bellmont desires is projected in place of the "child," as Frado is reconceived as a creature always-already capable of perpetual labor.[91] In consequence, she is to be multiplied rather than matured, as Mrs. Bellmont indicates when she continues: "I have so much trouble with girls I hire, I am almost persuaded that if I have one to train up in my way from a child, I should be able to keep them awhile" (16). Mrs. Bellmont's revision, in this statement, of Biblical sentiment, the mandate to "train up a child in the way he should go" (Proverbs 22:6), substitutes for future-oriented religious discipline a course that stresses multiplication ("one" becomes "them," echoing her desire for a dozen "niggers" to serve her) and retention (being "ke[pt] awhile"). If the sentimental figure of the "child" is destined to move forward in time, reproducing the family, Frado is here marked not for that transgenerational narrative but for a different mode of breeding: a forced replication in static space. Mrs. Bellmont's "training," as it turns out, is highly effective in this respect; a few years later, she resists the suggestion that Frado might relocate to James's house because she is simply too profitable to lose, having learned to do "the work of two girls," and by the time Frado's indenture expires, she has been further cleaved, now holding several places around the household: "man, boy, domestic, housekeeper, etc." (50, 64).

Mrs. Bellmont's cruel treatment of Frado has been described by many critics as both un- and antimaternal. Within the model of acquisitive domesticity that she seeks to sustain, however, it is wholly consistent with her position, as she views Frado in no relation to a "child" who might require, say, nurture, education, spiritual conversion, or even social elevation, this last being the end she seeks, with Frado's labor, to achieve for those whom she does comprehend as family—a narrow band limited to marital and blood kin, her husband and children (but not Frado, the other hired hands, her husband's spinster sister Abby, or her son Jack's orphan bride Jenny). Frado, from this perspective, is again multiplied, made to serve a double function. She garners a racialized social capital for the Bellmonts, elevating their status from ordinary to what Robert Reid-Pharr identifies as supremacist whiteness, a positioning based explicitly on racial domination and possession (as revealed both in Mrs. Bellmont's plantation-style desire for a "dozen [niggers]" and Jack's prediction that his sister Mary would try to impress her friends by bragging to them about "*our* nig" [26, emphasis in original]), even as she produces additional economic wealth. Insofar as neither operation is teleological, moreover, her labors must be interminable. Frado's revision from "child" to "our nig" thus substitutes for the developmental separation-and-repetition of the middle-class girl-child a spatialized time predicated on complete suspension within the household. Indeed, we can identify Frado herself not as domesticated (the destiny of the middle-class daughter) but as *house-held,* a *retained* temporality emphasized even in the way she is permitted to occupy the Bellmont house—relegated to a garret located in the "L," an attachment to the main house that also holds the kitchen.[92] Farmhouses with L attachments stood in the early nineteenth century as signs of modernization, as they structured a separation between "work" and "family" spaces and thus between temporal arrangements of domesticity, the toil of the agrarian kitchen and the genteel urban leisure associated with the sitting room, which Mrs. Bellmont forbids to Frado.[93] The "old homestead's" move forward toward middle-class gentility is predicated, by the matriarch, on Frado's perpetual retention as support for their progress. Warned by Jack that Frado will soon outgrow her tiny room, the matriarch replies, "When she *does,* she'll outgrow the house" (17).

The other Bellmonts' attempts to mitigate Frado's apprehension by Mrs. Bellmont fail to improve her position precisely insofar as they generate no substitute narrative for her. Though at first Mr. Bellmont insists on treating Frado as a child by sending her to school, his wife declares her education completed after just three years, when she has reached a more conventional age for indenture, and withdraws her to work full-time at home, declaring that Frado's "time and person belonged solely to her" (41). The "relief" offered by his sister Abby and the invalid daughter, Jane, who, conforming to the genteel model of charitableness, attempt to succor Frado's spirit through kind works and sympathy, always arrives after the fact, never preventing the abuse to her body that accumulates over years until it creates permanent damage. Even the dog that Jack buys the girl as companion is used by the family to track Frado when she escapes to the swamp, enabling them to thwart her plan to "stay out here and die" by forcing her return to the house. Indeed, their attempts to conform to genteel sympathy are mocked by Mrs. Bellmont's use of Frado's body as an emotional prop; whenever she is upset, "a few blows on Nig seemed to relieve her of a portion of ill-will" (41). This abuse of Frado as a means of regaining composure enables Mrs. Bellmont to approximate one of the requirements of the sentimental-domestic mother, the need to maintain an even temper for the sake of the deep future. Notably, maternal advice manuals recommended, for the woman who had trouble refining her feelings, the supplementary support of prayer. Mrs. Bellmont's situation of Frado as a substitute, in this light, identi-fies the girl ironically as another instantiation of the sacred, the figure who may be sacrificed—a move that does not, as we saw with *The Wide, Wide World,* unsettle the assumption of perfect synchronicity between sentimen-tal origins and spiritual ends but rather insists that both timeframes predi-cate their movements both in relation to one another and also *against* those bodies that remain permanently asynchronic.[94]

Though Frado's unsentimental suspension within the bare space marked as having "no mother, no home" continues unrelieved for years, the forma-tion of an affectionate attachment does, temporarily, succeed in altering Frado's place in time. This change is initiated when the long-lost son James returns home for a visit, arriving during Frado's attempt to run away. No-tably, this arrival also occasions the novel's last overt mention of Mag, in Frado's aforementioned wish that she "had [her] mother back" to protect her from Mrs. Bellmont's abuse; the comment is uttered in a conversation in which Frado requests James's protection and receives, in response, moral counsel—"You must try to be a good girl"—the insufficiency of which she immediately recognizes (51, 50). Nevertheless, in the wake of this encoun-ter, Frado begins to accumulate sentimental memory; when James departs, "the remembrance of his kindness cheered her through many a weary month" (52). When, moreover, she learns of his impending marriage, she begins to imagine herself moving toward a future distinguished by improve-ment, in the hope that James and his wife will take her in. James's response to Frado's misery, in turn, accumulates a certain momentum over the years. His initial sympathetic replication of her moroseness (the narrator notes that after their first meeting, in the wake of Frado's escape to the swamp, it takes several days before James can manage to face the round of social visits that he had previously planned) gives way, on his second visit home, to a historical appreciation of her plight as indicative of contemporary race rela-tions, leading him to desire both Frado's growth as an individual and a change in the course of the nation. The spectacle of the grief that Frado can confide only to her dog, Fido, moves James to wish for the power to make history. After overhearing her mourning the ceaselessness of her toils, he observes to his Aunt Abby, "But to think how prejudiced the world are toward her people; that she must be reared in such ignorance as to drown all the finer feelings. When I think of what she might be, of what she will be, I feel like grasping time until opinions change, and thousands like her rise into a noble freedom" (41). James appears to succeed where the kindness of the other Bellmonts fails because he possesses both a will to continuity and, as an independent property-owner, a degree of power to enforce it. But instead of the epochal transformation that he dreams of, he pursues a course of individual elevation, encouraging Frado to "hope for better things in the future" and planning, in concert with his wife, to take her to live with them, although the capacity—ward or servant—in which she might do so is never clarified (42). This promise of improvement is, however, mitigated by its limited assessment of the need for transformation. James's sympathy with Frado, as Xiomara Santamarina points out, reductively frames the origin of her grief, responding only to racial "prejudice" without considering the economic exploitation to which it is joined (and which Frado's lament cannily recognizes: "Work as long as I can stand, and then fall down and lay there till I can get up . . . and then it is, You lazy nigger, lazy nigger" [75]).[95] Consequently, James's plan of "elevation" is incompletely rendered, coupled only to an indistinct "hope for better things in the future" (76). His vague optimism is, however, countered long before it is uttered, undercut by the extended narratorial reflection on time that opens the chapter introducing James. Following an epigraph drawn from Byron's *Hours of Idleness* that dwells nostalgically upon the friendships of youth, the narrator comments, "With what differing emotions have the denizens of earth awaited the arrival of to-day" (40), and goes on to tally various modes of viewing time's passage, from the anguished suspension of the sufferer, to the regret of the pleasure-seeker, to the impatience of youth, to the time-starved anxiety of "busy manhood." The heterogeneity of feeling, however, is unified by dissatisfaction with the present and a desire for difference. Marking the universal wish for something *more* from time, the narrator moves into her particular case the peculiar duration of Frado's disconsolate pre-James existence, in which three years with the Bellmonts "seem a long, long time" (41). The mood of restless anticipation evoked in the opening paragraph links implicitly to James's imminent befriending of Frado, a change, we may assume, for the better; yet the cynical tone of the narrator in these lines insinuates that such expectations are inevitably thwarted, enclosing the optimism that Frado's encounter with James generates in story-time within a pessimism that attaches itself to the reader's present tense.

And in the long run, the relationship between the two characters does not fail to disappoint. Despite his invocation of sentimental rhetoric, James provides no foundation, familial or otherwise, from which Frado can be "launched" toward a different future. In fact, the only significant change in Frado's relation to the future comes about as an indirect result of the *collapse* of James's efforts to arrange it; for as it turns out, James lacks time to change Frado's living conditions, since he soon realizes his death is imminent. As a substitute, he launches a full-scale spiritual conversion drive, using his impending death as lure by promising that her obedience and devotion will enable them to meet "in a *heavenly* home together" (95). Yet this effort is destined to fail as well. James's typically sentimental invocation of the afterlife in domestic terms is predicated upon a narrative sequence wherein heaven returns as the perfection of idealized earthly origins, but this narrative, as we have seen, is one from which Frado, who has "no mother, no home," has been continually held apart. Hence, just as Frado's father's inspirational deathbed scene proved scant inheritance against Mag's isolation, James's blessing seems to lack staying power against his mother's will to maintain Frado as perpetual sacrifice. Frado's intense mourning after James's death initially follows the sequence intended in his spiritual instruction, as she becomes a regular attendant at meeting and spends her scant free time praying. Her attention to the celestial future is, however, at once inspired and attenuated by its origin in personal attachment. Since it is James, the narrator reminds the reader, who anchors Frado's investment in heaven, her desire for redemption weakens when Mrs. Bellmont announces that Frado will never be able to meet him there because she will never get as "high up" as James, marking the continuity, in her imagination, between the carefully maintained temporal hierarchies of the middle-class domestic sphere and their spatial manifestation in the afterlife, as though L attachments were also features of heavenly homes (100). When this announcement alone fails to halt Frado's devotion, however, Mrs. Bellmont threatens immediate violence, and Frado consequently "resolve[s] to give over all thought of the future world," less from fear of another beating than from the desire not to be stuck with Mrs. Bellmont, who also professes Christianity, for all eternity (104).

Once Frado turns her attention from the imperative of self-deferral exacted by the ideal of the "heavenly home," however, she finally succeeds in gaining some momentum in the present. Not long after she is talked out of religious devotion, Frado, finding herself threatened with yet another assault, acts to interrupt the mistress by promising to cease work forever if she is struck. In the wake of this episode, Frado contemplates leaving the Bellmont household, especially after the death of the favored Bellmont daughter, Mary, fails to produce any change in the behavior of her grief-stricken mother, leading instead to a brief respite followed by a redoubling of her persecution. Yet Frado worries that racism will prevent her finding another place, a worry exacerbated by Abby, who insists that Frado will not find such "good friends" elsewhere, and so she determines to remain through her "period of service" (108, 109). This episode, which begins, as Santamarina emphasizes, with Frado's transformative recognition of the ability to leverage the value of her own labor, concludes with the generation of a timeframe in which such leveraging is possible: one that comprehends Frado as not terminally but temporally bound to the Bellmont home.[96] Countering Mrs. Bellmont's assertion that Frado's "time and person belonged solely to her" (41), Frado's decision to remain until her period of service expires when she turns eighteen points out, for the first time in the novel, that it *will* expire, and the reflection projected back from that definite future moment offers her purchase on that "time and person" at present. In this light, Frado's reconception of the future as neither a vague "hope" for elevation nor posthumous reward provides her with some traction. Santamarina transposes this retemporalization to the novel as a whole, which she reads as unsentimentally generating, out of the very depths of middle-class white domesticity's "familiariz[ed] domination," a black working-class ethic in which "striving in labor [appears] as an end in itself."[97] This framing also makes legible an assessment of Wilson as conducting a comparable retiming of the contemporary discourse of African American racial "uplift," which, in its insistent linking of self-elevation with upward social mobility, deferred the promised uplift, for the overwhelming majority of black workers, to some indefinite point in the future; in contrast, the model that Wilson pursues, by rendering black workers' empowerment independent of a model of "achievement" predicated on middle-class accumulation, returns uplift, now comprehended as both a consciousness of the interlocking systems that degrade black labor and a revision of that labor as empowering in itself and not in its deferred accumulation, to a *now* understood as any moment in which such a realization might take place.

Yet although this perspective on the novel disentangles Frado's labor from its (de)valuation by the domestic "tyrant" Mrs. Bellmont (107), Wilson's assessment of the emotional time-values deployed in sentimental culture is, I would argue, less decisively transformative: what the novel exposes as a false deployment of familial emotion bent on securing Frado as domestic worker coexists uneasily with its universalized depiction of "that arbitrary and inexorable tyrant," love, which shadows her own marital history with the unsettled specter of the maternal past (127). In the novel's brief final chapter, "The Winding Up of the Matter," Frado, having recovered from a period of debilitating illness brought on by Mrs. Bellmont's abuse and entered on a course of self-improvement, meets and marries Samuel, ostensibly a fugitive slave, drawn by both the similarity of their experiences and "silent sympathy" with his unbroken self-esteem (127). Initially, then, Frado appears to have improved on Mag's life by rejecting the romance of marital "elevation" to "ease and plenty," the fantasy that drew Mag to her elite seducer, in favor of self-elevation and a subsequent coupling enacted on the basis of sympathy; hers appears as a marriage for the modern woman, contrasting the dated dreams of the mother (5). Yet the ideal of sympathy turns out to be as deceptive as Mag's fantasy of ascension. Samuel confesses that the slave past that Frado had seen as a parallel to her own experience is an invention and then abandons her, pregnant and penniless. Though he returns, for a time, after their son's birth, he ultimately dies of yellow fever, leaving Frado, once again beginning to break down, forced to board the child in order to find work. In a sense, then, Frado reiterates Mag's history, ending, as Reid-Pharr points out, "precisely where Mag began": a compulsory repetition underscored by the melancholy resonance of the Biblical epigraph to the chapter, "Nothing new under the sun" (126).[98]

Although Mag's name disappears from the narrative with the arrival of James as affectionate attachment, her story's untimely return in Frado's adult life underscores the apparent failure of sentimental attachment to provide Frado with any substantive purchase on time. Yet at the same time, the repetition that marks Frado's adult history recalls the near-unthinkability of doing without the fantasy of a selfhood grounded in feeling, a fantasy required, in a culture permeated by the chronobiopolitical logic of sentiment, to generating oneself as *human.* To abandon sentiment as such is, in effect, to risk reduction to the asynchronic sensationalism that Thomas Jefferson, as we saw in the first chapter, projected onto the black body and that Mrs.

Bellmont apparently adopts in her belief that Frado is unfitted for social functions other than repetitive labor.[99] In this light, the narrator's description of love as an "arbitrary and inexorable tyrant" reflects not simply an individual susceptibility to seduction but also the coerciveness of a broad cultural investment in a fantasy of affectionate origin: either one yearns after the developmental trajectory that marks the directed life-narrative of the middle-class subject or one capitulates to the atemporality of merely existing. The epigraph from Ecclesiastes, however, challenges this opposition, which corresponds to the distinction we earlier saw between "bare" life and the good life, the life of those who count as subjects, precisely by introducing another timeframe into the novel: that of the transience elaborated in Ecclesiastes. From the perspective of the Ecclesiastes speaker (whom Wilson identifies as Solomon), grief emerges not from a longing for the unrecoverable past but from the melancholy of wisdom's dual perspective on the future, as at once thoroughly known and unknowable. The temporal collapse stressed in the epigraph (from Ecclesiastes 1:9, which reads in full, "That which has been is that which shall be; and that which has been done is that which shall be done: and there is no new thing under the sun") is not a particular but a universal condition for the speaker, who emphasizes both the completeness of eternity and the incompleteness of human knowledge, particularly concerning the afterlife. The speaker's affirmation of transience both echoes and differs from the emphasis featured in the Puritan approach to death: for both, the consciousness of life's fleetingness should alter behavior, but the Christian concern with *how* one will spend eternity is displaced in Ecclesiastes by the prior question of *whether* humans access it at all.

Wilson's citation of Ecclesiastes in her final epigraph, then, complicates the distinction between bare and directed life by exposing directedness as itself an act of the imagination—a move that recollects the activation of the present that we earlier saw in Santamarina's analysis of the novel's ethic of work. Wilson's challenge to the sacred foundations of sentimental culture transforms the model of the temporal wound that culture posits at the origins of the subject, by opening it both to maternal anachrony and the asynchronicity of the house-held body—a move that recasts the fantasy of timeless origin as the impossibility of assured telos. In effect, then, *Our Nig*'s shattered adaptation of sentimental-domestic structure emphasizes what Lauren Berlant terms "the not-necessary continuity between pragmatic (life-making) and accretive (life-building) gestures."[100] Frado, at the novel's close, has reached no telos, only a stopping place where she presents herself to the reader as the novel's narrator and appeals, as an invalid, for "sympathy and aid"—maintaining, at the same time, that she will never cease to track the movements of the family who mistreated her "till beyond mortal vision" (130). The last paragraphs thus both proclaim the tenuousness of Frado's continued existence and affirm an intent to keep going, leading to a sense that, as Gates comments, "*Our Nig*'s tale ends ambiguously, if it ends at all."[101] The uncertainty of this ending stands as a re-collection of the melancholy time that marks the epigraphs, pointing toward the conviction that what matters is neither origin nor telos but the effects, both momentary and momentous, of the way one moves through time.

Conclusion: Anachronistic Futures

If the sentimental fantasy of the home supported a fundamental shift in time's direction, from the perpetual stability marked by aristocratic stasis to a progressive, forward-moving time balanced by the affections of (maternal) nature, then the turning of the mother toward anachronism at once exposes the melancholic incorporation of other microhistories inscribed on women's bodies and gestures toward the development of other ways of occupying and of marking time. In this light, maternal anachronism may serve as a corrective to the ahistorical affective stance that has come to characterize American sentimentality, where the appeal to deep feeling, feeling whose force and magnitude arrests the flow of time, is not necessarily linked to any particular historical critique. Instead, the suspension of time in feeling, rather than opening a new perspective on history, itself comes to serve *as* critique, a stance that has resulted in a certain political paralysis. Both Wilson and, to a lesser extent, Warner sketch alternatives, as their resistance to the mastery of closure underscores the demand for other narratives and other timeframes in which to render them. Yet both works, insofar as they find themselves implicated in the foundational fantasy of sentimental culture, cannot help but engage a melancholia that they also resist, precisely because, I suggest, the form of the affective subject—the subject who counts, whose life appears as directed rather than "bare"—is linked above all to the form of the normative family. In the next chapters, accordingly, I will consider the extent to which that fantasy itself may be displaced, distancing sentimentality without abandoning the feeling body and thus expanding the ways in which figures who have been denied the comforts of affective heritage might nevertheless be seen to generate another kind of future.

4

Slavery's Ruins and the Countermonumental Impulse

> This Fourth of July is yours, not mine. You may rejoice, I must mourn. . . .
> Whether we turn to the declarations of the past, or to the professions of
> the present, the conduct of the nation seems equally hideous and revolt-
> ing. America is false to the past, false to the present, and solemnly binds
> herself to be false to the future.
>
> —Frederick Douglass, oration delivered in Corinthian Hall,
> Rochester, New York, July 5, 1852

What kind of a difference might the time of mourning make to national history? Frederick Douglass's deployment of the rhetoric of lamentation, in a
speech delivered in Rochester, New York, now known as "What to the Slave
Is the Fourth of July?" provides an unexpected answer to this question. The
distinction that Douglass emphasizes in the first two sentences of the passage cited in the epigraph, a distinction that is at once possessive and affective, develops the shift in perspective cited in the speech's eventual title:
what Douglass describes as an effort to "see this day, and its popular characteristics, from the slave's point of view."[1] Douglass challenges the unquestioned historical significance of this monumental occasion by recalling the
present-tense melancholy that it obscures, amplifying the way the "jubilee
shouts" of the holiday do not simply distract listeners from the "mournful
wail of millions" but actually augment the pain behind that cry as they
dramatize the distance between nationalist celebrations of progress and the
slave's asynchronic suffering (368). The speech mines the emotional archive
of sentimentality as a means of contesting the nation's indifference to the
slave's situation, insisting on critical action, not celebration, as the response
proper to the date.

But the temporal force that distinguishes Douglass's speech—its insistence on the time that he calls *now*—does not emerge, crucially, from its citation of mournfulness alone, since the conventional rhetoric of mourning,

which valued the past without necessarily effecting any change in the present, would not in itself generate that transformative force. The temporal structure of individual mourning corresponds, as I will show in this chapter, to the cultural work done by national-public memorial; both sacralize foundational virtues—the freedoms of the nation, the affections of the family— to legitimate the forward movement of national history. Yet it is precisely the conjunction of history and virtuousness that Douglass, in his speech, wishes to unsettle, insofar as this conjunction underwrites the very complacency that prolongs the mournfulness of the slave. Hence, his citation of grief is not an opening to reparative feeling-in-common, an appeal to persuade his audience to weep along with him. Instead, his deliberate deployment of the grief of the slave and the lingering mournfulness of the freedman develops an essentially *countermonumental* perspective on the legacy of the American Revolution. The belatedness emphasized in Douglass's July 5 speech ironically quickens the pace of its relation to the present, as his scorching exposé of white American hypocrisy sidesteps the sentimental possibility of sympathizing with the mourning of the slave precisely insofar as such universalizing appeals to affect mystify conceptions of time. The desire to correct this mystification, as I will show, leads to the countermonumental nature of the speech's revision of conventional tropes of mourning toward the temporal detonation that would, in Benjaminian terms, "blast open the continuum of [American] history." In this sense, the countermonumental perspective links the speech to the distinct *temporal* force that Foucault assigned to the notion of countermemory: that of prompting the "transformation of history into a totally different form of time."[2] The subject of the countermonument is less the truth content of a given event than the formal arrangement of time around the event; in response to the sacralizing appeal of the monumental, the deliberately untimely countermonument marks out spaces in which damaged time becomes visible.

In this chapter, I want to think through the countermonumental perspective by considering three 1850s challenges to the imperial logic of slavery: Douglass's 1852 oration, Frances E. W. Harper's 1854 poem "The Slave Auction," and Herman Melville's 1855 novella "Benito Cereno," all of which, I argue, simultaneously contest the temporal silencing effected in monumental historiography and force the sentimental heart to skip a beat. My point of departure here is a conviction that countermonumentalism, a term usually associated with postmodern challenges to the monumental aesthetic, should be understood not as a late-twentieth-century cultural form but as a trans- and counterhistorical strategy. Although the self-consciously post-modern countermonument may be a recent cultural development, I contend that the countermonumental *vision*—the assurance that past, present, and future are linked not in a single linear narrative but in an ever-evolving array—and the countermonumental *impulse*—the demand for historical memory to work through this linkage without relying on amnesia or subscribing to a redemptionist teleology—have much longer histories. Accordingly, I examine the way these three mid-nineteenth-century writers worked not only to counter the monumental erasure of certain perspectives on the nation but also to transform the chronobiopolitical structures encoded within liberal-sentimental responses to slavery. Countermonumentalism, as I will show, offered these writers a way of rejecting both the public monument's refusal to concede the ambivalence of the national past and the insistence on affective simultaneity inscribed in works such as Stowe's *Uncle Tom's Cabin,* insofar as such works ultimately offer a reductive account of the possibilities of the future by sacralizing the forms of the middle-class family.

Before beginning this analysis, however, I would like to pause momentarily to reflect on the form of the critical encounter that I orchestrate within this chapter. My assessment of the countermonumental impulse at the middle of the eighteenth century casts it as a response to the emergent sexual logic of two American monumental forms: the public monument's appeal to the durability of the self-sufficient nation and the constitutive incompleteness of the sentimental subject, which established complementary inheritances of nature and nationality. In contrast to a sentimental reformist discourse that sought to correct the former by opening it to the truths revealed through the suffering of the latter, the countermonumentality of the writers I consider challenges the received logic of both temporal frames—but that does not mean that these challenges were themselves temporally identical. In fact, I demonstrate just the opposite, as I examine first Douglass's ironic exposure of the nation's lack of cohesion as an effect of the monument's alienation of action, then Harper's challenge to the sentimental resistance to sexuality in the name of familial feeling and the consequent reworking of sentimental simultaneity into a radical appeal to *contemporaneousness,* and finally Melville's working-through of the melancholy traces of the lingering past. Hence, as the reader will observe, the pace of the critical time that I associate with the countermonumental perspective changes markedly across the course of my chronological move "forward" from Douglass's requicken-

ing of the Revolution to Harper's lyrical emphasis on the protracted bereftness of the slave's heart to Melville's experimental narrative, in which time
grinds almost to a halt. That shift in pace also corresponds to a repeated resi-
tuation of the rhetorical emphasis on the necessity of countering slavery.
Whereas Douglass's oration explicitly engages antislavery as a historical social movement and assures its audience that there are "forces in operation,
which must inevitably work the downfall of slavery," neither Harper's poem
nor Melville's tale posits its critique of the slave system in terms this explicit. "The Slave Auction," rather, allows the spectacle named in its title to
speak for itself and then moves to caption and revise the reader's expected
response, and the relation of "Benito Cereno" to the movement against slavery is so muted as to be fugitive; indeed, despite the laudable labor of a number of twentieth-century critics in making a critique of slavery appear in
"Benito Cereno," the story itself might yet be said to remain agnostic on
the question of action. My intent in collecting these three works under the
rubric of countermonumentalism is, however, not to assess their relative
merits in relation to a given understanding of committed art; by constellating these texts, I mean rather to think through the very possibilities and limitations of critical-historical assessment. Accordingly, I return, at the close of
this chapter, to a consideration of the temporality of critique itself.

Monumental Pedagogy and the Sexing of National Time

The antebellum American inclination to monumentalism developed, as Russ
Castronovo has demonstrated, as a way to address the need for historical
memory in the search for a distinctively American cultural identity.[3] Monumentalism supports the work of nation-building by creating, through the
manipulation of a mythical past, a feeling of national belonging. The monument, accordingly, speaks of timeless truth across time; as Daniel Webster
proclaimed at the 1825 cornerstone ceremony for the Revolutionary War
memorial atop Boston's Bunker Hill, the monument's project was to "proclaim the magnitude and importance of [the American Revolution] to every
class and every age."[4] As Webster insisted, the time of the monument would
be both foundational and exceptional: commemorating the sacrifices of the
Revolutionary "fathers," the monument would allow future citizens to recollect themselves in relation to this sacralized moment, remembering to
"Thank God, I—I also—am an American!"[5] The monument's appeal to the
sacred time of the nation thus situates its audience at once within its own

historical moment, conscious of its temporal distance from the events commemorated, and dissolved into another moment where they are gathered together with all other citizens, past and future, in relation to the timelessness of origin. The mode of simultaneity produced by the monument's gesture toward the foundations that supported and stabilized the nation's progress through time emerged in numerous antebellum projects seeking to enshrine for all time the significance of the Revolution.[6] The capacity to monumentalize was, indeed, understood by nationally minded thinkers as not only exemplifying but actively promoting the ongoing work of the civilized nation. Antebellum supporters of the monumental drive argued that whereas a hereditary aristocracy could manifest itself in familiar signs like the body of the ruler, an ideal so abstract as democracy needed to be supported by "something tangible, to cling to."[7] Participants in the debate were divided, however, as to the form that such monuments should take. Some, like the aforementioned observer, held that the nation should be depicted as a "kind mother"; others insisted on allegorical representations (eagles, crowned figures of liberty); and still others held that sepulchral forms would best indicate the humility with which the young nation accompanied its commemorative visions, thus avoiding further conflict with the more established European powers.[8] But the voice that would resound loudest in this period was one that sought a direct, vigorous, and awe-inspiring monumental pedagogy. Allegory, these commentators insisted, was too abstract and too dependent upon the observer's interpretation; instead, they stressed a need for forms that directly impressed the observer with their significance. This position would characterize the debates over both the Bunker Hill Monument and the D.C. Washington Monument, each of which saw a strong inclination toward what Tocqueville, in *Democracy in America,* described as the tendency to picture the democratic nation as "vast" and "extend[ing] indefinitely."[9] This spatiotemporal expansiveness meant, of course, that the young nation often embarked on projects that struck observers like Tocqueville as both extravagant and impractical; and indeed, despite the vociferous patriotism with which supporters of the aforementioned structures sounded the drive for contributions, both were left incomplete for years—the latter for over a quarter century—as the result of funding and strategic delays.

As the inclination toward sentiment and awe in the developing monumental consciousness might suggest, monumentality's proposed solution to the problem of national-historical pedagogy depends as much upon forgetting as it does upon remembering. The monument's pedagogy of self-consolidation is facilitated by reductive, monologic, and imprecise versions of historical events; its task is not to *teach* history but to instruct people how to *feel* about it: inspired, reverent, and moved to appropriate action in their own historical moments. In this sense, as Friedrich Nietzsche observes, "monumental history, since it disregards causes as much as possible, could without much exaggeration be called a collection of 'effects in themselves.' "[10] Emphasizing effect and eliding cause, the monument follows the consolidating tendency that I have shown to inhere in with the discipline of mourning in the nineteenth century—it functions, in effect, as a string tied around the finger of the national public to remind it of its own self-image. What Nietzsche aptly terms the "approximate" nature of the monumental, then, not only creates a deliberate imprecision about the dynamics of history but induces other kinds of forgetting as well: circumscribing the limits of critical engagement with the past by transmitting a *completed* account of its significance. Naturalizing the power exercised through political domination by deflecting it onto aesthetics, the monument imposes closure on historical events by declaring for all time what they mean. Hence, Nietzsche's insistence that "whenever the monumental vision of the past *rules* over the other ways of looking at the past . . . the past itself suffers *damage.*"[11]

The silencing of deviant readings of the past in the temporally stabilizing pedagogy of the monument also works to naturalize the sexual arrangement that we earlier saw outlined in Elizabeth Maddock Dillon's account of the gendered narrative of liberalism.[12] As the public monument's pedagogy of awe encouraged reverence for the Revolutionary "fathers," that is, it supported the temporality of nationhood as a complementary division between the linear, accumulative time of public life and the regenerative time of the private sphere. The antebellum inclination to commemorative forms that bespoke the "lofty grandeur" of the ideals associated with the Revolution— the Classical column and the Egyptian obelisk—can be understood, in this light, not simply to furnish those relatively new ideas with an awesome duration by projecting their significance backward in time but also to support their implicit appeal to an independent and self-possessed masculinity, one suggested not only in the gender of the soldiers and fathers commonly cited by the monument as "founding" the nation but also in the structure of the monument itself, as the temporal form proper to public life. In fact, the obelisk appeared to many antebellum observers to be superior to the column in this respect, not only because it antedated the Classical-era column and thus provided an even longer duration to the idea of the nation but also because, as the sculptor Horatio Greenough observed, the form of the obelisk seemed "complete in itself."[13] Greenough's vision points us again to the monument's aspiration to completeness in its narration of national history. Not only would the short span of national existence be strengthened through its association with an ancient mystique, but this mystique itself would work to obscure the tenuousness of the monument's claim to timeless truth, replacing the transhistorical appeal of the Classical column, which implicitly bespoke the duration of democracy, with one based entirely on the logic of form.

The ostensible self-containment of the masculinized national public should not, however, blind us to its implications for the timing of American private life. Rather, as Greenough's proto-Lacanian account of the monument's significance for democracy itself might suggest, this account of publicity was nevertheless dependent on the prioritizing of the affectively coded privacy that it appears to disavow. In this light, we can understand the reverence for the nation's fathers encoded in the awe-inspiring pedagogy of the public monument as both complementing and supported by the reverencing of the family in sentimental culture—a reverencing that, as we saw in the preceding chapter, enshrined maternal feeling as most clearly indexing the sacred truth of human affection. Yet their complementarity does not indicate a parallel, precisely to the degree that, as I have shown, the maternal form is *not* understood as complete in itself—rather, it is understood to be completed by the child to whom its affections are naturally directed. The constitutive incompleteness of the affective subject should not, however, blind us to the way sentimental culture participated in the temporality of liberalism by reproducing, within the regenerative time-space of the home, the conditions of the national simultaneity to which the public monument appealed. For the universalizing appeal of feeling, as we have hitherto seen, effaced the historicity of modernity's sexual arrangement of time through its appeal to the timelessness of the natural affections, while privileging those arrangements as the cumulative effect of progress. What I am arguing, then, is that sentimentality must be understood as the way the monumental makes itself at home in the nineteenth century. While the tender memorials of sentimental culture substitute the comfort of fellow-feeling for the public monument's pedagogy of awe, the parallel insistence on the timelessness of proper feeling and their facilitation of the observer's self-consolidation establish them as linked temporal modes—conjoined by the heteroreproductive structure that sutured publicity to the private sphere, a structure that manifests within the logic of inheritance. The historical conjunction that I am identifying here as sentimental/monumental, then, worked to stabilize the American future by establishing complementary inheritances of nature and nation.

It is precisely the value of this inheritance, however, that the antislavery movement sought to question. As Frederick Douglass argues in the passage that forms the epigraph to this chapter, viewed from the perspective of the slave (a condition that was also positioned as heritable) the conventional reverence accorded to the national past appears in quite another light. Yet the familiar antebellum forms of the public monument, as Kirk Savage points out, resisted the interrogation that antislavery activists sought to open, not only in their insistence on reverence but also in their formal reliance on a completed framework indexing self-possession. For this reason, as Savage suggests, the aesthetics of the antebellum abolition movement tended, instead, toward the sentimental. Savage traces the history of nineteenth-century monumental representations of slavery to the image adapted from the logo of the British Anti-Slavery Society: a figure of a shackled male slave kneeling in supplication, captioned by the words, "Am I not a Man and a Brother."[14] The affecting image of the supplicating slave operated not only through the appeal to compassion but also in the familial appeal of the caption. In this sense, the sentimental antislavery monument turns the temporality of liberalism back on itself; it demands that the public witness remember the foundational feeling-in-common associated with the private sphere and, consequently, apply that feeling to effect change in public. The logic of this liberal-sentimental antislavery appeal—the deployment of a familialized human "nature" to correct the errors of the nation—is, of course, quite familiar to the contemporary reader by virtue of its application in Harriet Beecher Stowe's *Uncle Tom's Cabin* (1852). Numerous recent critiques of Stowe's sentimental strategies have interrogated both the appropriative dimension of sympathy and the political passivity imputed to her suggestion that the foundation of all opposition to slavery is "feel[ing] right" (a phrase so commonly cited in contemporary challenges to sentimentality that one might reasonably conclude that Stowe represented feeling as the *only* action that the citizen should take against slavery, rather than, as the afterword makes clear, the *minimum* form of action, the one thing that "everyone" can do, even if they cannot vote, teach, or actively campaign against slave laws, activities the afterword also endorses). A critical trajectory that addresses the afterlives of *Uncle Tom's Cabin*, running from James Baldwin's seminal

"Everybody's Protest Novel" to Lauren Berlant's recent "Poor Eliza," points out that this minimum form remains problematic for the way it resonates against the monumentally supported structures of liberal subjectivity to perpetuate a politically traumatized national public. That is to say, familiarity with the exceptional temporality of the sacred as it founds national life through (public) monumentality and (private) sentimentality has trained the American citizen to conflate participation in the temporal suspension peculiar to moments of intensified feeling with political action so thoroughly that the intensive reacquaintance with wholly familiar forms of social organization in those moments can feel somehow *different,* as though the enlivening of the affections were not possibly but automatically a means of making change.[15] Since the works by Douglass, Harper, and Melville discussed in this chapter may also be understood as part of the critical afterlife of *Uncle Tom's Cabin,* I will pause here to examine the form taken by Stowe's maternalist citation of sacred simultaneity in order to illuminate the countersentimental dimension of the later writers.

Stowe's novel, as Philip Fisher has observed, is a paradigmatic attempt to repair the damaged fabric of national life—a fabric that is, as I have been arguing throughout this book, as much temporal as it is spatial. In this sense, the characteristically sentimental deployment of feeling as a means of reassembling what Fisher calls "damaged social space" into a utopian whole is, as I will demonstrate, equally concerned with the problem of damaged *time* that we have come to know as historical existence.[16] Indeed, Stowe's preface to the novel's first edition directly links the two, pointing to the "better day dawning," observing that fiction's corrective emphasis on the "common and gentler humanities of life" is both the sign and the instrument of this new era, and looking optimistically forward to the "time [to] come" when her book will be valued "only as [a] memorial of what has long ceased to be."[17] The preface thus confidently predicts the eventual obsolescence of the novel's sense of urgency even as the narrativity associated with its dominant structures of feelings—grief and its mirror image, hope—underscore its vision of the faulty social progression sustained by an imbalance of temporal principles, suggesting that feeling must be oriented *reproductively* to set time aright. In this light, Jane Tompkins's polemical contention that *Uncle Tom's Cabin,* as the type of the nineteenth-century popular domestic novel, represents "a monumental effort to reorganize culture from the woman's point of view" resonates in a distinctly temporal register as well; for it is precisely an alliance of the temporal suspension of the monumental and the repetitive-cyclical time of the family, figured in the novel as the necessary coupling of mothers and children, that enables the novel to reimagine history as such.[18] The novel argues, in effect, that "feeling right" is not only feeling in harmony with "the sympathies of Christ" but also feeling *like your mother taught you to feel*—a sacred form of feeling that is at once natural and familially installed.[19] This principle of ever-changing sameness organizes what Tompkins identifies as the essentially typological mode of narrative development in Stowe's novel, the way that succeeding episodes add to and amplify, without radically altering, the revealed truth of the novel as a whole.[20] Narrative time moves forward in the novel in order to catch up with its originary truth —a mode of proceeding that recalls its affinity to the monumental. Crucially, this process, for Stowe, is not simply linear-generational; even as mothers teach children, children teach mothers, and mothers (as Eliza's strategic exchange with the mournful Mrs. Bird, which draws upon her own prior training by her mistress Mrs. Shelby, exemplifies) tutor other mothers, creating regenerative exchanges that will ultimately enable familial affection to correct the problem of American history—a problem set into motion by the split in the nature of time effected by the American democratic experiment. For "nature" in the novel is not simply the originary sign of the regenerative maternal drive; it comes, as well, to refer to the desire for freedom of the self universally promised but unequally delivered by the democratic nation-form. The (male) slave's desire to be free is acknowledged by other men in the novel as a *natural* desire, and public indifference to this drive for freedom is, accordingly, seen as a crime against nature, preventing the desirable growth of the individual repeatedly echoed in images of the mother's fond attentions to the development of the child. But the desire for freedom of the *self* also presents a potential problem within the maternalist framework of this novel, as the example of Marie St. Clare makes clear. Marie's "hysterical" bodily ailments, the narrator suggests, stem from a disordered will, whose perversity is the effect of that excess of freedom allotted to the privileged classes and their consequent abuse of it in habits of self-indulgence. The imbalance of individual growth and responsibility to others figures as the historical result of the nation's excess attention to a profit-oriented model of progress, to the detriment of the regenerative and regulatory principles of nature.

Accordingly, the conclusion—or, given the form of its temporal movement, we might say the *completion*—of *Uncle Tom's Cabin* insinuates the corrective influence of "natural" maternal affection into the time of public life in two ways: through the reproductive logic of generations and through the complementary logic of the heterosexual couple. The former is exemplified in Stowe's "Concluding Remarks," in which the narrator links affective re-form to a slow process of change, figured, significantly, as a national scene of child-raising, declaring, "if the mothers of the free states had all felt as they should, in times past . . . the sons of the free states would not have connived at the extension of slavery, in our national body" (624). The developmental time of childrearing, the narrator implies, will settle the future of slavery through recourse to the natural progress of generations, which will gradu-ally move the desire to repair the temporal/familial damage enacted by the peculiar institution into the public sphere. The concluding address to the reader thus outlines social change as a *(re)generational* process, incorporating affective time into the linear development of the nation. In turn, the novel uses the complementary logic of the heterosexual couple to millennially complete this temporal transformation on a global scale, as it sends George Harris, along with his wife, Eliza, to Africa to engage in missionary work. George's plan for African regeneration privileges the maternalist temporality that the novel repeatedly endorses; he insists that while the ready-made model of Western democracy, applied in Africa, will allow the rapid growth of democracy there, the fundamentally maternal nature of the black body (Africans, in George's view, are, "[i]f not a dominant and commanding race, . . . at least, an affectionate, magnanimous, and forgiving one" [611]) will prevent the profiteering public indifference that marks American progress. The projected rise of a Christian African nation will herald a new, posthistor-ical era; contemporary historical conflicts are, from this millennial perspec-tive, "but the birth-pangs of an hour of universal peace and brotherhood" (611). Significantly, however, George admits in his letter that he alone might be physiologically unfit for the task because of his white blood, the inherent "hastiness" of which would make him "feeble" for the task of regeneration were it not for the presence and faith of Eliza, which "restores" him and keeps him on course (611). The domestic-marital balancing of time in this couple both prefigures and enables the planetary revolution in time pre-dicted in the preface, first modeled in domestic space in the ninth chapter and extended by the narrator to the nation (and its readers) in the after-word. Here, then, we can observe the way the sentimental at once comple-ments and seeks to correct the sacralized foundation of the nation com-memorated in the public monument—recalling Tompkins's apt characteri-zation of this work as "a monumental effort to reorganize culture from the woman's point of view"; it posits the complementary familial coupling of man and woman, as well as that of mother and child, as the forms most suited to accomplish the millennial regeneration of time that, in the name of the exceptional American family, will bring about the end of history.

Untimely Perspectives: How the Countermonument Tells Time

The problematic inscriptions and equally problematic erasures of monumentalism lead many people to discard the monumental project altogether. Melville's Pierre echoes this dismissal as he announces,

> Hitherto I have hoarded up mementoes and monuments of the past . . .
> but it is forever over now! If to me any memory shall henceforth be dear,
> I will not mummy it in a visible memorial for every passing beggar's dust
> to gather on. . . . [N]ever more will I play the vile pigmy, and by small
> memorials after death, attempt to reverse the decree of death, by essay-
> ing the poor perpetuating of the image of the original.[21]

Pierre's disillusionment with the past (or, more precisely, with his father's history) leads him to rebel against the project of memorialization, representing it as a "primitive" attempt to deny the passage of time. Believing that he cannot find any "visible" form that will preserve memory without "mummifying" it, Pierre chooses instead to burn his mementos and declares himself to be "ever present," without past or future. This idealization of the present in place of the past is replicated in Lewis Mumford's well-known modernist critique of the monument in *The Culture of Cities*. Mumford declares the monument to be aligned with "death and fixity" and insists that the modern world, in contrast, is "oriented to the cycle of life."[22] Like Pierre, he derides the monumental impulse as primitive and childish and announces that the modern world has outgrown it. Mumford's refusal of the monument defies the authority of its "timeless" projections, repudiating the past's power to dictate the terms of the present.[23] In its most severe form, however, this refusal to give space to public memorial does not fully liberate the present from the tyranny of the past—it simply hyperinsulates it, transposing the logic of sentimental privacy to the timeless time of the unconscious, making critical dialogue about the significance of the past impossible. The refusal of the monument, that is, does not erase but merely displaces monumental history; rather than desacralizing the power of the past, it melancholically denies it.

What I have identified as the countermonumental perspective, in contrast, seeks to open a dialogue between monumental timelessness and the registers of the historical unconscious. In considering the appearance of countermonumentalism over a century before the period conventionally associated with the term, I am, in effect, seeking to resist the linear-progressive framework that guides Mumford's alignment of the time of modernity with that of "life," in contrast to the deadening fixity of the past. Instead, I suggest that the work of nineteenth-century writers who sought to transform the suspension of historical time encoded within sentimental responses to slavery may be effectively understood in relation to this critical paradigm. As a means of illuminating their challenges, then, I want to turn briefly to an examination of recent European countermonumental installations. Described by James Young as "brazen, painfully self-conscious memorial spaces . . . conceived to challenge the very premises of their being,"[24] countermonuments refuse to "tell people what they ought to think" about the past and thus to relieve them of the burden of thinking it.[25] Rather than facilitate the self-consolidation of the viewer in relation to an already-agreed-upon understanding of the past's significance, Holocaust countermonuments have consistently sought to disorient their observers, emphasizing the viewer's implication in a historical narrative that remains unresolved.[26] In an effort to restructure the terms of audience response, these countermonuments deploy forms that amplify the play of time, privileging displacement and/or evanescence in order to highlight the damaged intersections of space and time sustained through the event.[27] The narrativity of the forms employed in these installations suggests that traumatic history is most effectively engaged not in the transcendence of a single symbolic image but from moment to moment, as one struggles to move through the memorial site or watches its appearance and disappearance.[28]

These projects illuminate the way the countermonument supplants the timeless symbolic appeal of the traditional monument with the destabilizing effects of both irony and allegory. The turn to allegory in countermonuments, in particular, reflects a desire to find ways of negotiating the relationship between past and present that depend neither on linear emplotments of time nor on its collapse into timelessness. Because allegory always stresses the temporality of the relationships it enfolds, referring insistently to a prior set of meanings with which it can never fully coincide but without which it loses its significance, it has proven a powerful tool at moments in history when the question of history itself engenders a temporal crisis.[29] Allegory, in Walter Benjamin's reading, is a "powerful" pleasure because it exposes the incompleteness of objects, gesturing toward a referential relationship that is both arbitrary and necessary. The functional instability of allegory's semiotic reveals history as a "script," a set of meanings superimposed over the debris of human existence; as in the ruin, in the allegory "history does not assume the form of the process of an eternal life so much as that of irresistible decay."[30] Yet the broken and uncertain forms that appear from the countermonumental perspective express, though not a blithe optimism, something like a hesitant faith in the possibility of the engaged critical dialogue that it hopes its temporally charged gestures will provoke. For if allegory is a mode in which, as Benjamin notes, "[a]ny person, any object, any relationship can mean absolutely anything else," then it emphasizes the necessity of making meaning of (rather than receiving meaning *from*) the countermonument, a process that will, like allegory itself, necessarily be dispersed across time.

In sidestepping the fantasy of completion, then, countermonumentalism resists the monumental vision of the national public as a boundless, simultaneous totality, merged within the unanimity of automatic response—the fantasy that also grounds sentimental appeals to the timeless truth of the human. Drawing on dispersed and disruptive allegorical forms, it reconceives audience as the space of interpretation—a space, that is, in which something like a critical counterpublic might continue to inform, reform, and reinvent itself and its relations. To do so effectively, however, countermonumentalism cannot simply deny the power of the sacralized image; rather, it seeks in effect to ruin that image, reopening the flow of time within it. Benjamin's comparison of allegory to ruin is particularly instructive in this respect. Ruins, it must be recalled, are of the class of monuments that Alois Riegl designates "unintentional monuments": artifacts that were not originally intended as commemorative but which become so over time. Hence, what the ruin commemorates is time itself or, more precisely, the passage of time, which creates what Riegl calls the "age-value" of the monument—a value that varies according to the historical self-image of a given era. If narratives of liberalism bespoke the commodity-form of American time-value in the antebellum United States as stable, predictable progress— a forward and upward-moving public working to make the young nation ascendant on the world stage, nurtured by the perpetuation of its human values in the private sphere—the countermonumental perspective sought to arrange matters to give that complementary formation a distinct shock through the recognition of slavery itself as an ongoing *interruption* to the mutually imbricated timelines of family and nation, a shock that entailed, in effect, the deliberate ruination of sacred forms of American nationality.

Now Is the Time: Douglass's "What to the Slave?"

In the 1852 speech with which this chapter opened, Frederick Douglass quite deliberately *times* his intervention into monumentalizing accounts of America, intervening not only in the content but also in the form of American public memory through his manipulation of belatedness. The question of belatedness was foregrounded in the speech's performance on the *fifth* of July, a calendrical displacement that dramatized Douglass's intentional distance from the usual matter of Fourth of July speeches; he implicitly refers to this delay in the apology with which his speech opens: "The papers and placards say, that I am to deliver a 4th [of] July oration. . . . The fact is, ladies and gentlemen, the distance between this platform and the slave plantation, from which I escaped, is considerable—and the difficulties to be overcome in getting from the latter to the former, are by no means slight" (360). Belatedness also marks the speech's structure, since its first half—a carefully considered review of the lasting significance of the American Revolution—receives a different cast as a result of the shift, midway through, to the slave's perspective—a retemporalization marked in the speech as "The Present" (366). Of course, Douglass's resistance to slavery would come as no surprise to his audience, and, since he spoke at a meeting sponsored by the Rochester Ladies' Anti-Slavery Society, it was one he might reasonably expect many of his auditors to share. His speech, in this sense, addresses itself as much to the failures of critical vision within the abolitionist movement as it does to the wrongs of slavery itself—highlighting, in effect, the extent to which many of slavery's opponents remained identified with the timeless "Americanness" perpetuated in Webster's ventriloquism of the Bunker Hill Monument's appeal, weakening the movement's ability to counter the social stasis that this ideal provokes. Douglass effectively anticipates and problematizes the conception of the counterpublic put forth by Nancy Fraser. Fraser sought to replace the assumption that there is a single, comprehensive, and continuous public sphere (the assumption of Webster's oration) with a vision of proliferating subaltern counterpublics generating democratic dialogue.[31] But since the populations that might compose various counterpublics are themselves unevenly temporalized, this model itself can offer no guarantee that subaltern counterpublics will be able to gain the kind of traction that might lead to transformative action. Douglass seeks to jolt his audience out of any too-complacent conviction that an antislavery counterpublic marching fearlessly forward could simply embrace its "lagging" members without modifying its own image in time and space. In the (retrospective) wake of Douglass's subsequent denunciation of the "American slave-trade, sustained by American politics and American religion" (372), then, the spatial and temporal differences that Douglass introduces between the present celebrations and the moment of the Revolution take on additional force:

> your fathers, who had not adopted the fashionable idea of this day, of the infallibility of government, and the absolute character of its acts, presumed to differ from the home government in respect to the wisdom and the justice of some of those burdens and restraints. They went so far in their excitement as to pronounce the measures of government unjust, unreasonable, and oppressive, and altogether such as ought not to be quietly submitted to. I scarcely need say, fellow-citizens, that my opinion of those measures fully accords with that of your fathers. (361)

The second half of the speech makes clear, for those who might have missed it at first, the irony layered into Douglass's final sentence, his endorsement of the Revolutionists' resistance to the burdens of an unjust government, which marks "this day" as occurring both in the past and the present. Yet this irony would likely have been audible the first time around; after all, Douglass had opened by highlighting the "distance" between platform and plantation and followed by tendering his congratulations to the audience on possessing a nation so young, "still lingering in the period of childhood," since the reformer could find hope in the fact that young nations remained yet "impressionable" (360). More important in this passage, then, is the way it serves to amplify the significance of the term with which it opens and closes: "your fathers." While Douglass consistently addresses his audience as "fellow-citizens," the gesture of distancing implicit in his repeated references, during this recitation, to "your fathers" and "your nation" becomes fully apparently as he brings the first section of the speech to a close by reminding his listeners that they themselves well know the history he is recounting, since "the causes which led to the separation of the colonies from the British crown . . . have all been taught in your common schools, narrated at your firesides, unfolded from your pulpits, and thundered from your legislative halls, and are as familiar to you as household words" (365–66). Closing the subject, Douglass remarks, "I leave . . . the great deeds of your fathers to other gentlemen whose claim to have been regularly descended will be less likely to be disputed than mine!" (366). This transition moves the speech beyond the specific focus on the hypocrisy of celebrating the Declaration of Independence in a country where an eighth of the population remained enslaved, rendering it a general interrogation of monumentalized celebrations of American history and American identity, in terms that point out both the widespread dissemination of this account and the mercenary egotism that underlies this circulation. Crucially, however, Douglass, while continuing to employ the rhetoric of fellowship, makes explicit the thinking behind his repeated references to "your" fathers—not only his disputed ability but also his disinclination to claim "regular" descent from them, to be simply annexed to the genealogy of an otherwise untransformed nation.

Douglass's resistance to both the monumental image of the Revolution as a self-contained and timeless victory over tyranny and to the rhetoric of the nation-as-family challenges the naturalized structures through which his audience has come to understand freedom, synonymous with Americanness, as their inheritance. This resistance to the accepted timelines of American history in this section also charges his suggestion, toward the close of the lecture, that the times are changing. Exploring the "tendencies of the age," Douglass observes that "no nation can now shut itself up from the surrounding world, and trot round in the same old path of its fathers without interference" (387). The development of trade and print culture, he observes, "annihilate[s]" space, so that "[t]houghts expressed on one side of the Atlantic are distinctly heard on the other" (387). Douglass's endorsement of modernity as a process that, pushed by commerce and speeded by new technologies, will bring the "all-pervading light" of human rights to all nations seeks to bring this observation home, as he compares the much-condemned Chinese practice of footbinding to America's own continued fidelity to "long established customs of hurtful character" (387). Intriguingly, the conclusion celebrates the potentialities linked to the modernization of global space—a celebration that both endorses the logic of progress and turns it back on the United States—even as it suggests a consequent and concomitant change in the nature of time. For time, in this speech, is not organized according to either linear-progressive or cyclical-generational frameworks; Douglass does away with these at the moment he punctures the "timeless" image of the Revolution, revealing himself as the deliberately irregular descendant of the Revolutionary fathers.[32] The time that most concerns Douglass, as I suggested earlier, is the time of the "now," the time that heralds his overt move into the spatial perspective of the slave, as he announces that his business is not with the past but with the present or, rather, "the accepted time with God and his cause, . . . the ever-living now" (366). Douglass reminds the audience that although they are free to gather inspiration from the deeds of the past, "now is the time, the important time" (366). The messianic charge of Douglass's now effects a quickening of the moment into the "living present," suggesting the temporality that Walter Benjamin (drawing on and absorbing into his logic, as Douglass does in the Fourth of July speech, the theological energies of the Old Testament) would also nominate now-time, or *Jetztzeit*, the distinctive actualization of the present that he understood as "shot through with chips of Messianic time."[33] For Benjamin, this stopped and yet energized temporality, which connected to the past in a manner radically distinct from that of the monumental historiographer, was the only moment from which one might write a revolutionary history. Douglass employs the now-time Benjamin describes, as his purpose in the speech is not to discredit the American Revolution for its incompleteness but, more precisely, to reactualize it—to yank the language of revolution out of the eloquent forms that rehearse and contain its significance and return it to the tense that he presents.

The belatedness that prompts Douglass's actualization of the "now" as a moment of radical *eventfulness* also authorizes his turn from the subtle irony that marked the first half of the speech to the "fiery stream of biting ridicule" that, he suggests, is the only ethical response to the belief that the slave's humanity and right to liberty, or the refutation of slavery as part of the "divine design," must be treated as points to be argued and proved. Douglass insists, in response to the demand for persuasion rather than denunciation, that "[t]he time for such argument is past. At a time like this, scorching irony, not convincing argument, is needed" (371). The shift from the emphasis on the grief of the slave, and on Douglass's own mournfulness in the face of the holiday, to "scorching irony," and the corresponding shift in the pace of the speech, insinuates a distinction between the temporalities corresponding to the affective states of grief and shame, one that we might follow in terms of Paul de Man's analysis of the relationship between allegory and irony. Following Benjamin, de Man identifies both allegory and irony as rhetorical modes that emphasize temporality, as distinguished from the symbol (the favored trope of the monumental), which masks temporality in its alleged transcendence of time. But irony, for de Man, functions rhetorically as the "reverse mirror image" of allegory. Whereas allegory, like mourning, turns to the past for its authority, always dependent on a prior significance with which it can never coincide in linear time but without which it loses its significance, irony, which signals, critically, a suspension of "the innocence or authenticity of our sense of being in the world," inscribes a discrepancy of meaning that is *instantaneous* and so is "[e]ssentially the mode of the present."[34] In this sense, we can understand the shift in the mood of the speech as a doubling-back on the distance that Douglass established between himself and his white audience: from belatedness comes the impulse to shake the nation loose from its complacent indulgence in monumental pieties—an impulse he proceeds to extend, successively, to the legal system and the American churches, refusing the conventional plea to leave the critique of religion out of abolitionist rhetoric. For, despite the nation's youth, the speech suggests, nothing American can be understood any longer as innocent.

Douglass's prolonged attention to "your national inconsistencies" works finally to re-create the form of national history as neither generational or monumental but perpetuated by the means of its recognition. In this light, the quickening of the speech into now-time can indeed be understood to emerge from Douglass's reference to the "heart within"—though not in the conventionally sentimental sense of the universalizing appeal to feeling that persuades the sympathizing witness of a common humanity, a mode of persuasion that Douglass will not undertake to validate. Rather, the "heart within" functions to guide the pulse of the speech, enlivening its apprehension of national time without subsuming that time to the logic of reproductive generationality. "What to the Slave Is the Fourth of July?" suggests, finally, that Douglass is indeed closely connected to the memorial holiday whose origins he claims to feel less interest in than his audience, through his messianic reawakening of its revolutionary significance. He is bound to the Revolutionary generation, however, not as its heir but as its *prophet*—a temporal involution that signals the complex and shifting modes of reconnecting past, present, and future that are, for Douglass, the only place where "hope" might be found.

The Weight of Time in "The Slave Auction"

The revolutionary quickening of Douglass's speech receives a crucial push, at one moment, from his dramatic narration of a horrifyingly thrilling scene that typifies the slave trade: the forcible driving from Washington to New Orleans of a "wretched" band of slaves destined to be sold at auction. Frances E. W. Harper's 1854 poem "The Slave Auction" foregrounds a similar dramatic scene, but to radically different ends; whereas Douglass's speech seeks to quicken the pulse of the nation, Harper's poem, in contrast, dedramatizes the pace of time, slowing it toward the gradual death of feeling. The deceleration of time in Harper's poem, however, does not appeal to the slow progress of regenerative generationality that we saw in the discussion of Stowe's monumental novel, to which, as Glenn Hendler proposes, "The Slave Auction" may be read as a deliberate response.[35] For although "The Slave Auction" also pits the profit-oriented indifference of public time against the regenerative appeal of interior temporalities, the poem eschews the (re)productive rebalancing of contemporary forms of time seen in *Uncle Tom's Cabin*, instead suggesting new forms of temporal connection as the necessary solution to the problem(s) of history. Foregrounding both the inability to resist the damage of linear time and the insufficiency of sympathy as a reparative tool, the poem may also be seen to challenge conventional assumptions about the generic temporality of lyric: its suspension of the flow of time in favor of the detailed examination of a particular moment. Sharon Cameron explains this as an ahistorical and perhaps antihistorical tendency of the genre, in which events are presented as "arrested, framed, and taken out of the flux of history." Indeed, Cameron speculates, "one might almost go so far as to say that in lyric poems history gets sacrificed to presence, as if the two were somehow incompatible.[36] We may, however, question the extent to which history can be understood as sacrificed to presence in Harper's poem. In fact, the reverse might ultimately be said to be the case, as the poem details the slow sacrifice of presence to a historical condition. Her poem thus historicizes what Cameron outlines as a temporality conceived against history as such, specifically locating what appears for Cameron an existential condition: the "victory" of the lyric, its "stunning articulation of the isolated moment," as underlaid by "despair of the possibility of completed stories . . . and thus of complete knowledge."[37] "The Slave Auction's" challenge to this vision of lyric temporality derives from what Mary Louise Kete has identified as nineteenth-century sentimental writing's mixing of lyric and narrative modes, for even though, as I will show, the poem contests the normative assumptions of the white middle-class sentimental culture that Kete examines, it does so in terms that reference that culture.[38] Harper's poem also corresponds to Wai Chee Dimock's recent analysis of the way the widely varying temporalities that circulate through what we know as American literature expose its global origins: as it details a moment in local time that is rooted in a transnational and long-range historical trade, "The Slave Auction" effectively supplements its lyric mode with an epic echo that underscores the epochal, rather than atemporal, status of experience therein.[39] This layered temporality, in turn, not only highlights Harper's distinctive countermonumental move in the poem but also calls our attention to the question of whether, in fact, broadly generic temporalities should be applied to historical instantiations of any particular genre. Virginia Jackson has recently suggested, contra Cameron, that the critical tendency to isolate lyric in space and time is itself a historical phenomenon rather than a generic truth, reflecting a twentieth-century emphasis on a "hypostatized lyric" as standing for "poetry in general."[40] Recent work by Jackson, Kete, and Max Cavitch articulates a nineteenth-century understanding of poetry as a social form implicated in concrete circuits of reproduction and circulation, a conception that itself complicates, if it does not entirely counter, any reflexive association of lyric with the eternal moment.[41] Thus, I read Harper's poem not according to the abstract temporality of a genre but as an intentional animation of form within time and history, one that works both within and against the monumentalizing tendency of sentimental culture.

We may now turn to the poem itself, which is reproduced here in full:

> The sale began—young girls were there,
> Defenceless in their wretchedness,
> Whose stifled sobs of deep despair
> Revealed their anguish and distress.
>
> And mothers stood with streaming eyes,
> And saw their dearest children sold;
> Unheeded rose their bitter cries,
> While tyrants bartered them for gold.
>
> And woman, with her love and truth—
> For these in sable forms may dwell—

Gaz'd on the husband of her youth,
With anguish none may paint or tell.

And men, whose sole crime was their hue,
The impress of their Maker's hand,
And frail and shrinking children, too,
Were gathered in that mournful band.

Ye who have laid your love to rest,
And wept above their lifeless clay,
Know not the anguish of that breast,
Whose lov'd are rudely torn away.

Ye may not know how desolate
Are bosoms rudely forced to part,
And how a dull and heavy weight
Will press the life-drops from the heart.[42]

The poem begins with a narrative speech-act that marks the initiation of an event in time, the opening of the sale of slaves, and then slows time to explore in detail the moment upon which the reader's attention has been focused. Crucially, however, the point in time that Harper's poem examines foregrounds above all the *impossibility* of stopping time, particularly for the bondswomen and men whose inability to determine the course of their own lives is underlined by the scene of the sale. There is, then, nothing sacred about the lyric moment in Harper's poem, in that there is no exception to history available within it; the profit-making productivity emphasized in this manifestation of historical time continues to resonate as affective narrative throughout the "stopped" moment of the sale, as the poem uses the suspension of external action to trace the *anticipatory* nature of the slaves' emotions—an anticipation that ends with their relocation alone and elsewhere.

The poem's apprehension of the problem of time is suggested in its repeated moves from exterior to interior—the depiction of categories presented as moments of human life in time (girls, mothers, husbands, children) followed by the speaking emotions experienced by each type of person during the scene of the sale. This characteristic move outlines the progress of the titular event by presenting its emotional traces, telling the story of the sale through the signs of anguish that it creates. The "private" temporalities of these emotions displace, but cannot delay or undo, the linear motion of the commercial event, as its inexorable onward movement effectively deprives emotion of any regenerative capacity. Instead, the time of feeling is itself arrested in the image of emotional death that concludes the poem, as the end of the slave auction is signified metonymically as the "end" of the auctioned slave whose "life-blood" is slowly pressed away. The slow time of mourning is, here, unable to create a corrective or compensatory movement; it produces only displacement, the sundering of affective bonds that cannot be regenerated by sympathy. The weight of the suppressed pain that follows the "rude parting" of the slave families has, as Harper insists, little in common with the consoling attraction of lingering grief conventionally posited in sentimental consolation literature, as it not only fails to revive the "human" spirit appealed to in the culture of mourning but actually contributes to the gradual death of the heart.

Part of this difference in the temporality of pain may be traced to the altered pacing of the sentimental figure of the family in the poem. Significantly, the scene of social and emotional violation that most closely figures the spatiotemporal damage of slavery within Stowe's novel—the severing of mothers from children—is delayed in "The Slave Auction" until its second stanza. The point of origin of the poem's affective logic, rather, is the temporally intermediate figure of the *girl,* whose defenselessness and anguish indexes an anticipation of the bodily violation of rape likely to follow from the sale. The affective/temporal break narrated in the poem thus appears *first* as the desecration of the physical body and only secondly as the shattering of affective/familial bonds. In this sense, the poem suggests that the inviolability of affective time, the foundation of the social bond, should be understood to originate not in the affective bondedness of the family but in the integrity of the body itself.[43] The sexual violation that awaits the trembling body of the girl is juxtaposed to other violations in the poem's later returns to the physicality of the body, figured in the "sable forms" of women, containing "love and truth," and men "whose sole crime was their hue / the impress of their Maker's hand." In these images, the dark skin of the slave operates not as a sign of "natural" biological difference, indexing a particular affective-corporeal orientation that, as we saw in chapter 1, was cited to buttress the asynchronic placement of the slave within the familialized framework of the nation, but rather as the mark of the body's disregarded sacredness. Blackness, in the poem, serves as a physical mnemonic for the divine design of the human. The time of the (black) body thus resonates distinctively in Harper's poem; it is not mere debris that threatens to disrupt the flow of time toward futurity, but rather the material index of the discarding of divine principles by a profit-oriented public to whom nothing is sacred.

This reimagination of the time of the body also resonates in the strategically disidentificatory move of the poem's last two stanzas, which connect the affective spectacle of the first four stanzas to the emotional experience of the reader, only to refuse the direct correspondence that the conventions of sympathy would trace between the two. Delineating, in two lines, the pain of loss that the reader may well have experienced, the poem nevertheless insists that this pain is not identical to the "anguish" of the "desolate" slave. This move, as Hendler observes, points to the "epistemological limits" of the "fantasy of experiential equivalence" encoded in Stowe's sentimental project—limits that are, I would emphasize, temporal as well as spatial.[44] For what the close of the poem refuses, crucially, is not the *possibility* of feeling for the other (for that feeling is actively solicited through the careful delineation of anticipatory emotion) but the spatiotemporal error of feeling for the other *as* the self—the principle of affective *simultaneity* appealed to in sentimental sympathy. Insisting on the specificity of the auctioned slave's emotions, the poem ruptures the monumental temporality of sympathy as it seeks to erode differences not only in space but also in time. Not incidentally, this disruptive direct address to the reader, which suspends the depiction of the slave auction, finally returns the poem to conventional narrative time, but in a different place, replacing the exterior scene of the sale with its interior aftermath. The poem's characteristic movement from exterior to interior is deftly (re)figured in the way the "life-drops" emphasized in its final line recall the tears of the bereft mourner in line 18; as the physical signs of mourning are relocated from the outside to the inside of the body, the violation of the body-for-profit encoded in the auction is again recalled. The tears of the heart do not function redemptively in this image; they neither enable a regenerative exchange of sympathy nor signal a physical dissolution into the general consolation promised by the afterlife.[45] The poem remains at once *in time* and untimely; since even its figuring of the sacred exception is attached to the always-already-violated space of the enslaved body, there is no realm of escape from the temporal damage that slavery figures in history.

The disruption of sympathy in the direct address to the reader, accordingly, allows closure to come about only as the final *displacement* of the poem's narrative progress, in which the time of the public event traces its lines in and through anticipatory and mournful bodies. This spatial move suggests a different temporal principle for sentimental readerly identification: not the (monumental) simultaneity of sympathy appealed to in *Uncle Tom's Cabin* but an idea of *contemporaneousness,* a being-together within time that would not require history to stop in order to correct the temporal damage it enacts. This suggestion of contemporaneousness rather than simultaneity as the basis for national action relocates the minimum possibility of responsive action for the witness of this spectacle; insofar as it shifts the framework of community from the sentimental/monumental ideal of *feeling* together in time across an infinite expanse of time to one of *being* together in time, the basis for response is no longer simply a question of "feeling right" but of acting correctly. As Harper's poem tracks the movement of commerce across feeling, it works to open the desire both to assess and to *interrupt* the event, to follow the course of its emotional traces and to arrest the progress of the sale before its termination. The latter desire, frustrated within the space of the poem itself, is referred to the contemporaneous space of the reader by means of the iterability of the auction, the commercial event, in market culture. The likelihood of its repetition in the world of the reader, that is, refocuses the desire for interruption opened in the poem. Although Harper's poem presents no specific plan for resolution of the historical problem of slavery, it frames the time in which resolution might take place differently, for the interruptive desire it solicits demands action in the present, as distinct from the gradual rebalancing of Stowe's generational/millennial schema.[46] The poem effectively insists on a new mode of time, coupling reflection and action, which is untethered to the gradualism of progress, the cyclical regenerativity of the natural, or the stasis of monumentality—a politicized time, one that comprehends the very condition of political action as a momentous dissociation from those temporal modes that limit historical change.[47] And significantly, the slowed time of the poem suggests a dedramatizing revision of revolutionary potentiality, by positing the moment of rupture as an ongoing intervention into everyday forms of recognition. In this sense, the politicized time Harper's poem suggests would be a distinctive time but *not* a time apart; that is to say, it is not a time to be sacralized but to be apprehended in relation to ongoing movements of change across public and private spaces. Despite the difference in the pace of "The Slave Auction" and "What to the Slave Is the Fourth of July?" the substitution of critical contemporaneousness for monumental simultaneity enacted in the closing stanzas of Harper's poem, no less than the demonumentalizing of the Revolution in Douglass's speech, suggests a countermonumental reconfiguration of the status of the present tense, one effected by a deliberate wresting-free of that tense from its naturalized place in the order of things.

Ill-Timed Perspectives: "Benito Cereno"

In comparison to the slowed pace that Harper foregrounds in her reworking of the present into a politically charged "now," Herman Melville's 1855 novella "Benito Cereno" might well be said to slow political time almost to a halt.[48] Indeed, so carefully layered is Melville's reworking of the story of a slave rebellion aboard a Spanish ship, which he had come across in Amasa Delano's 1817 *Narrative of Voyages and Travels in the Northern and Southern Hemispheres,* that readers have often been unsure what, if any, perspective the story provides on the question of slavery. The limited critical response to the tale at the time of its publication suggests that it was viewed as a thrilling adventure narrative; in the twentieth century, some critics have argued that the tale itself repeats the dehumanization of the slave figured in the gaze of Delano; others, recognizing the story as containing an antislavery argument, nevertheless fault Melville for privileging aesthetic experimentation over political action.[49] It is not my intention here, however, either to uncover the "truth" of the tale's position on slavery (the story, I believe, may be read as privileging an antislavery perspective whether or not that was intended) or to defend Melville's "subversive" method, but to consider the way his story resonates within the constellation that this chapter has constructed. Accordingly, the need to comprehend that resonance as both vital and provisional will form part of my argument.

Melville's skepticism, in 1855, about the capacity for critical thought in his own historical moment is well documented.[50] "Benito Cereno," in light of that skepticism, can be read as a kind of shock treatment—an attempt to jolt the reader out of received thought patterns, uncritical habits learned from exposure to self-satisfied accounts of Americanness and to sentimental celebrations of the regenerative power of private feeling. Rejecting alike the redemptive pedagogy of monumentalism, the melancholy silences of antimonumentalism, and the consolations of sentimental sympathy, "Benito Cereno" intervenes in American history by fragmenting it, breaking it apart and rearranging the pieces so that the very limitations and possibilities of time become visible in its narrative spaces. The tale's countermonumentalism manifests, in particular, in its critique of the flawed interpretive habits of the two ships' captains, the American, Amasa Delano, and the Spaniard, Benito Cereno. The narrative positions the Spaniard and the American alike as seeking ways to assert a sense of absolute control in a world of flux, a world where signs are never simply self-evident and time acts to aggravate, rather than ameliorate, their tendency to disseminate multiple meanings. Neither captain can cope with this multiplicity, and their incapacity is revealed as an effect of the limited and unproductive temporal orientations associated with each character. Delano's monumental amnesia and Cereno's antimonumental melancholy both appear as painful modes of mismanaging relations to the past, a damage linked to the historical violence that the tale exposes and condemns.

Critics of "Benito Cereno" have long identified Amasa Delano's interpretive dysfunction as central to Melville's purpose in the narrative.[51] Delano's inability to recognize the slave rebellion aboard the *San Dominick* should, I propose, be understood as a temporal disability—an effect of what Nietzsche terms the historical "damage" sustained in the monumental mode of history. The past, as Delano knows it, is never very complex, its lessons are self-evident, its separation from the present is anchored by a few, select timeless truths, and its proper use is always self-consolidation. Accordingly, Delano approaches the story he hears aboard the *San Dominick* as one would understand a monumental history—the representation of an event that has *already happened,* whose significance is self-evident and timeless, and to the aftermath of which he responds, as a good citizen should, with benevolent action, an attempt to succor the unfortunates. Indeed, the narratorial emphasis on Delano's benevolence and sympathy throughout "Benito Cereno" suggests, as Peter Coviello has recently argued, that Melville, in response to works like *Uncle Tom's Cabin,* frames Delano as a sentimental reader, whose self-affirmative recognition of supposedly familiar forms aboard a strange ship enables an "often grossly self-satisfied ignorance."[52] For while both Delano's mistaken belief in his own distance from the catastrophe that has befallen the *San Dominick* and his attendant insistence on a romantic-racialist (mis)understanding of the relation between race and power are reinforced throughout the narrative by the dual temporal gestures he adapts from monumentalism—its simultaneous promulgation of "timeless truth" and its assurance that, as Delano argues in the tale's final pages, "the past is passed"— his citation of sentimental postures and rhetoric suggests the extent to which, as we have seen, the monumental makes itself at home in the nine-

teenth century with the help of the sentimental, allowing him to miscon-
ceive his alienation as human charitableness.

The deliberately countermonumental construction of time through the
story's exposure of Delano's problematic perspective is emphasized in his
first view of the *San Dominick*. This vessel, a Spanish ship once belonging to
the Royal Navy but now in use as a merchant ship transporting "negro
slaves, amongst other valuable freight" (36), appears to Delano as a floating
ruin, laden with "relic[s] of faded grandeur . . . left to decay" (37). This vision
of the slave ship as a ruin offers a critical apprehension of the narrative's
complex temporal strategy, the way it at once inhabits and exposes Delano's
monumentalism. For the cultural significance of the passage of time indexed
by the ruin is *not* timeless; it changes according to the understanding of the
past favored in each era. Whereas the ruin (as Benjamin, following Riegl, has
pointed out) spoke to the Baroque viewer of the pain of loss, bearing witness
to present decline from some bygone era of glory, by the nineteenth century
viewers were inclined to see ruins in accordance with their own sense of history, framed by a progressive view of civilization in which the cyclical rise
and fall of great powers drove humanity ever upward.[53] Delano, as we see
later in the story, shares this perspective and is inclined to interpret whatever he sees as evidence of the "natural laws" on which this theory of history is based. Accordingly, the ruined Spanish ship, for Delano, testifies to
the natural and inevitable decline of European imperial power and, con-
comitantly, to his own ascendancy, as a hard-working but soft-feeling American, on the world-historical stage.

In line with this view of the Spanish ship as a ruin, Delano understands
what he sees aboard the *San Dominick* as fundamentally *other* to him in a
temporal sense. Hence, he believes the "common tale of suffering" that the
San Dominick's passengers offer "in one language, and as with one voice"
(38), to be effectively over once he arrives to hear it. Though he is called
upon to assist in the aftermath of the unfortunate events that have befallen
the *San Dominick* (supposedly, a long, immobilizing calm coupled with a
plague that killed many of the crew members), he is not himself implicated
in those events; he attends and reacts to the story but believes he bears no
responsibility for it. To say that Delano understands himself only to bear
witness to the story aboard the *San Dominick,* however, is not to say that he
does not believe that it is in the end all about *him*. Rather, his compassionate
response to the *San Dominick*'s distress confirms, for him, the already-agreed-
upon version of what it means to be a good citizen-sailor. Indeed, his self-

satisfaction suggests a certain autoerotic dimension to the narcissism of sentiment; for though the traumatized Cereno seems hardly to appreciate his charity, Delano's approval of himself makes up for the Spanish captain's indifference: "a sort of saddened satisfaction stole over Captain Delano at thinking of the kindly offices he had that day discharged for a stranger. Ah, thought he, after good actions one's conscience is never ungrateful, however much so the benefited party may be" (83). The American's sympathy-inspired good works, in this sense, serve as the means for his pleasurable self-consolidation across the temporal gap separating him from the Spaniard's ruined world.

But Delano's sentimentally and monumentally "appropriate" response to the spectacle before him is disrupted by the repeated intrusion into his consciousness of a shadow-story, one that represents the *San Dominick*'s history as unfinished. In this version of the story, Delano appears not as a self-satisfied witness to events that are historically outside his experience, with which he can make contact only through the operation of sympathy, but as an anxious guardian of his own radically uncertain future. Observing a number of details that he cannot quite interpret, yet which appear to him to possess a "lurking significance" (54), Delano begins to suspect a "sinister scheme" (55) aboard the ship. In the shadow-story opened by Delano's suspicion, the history of the *San Dominick* no longer appears as an explained and contained fact but as a series of multiple possibilities bent upon perpetuating themselves in his own moment. Thus, instead of contemplating the ruins of the ship from a safe (temporal) distance, Delano suddenly finds himself engulfed by them. Gazing at a mossy balustrade that "seemed the charred ruin of some summerhouse in a grand garden long running to waste," he imagines that he is "in some far inland country, prisoner in some deserted chateau, left to stare at empty grounds and peer out at vague roads where never wagon or wayfarer passed" (61–62). This paranoid fantasy inverts his sentimental self-consolidation, situating him as vulnerable to the latent possibilities of the inconclusive narrative. The constant slippage between his initial self-satisfied sense of closure and the suspicion of an ongoing plot so disorients Delano that he compares his distress to a sort of mental "sea-sickness" (64), suggesting that the inability to maintain monumental orientation threatens to pull the (historical) ground out from under him. In light of the story's conclusion—in which Delano's suspicion is seemingly confirmed, as the moments of incoherence that he witnesses are revealed to be the effect of a carefully designed attempt by the rebel slaves to gain time, to persuade Delano that everything is "normal" aboard the *San Dominick* until night falls and the rebels can safely attack Delano's own ship—we might therefore conclude that Delano's paranoid moments are the ones in which his vision is most accurate. Yet this conclusion would be misleading, insofar as Delano's paranoia should rather be understood as another mode of self-consolidation. While it inverts the sentimental fantasy that the subject may be completed through affective identification with others, his paranoia fails to counter the conviction that witnessing is itself a mode of perception whose horizon is the subject. That is to say, the suspicion that Delano cannot quite abandon is, finally, another way in which the *San Dominick*'s story *is* really all about him, as the object of a conspiracy that he characteristically imputes to Cereno rather than to the slaves, whom he never sees as agents. His paranoid version of the *San Dominick*'s story would *end* with his death, whereas a longer view—one that achieved the decentering of Delano that he himself cannot imagine—might instead see him as simply *incidental* to that story. Delano's perspective, ultimately, falls into the pattern of historical denial that we have come to know as American exceptionalism, one that both affirms the complementary linear-cyclical view of history cited earlier and denies its significance for the United States, which must always remain *ascendant*.

In an effort to ward off these suspicions and reorient himself to his initial position of distanced observation, Delano uses the racial spectacles before him to prop up his customary sense of time. Worrying that the captain before him might be an imposter, he is calmed by catching sight of Cereno's profile, "whose clearness of cut was refined by the thinness incident to ill-health, as well as ennobled about the chin by the beard. Away with suspicion. He was a true offshoot of a true hidalgo Cereno" (52–53). Cereno's "typical" physiognomy is part of the repertoire of uncomplicated visual signs through which Delano naturalizes social space. The hidalgo profile is a causeless effect that explains Cereno entirely, essentializing the nobility of the nobleman and erasing the history of power and domination that constructed it as nobility in the first place. Delano's naturalization of nobility is complemented, in the attentions he gives to the black characters, by his nobilization of nature. Confused by the strange behavior of one of the Spaniards, Delano stabilizes his sense of self by taking in the "pleasant sort of sunny sight" (60) of a young Negress breast-feeding a child, which he reads as "naked nature . . . pure tenderness and love" (61). His voyeurism is rendered "innocent" by his citation of sentimental forms, which deflect the possibility of sexual desire by insisting, instead, that this moment is about the timeless value of maternal affection and, as a result, stabilize Delano's location in time. Under Delano's gaze, the black woman becomes a monument to the naturalness of human affections, relegated, within the space of the ship that the bachelor-sailor understands as constitutively masculine, to the indefinite anteriority of the noble savage; he locates in her a "nature" that reads as always anterior to civilized self-possession even as it regenerates the civilized subject. By interpreting race and maternality as alike part of nature, Delano manages to naturalize historical positions, looking away from signs that confuse him and instead idealizing the spectacle of "the black upholding the white" (45) as a beautiful and natural relationship.

Delano's sentimental-monumental readings of racial spectacle as reflecting the "natural" order of things are ironically inverted in his vision of Atufal, the "colossal" rebel who plays the part of a shackled slave, as taking monumental form. Having decided to take charge of the hull, Delano is startled, as he walks on deck, by "the unexpected figure of Atufal, monumentally fixed at the threshold, like one of those sculptured porters of black marble guarding the porches of Egyptian tombs" (78). This fleeting glimpse of a sculpted, rather than "natural," monument, which follows soon after Delano's vision of Babo as a "Nubian sculptor" (74), here signifies both artifice and truth; that is, it suggests simultaneously the (historical) constructedness of the scene that Delano misunderstands as the natural order of things and the (historical) reality of the violence that has turned the ship into a floating tomb. After a moment of disorientation, however, Delano decides to read Atufal's monumental presence not as a trace revealing the artifice of the social forms that surround him but as a sign proclaiming that all is still in order upon the ship. The shackled slave confirms, for him, the image of Cereno's command, upon which his own sense of security depends.

The centrality of monumentalism to Delano's identity is emphasized as he maintains, toward the end of the narrative, that although his initial reading of the ship was proved utterly wrong, it was still the best one, because it ended up saving his own life, allowing him "to get the better of momentary distrust, at times when acuteness might have cost me my life" (101). His monumental ignorance allows the American to frame his own survival as the inevitable and necessary result of history. Delano insists on enforcing a recollection of the rebellion that emphasizes the victory of the whites— advising Cereno to forget the rest. This survival strategy is supported by Delano's facility in the kind of unconflicted mourning demanded by the monument, which imposes closure rapidly in order to transmit that resolution to the ages. His advice to Cereno—"The past is passed. Why moralize upon it? Forget it" (101)—is based on this kind of mourning, which averts the complications, painful contradictions, and lingering attachments that would come with working through the experience. In support of his view, Delano once again calls upon nature, illustrating the process of forgetting by pointing to the bright sun, blue sea, and blue sky, which, he asserts, "have turned over new leaves" (101). The awkward twist of phrase in the middle of Delano's sentence ironically highlights the artificiality of his reliance upon natural metaphors, not simply because sun, sea, and sky all lack leaves but because his appeal to the "naturalness" of forgetting as a way of negotiating one's existence in time collapses a number of distinct temporal tropes—the "eternal" time of the sea, the fickle alternations of sky, the diurnal pattern of the sun, and the seasonal model of renewal—against a text-based model of moving forward. The aesthetic painfulness of this phrasing, that is, points the reader to the way Delano continues to do damage, as he clumsily conflates these different modes of time into a single effect organized by a simple and unbridgeable distinction between *then* and *now*.

The significance of this conflation escapes Delano, who, the narrator reminds us, is "incapable of satire or irony" (51), unable to grasp more than one level of meaning or mode of temporality at a time. Cereno, however, feels the pain in Delano's sentence acutely and responds by insisting on the continued presence of the past in the form of human memory. Cereno's insistent juxtaposition of "now" with "then" emphasizes his consciousness of his own temporal dislocation. Like his ruined ship, Cereno appears as a remnant of the imperial past, recalling, for Delano, "his imperial countryman Charles V" (41). Along with this located historical referentiality, Cereno also embodies an indefinite temporal alterity, which situates him as somehow *apart from* the present. His responses to Delano's questions are muted and delayed, he appears to suffer flashbacks, and he reacts to Delano's presence "like some somnambulist suddenly interfered with" (43). Cereno's apparent inability to coincide fully with the present that he inhabits marks him as melancholic, suspending the past within the present, powerless to complete the work of mourning that would put an end to this suspension. This resistance to abandoning the past counters the blithe violence of Delano's forgetting, but Cereno can make no more use of history than Delano, because his melancholic silence provides no way for past and present to enter into generative dialogue. Although the Spanish captain, at the end of the tale, speaks unreservedly about his past suffering, he refuses consolation, countering Delano's suggestion that he think of the trade-winds as "human-like healing ... friends" with the response, "With their steadfastness they but waft me to my tomb" (101). Cereno's dismissal of Delano's gesture toward "healing" repudiates the American's sentimental personification of these natural forces and the parallel naturalization of economic history implied in the very notion of the trade-wind, renouncing the romanticized vision of the (slave) trader working in harmony with nature. Yet the only thing that the Spaniard can put in place of this romantic vision is his imminent demise. Cereno's melancholy rejection of Delano's monumental forgetting replaces his appeal to eternity with an insistence on decay, as in the Baroque allegory. But instead of using this revision of history as a means of intervention, Cereno flees into the security of his own allegory. Identifying himself as the corpse of the untimely, he collapses the temporal distance that allows allegory to speak as such. Looking (back) on himself as a ruin, Cereno cannot reconceive his own place in time as having anything to do with a future; instead, his melancholy ends in his own mute death. In this sense, we can see Cereno, no less than Delano, working not to enliven but to damage his relationship to the remembered past. Delano manages to do so by purging the troublesome parts of history from his own memory; Cereno, in contrast, abandons himself to the past and so removes himself from history. The limitations of the two captains' temporal perspectives deny interpretation the ability to move toward a vitalized but radically indefinite future, pointing, instead, only in the direction of self-consolidation or self-annihilation.

In marked contrast to the temporal tidiness of Delano's amnesiac perspective, "Benito Cereno," like its namesake, makes a mess of time. This disorder begins with the narrative, which is, as its narrator acknowledges, not "set down in the order of occurrence" but "retrospectively or irregularly given" (100). Even the signs marking the regular progression of clock-time, the ritualized parading of Atufal in chains and the sounding of the ship's bell, which rings "with a dreary graveyard toll, betokening a flaw" (49), register their own wounded limitations. The narrative's resistance to the dominance of either linear-historical or simultaneous-monumental time suggests that the past can only be effectively engaged if one is able to work with a notion of time as discontinuous and fragmentary. This refusal of orderly progression enables the texture of time to fluctuate throughout the tale: now slowed to a trancelike near emptiness, now suspended in moments overstuffed with significance and quivering with multiple possibilities. Indeed, these two temporal states are frequently mapped onto an identical narrative space, as the "retrospective" perspective, adopted once the rebellion has been revealed, locates in precisely those passages where Delano saw nothing much happening a tangle of intensely present possibilities. In this sense, the space of the story, as Philip Fisher has observed, "suffers from simultaneity."[54] The sheer painfulness of this kind of simultaneity, however, marks it as an ironic re-citation of the "simultaneity" enfolded in the timelessness of the monumental or the comforts of the sentimental. It is within this kind of simultaneity, which registers the erasures, elisions, and approximations of monumental time, that history can be understood not as the means of (national or personal) self-consolidating but rather as, in Frederic Jameson's apt phrase, "what hurts": that which resists, opposes, and dissolves individual and aggregate attempts at transcendence.[55] Melville's awareness of this damage accounts for his approach to Amasa Delano's 1817 narrative, which attempts neither to confirm Delano's original text nor to refute it but to *fragment* it, breaking apart the earlier document to reveal its contradictions and to multiply the historical referents behind its allegorical gestures. This multiplicity emphasizes the purpose of countermonumental allegory, which is not to rewrite history by substituting one story for another but to make known the partiality of the substitutions that pass as official history. Melville's revision of Delano's purportedly historical narrative reshapes it into a history of (and in) the present.

This fragmentation of Delano's narrative (and of "Benito Cereno" itself) is most visible in the legal documents that interrupt the story, which induced the editor of *Putnam's Monthly* to lament Melville's inability to write a "connected tale."[56] The disconnections introduced by these documents, however, are precisely the point of this section, as the narrative emphasis on their fragmentary appearance suggests. Where Delano's transcript identified the court documents as representing the whole truth—"officially translated, and inserted without alteration, from the original papers"[57]—Melville's tale declares that they are "extracts . . . selected, from among many others, for partial translation" (89). The alterations that Melville makes in the text of the documents themselves further emphasize their disintegration. Some of these changes are clearly designed to multiply the narrative's allegorical possibilities; most notably here, Dago, one of the rebels, identified as a "caulker" by profession in Delano's text, is described in Melville's as a "gravedigger" (90). Melville's revisions, as Susan Weiner has argued, throw both the veracity and the referentiality of the legal text into doubt. Not only do the changes that he makes to the deposition challenge the authority of the "real thing," but his decision to avoid revealing the "source" for his narrative also compels the reader to speculate on its historical referent(s).[58] While Melville's readers in 1855 might well have been unaware that the novella was based upon a putatively historical account published three and a half decades before, they would likely have had in mind other slave uprisings on U.S. soil, from Gabriel's Rebellion to Nat Turner's abortive revolt; moreover, the alteration and invention of detail in "Benito Cereno" deliberately invites other events, such as the Haitian revolution and the *Amistad* incident, into its historical overlay as well. These manifold historical references can serve to discourage the reader from severing the present-tense world from the "past" represented in the tale, since, unlike a singular citation, the dispersed allusions resist closure, making the subject of the narrative appear as ongoing. This dispersion also allows Melville to retemporalize the maternal body in his tale. In Delano's account, the court decides to view the slave women and children as "innocent" of the conspiracy, whose violence and cunning it understands to be the product of the male slaves alone (although these "non-conspirators" are nevertheless punished by being forced to watch the execution of the ringleaders), but Melville's reworked version represents the women as not only "knowing to the revolt" (98) but also as active participants within it, noting their desire to torture as well as kill the Spaniards executed in the course of the rebellion and commenting that during the battle with the American sailors, they encouraged the fighting by singing "melancholy songs to the Negroes, and . . . this melancholy tone was more inflaming than a different one would have been" (98). This information recasts Delano's earlier observation, stimulated by the sight of the breast-feeding woman, that the ship's Negresses, "like most uncivilized women . . . seemed at once tender of heart and tough of constitution; equally ready to die for their infants or fight for them. Unsophisticated as leopardesses; loving as doves" (61). The revelation of the conspiracy, of course, points out the temporal blindness emphasized within the narrator's representation of Delano's strategies of sentimental self-consolidation; his inability to reconcile his own observation of deadly maternal toughness with his impression of the breast-feeding spectacle as both "pleasant" and "quite sociable" appears, in the wake of subsequent events, deeply ironic (60). Yet while the revelation of a secondary meaning within Delano's sentimental paean to the noble savagery of the slave-mother suggests the deliberate refusal to see the contradictions implicit within the affectively active but socially passive ideal of the all-protective mother—suggesting, in effect, a sentimental *denial* of the agency inherent in a figure constituted entirely around the future of the child—the deposition takes this challenge to the sentimental temporality of the mother a step further, since the existence of children is nowhere there cited as an alibi for the women's ferocity or their melancholy contributions to the battle. Hence, although the reader could be *expected* to connect the women's violence back to the figure of the mother, nowhere is the reader *directed* to do so—an omission that shadows forth the possibility of female action on behalf of the self rather than the child.

While the fragmentary remains of Delano's narrative within Melville's tale contest both the conception of history as a lost totality calling out to be monumentalized and the naturalization of the family based on the historically instituted construction of a complementary heterosexuality, the deliberate insertion of countermonumental spectacles constructed not from textual but from *human* remains both follows and inverts the logic of sentimental critiques of the slave system; it emphasizes the human costs concealed behind this conception without associating that emphasis with the values associated with privacy—for these spectacles remain inseparable from their deliberately public placement in the narrative. The first of these spectacles is the suspended skeleton of the slaveowner Don Alexandro Aranda. In Amasa Delano's narrative, the rebels, who believed their freedom would only be secure if they killed Aranda, were said to stab him and dispose of his body by tossing it overboard. The pragmatic violence of Delano's account is replaced by allegorical violence in Melville's revision, however, as Aranda's burial at sea is replaced with his unburial. Concealed for most of the first part of the narrative, Aranda's prematurely exposed bones are revealed, at precisely the moment it becomes clear that the black "slaves" are actually rebels, to be affixed to the prow of the ship, where they have been put in place of the ship's original figurehead, "the image of Christopher Colon, the discoverer of the New World" (93). Under the skeleton, the cryptic message "Follow your leader," in Spanish, has been written. The deposition fragments explain that Babo has arranged this spectacle and then used it in a ritual of intimidation, showing Aranda's bones to Cereno and the other Spaniards, asking each of them in turn "whose skeleton that was, and whether, from its whiteness, he should not think it a white's," and then advising them that resisting his authority will cause them to "follow [their] leader" (93).

Sanborn has provocatively argued that the melancholy spectacle of Aranda's skeleton turns the nineteenth-century fantasy of sentimental mourning inside out. Sanborn identifies Aranda's bones as recalling the Puritan funerary emphasis on skeletal forms, thus representing "the recursion of a pre-sentimental understanding of the relation between body and spirit. No longer the symbol of personality, the corporeal self has become, once again, a purely indifferent sign."[59] The story's return to this older iconography of death thus reverses the historical development that I outlined in chapter 1 as marking the retemporalization of the body in the nineteenth century, from the Puritan theological emphasis on transience to the affective/sexual continuity established in the name of grief. The skeletal sign, in this sense, mocks the redemption of loss by meaning promised in both sentimental appeals to grief and monumental configurations of completeness. We should recall, however, that the Puritan death's head is also layered upon earlier mortuary iconography, the late medieval *danse macabre*. Whereas the dance of skeletons deployed death as a compensation for living, emphasizing its indifference in contrast to worldly differences of wealth, fortune, and social position, the Puritan revision reinflected the moral pedagogy associated with this sign, insisting upon the one difference that mattered in death —the distinction between election and damnation—and thus stressing not only the inevitability of death but also the irreversibility of postmortem judgment.[60]

In Melville's resurrection of Aranda's bones, then, the "impartial" authority of "divine judgment" is replaced by an emphasis on human judgment, which is always interested and located. What Sanborn terms the skeleton's "indifference" allows it to perform crucial differentiating work within the story. The skeletal countermonument undoes the sentimental-monumental fantasy of universal feeling, which may be linked to the isolation of "timeless" significance associated with the work of the symbol, and emphasizes instead the radical *proliferation* of invested meanings around Aranda's uncovered bones. Babo's ironic question concerning the skeleton's identity —whether its whiteness proves it a white's skeleton—supplants the color white, as an ostensibly neutral physical description of bones, with the identity of whites, whose investment in racial violence brought about this inversion. Though the distinction between whiteness and blackness had worked to naturalize racial hierarchies, permanently securing freedom and privilege to Aranda and the other whites, the "shadow" that the Negro casts from this perspective is the end of whiteness as such: its exposure not as timeless natural fact but as a generational-historical formation, an effect of hereditarily organized power. For the blacks, then, the skeleton operates as both an emblem of their freedom, realized in the death of whiteness, and a symbol of their power over the Spaniards, secured by the threat of death. Accordingly, for the Spaniards, the skeleton is both a sign of their bondage and a warning signal. Cereno reads the skeleton as a melancholy reminder of his own emptiness. Covering his face as the skeleton is exposed, he cries out, "'Tis he, Aranda! my murdered, unburied friend!" (86). The temporal suspension of the skeleton—murdered but unburied—figures Cereno's own melancholic dislocation, his lack of place in the present tense. Yet Cereno's use of Aranda's name demonstrates his resistance to the suspension of Aranda's identity in death enforced by Babo's revolutionary act, which not only unburies the bones but also unnames them. After placing the bones on the prow of the ship, Babo repeatedly asks the Spaniards *whether* they know whose skeleton it is rather than telling them, questioning rather than confirming its (and their) identity. His message here—that the bones could as easily be theirs—strips Aranda of particularity and reduces him to type. Only after the rebellion has been put down and Babo executed are the bones again collected under the sign of Aranda as, "recovered," they are interred in a vault at St. Bartholomew's Church. The representation of this burial as a *recovery* underscores the workings of power in the writing of monumental history, which purports to heal the damaged forms of the past even as it enacts damage in the very gesture of "healing." This perpetuation of destruction under the guise of restoration emerges from the Americans' monumental reading of the skeletal spectacle. Ignorant of Babo's commentary exposing the contingency of racial identity, the Americans read Aranda's skeleton as embodying an affiliation that they understand as always-already racialized. As they prepare to retake the *San Dominick,* the skeleton appears to the American sailors to be "beckoning the whites to avenge it"; in response, the ship's mate bellows "Follow your leader!" as the Americans board (88). Representing the purpose of their attack on the ship as the reclamation of Aranda's dead body more than the reenslavement of the Africans' live ones, the Americans read whiteness as a given, the "natural" basis of alliance between Europeans and Americans against Africans. The racialized (re)consolidation of Don Aranda, then, marks the silencing of the play of differential meaning around the unnamed bones by the emergence of a victorious differentiating power in the Americans, whose military force underwrites the legal resolution of the rebellion.

These located readings emphasize the partial and limited nature of interpretation within the world of the story (and that of the reader), but the function of the skeleton in the narrative as a whole moves in the opposite direction, highlighting the uncertainty of the allegorical register in which it operates. One way of reading the skeleton—as gesturing toward the idea of death—is suggested by the narratorial description of the bones as "death for the figure-head" (86). The association of the skeleton with the idea of death parallels the narrative with the message of the *danse macabre*: a reminder that regardless of race or social location, enslavement or freedom, all are equally subject to death. This reflection on transience situates "Benito Cereno's" ethical implications within a postsentimental conception of human community based on finitude, making it possible to read the narrative as deploying the inevitability of death to insist on justice in the present—a conception of community that we might understand in relation to my earlier discussion of contemporaneousness in Harper's own postsentimental poem. The reading of the skeleton as a figure insisting on the erasure of racial difference echoes Babo's ironic commentary on the skeleton, which annulled white privilege by matching social whiteness with its skeletal counterpart. Yet this emphasis on death as dissolving racial difference also makes race merely one among a number of differences expunged by death, disregarding the historical specificity of the bloody power struggles waged in the name of race and turning the narrative's suggestive exploration of racial history into a negation of that history.[61] To read the skeleton as simply allegorizing the human condition, then, risks producing an ethical interpretation of the narrative at the expense of a historical one, sacrificing materiality for universality, whereas the ultimate challenge of the countermonument, as I have suggested, is to find ways of expanding the horizons of what appears as "historical" thought. Melville's location of the skeleton in the place formerly occupied by the figure of Christopher Columbus, identified in the narrative as "the discoverer of the New World" (93), returns a (broadly) historical frame to the allegory. The narrative's substitution of death for Columbus is, in this sense, an allegorical equation designating an epoch of violence masked as progress, the effects of which never quite catch up with its own self-image. The gap between Columbus's displaced figure and the displayed skeleton outlines the historical erasure of this violence in reverse. In this sense, the skeleton signifies not the idea of death as a universal future but the materiality of death in the occluded past; in place of the gesture toward death's inevitability, this reading insists that history could have happened otherwise—that although death in general might not be avoidable, specific deaths, untold millions of them, were.

Two possible allegorical readings of the skeleton's significance thus circle around one another, suspending the figurehead between past and future, between experienced "history" and idealized "truth." The divergent directions of the allegory are therefore connected in an ironically doubled present tense. Paul de Man's aforementioned examination of the temporality of irony argues that it works, like allegory, to demystify the transcendental symbol and to emphasize a "truly temporal predicament." Yet the temporality of irony, as we saw, is the "reversed mirror image" of that of allegory.[62] The mode of the present is associated, in "Benito Cereno," with Babo, mastermind of both the rebellion and the deceptive show staged for the American, whose perpetual presence recalls Cereno whenever his mind has "wandered" into traumatized reflections on the past. Babo's skill as ironist enables him to locate freedom within the very rituals of slavery, as his inversion of the "significant symbols" of padlock and key demonstrates (51); his subterfuge evokes a duplicity of meaning from even the most single-minded commentary, as when he inspires Delano to announce in admiration that he cannot call Babo a slave (45). Even Babo's silence at the end of the tale speaks ironically, supplanting the legal suppression of his voice with a willfully resistant enactment of that condition.

The final scene of "Benito Cereno" confirms Babo's posthumous position as the "reversed mirror image" of the allegorical skeleton. Executed to excess (his body is dragged, hung, and then burned), Babo nevertheless remains a living presence at the end of the narrative:

> [Babo's] body was burned to ashes, but for many days, the head, that hive of subtlety, fixed on a pole in the Plaza, met, unabashed, the gaze of the whites; and across the Plaza looked toward St. Bartholomew's church, in whose vaults slept, then as now, the recovered bones of Aranda; and across the Rimac bridge, looked toward the monastery, on Mount Agonia without; where, three months after being dismissed by the court, Benito Cereno, borne on the bier, did, indeed, follow his leader. (102)

The ritual public display of Babo's severed head references a common fate for slaves convicted of inciting rebellion (which, in fact, was precisely the sentence meted out to five of the rebels by the Spanish court in Delano's account); it is meant to serve as a warning to observing blacks in precisely the way that Babo used Aranda's bones as a warning to the whites.[63] Yet Babo's "unabashed" gaze turns this symbol of defeat into an ongoing critique, just as his rhetorical juxtaposition to the remains of both Aranda and Cereno in this *tableaux mortant,* enfolding time within and through the gaze of those violently excluded from official history, challenges the narrative arrangement of the rebellion that would locate closure in his execution. Babo's exceptional position, that is, recalls the duality of the sacred as it signifies not only that which we hold most holy but also that which cannot be touched without profanation, an ambivalence tied to the extraordinary historical violence executed under cover of this term. But it also emphasizes the critical possibilities that can emerge from a deliberate refiguring of exceptional temporalities. If Babo's execution refounds the civilized order by projecting him into the category of the exception, his refusal to remain quietly dead there—his prophetic insistence on looking back at the future as past—also suggests what might happen when a presumably stabilizing manifestation of sacred time is instead given the force of untimeliness.

Babo's asynchronic status, in this sense, allows the final sentence to draw together three disparate moments in time, enacting a conjunction that does not exist within the space of the diegesis.[64] In the complicated time zone established in the sentence, the collapse of past, present, and future deaths into the space of a "then as now" spanning an indefinite period of time creates what Benjamin might identify as a dialectical image, enclosing "time filled by the presence of the now . . . blasted out of the continuum of history."[65] The now-time of the dialectical image, as I suggested earlier, stops time in a different manner than the timelessness of the monument; the lack of reconciliation between its different elements beckons instead toward the ongoing production of historical consciousness. The image, which brings together both types of allegory suggested by the skeleton-figurehead, the allegory of ideas (realizing the universality of death in the deaths of all three characters) and the historical allegory (since even death here does not erase imperial/racial hierarchies), ties these gestures to the past and the future together in its unabashed insistence on the present. Significantly, however, the American is excluded from the *tableaux mortant*; indeed, the final paragraph of the story appears to have forgotten Delano entirely. This omission conveys the inability of the sentimental/monumental perspective to grasp the content of history effectively. Babo's enduring gaze might, as some critics have suggested, imply that the American's escape from confronting the implications of this scene of death may be only temporary, but the image itself cannot predict the future—it can only insist on its connection to the "then as now." This insistence does not, however, abandon the future to "fate" but underscores its radical dependency on present-tense action. And it is this provocation—the suggestion that time *will* tell, but only if we rethink how we listen—that is the effect of the countermonumental perspective.

Of course, not all of "Benito Cereno's" readers have patiently accepted this dictate. C. L. R. James, for instance, has argued that "Benito Cereno," though one of Melville's finest works, is, in the end, too self-consciously formal, reflecting "the shallowness of modern literature." For James, the tale's attention to form suggests that Melville had "lost his vision of the future" because he did not invent any "new type[s] of human being" in its characters.[66] James's insistence on the non-newness of the dramatic personae may overstate the case; as Arnold Rampersad suggests, the revolutionary Babo might indeed be counted as a new kind of character in American literary history.[67] Pinpointing Babo's literary-historical status does not of itself, however, answer James's charge of "shallowness," which attaches not to character but to form.[68] But James's investment in the humanness of character over the ostensibly inhuman matter of form, and his consequent frustration with Melville's inversion of this valuation, may well have caused him to miss the direction of Melville's "vision of the future," which is projected, like Babo's gaze, outside the diegetic frame of the tale. The manipulation of hyper-self-conscious forms and the failed perspectives of deliberately static characters in "Benito Cereno" do fill the narrative with a sense of exhaustion, yet this exhaustion need not be seen as reenacting, on the authorial level, Cereno's shattered abandonment of the future. Rather, the breakage of the fragmentary narrative reveals an effort to create, in its interstices, not a new kind of character but a new kind of *reader*. This reader, unlike Delano, would resist reading as a form of self-consolidation and would instead view the necessarily dispersed and uncertain attempts to read the narrative as establishing an understanding that is always provisional and subject to change.

The provisional nature of this interpretive labor has meant, as I noted at the outset of this section, that critics have often been painfully unsure what to think of "Benito Cereno." I want to add, by way of conclusion, that I am not attempting, in constellating what I have identified as the counter-monumental antislavery perspective in "Benito Cereno" with the works of two explicitly committed writers, Douglass and Harper, to solve the problem of Melville's "quietism" in relation to political debates on slavery in the 1850s once and for all—for that quietism itself, as Maurice Lee elegantly demonstrates, has ongoing meaning. Lee's caution in response to twentieth-century readers' celebratory assessments of the belated "truth" of Melville's tale should remind us of the advisability of continued wariness about the histories implied in our critiques: that the discovery of the "now" in Melville's story—a now connected by James and other critics to contemporary anticolonial and anti-imperial struggles—not be enacted in a manner that implies that, as Lee puts it, "Melville apparently speaks to *us* at the expense of an earlier *them*."[69] The problem with assuming that *we* are the readers who can finally complete "Benito Cereno"—or "The Slave Auction" or "What to the Slave Is the Fourth of July?"—is that by doing so, we would fall into an error of monumental proportions, overlooking these three texts' most lasting contribution to debates over the politics of memory: the necessity of continually interrupting foundational narratives of nation and family insofar as they posit the timelessness of the sacred to cover over the exceptional time of the sacrifice.

Conclusion: Engaging Moments of "Danger"

Earlier in this chapter I opened the question of how the countermonument tells time by reviewing the critical gestures made by a number of late-twentieth-century Holocaust countermonuments.[70] Of course, the counter-monumental projects constructed from the 1970s through the 1990s in relation to the Holocaust and the temporality of 1850s critiques of U.S. slavery would seem to differ in one crucial respect: in the latter case, the specific social problem being addressed was not "over" in any sense of the word. Yet to pose the difference in this way omits the very challenge to logics of completion inherent in the countermonumental perspective: its insistence on problematizing the belief that the termination of a specific event marks its conclusion. The driving impulse behind the countermonumental trend in post-Holocaust commemorative work, for instance, was a conviction of the potential danger of succumbing to the relief that the Holocaust has ended. For this reason, I close this chapter by reflecting on the comparable critiques of the monument enacted in two twentieth-century revisionary projects: Horst Hoheisel's proposal to blow up Berlin's Brandenburg Gate and the alteration of Lincoln Park in Washington, D.C., through the addition of a statue of Mary McLeod Bethune.

Hoheisel's polemical 1995 proposal, which he entered in Germany's national competition for an official memorial to the Jews murdered in the Holocaust but which was, unsurprisingly, not chosen, appears to constitute its effect around the spectacular impact of a single act. As James Young put

it, "Rather than commemorating the destruction of a people with the construction of yet another edifice, Hoheisel would mark one destruction with
another destruction."[71] Yet this emphasis on the most dramatic moment of
Hoheisel's proposed countermonument occludes the multiple continuities
contained in the proposal. Indeed, the history of the Brandenburg Gate suggests the malleability that the iconography of the monument is designed to
efface. Originally commissioned in the late eighteenth century to replace an
earlier city gate, the neoclassical Gate, which supports a figure of the God-
dess of Victory carrying peace into Berlin, expressed a protonationalist vision that was taken up and reconfigured in a number of historical settings:
as a sign of Napoleonic victory over Germany (Napoleon's forces removed
the figure of Victory and carried it back to France); as a prominent prop for
Third Reich iconography; as part of the Berlin Wall; and finally as a symbol
of the end of the Cold War. Hoheisel's proposal can be understood as taking
part in and reinflecting this chain of events: the commemorative explosion
of the gate, in this light, echoes prior reconfigurations, amplifying the way
they themselves signal the *historicity* of the nation's purportedly timeless
self-image. Moreover, the high drama implied in the explosive gesture was
not, crucially, the end of the proposal. Hoheisel included a specification that
the wreckage of the gate be ground to dust, sprinkled over the site, and
marked with commemorative plaques. In this way, visitors to the site would
continue to interact with the history of the gate by literally walking through
the remains of the monument, an interaction that would model an ongoing
process of meaning-making.

For that reason, Hoheisel's proposal, I suggest, should be engaged not
only as a dramatic rearticulation of the past but also as a rather more pedestrian one—one that suggests, along with the writings I have discussed in
this chapter, that "revolution" can also be experienced in ordinary time,
though only when that time is itself experienced differently. What Hoheisel's, Douglass's, Harper's, and Melville's works exhibit in common is the
work of ruination: the effort to dig up, expose, and, crucially, not erase but
redistribute the buried foundations of the nation's self-image as it resonates
across both public and private "spaces." That said, however, we should keep
in mind that a version of the pedestrian interactivity which I have cited as
key to the intervention proposed in Hoheisel's countermonument is already
in place in many recent invocations of memorial, in a way that may finally
sustain traditional monumentalism. In the wake of the surprising public response to Maya Lin's Washington, D.C., Vietnam War Memorial, the move

to incorporate spaces of "interactivity" in memorial installations has become increasingly familiar; American memorials, in particular, appear to place a great deal of faith in the usefulness of offering paper, index cards, or other places where visitors might inscribe their responsive thoughts. This aspect of contemporary memorial seemingly replaces the belief that the monument's audience all think alike about its meaning with an insistence on the democratic plurality of the audience's thoughts. Yet although this move may have a significant reparative effect on the ability of the memorial to console the viewer, its logic remains continuous with forms of nineteenth-century consolation insofar as both assume that a benevolent collective effort in the present may help "cure" ongoing emotional damage.[72] The ostensibly democratic "dialogue" taking place in the collection of the memorial-viewers' responses lacks a specifically dialogic component, insofar as the collection of responses itself is assumed to be the significance of the gesture, rather than a space where signification may itself begin to be assessed. Accordingly, the putative interactivity of much contemporary memorial corresponds, finally, to the liberal structuring of the complementarity of public/private forms established in the nineteenth-century monumental/sentimental coupling; by "making space" for viewers' responses but failing to make a time in which those responses might be more effectively engaged, the interactive memorial simply complements the sentimental assumption that the point of the past is to complete the observing subject.

A rather less dramatic response than Hoheisel's to the imperial implications of national monumentality is visible in the 1974 addition to Lincoln Park. That park (then Lincoln Square) had seen the unveiling, in 1876, of the Freedmen's Memorial Monument, a commemoration of the end of slavery in the United States designed by Thomas Ball, a white sculptor, and built through the fundraising efforts of former slaves. Ball's memorial depicts an upright Abraham Lincoln symbolically emancipating a male slave (whose figure is modeled on Alexander Archer, believed to be the last person captured under the Fugitive Slave Act); the representative freedman is depicted in the act of shaking off his chains and just beginning to rise from a kneeling position (an action that yet leaves him seeming to kneel before a white man). The freezing-in-time of this symbolic relationship between an imagined benevolent, upright (white) nation and the beleaguered but slowly rising African American has drawn sustained criticism, beginning with Frederick Douglass's 1876 speech at the unveiling.[73] Hence, the addition, nearly a century later, of a statue commemorating Mary McLeod Bethune opposite the Freedmen's Monument was construed by many as a deliberate response to the earlier installation.[74] The Bethune sculpture (which is also the first statue in the capital to depict a historically existing woman rather than an allegorical female figure) shows the standing educator, who was herself the child of freedmen, handing a tablet to two children, who represent the rising generation. The addition of a figure of a woman and two children to the masculine-nationalist symbolism of the Freedmen's Monument might seem simply to reinstall a heterofamilial model as the sign of the nation's future. But the children in the statue are, crucially, Bethune's students; hence, the statue's conventional reproduction of the monument's pedagogy—as itself a monument *to* pedagogy—might instead be understood to introduce a potential variation into the figuring of the child, though it is one that resonates critically only if we alter the conventional framework of teaching as yet another kind of "generational" succession and permit it to resonate otherwise in time.[75] One potential model for this alteration emerges from a rereading of the statue's inscription, a passage from Bethune's last will and testament, where, among the list of things Bethune "leaves" to her students are included "love," "hope," and "a thirst for education."[76] What arrests attention in this inscription of inheritance is the conjunction of the language of an optimistic futurity—the language of "hope"—and invocations of both affective attachment and bodily desire. Although the statue itself leaves implicit the generational structure of futurity, its direct response to a century-old invocation of "gradualist" national change also offers a potential reconfiguration of the logic of generation, as the passing of time is marked by the crossing of desiring bodies in space, leaving open the possibility of developing other modes of connection and communal inspiration.[77] That potential is amplified if we recall Samuel Delany's analysis of the public park as a space open to "contact" relations, those that need not fall into the more conventional forms of association that he calls "networking," a term that, I contend, aptly characterizes conventional structurings of both "national" and "familial" heritage.[78] But this kind of reconfiguration is only possible, finally, if we resist both the desire to hold tightly to reparative visions of monumental and memorial installations as making possible the reconsolidation of familiar forms (of subjectivity, citizenship, or memory) damaged by the passage of time *and* the impulse to have done with them by (melo)dramatically blowing them up, and work instead to amplify, even among the most "ordinary" invocations of the monument, the resonant echo of other possibilities for living among the ruins.

5

Representative Mournfulness

Nation and Race in the Time of Lincoln

> Strange (is it not?), that battles, martyrs, agonies, blood, even assassination, should so condense—perhaps only really, lastingly condense—a Nationality.
>
> —Walt Whitman, "The Death of President Lincoln"

In 1878, two years after the publication of Whitman's *Memoranda during the War,* the poet's friend John Burroughs wrote to him from New York, inviting him to give a talk on the anniversary of Lincoln's death. Though poor health prevented Whitman from carrying out the plan that year, on April 14, 1879, he managed to present the first version of his lecture on the death of Lincoln, which he would deliver a number of times over the following decade. To his dramatic depiction of the main event promised in the lecture's title —the scene of assassination and its panicky aftermath, adapted from *Memoranda*—the poet appended the hypothesis that the episode, in the end, would prove most significant *as* drama; its "flash of lightning-illumination" would highlight "those climax-moments on the stage of universal Time, when the Historic Muse at one entrance, and the Tragic Muse at the other, suddenly ringing down the curtain, close an immense act in the long drama of creative thought, and give it radiation, tableau, stranger than fiction."[1] Whitman's theatrical language locates this nation-making event outside the traditional narrative mode of conventional historiography, and indeed, outside language itself; he argues that the spectacle of Lincoln's death furnishes "a cement to the whole People, subtler, more underlying, than any thing in the written Constitution" by providing a "first-class tragic incident thoroughly identified with that People, at its head, and for its sake."[2]

The identification of the sixteenth president with "the people" is a familiar enough move in the memorial discourse for Lincoln, which stresses his extraordinary, and historically new, *ordinariness.* His distinction was that of exemplifying the possibility of an American life, of rising from an undistinguished family in the nation's backcountry to a seat at its center without (as his eulogists repeated again and again) losing touch with the virtues and the values of the common citizenry from which he had emerged. The memorial discourse thus emphasizes what we might call Lincoln's *representativeness*. The representative individual, for Ralph Waldo Emerson, was one "who is what he is from nature, and who never reminds us of others," yet who somehow "must be related to us, and our lives receive from him some promise of explanation."[3] In effect, the representative individual reminds us not of others but of *ourselves*—the fuller, better selves that circumstance may circumscribe but to which democracy promises at least the possibility of unfolding. Emerson's own 1865 eulogy for Lincoln identified him along precisely these lines, as "the true representative of this continent, . . . a heroic figure in the centre of a heroic epoch, . . . the true history of the American people in his time."[4] But as Emerson's language implies, Lincoln both kept pace with American history and moved, predictively, ahead of it: "Step by step he walked *before* [the people]; slow with their slowness, quickening his march by theirs."[5] The double temporal movement sketched by Lincoln's life-history is that of actualizing the potential of the nation, of embodying the becoming-possible of its best qualities. As the Reverend C. M. Butler of Philadelphia insisted, "we loved him as a second and better self—the possible self which we wished to be."[6]

There is, of course, nothing new in the tendency of the 1865 eulogies to posit Lincoln's character as one toward which the nation should aspire, since, as I have earlier observed, the insistence on using the "enkindled affection" awakened by recent grief to drive home the necessity of identifying with the dead's best qualities is central to nineteenth-century mourning culture. Nor is there anything new in the drive to posit the language of mourning as publicly significant, for nineteenth-century Americans frequently deployed the rhetoric of grief in response to the death of a public figure as a means of bonding and regenerating the nation, beginning with the national insistence on the patriotic duty of sorrow articulated in the wake of George Washington's death.[7] What makes Lincoln's case distinctive, I argue, is the particular quality of the affective rhetoric exhibited in the 1865 eulogies, which stressed as part of his illustrious career an especially developed capacity for feeling. Americans were exhorted to identify intimately with Lincoln in the national commemorative ceremonies following his assassination; they were, specifically, encouraged to grieve him by *identifying with his own grief,* and to use that recollected grief as a means of strengthening the progress of the nation. In this sense, the appeal to the Lincoln image posited not simply a better and stronger selfhood as the mourning nation's destiny but also a kinder and gentler one. And the fact that this regenerative kindness was most frequently accessed, in the eulogies, through reflections on the President's characteristic mournfulness posits his capacity for nationally significant sentimentality in a distinctive temporal mode, shading the proud look back at the nation's timeless origins with a tint of regret that itself, paradoxically, became part of that nation's monumental pride. In this way, the eulogies suggested, Lincoln's extraordinary martyrdom refounded the nation: he fathered it again by, in effect, mothering it.

Hence, the gestures toward the extraordinary time of Lincoln's life and death—what Emerson depicts as a "heroic era"—became charged with a peculiarly resonant sense of time, one that came to signify apart from, and yet within, the narrative of national history taken as a whole. The national temporal alterity accessed through the figure of Lincoln was associated, in Walt Whitman's writing, not only with his spectacular death but with this affective peculiarity of his "nature," which gestured, in its insistent mournfulness, toward a past that exceeded the conventions of the present. In a passage from *Memoranda during the War,* Whitman comments on the melancholy appearance of the president, "I see very plainly ABRAHAM LINCOLN's dark brown face, with the deep cut lines, the eyes, &c, and always to me with a deep latent sadness in the expression."[8] Whitman muses, "None of the artists or pictures have caught the deep, though subtle and indirect expression of this man's face. There is something else there. One of the great portrait painters of two or three centuries ago is needed."[9] The expression that Whitman read as remarkably untimely—a sadness so pronounced that decorum could not hide it, yet so subtle that the dead must be called up to reproduce it—appeared, to many observers, entirely timely during the years of the Civil War, when sadness was a historically appropriate feeling. Lincoln's mournfulness thus read as another demonstration that he belonged above all to the people; the melancholy face of the President reflected, to a bereaved public, its own intense anxiety and grief. Yet Whitman's emphasis on the unexpressed "something else" that lurked within the President's mournful expression suggests a distinction that sets it apart from the daily life of the country. His melancholy exceeds the history of the American aesthetic tradition, opening the nation not simply to the possibility but to the *necessity* of another form of time that might "capture" its significance.

In this chapter, I show how the retrospective mode associated, in Whitman's writing, with the sixteenth president intersected, in the eulogistic discourse that followed his assassination in 1865, with the proleptic function of his representative status to create a distinctive monumental vision of national mournfulness. In highlighting this vision, I develop an analysis of affective nationality that closely considers the peculiar temporality of national "feeling-in-common" by emphasizing the duality implied in the interaction of mourning's backward gaze and the progressive direction of patriotic nationalism. In the eulogistic discourse, the messianic love that Lincoln offered the nation—a love that revealed itself, above all, in his willingness to mourn the nation's losses—functions as a substitute for the as-yet-unfulfilled realization of democracy's promise. Yet despite the insistence in the 1865 eulogies on exemplifying Lincoln's democratic orientation by enshrining his (belated) commitment to emancipation, the imagined nation that he moved "before" during the war years, as Frederick Douglass remarked in 1876, remained, in form, essentially a white one.[10] Hence, the ability of affective nationalism to incorporate the very problems it purports to address is also part of my focus. I link this capacity to the manifestation, in the deployment of mournfulness as a mode of utopic national critique, of the unreconciled duality described earlier: an effectively melancholic melancholy. For if, as Giorgio Agamben has argued, melancholia's tenacious refusal to abandon attachment to a past object "offers the paradox of an intention to mourn that precedes and anticipates the loss of the object"—an object, Agamben suggests, that is not *lost,* per se, because it was never possessed, and perhaps never existed—then its past-directedness contains an oddly proleptic dimension, suggesting a prolonged effort to change the future by refusing to abandon the past.[11] In its attempt, in effect, to *mourn something into existence,* melancholia is endowed with a particular creative capacity, an ability to create space, in Agamben's terms, "for the existence of the unreal."[12] Yet the generative capacity of this space is hampered by the projection of that unreal into a time that is unrealized, as it depends on what I identified in chapter 4 as the sentimental tendency to produce a sense of affective simultaneity that lacks directedness. In this light, the affect-image of persistent mournfulness associated with the failures of democracy in historical practice—an affect-image that finds fetishistic expression in the picture of the sad-eyed Emancipator—reveals the simultaneous embrace and surrendering of the horizon of its own critique.

The monumentalization of affective leadership in the eulogies for Lincoln has had a prolonged and increasingly diffuse afterlife. Indeed, if the American public has become addicted to watching itself mourn, if participation in mournful rituals of national remembrance has become one of the most familiar ways in which it articulates to itself its co-presence *as* a public, then this, I suggest, is the end result of a nationalism whose always-ambivalent relation to the state has caused it to invest itself more strongly in the redemptive power of the people's collective emotion than in the belief that democracy will ever fully manifest itself through legal practice.[13] Lauren Berlant's reading of the complex political significance attached to the overwhelming public responses to death of national figures who signified as "political" only through displacement, figures such as John F. Kennedy Jr. or Princess Diana, identifies in this phenomenon "something like a lost revolutionary wrinkle in time, as the articulation of the sacred *against* the political," which appears "not as sovereign but as fallen law."[14] The structures of this mode of response—which is, as Berlant points out, in essence a political critique, albeit one rendered in terms that express political discontent as personal loss and woundedness—are, I propose, already present in the national mourning for Lincoln, though in an altered form given the distinct nature of the historical circumstances: not that Lincoln, as president, was directly linked to the state (for, as we will see, his virtues were often sacralized against the state) but that his death came during wartime, when the nation could bond together against a designated enemy, and not just its own underarticulated collective disappointment with democracy. Yet that disappointment, too, resonates through the rhetoric of mourning the fallen president, emerging in a preoccupation with his own desire for justice, a desire understood as rooted in personal affection rather than legal abstraction.

What I am calling the "time of Lincoln" thus has both a historical and a transhistorical resonance: it invokes at once the historical period associated with Lincoln's presidency and assassination and a transtemporal, quasi-reformist mode of national belonging. This mode, as I will show, was consolidated in and through the modes of representative mourning opened by Lincoln's own memorial speeches during the Civil War and then extended in the wake of his assassination to incorporate the appeal of the Lincoln-figure to a redemptive Americanness—forms of monumentalization that complicate the account of depersonalized serial nationality that Benedict Anderson has developed in his seminal work on forms of national memory. Indeed, the sacralization of personal feeling modeled in sentimental nationality—a model that, as I show, cites Biblical precedent in order to *exalt* the time of affect—incorporates both of the gendered modes cited in the preceding chapter, the "public" nationalist appeal of the monument, which emphasized the completeness of the nation, and the "private" affective mode associated with the sentimental family. As a consequence, however, the forms of nationally significant feeling established in the popular eulogistic discourse ironically perpetuated the asynchronicity attached to the figure of the black slave even as they sought to celebrate emancipation. In contrast, African American responses to Lincoln's assassination sought to depict black grief over the assassination as both a mode of affirmative national belonging and a form of affective labor that could allow African Americans to move forward in national time—a movement that was, as I will show via a reading of Elizabeth Keckley's 1868 memoir *Behind the Scenes: Thirty Years a Slave and Four Years in the White House*, hampered by the national reluctance to address the sexual dimension of racial subjection.

Sacred Time and National History

For Whitman, the kind of dramatic moment represented by Lincoln's death brought ordinary time to a standstill, turning history into a "tableau." Eventually, however, he believed that such radiant spectacles would be reinserted into genealogical time, becoming the nation's "most important inheritance-value."[15] Benedict Anderson's influential study of modern nationalism, *Imagined Communities,* considers precisely this mode of using the dead to order the nation in time. The nation's dead, for Anderson, take on a monumental function, creating a motionless time-space of identity between past and present that supports the day-to-day work of progress.[16] Anderson asserts that monumentality allowed modern nationalism to mitigate the temporal threat posed by the revolutionary rupture that founded the nation, which threatened to confound the continuity of national narrative; postrevolutionary nationalist genealogy buries its origins, so to speak, by conscripting the dead into its history. In this way, Anderson explains, nationalist commemoration entails "a curious inversion of conventional genealogy [which] start[s] from an originary present."[17] Although Anderson glosses the mechanics of this inversion, we may surmise that it is enabled by the temporal slippage entailed in identifying with the dead. For as he stresses, the deaths that found the nation (typically "exemplary suicides, poignant martyrdoms, assassinations, executions, wars, and holocausts") are those that the citizenry can recognize as in some sense its *own.*[18] Hence, while the citizens, located in serial time, are cognizant of their historical distance from the exemplary dead, the consolidation that Whitman describes as the "cementing" effect of national death functions precisely by drawing the people together, with the dead and with one another, in relation to national principles that occupy another form of time—what we tend to call the "timeless" or "eternal" truths of the nation. In this sense, as I argued in the preceding chapter, monumentalism seeks to stabilize the nation's progress through time by representing its ideals as always-already *completed* in its foundational act; its forms seek, accordingly, to emphasize this completeness over and above the ruptures associated with death.

In a later essay furthering his speculations on nationalism's relation to the dead, Anderson points out that one of the monumental forms favored by official nationalism is the National Cemetery, whose spatial organization of the dead reveals the evolution of a statistical conception of the "people." This form, he asserts, was first pioneered at Gettysburg in 1863.[19] I want to extend and, partially, to challenge Anderson's analysis by examining the *temporal* relation of the nation to its dead, and its relation to the monumental dimension of nationalism, framed in the renowned short speech delivered by Lincoln on that site during the November 19, 1863, dedicatory ceremonies. Lincoln had been invited to the ceremony only to deliver a few corollary remarks, a kind of governmental footnote to Edward Everett's keynote oration, which lasted two hours.[20] The time of national crisis that occasioned the Gettysburg dedicatory ceremony is stabilized (grounded, as it were) by the deliberately monumental association of time with place in both speeches. Everett's speech works through the history of democracy, beginning with a description of the cemetery at Marathon in ancient Greece, which locates soldiers' graves precisely where they fell in battle; he uses this description to make an analogy to the Gettysburg cemetery, which was designed in the same way, and then moves into an extended review of the battle in which they fell and its importance to the conflict in which the nation was then engaged. In place of the global history of democracy that Everett traces, however, Lincoln's brief remarks endow the location with a different sort of temporal transcendence; the nation, rather than democracy, becomes the transtemporal event in which the audience is invited to participate. The site identified in Lincoln's speech expands in space, rather than in time, and it does so, ironically, by seeming to *contract*; the locus of action in the speech narrows, from "this continent" in the first sentence, to "a great battle-field," to "a portion of that field," to "this ground," finally becoming simply "here," a word repeated eight times in the speech, with seven of those repetitions occurring in the last four sentences alone.[21] But although the immediate referent of "here" is the space of the cemetery itself, it is also, in a deferred sense, the *taking-place* of the "new nation [brought forth] on this continent" introduced in the address's opening sentence, linked to the present location by a pronominal echo effect. The cemetery is thus both a physical portion, a part, of the nation and a symbolic representation of the whole, just as the present is at once a transient moment, a piece of time, and a highly significant instance of the ever-unfolding *event* that is the nation.

The conversion of the present moment into a place of memory, a place apart from ordinary time, takes place in the address's eighth sentence, which reflects on its own place in history: "The world will little note, nor long remember what we say here, but it can never forget what they did here."[22] Latter-day commentators on the address often point to the ostensible irony of this sentence, which has, over time, become technically incorrect; most Americans can recite at least part of Lincoln's speech, but few know much about the Battle of Gettysburg itself. Yet accounting this development as ironic posits a distinction between words and deeds that is out of place in the logic of monumentality. The essence of the soldiers' action is not the particularities of the battle but the consecration of a symbolic site; in this sense, Lincoln's words *contain* the soldiers' deeds by defining them and rendering them (com)memorable. In urging his audience to carry on their unfinished work, Lincoln is, as Priscilla Wald has observed, asking them to become "symbols of the nation."[23] Nationalist action, here, is a process of *becoming symbolic*; it enables citizens to mimic the temporal transcendence of the symbol, rising above particularities to align themselves with monumental time.

Although the address initially foregrounds revolutionary rupture in its opening emphasis on the founding of a *new* nation, its appeal to the monumental offers a reassuring continuity, rhetorically creating a sense of American newness as an unbroken, unbreakable tradition. Hence, the "new birth of freedom" promised in the final sentence resonates not as a departure from the past but as a confirmation of it, a rebirth of the newness that is the nation's tradition, rendering the nation's present tense, in effect, a *taking-place* of already-known principles originating in that past.[24] The address creates this impression of spatiotemporal continuity by enfolding the present within the ongoing action emanating from the past, an enfolding effected most notably in the much-remarked rhetorical inversion in the middle of the address: "we cannot dedicate . . . this ground. . . . It is for us the living, rather, to be dedicated here to the unfinished work which they who fought here have thus far so nobly advanced."[25] The inversion performed in this sentence transposes the present-tense concrete act performed by the President and his audience—the dedication of the cemetery—into the timeless work of the infinitive, locating the present as a necessary moment in the unfolding of an action already under way. The dedication to the "unfinished work" carries the present forward, that is, toward a destined future: not simply the completion of the war but the temporal completeness of the nation-form.

The Gettysburg Address is noteworthy for its omission, in an era that aligned mortality with a distinctly sentimental pedagogy, of the deliberate solicitation of personal feeling that characterizes the nineteenth-century rhetoric of grief. Everett's address contained a number of such flourishes, but the closest Lincoln's speech comes to the language of emotion is his reference to "devotion" to the nation. Although the address represents the nation as a living entity, it is one that, despite repeated births, strangely lacks a body; or rather, it might be more accurate to say that the national body, birthed under masculine agency, emphasizes a vision of *endurance* over appeals to corporeal vulnerability and transience. Lincoln's address accordingly works even harder than the cemetery to keep the physical bodies of the nation's dead soldiers out of sight. Like the Gettysburg cemetery itself, then, his speech can seem strangely ahead of its time, looking forward from its location in the mid-1860s to the twentieth-century cenotaphic nationalism that Anderson considers as an index of the statistical abstraction of the citizen. Anderson's insistence on the anonymity of the citizen, derived from an electoral conception of the citizen as a "substitutable symbolic integer" organized horizontally, in token of democratic equality, takes shape, in his assessment, in the even horizontal rows featured in so many twentieth-century national cemeteries.[26] The address's affinity with an abstracted, horizontal-conceived equality (rather than, say, a meritocratic apportioning of citizenship on the basis of differing degrees of heroism or passionate national feeling) manifests in its rhetorical leveling of "these dead,"[27] who are, in the speech, differentiated only from the living, not from each other. Collected in this way, the dead lose all specificities, including both the spatiotemporal distinctions maintained in burying them *at* the site of death (which Everett's speech emphasizes) and the fundamental political split between the Union and Confederate forces—also represented, in much contemporary Northern writing, as a temporal difference between a properly progressive North and a backwardly aristocratic South. The address's avoidance of the body, either as symbol of the Union or in the rhetoric of deep feeling, distances corporeally linked specificities that might otherwise puncture or pervert its unbroken national/monumental continuum, introducing potential variations in the course of (national) time.[28]

This resistance to specificity recalls the way that, as Marc Redfield, in an analysis of Anderson, affirms, the presence of the (dead) body fundamentally troubles nationalist attempts to abstract the death of the symbolic citizen by making visible the loss of a specifiable person, and so "mark[ing] death's resistance to its own universality, recalling the inassimilable particularity and finitude of this death, the absoluteness of an irrecuperable loss."[29] Redfield's observation may serve to point us toward a distinction between sentimental and serial nationalisms that parallels the distinction between "public" and "private" simultaneities that I discussed in the preceding chapter, insofar as the sacralization of personal feeling complicates the chronological distinction upon which Anderson founds the modern nation. Within the framework of the nineteenth-century culture of mourning, each person is irreplaceably beloved to the survivors, who never get over the lingering pain of the particular loss; hence, grief, more than death, is what becomes universalized, not as a disembodied abstraction but as a shared testimony of nature to human origins, though, as we have seen, certain asynchronically disposed corporealities were held to impede that sharing. Indeed, we might say that Anderson's emphasis on serial nationality itself moves too quickly to dispose of the body, neglecting to fully consider the way the solicitation of personal feeling supports nationalisms that might be more accurately typed as affective rather than abstracted. For as Redfield also notes, the typical commemoration of soldiers as the nationalized dead itself partly mitigates the abstraction upon which Anderson insists, since soldiers are traditionally assumed to be male. As a result, Redfield argues, national mourning becomes the task of the feminized and, significantly, the maternalized subject: the bereft mother, grieving within the domestic sphere, is the implicit complement of the publicly commemorated fallen soldier, and "mourning is her destiny . . . because continuity is her function."[30] The mother-as-mourner is the soldier's ideal complement, from the standpoint of either sentimental or statistical nationalism, because her loss registers as primarily emotional, whereas the image of the bereaved spouse or child introduces more immediate economic questions—although the extensive losses sustained in the Civil War rendered it impossible to ignore these other domestic counterparts. In either case, however, the implicated mourner extends the "completed" narrative of public nationality by pairing it with a privatized story in which affective incompleteness becomes the principle of the nation's continuation in time.[31]

This pairing is itself paralleled in the convention of coupling Lincoln's brief address at Gettysburg to his less condensed, though still concise, Second Inaugural Address, delivered on March 4, 1865 (visible, for instance, in the Washington, D.C., Lincoln Memorial, where the two speeches are inscribed on opposing walls in front of a statue of the seated president). Counterposed to the abstracted monumentalism of the Gettysburg Address, the Second Inaugural, Lincoln's last major speech, can seem positively heavy with the flesh. The corporeality of the Second Inaugural attaches in particular to two issues merely glossed in the Gettysburg Address: the ongoing trauma of the war itself and the question that the Gettysburg speech subtly installed at the heart of that war, that of slavery. Delivered when the outcome of the war was yet uncertain, the Gettysburg Address moderated its references to the conflict—the war itself became a "testing" of the nation and the act of being killed in battle, "the last full measure of devotion."[32] But in early March of 1865, the surrender of the secessionist forces appeared imminent. With this promise of closure, Lincoln could represent the war as a *limited* rupture in national time—a traumatic historical wound, vast in its magnitude but capable of recuperation. The Second Inaugural accordingly emphasizes the awe-inspiring suffering of the living over the timeless principles underwritten by the dead. Mining the rhetorical archive of sentimental culture, it foregrounds the language of affect and authorizes national action through an appeal to divine law. The centerpiece of the Second Inaugural is the rendering of the Civil War as an exemplification of Matthew 18:7: "Woe unto the world because of offenses! For it must needs be that offenses come; but woe to that man by whom the offense cometh!" Lincoln identifies slavery as the "offense" that, "having continued through His appointed time, [God] now wills to remove."[33] Human suffering becomes a divinely ordained medium of compensatory exchange: "this terrible war," according to Lincoln, is the "woe" that the nation must suffer for the offense of slavery, itself a conversion of the bodily pain of blacks into the earthly material gain of whites who "[wring] their bread from the sweat of other men's faces."[34] The long history of bodily and emotional suffering that slavery represents is called into play directly in the speech, diminishing, by comparison, the relatively short duration of both the war and the nation itself:

> if God wills that [the war] continue until all the wealth piled by the bondsman's two hundred and fifty years of unrequited toil shall be sunk, and until every drop of blood drawn with the lash, shall be paid by another drawn with the sword, as was said three thousand years ago, so still it must be said "the judgments of the Lord, are true and righteous altogether."[35]

The Second Inaugural's revision of the cause of the war—from "testing" the durability of national principles to expiating the sin of slavery—opens a temporal frame larger than the one invoked in the Gettysburg Address, dislocating the historical importance of the Revolution in its graphic depiction of the still-older material practice of chattel slavery. Yet the extensive duration of the slave's suffering is itself diminished in relation to the longevity of Biblical truths, whose citation encompasses the ostensible history of civilization and whose resonance within Psalm 19, quoted at the end of the passage, invokes the completeness of the divine eternal plan. The affective language of embodied suffering thus calls into play a sacred temporality different from the protomodern monumental nationalism that resounds throughout the Gettysburg Address; in contrast to the symbolic tropes favored in the Gettysburg Address, the theodicity at the Second Inaugural's core aligns it with the messianic temporality of exegetic allegory, in which all earthly experience is the exemplification of Biblical principles. Its vision of timelessness aligns American national history and the monumental appeal of democratic truth with the dictates of divine law. At the same time as they decenter the nation, then, the Biblical appeals in the speech also authorize that nation's historical actions, providing spiritual compensation for the physical and emotional suffering of the war.

After the reference to Psalm 19, the Second Inaugural relocates itself according to the narrative of national history with which it opened, the story of the war itself. Significantly, however, it makes space for a continuation of the exceptional time invoked in the exegetic allegory by way of feeling. Its final paragraph moves to bring the temporal rupture represented by the war to a close, exhorting the citizens to "strive on to finish the work we are in, to bind up the nation's wounds, to care for him who shall have borne the battle and for his widow and his orphan, to do all which may achieve a just and lasting peace among ourselves and with all nations."[36] The restoration of linear-historical time is brought about through the language of regeneration: physical healing for the veteran and emotional healing for the bereaved. The speech surrounds the potential interminability of the war's awesome degree of woe, the suffering that sacralizes the nation's efforts, within a narrative of loss and recuperation that will restore the nation to corporeal and temporal wholeness, miming the reparative work of mourning. Yet unlike the temporal transcendence of the nationally symbolic *death* in the Gettysburg Address, the allegorical authorizing of national *suffering* in the Second Inaugural cannot be fully reconciled with the public history of the nation. For whereas, as Paul de Man notes, the symbol encapsulates the fantasy of transcending time, allegory, by virtue of its dependence on a *prior* narrative, demonstrates the irreducibility of the temporal gap that makes its mode of signification possible. The time-space of divine woe may coexist, in the speech, with national history, but it cannot be dissolved into the timeline of the nation.

The temporality of the body that suffers for the nation, then, differs from that of the one that dies for it; the latter may be dissolved into an abstracted monumentality, but the former maintains, if not an individual, a personal particularity—the particularity *of* the "personal"—that gestures insistently toward the painful passage of time, the cause of its suffering. The nation may be repaired in space, its wounds healed, its wartime division eradicated, but the periods of nationally significant suffering—four years of war, two and a half centuries of slavery—remain as a time apart, signifying, through the experience of redemptive pain, the value of the ideals of unity and freedom to which they appeal. The sacralizing of suffering, like the monumentalizing of the mourner, thus deploys the affective fallout of time as a means of emphasizing the timelessness of the ideals it embraces, providing both the opportunity and the necessity for the periodic renewal of that which is postulated as foundational about the nation. In the prolonged suffering of the slave and the lingering grief of the survivor, the presumably secular frame of American nationalism (as modern nationalism, in Anderson's view, is always akin to religious feeling but never identical to it) inclines toward the divine, though this divinity, significantly, is associated with the capacities of a redeemed humanity: the capacity to bleed and to weep and thus to bind together fellow-sufferers. And although Lincoln's insistence, in the Second Inaugural, on the collective significance of this exceptional time would shortly find a singular corporeal form—the image of the martyr-president himself—that corporeal singularity would nevertheless remain linked, in the popular imagination, to the belatedness of the particular suffering figure whose forms of regeneration were not specified at the close of the oration: the (ex-)slave.

The People Weeping: Representative Mournfulness and National Feeling

A little over a month after Lincoln delivered his Second Inaugural Address, the hopeful movement toward national restoration and healing that it expressed was fractured by his assassination. Lincoln's death became the occasion for an unprecedented exercise in national mourning, one that sought to bring closure to the national disruption occasioned not simply by the assassination of the president but by the prolonged and bloody conflict as a whole. The sermons and eulogies produced during this period exerted a strong influence on public opinion about how the nation should proceed after the war; many Northern clergy, in particular, urged a course of harsh retribution against the South, replacing Lincoln's insistence on leniency with a call for vengeance.[37] But these eulogies also laid the foundation for the particularly resonant image of Lincoln that exists in national memory, transforming him from a president about whom public opinion was deeply divided into a symbol of national unity. They accomplished this rapid transformation not by circulating new information about him but, as Barry Schwartz has observed, by "generating an emotional context in which people felt differently about what they knew about him," turning known *facts* about Lincoln into newly appreciated *truths*.[38] The new "emotional context" created during the national mourning for Lincoln incorporated, significantly, a particular context for understanding the national significance of emotion, including those of the President. A number of the memorials depicted Lincoln as unusually sensitive to the nation's sorrows. This sensitivity explained and legitimated the extraordinary anguish that, they maintained, the citizens felt in response to his death. And while some urged Americans not to overvalue their emotional responses to the event, most allotted feeling for the President a significant measure of importance, depicting grief as a measure of national belonging.[39] In this sense, the eulogistic discourse is remarkable for its resonant continuities—continuities that, significantly, resounded across speeches and writings emanating from both officially Christian and nominally secular sources. Though the sermons preached in Northern Christian churches, in particular, displayed a penchant for allegorizing Lincoln as a Christ-like figure and, accordingly, for deifying his wounds, that tendency was also marked in the rhetoric emanating from extrareligious authorities. The eulogistic image of the sacrificial leader thus indexes less the nationalist secularization of an "originally" religious image than the naturalization of that ideal—the transubstantiation of divinity into affectivity that characterized the nineteenth-century culture of sentiment.

Prior to his assassination, differing assessments of the President's capacity for feeling circulated. In some visions, his humble origins and "folksy" persona translated into an unrefined, even boorish insensitivity, a tragic (from the war-torn nation's perspective) lack of the sympathy that oriented the middle-class subject. An 1864 political cartoon makes this point forcefully. In the cartoon, the nation, personified as Columbia, appears before the President demanding the (impossible) return of her "500,000 sons"—the number of the war dead. Lincoln, his long legs slung awkwardly over the back of a chair, responds, crushingly, "By the way, that reminds me of a story."[40] In other visions, however, the President possessed the deep, even morbid sensitivity that came with a depressive personality. Friends and associates frequently commented on his "peculiar melancholy," reading it, as Whitman had, in the very lines of his face and body. According to Joseph Wilson Fifer, "[Lincoln's] melancholy seemed to roll from his shoulders and drip from the ends of his fingers."[41] Lincoln himself contended that his propensity for melancholy should be considered a misfortune, rather than a fault; following the contemporary medical understanding of depression, he believed his emotional tendencies resulted from a physiological disorder.[42] The biographical discourse on Lincoln has repeatedly singled out this depressive tendency as part of his success, beginning with the work of William Henry Herndon, one of Lincoln's associates, who coauthored the massive biography of the President first published in 1889, and continuing up through the present day, as exemplified in the 2005 study *Lincoln's Melancholy: How Depression Challenged a President and Fueled His Greatness*.[43]

In the immediate wake of the assassination, however, the President's reputation for depressiveness was revised into a skilled capacity for *mournfulness*, an unusual sensitivity to the tragic resonance of the conflict. In this context, Lincoln's emotions appeared as a form of sentimental leadership, making him, in effect, a role model for a feeling nation. Eulogists emphasized the extraordinary depth of the President's pain. Charles Everett challenged his audience, "Who mourned like him, for our country's sorrow? Who shed such bitter tears over her sons fallen in battle? Who felt with such keen agony the woe of each repulse?"[44] Lincoln's extraordinary mournfulness, in these accounts, was the effect of taking on massive national losses as personal, sympathetically mourning each individual death. The exceptional capacity for feeling attributed to Lincoln as the nation's Mourner-in-Chief emphasized the fundamentally *democratic* orientation of the President's emotions. Displaying a kind of superhuman humanity, he was said to care for each of those fallen "sons" as though they were his own. Henry Ward Beecher insisted,

> There has not been a poor drummer-boy in all this war that has fallen for whom the great heart of Lincoln would not have bled; there has not been one private soldier, without note or name, slain among thousands, and hid in the pit among hundreds, without even the memorial of a private burial, for whom the president would not have wept.[45]

This contention that Lincoln's grief was distributed equally among all soldiers also resonated against the nation's memory of the death of his own son, William, in 1862, suggesting that in the eyes of the true patriot, all sons were as important to the nation as the President's child. Some eulogists made this equation explicitly; Gilbert Haven, for example, claimed that Lincoln "felt a deep and individual regard for each and all; he wept over the nation's dead boys at Gettysburg as heartily as over his own dead boy at Washington."[46] The equation of personal and national grief here rewrites recent history, turning the Gettysburg Address's impersonal language into a rhetorical bout of weeping that confirmed the President's deep, and deeply democratic, feeling for the country. Accounts like this worked to legitimize the exercise of presidential power in ordering the nation to war. Their collapse of death's specificities into the unity of mournful feeling glosses the distinction between the demise of a child from fever and deaths sustained in war, effectively naturalizing the latter. Lincoln's deep personal grief over all these losses further mitigates any blame attaching to him from them:

> We felt—we knew—that he suffered a thousand deaths in the destruction of the brave lives he had summoned to his country's defense, that he sympathized with every mourner in this mourning land, that he called us to no sacrifice which he would not gladly have made himself,

that his heart was with the humble and the oppressed, and that he had no higher wish than to see his people peaceful, prosperous, and happy. He was one of us—one with us. [J. G. Holland][47]

Emotional suffering appears here as the common denominator of national love, that which demonstrates most efficiently the President's affection for others; as the people's equal in feeling, Lincoln cannot have arbitrarily abused a disproportionate degree of power.

The image of the mournful President, moreover, permitted a peculiar intimacy between the people and their president, an intimacy that served as a means of democratic distinction. One oft-cited story used a solider to validate the tender manliness of Lincoln's mourning, reporting the testimony of a colonel in the Union army who, at the end of ten days spent working with Lincoln, declares, "I found that I was in love with him, and I could not help it."[48] The President's seductiveness is set down to his unexpected and touching query, one afternoon, as to whether the colonel ever finds himself addressing loved ones who are dead. When the colonel admits that he does, the President announces that he is glad to hear it, for he himself holds daily conversations with his dead son, which are a great solace to him. The "love" excited in the soldier by the revelation of his commander's sentimental mourning is at once a personal sympathy, connected to the individual's experience of loss, and potentially reproducible by any citizen-mourner who wants to identify his or her feelings with the President's. The fact that Lincoln mourns his son just as the rest of the citizens do theirs gives ordinary expressions of love and grief a new proximity to power. This affective authority is represented, in the eulogies, as an innovative form of political association:

Never did a great people so universally recognize and repay such love in its ruler. Never did a ruler so love his people. . . . All the great leaders of the revolution, all the great living leaders, reform, civil, and military, are devoted to the idea that controls them: this to liberty, that to union; this, America's glory, that, her destiny; this, philanthropy, that, piety; this, justice, that, honor; this, empire, that, prosperity. Not one of them can in a peculiar, profound, and personal sense be said to love the American people. . . . Not that they do not love the nation; far from it. All have, all do; but it is a general, not a special regard; an affection that reveals itself in other forms than mere love. Not so with our great President. He held every one in his heart of hearts; he felt a deep and individual regard for each and all. [Gilbert Haven][49]

Lincoln's love heralds an American second coming: the arrival of a postpolitical nationalism characterized by a substitution of the unifying power of affection for the divisive and uncertain labor of statesmanship, the selfish pursuit of power and glory, and the abstracted dedication to ideas. His affection, in effect, *enlivens* the nation, transforming it from an abstract "idea" to a people.

The narrative of national love installs this newly arrived principle as retrospectively *foundational* by coding it in the language of domestic affection, as eulogists insisted that Lincoln was "singularly identified with us all . . . like a relative—one of your household."[50] The mourning for the President took on deeply familiar contours. Henry Ward Beecher declared, "Every virtuous household in the land felt as if its first-born were gone. Men were bereaved, and walked for days as if a corpse lay unburied in their dwellings. There was nothing else to think of."[51] The new spirit of love of, by, and for the people incarnated in the President thus signifies, in line with the temporality of middle-class privacy, as *prior* to partisan politics; indeed, as many of the eulogies suggested, the people's affection for Lincoln remained, like familial affection, entirely apart from their assessments of his political career, about which public opinion remained divided.[52] Gilbert Haven, who had criticized Lincoln during the war for his failure to move more quickly on emancipation, declared that the people "knew that his judgment was often at fault, however carefully he exercised it; that sometimes even his strength of purpose almost trembled under the fearful pressure to which it was subjected; that his pleasant smile became sadness, and the sunny wrinkles were channels for many tears." But the very fallibility of the president was, for Haven, an index of the deeply *human* affection he was able to exact from the nation, which "rested in his loving arms" throughout the war, secure in the knowledge that, like a mother's, Lincoln's love was eternal and unwavering:

> His most patient heart allowed every head to lie upon its broad, soft pillow. The people felt the throbbings of that heart warmly beating for them, and, like a tired child on its mother's bosom, sank confidently to rest. Far more than his sagacious judgment, incorruptible integrity, and playful humor, did his deep affection for the nation support and carry us through this darkest night of our history. It is not his mother's knowl-

edge of what is best for him, not her lightsome nature, not her unceasing faithfulness, that makes the sick child commit himself so confidently to her arms. It is her love that makes him trustful. Her judgment may err, strength may yield, joy may flee, but love never faileth. Many waters cannot quench it nor floods drown it. His greatest weakness only increases its strength. His dying makes it live forever.[53]

The maternal affection of the President for the people results, for Haven, in a leader whose affection could be trusted above his rational capacity for leadership: a president who was uniquely fitted to lead the nation through a trial, at which time it needed love above all.

In accordance with their relocation of the *space* of national regeneration to the family hearth, the 1865 eulogies reshape the monumental *time* of the nation using sentimentality's characteristic inflections. Figuring isolated moments of intensified emotional experience as privileged instances of American history, they work to transport deep feeling across time, protecting it from both political turbulence and mortal transience. Beecher described the sorrow that attended Lincoln's death as the perfect form of memorial:

> Rear to his name monuments, found charitable institutions, and write his name above their lintels; but no monument will ever equal the universal, spontaneous and sublime sorrow that in a moment swept down lines and parties, and covered up animosities, and in an hour brought a divided people into unity of grief and indivisible fellowship of anguish.[54]

The monumental significance of this wave of grief, according to Beecher, is its ability to dissolve ideological differences in emotional unanimity; as a spontaneous event, it will always overshadow even the sincerest intentional efforts at memorialization, privileging the temporal transcendence of the memorable moment over the centuries-long endurance of an edifice or a shrine. The preface to a volume in which Beecher's sermon was reprinted, a collection of sermons preached in New York City in the weeks following the assassination titled *Our Martyr President,* insisted that national feeling both could and should transcend time, depicting its own contents as a contribution to American affective history:

> When the flowers have many times bloomed and faded on the grave of our martyred President; when the banner of Peace floats over every acre

of the broad territory of our glorious Union; when the hearts that felt the pangs of awful bereavement are still, men will assent to the facts recorded by the historian, but they cannot feel with the generation whose bosom received the fiery darts, unless they come in contact with their feelings.[55]

The monumental grief that Beecher represented as an appropriate memorial for the President is here seen as a good in its own right, a death-defying ability to make the nation meaningful by facilitating affective contact across generations. This transgenerational contact, a vitalizing supplement to the "facts recorded by the historian," offers a kind of embodied knowledge that will keep the pain of the moment alive. The attachment of the Lincoln eulogists to this expression of national affect is indicated in their repeated, reverential caressing of the suffering bodies of Americans whose grief spoke more clearly than words could: "Trembling lips, tearful eyes, saddened countenances, and suppressed tones, evinced the unspeakable emotions of the soul. . . . America mourns as she never mourned before."[56] Moments of intense suffering take place, in this view, in the exceptional time-space set aside for the surfacing of deep feeling, which escapes conventional historical representation in its unspeakable intensity, its resistance to the linear order of words. This time-space is transient, yet opens in its time-warping intensity onto a seeming endlessness. J. G. Holland's eulogy, delivered in Springfield, Massachusetts, at a ceremony timed to coincide with Lincoln's burial in Springfield, Illinois, represented this peculiar temporality as the nation moving through a different element:

> Only the surface of the soul, like the surface of the sea, is vocal. Deep down within every one of our hearts there are thoughts we cannot speak —emotions that find no language—groanings that cannot be uttered. The surprise, the shock, the pity, the sense of outrage and of loss, the indignation, the grief, which bring us here—which have transformed a nation jubilant with hope and triumph into a nation of mourners— will find no full expression here. It is all a vain show—these tolling bells, these insignia of sorrow, these dirges, this suspension of business, these gatherings of the people, these faltering words. The drowning man throws up his arms and utters a cry to show that he lives, and is conscious of the element that whelms him; and this is all that we can do.[57]

As we saw in earlier chapters, deep feeling is associated, in the nineteenth-century culture of mourning, with a distinctly materialized experience of time. The sensuality of grief is reinflected in Holland's remarks as a kind of slow-motion crisis; the oceanic depth of suffering experienced by the nation produces a thickening of time, comparable to moving under water, that limits the kind of action that can be taken to those expressing the otherwise inexpressible depths of human feeling. But although such feelings cannot themselves be communicated in language, they can nevertheless be shared through the rhetoric of feeling-in-common that crosses both space and time, bonding the nation together across regions and generations; the isolated drowning man, in this sense, becomes the "we" whose collective experience of pain itself becomes the consolation that will assure that the nation continues to live.

For although the space assigned to this intensity of mourning was coextensive with that of the nation, its *time* was understood to be of limited duration, as even the most emotion-laden of the sermons insisted, in line with nineteenth-century mourning conventions, upon the liminality of the national dwelling-in-trauma. Beecher, for instance, speaking a week after Lincoln's death, follows his insistence on the monumental status of the national sorrow by admitting, "For myself, I cannot yet command the quietness of spirit needed for a just and temperate delineation of a man whom goodness has made great"; this delineation must, he declares, be left for "another occasion."[58] Even as they dilate upon the intensity of their listeners' grief, the speakers remind them that these depths both will and should soon pass. Nationalizing the conventional Christian insistence on the consolation of heaven, they advise the citizen-mourners to sublate their sorrow, recommending, as Beecher does, that it be used to "kindle anew their zeal and patriotism."[59] Addressing an audience in New York's Union Square while Lincoln's corpse lay in state in City Hall, George Bancroft speculated that "[t]he country may have needed an imperishable grief to touch its inmost feeling," but he insisted that this "[g]rief must take the character of action."[60] In the context of mourning Lincoln's assassination, then, the familiar American ambivalence about the embodied temporal play of emotion in grief articulated itself through a specific historical dilemma: grief seemed both especially *relevant* as a response to the highly visible death of the President, as well as the accumulated psychic toll of a long and bloody war, and especially *risky* at a moment when displays of national strength and solidarity were deemed essential to prevent a relapse into sectional conflict.[61]

Accordingly, the "great national sorrow" was organized into acceptable forms of mourning, given orderly distribution across both space and time, as the sermons and eulogies posited consolation for the nation's loss by exhorting their audience to translate their sensations of sorrow into a future-directed present-tense patriotism dedicated to restoring the nation to its original unity.

Yet these gestures of containment are not entirely moves toward closure; for while the national period of mourning for Lincoln worked to order feeling toward a renewal of "action," it also sought to establish the monumental significance of national bereavement, what Bancroft called an "imperishable grief," in order to remain permanently in touch with what this sorrow signified. The conventional insistence on the tendency of grief to linger was thus assigned official space, held open, as the preface to *Our Martyr President* suggests, by the eulogistic texts themselves, which lastingly embodied the sorrow of a suffering nation, and also by the bodies that those texts imagined as permanently in sympathy with their project. Most noteworthy was their establishment of the President himself as the nation's primary designated mourner, a characterization that situated him as the permanent figure for their lingering grief. The rhetorical suturing of Lincoln's melancholy to the woes of the nation, that is, allowed the image of the mournful president to carry some of the ongoing weight of national feeling. The preservation of Lincoln's mournfulness in the image of the sad-eyed leader, permanently available to be tapped as a fund of "sympathy" for the downtrodden and as a surplus source of "love" for all citizens, allowed the mourner-president posthumously to take his place as a figure of the sentimentality imagined as necessarily proximate to a democratic nation; his sorrow would stand forever as a reminder to that nation, taking the measure of the gap between democracy's theoretically limitless potential and its inequalities in practice. This vision of the "minor," sentimental Lincoln coexists with the active, heroic image of the president that, after the turn of the century, came to dominate the memorial tradition. While Lincoln the action-hero points toward the kind of decisive patriotic action to which nationalism exhorted the citizenry, the mournful Lincoln complements this image as a kind of passion-hero: standing in the place of the nation's conscience, he points toward the rifts that action leaves unmended, even when it moves to close them.[62] The two bodies of the dead president, in effect, occupy two distinct time-spaces: one, the rail-splitter, is aligned with a future-directed vision of hard work and progress, while the other, the one described as maternal, dreamy, or childlike, idealizes the world of feeling, embodying the exceptional moments in which the nation pauses to indulge in self-reflection.

The legacy of the Lincoln memorial discourse was, then, a posthumous bifurcation of the President that managed both to set American grief in motion, narrativizing it into productive mourning, and to set it monumentally *aside,* preserving an affective space in which the timeless value of the nation's highest ideals could be most effectively demonstrated by the pain experienced when it falls short of them.[63] The sacred status of that time-space is conveyed both by the eulogists' repeated assertions of Lincoln's Christianity and by their many comparisons of the President to Christ—specifically, to the feminized, affectionate image of Christ that emerged in the nineteenth century.[64] As Haven insisted, "Without profanity we may say Abraham Lincoln is love. By that nature will the future hail him." Ralph Waldo Emerson placed the same equation into the mouth of a stereotyped black speaker, who testified to Lincoln's divine transcendence by exclaiming, "Massa Linkum am ebery where."[65] Lincoln's wound-bearing body was, however, not the only one situated in this monumental time-space by the postassassination eulogies. Rather, as Emerson's use of dialect might indicate, the "peculiar, wild, and touching" intensity of black grief seemed, in the imagination of many white eulogists, to speak beyond conventional forms of consolation, locating African American mourners in an affective-temporal national annex, at once irrefutably American and held apart from the progress of the nation.[66] Black mourning for Lincoln, especially among freedmen, was, the eulogists asserted, particularly intense even in a nation universally laid low by sorrow; as the Reverend E. B. Webb predicted, "there will be mourning in the camp, and mourning on the prairies, and far away over the mountains; but nowhere keener anguish and disappointment than among the sable hosts whom his noble heart and hand has freed."[67] The memorial discourse for Lincoln nationalized the Romantic fascination with the "peculiar" mourning customs of African Americans, projecting the ideal form of grief's prelinguistic eloquence onto the mournful black body as spectacular testimony to the depth of the national anguish caused by the assassination. J. G. Holland's eulogy, for instance, suggests that Lincoln's truest monument would not be simply the American but specifically the African American response to his death:

> We who are white know little of the emotions which thrill the black man's heart to-day. There are no such mourners here as those simple

souls among the freedmen who regarded Mr. Lincoln as the noblest personage, next to Jesus Christ, that ever lived. Their love is deeper than ours; their power of expression less. The tears that stream down those dark faces are charged with a pathos beyond the power of words.[68]

The deeper feelings and weaker powers of expression attributed to black mourners here enable them to bypass the emotionally muting conventions of civil society, speaking directly from the bleeding heart of the nation.

Holland goes on to insist that white Americans may join hands "in perfect sympathy" with black mourners, since, if their grief is less spectacular, whites nevertheless owe Lincoln equal gratitude for redeeming them from responsibility for the "sin" of slavery.[69] For other white eulogists, however, even such sympathetic gestures failed; the imagined testimony of the grieving black body, instead, produced a racialized break in their ability to console:

You I can comfort; but how can I speak to that twilight million to whom his name was as the name of an angel of God? There will be wailing in places which no minister shall be able to reach. When, in hovel and in cot, in wood and in wilderness, in the field throughout the South, the dusky children, who looked upon him as that Moses whom God sent before them to lead them out of the land of bondage, learn that he has fallen, who shall comfort them? O, thou Shepherd of Israel, that didst comfort thy people of old, to thy care we commit the helpless, the long-wronged, and grieved. [Beecher][70]

I think, more than all, of the poor freedmen, when they hear of the President's death. How they will wonder and will wail! They called him "Father," as if it were part of his name. Oh, they believed in Abraham Lincoln! . . . His name was a spell to quiet or to rouse them. What will they do, now he is dead! Alas! alas! for the weeping and the wonder they will have, when they know how he died! [Robinson][71]

Intense as is our grief, who shall fathom the sorrow of those to whom he brought the boon of freedom, when they shall learn of the death of their liberator? What wails shall mingle with the voices of the sea along Carolina's shore! Miriam's timbrel in a moment drowned in Rachel's cry of anguish! [Cuyler][72]

Black grief over Lincoln's death is envisioned, in these passages, as a sublime spectacle of communicative speechlessness: the oceanic testimony of the body in anguish, too profound for mere words and thus resistant to the solace offered by white eulogists. The spectacle of black mourning, however, offered consolation for the rest of the nation, as it provided a vehicle for the preservation of its deepest, truest feelings, permitting it to move on toward the work of national healing that Lincoln, in his last major speech, had endorsed. Touched by spiritual as well as natural significance, black feeling completed the circuit of affective exchange when the words of whites failed to make the connection. Following his dramatic depiction of the fathomless grief of the freedmen, T. L. Cuyler's eulogy uses the speech of a black woman to endow the national trauma with spiritual significance:

> "Yes, sah," spake out a gray-haired Aunt Chloe—"yes, sah! Linkum's dead! They killed our best friend. But God be libin yet. Dey can't kill him. I'se sure of dat!" . . . In that poor freedwoman's broken ejaculation, "Linkum dead—but God, God still libin," I find the only solace for your smitten heart and mine.[73]

The "broken" speech of the freedwoman, in Cuyler's anecdote, can heal the hearts of the nation's (white) citizen-mourners insofar as the sacred truth it references exists beyond—or rather, before—language. The spiritual solace that she provides in this anecdote, that is, offers consolation on a parallel plane—the work of the nation can go on in time precisely because the work of the divine is eternal. As with Lincoln's insistence on the completeness of the Absolute in the Second Inaugural, the spiritual speech of the freedwoman points to a temporality that both exceeds and enables the progress of the nation. Yet although many of Lincoln's eulogists sought to underscore the inclusion of the freedman in the Second Inaugural's exhortation to "bind up the nation's wounds," the appeal to the grief of the freedman tended nevertheless to function similarly to the citation of the slave's suffering in Lincoln's last major speech; African Americans were embraced as spiritualized reminders of the nation's "imperishable grief," only to be left behind as guardians of that grief while the eulogies imaginatively moved the rest of the nation toward patriotic closure.[74] Black mourning for Lincoln spoke, in their consolatory narratives, not to the active future but to the sacred work of preservation that accompanied and underwrote the nation's lived history.

The image of anguished black mourning for Lincoln thus complemented the divine mournfulness ascribed to the President himself; both appeared as the embodiment of a representative sense of national mournfulness, the melancholy image of historical trauma to which ordinary citizens might periodically return in order to affectively reorient themselves toward the future as a redemptive space of possibility. The historically counterfactual *promise* of the fully democratic nation at play in the embrace of such sentimentalized images of national mournfulness was revered above the move to complete it, since, in effect, such images did so precisely by containing, alongside the memory of history's pain, an implicit testimony to the democratic nation's unique capacity to notice and remediate that pain—a testimony that was embraced as its own actualization. Both the sad-eyed Emancipator and the weeping freedman were rendered peculiarly static by their ability to commemorate failure as a form of success, as they gestured toward a nation whose timeless power of love exceeded the historical reach of its laws but whose painful failure to live up to its own unrealized democratic ideals could always be cherished as the intimation of a future in which, like a beloved and promising child, it somehow, someday might.

Feeling National: Black Remembrance and the Temporalities of Grief

Against this sentimental vision of representative mournfulness, African American eulogies for Lincoln assigned a different temporality to black grief in response to the President's death. Black eulogists maintained the popular emphasis on the distinct intensity of African American mourning for Lincoln, affirming that, as the Reverend Jacob Thomas, an A.M.E. minister from Troy, New York, insisted, "We, as a people, feel more than all others that we are bereaved."[75] Yet this intense bereavement, for Thomas, provided an avenue for African Americans to participate actively in the nation, as he imagined that grief as a kind of affective citizenship, furnishing a new means of present-tense connection to other Americans: "Abraham Lincoln is no more, and we mingle our tears with that of the mourning widow and bereaved friend."[76] Thomas's image of mingled tears resisted the tendency to set black grief apart in time and space—a tendency shared by white-authored eulogies and the organizers of some of the funeral observances taking place around the country. Yet the idea of national emotional unity emphasized in this ritualized mourning for Lincoln itself furnished African American writers with arguments against such moves to segregate black grief. In response to the threatened ban of African Americans from the funeral procession for Lincoln in New York City, for instance, J. Sella Martin wrote to the *New York Evening Post* demanding, on behalf of black mourners, the "much-coveted though melancholy satisfaction of following the corpse of the best public benefactor the country had ever given them." Martin's letter turned whites' chronobiopolitical assessment of black grief as indexing a lesser stage of civilized development back around on those who wished to keep it out of sight; insisting that Lincoln would have wanted African Americans to participate in the procession, Martin commented, "In the lowest forms of civilized life, the most puerile wishes and most insignificant directions of the dead are carried out. . . . shall the most highly civilized people do what the most barbarous would scorn to be guilty of doing?"[77] The conventional nineteenth-century call for civility in commemoration underlay and helped to regularize the "spontaneous outpouring" of national grief embodied in the enormous weeping crowds that thronged Lincoln's funeral train at every stage of its sixteen-hundred-mile path; media reports of the ceremonies, as Barry Schwartz points out, invariably emphasized the solemn, ritualistic orderliness of the procession itself even as they detailed the emotional response of the masses, as though the two offset one another.[78] Martin's insistence on permitting African American participation as a measure of the nation's civility reinflects the call for "civilized" displays of feeling to develop a call for civil rights.

African American eulogists used the image of black mournfulness for Lincoln to challenge and qualify the popular vision of the nation across time as well. Black eulogies redeployed conventional comparisons between Lincoln and other monumental figures of national history, such as George Washington, to offer a critical take on American history. Schwartz argues that the comparison of Lincoln to Washington in many eulogies reflects a general sense that the Civil War represented a turning point in American history similar to the American Revolution, so that such equations "were statements not about the equivalence of the two men but the equivalence of two heroic generations."[79] African American appeals to this equation, however, subtly remapped American historiography so that the heroism associated with the present highlighted and implicitly rebuked, rather than compensating for, the failures of the past. For instance, Joseph Prime, a black Presbyterian minister, used his eulogy for Lincoln to alter the nationalist genealogy drawn in many white-authored sermons, which placed Lincoln a close second to

241

George Washington in the pantheon of national heroes; Prime observes, rather, that Lincoln was superior even to George Washington in many respects, including "moral integrity," and argues that, although "the American people have reason to rejoice in the life and labors of a Washington, the colored people of our country have a much greater reason to rejoice that Abraham Lincoln was permitted to occupy the executive chair."[80] Jacob Thomas, similarly, uses black affection for Lincoln to challenge the historical oversights of American democracy. After pointing out the particular intensity of grief in the black community over the assassination, he goes on to observe,

> We had learned to love Mr. Lincoln as we had never loved man before. . . . He had taught us to love him. The interest he manifested in behalf of the oppressed, the weak, and those who had none to help them, had won for him a large place in our hearts. It was something so new to us to see such sentiments manifested by the chief magistrate of the United Sates that we could not help but love him. Is it to be wondered at that we mourn to-day?[81]

African American mourning for Lincoln becomes, in this account, not simply a testimony to the greatness of Lincoln but also a critical assessment of the failures of those who preceded him. Citing the historical *novelty* of Lincoln's regard for African American rights, and not simply that regard itself, as the cause of black affection and consequently black mourning for Lincoln, Thomas critiques the conventional assumption that this new regard constitutes an automatic return to the nation's foundational principles. Thomas's understanding of African American affective response as resulting from the distinction of Lincoln's embrace of the oppressed thus reworks the temporality of the President's messianicity that characterized the popular eulogistic discourse; in Thomas's assessment, the new contribution that Lincoln has made to the course of history is not simply the realization of democracy's general affection for the "people" but a specific and directed interest in the redistribution of justice. The distinctly revolutionary status of this contribution is further emphasized in the comparative framework that Thomas constructs for the President's significance. As in many other eulogies, Lincoln is counted as one of the two most important figures in American history—but the other, in Thomas's sermon, is not George Washington but John Brown. The tragically untimely death of the sixteenth president thus articulates the execution of Brown as another foundational national martyrdom, whose significance may be better understood in a more enlightened future.

The counterhistory developed in accounts like these rendered black mourning for Lincoln a vehicle for African American national agency in the present tense, as it provided the occasion both for the contemporary racial integration of the nation and for revision of its most cherished narratives. Avoiding the domesticated rhetoric that retrospectively installed Lincoln's love for the people as foundational, these African American eulogists acclaimed Lincoln as the Emancipator without suggesting that his existence somehow compensated for the losses of history. His death, instead, provided the occasion for a critical reassessment of the national past that emphasized its shortcomings as a mnemonic device to prevent their repetition. The refusal, in such accounts, of the sentimental temporal split assigned to national mournfulness implies a critique of its melancholy mystification of history, which emerges from the need to represent the unreal—the fantasy of an unimpeded operation of democratic ideals—as a *lost* reality, something always already in existence. Cognizant of both the historical newness of racial justice and the strong possibility that the "timeless" principles of democracy, in the case of the freedman, might continue to fall short, the black writers cited here avoided sacralizing the temporal split that enabled the nation to embrace national ideals as temporally transcendent while appealing to their failure in time as, paradoxically, an assurance of their timelessness. This refusal of historical mystification, and the consequent lack of distinction between affective and progressive labor on behalf of the nation, allowed African American eulogists for Lincoln to cite the rhetoric of affective nationality as an explicit critique of sentimental genealogies of national ideals, positioning democracy as a valuable aspiration without succumbing to the tendency to double-time its foundations.

Whereas these African American eulogists tended, in the immediate aftermath of Lincoln's assassination, to distance the time-stopping effect of sentimental nationality that dominated the eulogistic discourse nationwide, the freedwoman Elizabeth Keckley, in her memoir, *Behind the Scenes: Thirty Years a Slave and Four Years in the White House,* published three years later, instead appropriated the monumental image of the mourner-president as a sign of national membership. Keckley, who bought herself and her son out of slavery through her labor as a seamstress, came to know the Lincolns by working as a dressmaker for Mary Todd Lincoln. This professional association permitted her intimate access to the First Family during the war years. In 1868, in the aftermath of the "Old Clothes" scandal, in which Mary Todd Lincoln, with Keckley's assistance, attempted to sell some of her clothing in New York in order to raise money, Keckley published the memoir, asserting that its revelation of the "secret history of [Mrs. Lincoln's] transactions" would serve to explain and vindicate the widowed First Lady's behavior, thus clearing Keckley's name as well.[82] In response to the negative publicity that Mary Todd Lincoln's actions had drawn, Keckley promised to provide the public with an intimate view of life with the Lincolns, implying that knowledge of their most secret life would repair their standing with the public.[83]

Ironically, however, despite Keckley's emphasis on the intimate nature of her narrative, a certain *lack* of intimacy within its pages—the lack of explicit engagement with her own emotions, particularly her grief—has provoked considerable commentary from contemporary critics, who remark, especially, its minimal description of her response to the Civil War death of her only child, George. Keckley says very little about her son's death, noting only that he had left Wilberforce Academy to enlist early in the war and that he was killed "on the battlefield where the gallant General Lyon fell" (76). She observes that his death was a "sad blow to me" and notes that Mary Todd Lincoln wrote her a kind letter of condolence (76). In his introduction to a modern edition of her text, James Olney observes,

> Keckley gives a good deal of space to the death of Willie Lincoln, which she renders in language that would not be out of place in Dickens or Harriet Beecher Stowe, but only glancingly and as a kind of footnote to Willie Lincoln's death does she reveal that her own only son had been killed in a battle. . . . It is as if the Lincolns—their speech, their emotions, their actions—were "important," in Keckley's view, in a way that she would never claim for her own actions or emotions.[84]

Though Olney suggests that Keckley simply minimizes her own emotional life in relation to the greater national importance of the First Family's feelings, other critics have seen Keckley's reticence on these matters not as diffident but as tactical. For instance, Rafia Zafar observes that Keckley, as a former slave turned entrepreneur, compromised to prevent her son from becoming once again an object of economic exchange; though she consented to sell her story, "her most personal memories [were] so important that they [could not] be offered for public consumption."[85] Beyond the pragmatic adoption of a self-defensive position by a black writer addressing a white audience, Keckley's slender account of her grief resonates as a deliberate attempt to buttress her own status as middle-class subject. Zafar points out that her reticence may be linked to a desire to counter the white perception of black emotional response to death as stamping African Americans as "heathens, or at best nominal or emotive Christians" incapable of genteel self-management.[86] Keckley's mild-mannered mourning is notably counterposed to the narrative's depictions of the "wild" grief suffered by Mary Todd Lincoln after both Willie's death in 1862 and Lincoln's assassination in 1865. It is almost as though Keckley deflects the corporeal effects of the "sad blow" onto the body of her employer as she chronicles the "convulsions" and "paroxysms" of Mrs. Lincoln's hysterical response to Willie's death, even reporting a scene in which the President warns his wife that if she cannot control herself, he may need to have her committed to an asylum (75).[87]

Alongside the memoir's careful negotiation of these contemporary social frameworks for the regulation of feeling, the varying temporalities of the nationalized body, suggestively indexed in the comparative chronology of the memoir's title, constitute a significant aspect of Keckley's strategic treatment of grief. Specifically, her reticence about her own son's death is amplified by her appropriation of the vision of representative mournfulness elaborated in the national response to Lincoln's assassination three years earlier, a move that enabled Keckley to assert her own national citizenship by implicitly comparing her own self-reliance to the President's celebrated self-making while using his renowned capacity for grief to preserve the significance of her own loss.[88] Echoing the popular eulogistic discourse, Keckley dwells upon the President's sorrow over young Willie Lincoln's death even as she underscores his democratic refusal to value his own emotions over those of other Americans. The latter emerges most forcefully in her report of a conversation between the President and his wife in 1863, two years after Willie's death, on the subject of their eldest son Robert's intention to enlist. Though Mrs. Lincoln, pointing to her recent bereavement, refuses to "make another sacrifice," the President argues, "But many a poor mother has given up all her sons . . . and our son is not more dear to us than the sons of other people are to their mothers" (87). Lincoln's insistence that the First Family's feelings count no more than those of other Americans not only emphasizes what the eulogies termed his actively democratic "sympath[y] with every mourner in this mourning land,"[89] but it also allows Keckley, implicitly, to add her own "sacrifice" to the national quotient—for though she does not remark it at this point in the memoir, the reader will recollect that she herself is one of the "poor mothers" who has no surviving children, as was reported in the narrative's preceding chapter. In addition to testifying to the national significance of Keckley's grief, Lincoln serves to illustrate its moving depth. Shortly before her report of George's death, she dwells upon his suffering as he looks upon Willie's corpse; looking on the President's "tall frame . . . convulsed with emotion," Keckley comments, "I did not dream that his rugged nature could be so moved" (74). Lincoln's renowned sensibility emerges, here, as a revelation in light of his "rugged" nature, demonstrating an emotional capacity superior to that of his putatively more genteel wife, whose hysterical hoarding of her mournfulness contested the demand for sympathetic circulation. Lincoln's momentary breakdown at the side of his son's corpse, in contrast, recalls the sensitivity supposed to cause soldiers and citizens alike to fall helplessly in love with him—an image that Keckley, her own eyes "full of tears," helps to preserve by freezing the moment in time:

> I shall never forget those solemn moments—genius and greatness weeping over love's idol lost. There is a grandeur as well as a simplicity about the picture that will never fade. With me it is immortal—I really believe that I shall carry it with me across the dark, mysterious river of death. (74)

As Keckley's intimate witnessing of the President's grief corroborates the sense of personal participation in Lincoln's emotional life that underwrote the nation's deep affection for its fallen leader, her framing of the scene in the rhetoric of recollection revives and perpetuates the commemorative insistence on sacralizing the President's sensitivity. She turns the moment itself into a sentimental keepsake, a time-transcending "picture" that she may retain for eternity. Yet this immortal picture of Lincoln's grief possesses a markedly cumulative temporality within the memoir. It at once implicitly reflects and predicts Keckley's own bereavement, which has occurred chronologically earlier but is revealed narratively later. In this sense, her conversion of intimate space into lasting time reworks Redfield's comprehension of the gendered politics of national sacrifice, in which the mournful mothers of the nation's dead sons are tasked with the labor of national continuity through the domestic maintenance of feeling. Lincoln and Keckley participate in a sequential exchange of continuities: just as his private weeping in the site of national domesticity, the White House, carries on her attachment to her son, her circulation of this image in the pages of her memoir extends that moment forward in national memory. The image gestures forward in narrative time as well, predicting Keckley's later response to the President's own death, a repetition underscored by the involuntary surfacing of the image itself as she, called to the White House to attend to the First Lady, becomes one of the first to view the President's dead body: "When I crossed the threshold of the room, I could not help recalling the day on which I had seen little Willie lying in his coffin where the body of his father now lay. I remembered how the President had wept over the pale beautiful face of his gifted boy, and now the President himself was dead" (140). The sequencing emphasized in this recollected chain of events is carried further as Keckley herself steps into the place that the President earlier held (and the one that thousands of citizens would, in the succeeding weeks, occupy), looking tearfully into the coffin at the face of the dead. Yet Keckley, significantly, refuses to remain caught in the other-time of the image that she "carries with" her. Rather, she lingers a moment, responds appropriately, and then moves on:

> I gazed long at the face, and turned away with tears in my eyes and a choking sensation in my throat. Ah! Never was a man so widely mourned before. The whole world bowed their heads in grief when Abraham Lincoln died. (141)

Keckley's movements, both rhetorically and narratively, at once underscore her synchronicity with the rest of the nation and reinflect its habitual arrangement of sentimental time. As she overflows with feeling, the scope of the passage itself widens to take in the whole world, preventing her affectedness from being perceived as temporally peculiar. Moreover, immediately in the wake of her introjection on this mournful moment in history, Keckley gets back to work, returning to Mrs. Lincoln's room to try to calm her hysteria. Hence, Keckley not only refuses to remain with the "martyred President" in the mournful time-loop in which the white commemorative discourse tended to abandon freedmen and women, she reproduces both black eulogists' insistence that African American mourning was a sign of synchronous citizenship and the nationalistic labor that the dead President himself had declared necessary to "bind up the nation's wounds" and move toward the future—that of caring for the widows and orphans that the war had left.[90]

Keckley's insistence in her memoir on making grief *work* in several temporalities at once points us toward a reconsideration of Jennifer Fleischner's critical assessment of the narrative's tendency to pile up emotional keepsakes, which "represent a mode of valuation based on powerful affective ties that are at odds with her narrative praise of self-reliance." For Fleischner, Keckley's attachment to the keepsake reads as fundamentally melancholic; Fleischner argues that this tendency, constituting a substitution of objects for object relations, reveals the ongoing damage caused by the dehumanizing suppression of mourning among slaves.[91] Although Fleischner is right to identify this suppression as a key aspect of the production of raced hierarchies of feeling, her assessment of Keckley's reluctance to express personal grief as melancholic sustains a singular narrativization of the mourning process that overlooks Keckley's creative manipulation of the temporality of affect. Keckley's preservation of her own deep feeling in the body of the President not only avoids the hysterical paroxysms to which the First Lady falls victim, but it also confirms her own fully synchronous national belonging despite the disproportionate period of her life spent in slavery, when most of the capital produced through her incessant labor is squandered by the white family that literally lives on her time.

Keckley's effort to show herself and other forward-thinking freedmen and women as keeping up with a solidly balanced, progressively middle-class, and nationally responsible pace of productivity (an effort the memoir implicitly contrasts not only to Mrs. Lincoln's lavish, extravagant waste of time and emotion but also, on the other end of the class spectrum, to those emancipated slaves whose "love for the past was so strong that they could not find much beauty in the new life so suddenly opened to them" and so "pined for the old associations of slavery" instead of working toward the future [99, 101]) was not, to say the least, warmly received by the national public. Her attempt to recast the national time-value of her life story—both the slavery and the White House years—as both consistent and cumulative was undermined before the book even appeared; increasingly melodramatic advertisements for the work, calling it a "literary thunderbolt," dilated upon Keckley's take on national history in sensational terms, eventually removing the "Thirty Years a Slave" section from the title and inserting words like "revelations" and "disclosures."[92] But the attempt to invest Keckley's narrative of advancement with the spectacular, spatialized temporality that Whitman envisioned as providing Lincoln's assassination with superhistorical significance apparently backfired. Reviewers attacked both the author and the publisher; the publisher was blamed for violating its own "respectable" standards by producing books of a "certain class," and the author was panned, parodied, and berated as "ignorant and vulgar."[93] When the *New*

York Citizen printed, in April 1868, a letter from Keckley declaring, in response to the aforementioned attack, that she had a right as a "free woman" to publish her work, it was simply negated by the paper's response, which announced that the real writer of both memoir and letter was a man who had become so thoroughly identified with the "servant girl" Keckley as to have descended to the standards "one would naturally expect to find among the slaves on a Southern plantation."[94] The paper effectively rolls back the clock on Keckley, replacing the "free woman" of her letter with the very type of anachronistic plantation-slave mentality from which she distanced herself, as though not only the thirteen years since her own emancipation but also the five years since the Proclamation had somehow passed the memoir by. Keckley's refusal, in her account of her "eventful" life (9), to stay quietly behind the scenes is thus met with an insistence on retrojecting her into a status she had transcended and a stasis she rejected, demonstrating a desire to keep her firmly behind the times.

The Now of the "I": Affective Nationality and the Exceptional Status of Sex

The backlash against Keckley's insistence on her own synchronicity intersects tellingly with the specifically sexual undertones attached to her association with the "Old Clothes" scandal. The outcry against Mary Todd Lincoln's 1867 attempt, supported and facilitated by Keckley, to sell some of her used dresses to cover her debts (an attempt that also led to the First Widow's involvement in a political blackmail scheme) repeatedly cited the shamelessness of Mrs. Lincoln's behavior. One writer, calling Mary a "mercenary prostitute," insisted that she misunderstood her "true mission as a wife and mother."[95] This rhetoric of sexual outrage returned in the critical response to Keckley's memoir the following year, as reviewers, labeling the book "indecent" and "shameless,"[96] complained, "nothing is sacred to this traitorous eavesdropper."[97] The tone of moralistic condemnation that marked this line of response to her work must, however, have resonated familiarly to Keckley, since, as her memoir itself shows, being placed in the role of the blameworthy sexual transgressor is something she already knew thoroughly from her experience as a slave. *Behind the Scenes*'s challenge to this particular national tradition precedes and underlies her memoir's celebration of her accession of the status of citizen. In this sense, I propose, Fleischner's detection of a "melancholic counternarrative" within the pages of *Behind the Scenes* is accurate after all; that counternarrative, I would argue, does indeed exist, although the grief it holds in cherished suspension originates from another source than those recognizable familial losses, the death of her son and the kinship ties broken by the slave system, that the narrative accounts.[98] Rather, Keckley's melancholy attaches itself, from the perspective of sentimental culture, to a most "unnatural" feeling—not the lamentable *death* of her son but the lamentable conditions surrounding his *birth*. Her ambivalence about her childbearing (though not about her son himself) troubles the conventional sentimental emphasis on the natural affections of the mother, insofar as that ambivalence forcefully recalls the way the violence of familial rupture, for the slave, is both preceded and sustained by the perpetual bodily violation that orders the reproduction of slavery across generations—an emphasis that, as I suggested in the previous chapter, retemporalizes the liberal-sentimental critique of slavery by placing the inviolability of the *body* before that of the family in its critique of the social. Keckley's narrative, conforming in its general outlines to the rhetoric of affective nationality, does not posit this revision explicitly; rather, it emerges only through the revelation of her own prolonged mourning in the wake of her son's birth, a birth that is itself directly implicated in these systematic violations. Her *open* retention of this mournfulness in the early chapters of the narrative, in contrast to her mediated preservation of the affective aftermath of George's death later in the memoir, indexes the critique that Keckley's grief leveled against the sentimental account of the nation's foundations.

Keckley's experience with intimate violence is introduced in her report of repeated whippings that take on increasingly sexual overtones. In one scene, she resists an assault at the hands of the village schoolmaster, whom she represents as an ally of her mistress, a woman who seems to want vengeance against Keckley for "something" (18). The unspecified resentment of her mistress is echoed in the nonspecific cause of the whipping threatened by the schoolmaster, who refuses to tell Keckley what she has done to provoke his displeasure. Keckley nevertheless makes clear to the reader the implications of the schoolmaster's demand that she remove her clothes in order to be beaten: "Recollect, I was eighteen years old, was a woman fully developed, and yet this man coolly bade me take down my dress" (19). When she refuses, demanding to know what she has done wrong, the schoolmaster tears her dress and beats her savagely; her complaint to her master, the Reverend Burwell, is met with blows, and the cycle of beatings continues until first the schoolmaster, then her mistress, and finally Burwell himself are

moved by her suffering to repent—though not, she reports, before the entire neighborhood has begun talking. Burwell's violent reaction to Keckley's
complaint insinuates the cause of the joint persecution: the mistress's re-
sentful suspicion of a sexual connection between Keckley and her husband.
Keckley, however, affirms her own moral superiority by declaring that the
neighbors held the abusive trio to be the ones at fault. She thus deflects allegations of sexual wrongdoing without directly declaring herself innocent of
any such charges—for to proclaim her sexual purity would be precisely to
miss the larger issue: that such predeterminations of guilt are enacted on the
basis not of Keckley's specific sexual history but of a history of sexualizing
race in America. And notably, though Keckley's prolonged suffering finally
succeeds in gaining her a respite from the violence of the trio, her "persecution" does not end here; rather, it takes on more explicitly sexual form as the
narrative continues:

> I was regarded as fair-looking for one of my race, and for four years a
> white man—I spare the world his name—had base designs upon me. I
> do not care to dwell upon this subject, for it is one that is fraught with
> pain. Suffice it to say, that he persecuted me for four years, and I—I—
> became a mother. (24)

The news of her son's birth thus appears in the gap that simultaneously con-
ceals and reveals another story—the memoir's palpable but effaced representation of her sexual exploitation as a slave woman. The stuttered repetition
of her "I" reopens the time that, as I observed in chapter 3, domestic-sentimental culture works to efface: the sexual prehistory of the middle-class maternal body. In this sense, the sentence produces the effect that, according
to Gilles Deleuze, characterizes stuttering in general: that of bringing the
body to the surface of language.[99] The structure of the sentence recalls that
body to history as well. Insofar as it offers an account of effects (I became a
mother) that do not directly "match" the stated causes (he persecuted me),
it invites the reader to consider the way the sentimental account of the family as founded in love obscures the course of the past. Keckley's rhetoric, in
this light, highlights this obfuscation by partially repeating it, allowing the
direct cause of George's birth to speak through Keckley's decision not to
"dwell" on the subject. Her declared reluctance to speak ironically renarrates
the form of the family by challenging its timing, pinpointing the sexualized
female body as the unspeakable origin of maternal affection. The impossibil-

ity, for the slave woman, of telling that story in what Harriet Jacobs, in *Incidents in the Life of a Slave Girl,* calls the "usual way" leads Keckley to confront a convention that she cannot openly dismiss and consequently seeks to disarticulate through the broken speech of the sentence's supposedly "shamed" stuttering. The gaps in the sentence effectively point the reader to a long and underspecified history of sexual "persecution" that operates both in Keckley's individual story and in the slave system in general. The repetition of the "I" thus suggests the way that Keckley's publication of an intimate secret is not, finally, a story about herself and a problem within her history; it is a story about the problematic structuring of national history, in which the desexualization of the middle-class white maternal body also works to dehistoricize the social origins of this sexual violation by forcing the "lascivious" black woman to bear the blame. Yet the archive of nationally resonant rhetoric that Keckley seeks to animate in the memoir contains scant material for telling a tale about the fundamental *impersonality* of such purportedly personal experiences. Accordingly, Keckley signifies this impersonality indirectly, by stuttering her "I," suggesting, in this repetition, a break between doer and deed, and between mother and child, in which the public's self-interested stake in maintaining the structuring silences of privacy might become visible.

Yet Keckley's stuttered "I," and the hesitancy of the sentences that precede the revelation of her son's birth, at the same time demonstrate a personal ambivalence about the confession itself, which touches on a yet-vexed emotional history, one that is never resolved within the narrative despite her eventual "triumph" over her enslaved condition: the affective aftermath not simply of being constantly required to suppress her feelings, nor even of being continually made available for abuse and violation, but of perpetually being placed in the position of *blameworthiness* with respect to that abuse and violation. Keckley follows her account of George's birth, accordingly, by tracing its affective legacy:

> The child of which [the unnamed white man] was the father was the only child that I ever brought into the world. If my poor boy ever suffered any humiliating pangs on account of birth, he could not blame his mother, for God knows that she did not wish to give him life; he must blame that society which deemed it no crime to undermine the virtue of girls in my position. (24)

Replacing the familiar rhetoric of joy in the aftermath of a birth with a story of heritable humiliation and sorrow, Keckley displaces the sentimental account of the family as founded in timeless love without directly negating it. Her account of George's inherited "condition" renders her own unwillingness to mother itself an effect of maternal tenderness even as insistence on her own blamelessness in the matter remaps the boundaries of the slave family, citing broadly social rather than narrowly familial origins for affective transmission; if her son comes to inherit a version of her own "humiliation," she argues, then his pain must be understood as the phantomatic inscription of gendered and raced imbalances in the politics of sexual shame.[100] Keckley indicates that what is to be blamed for her son's inherited suffering is, finally, the scandal of his white father's blamelessness in the world's eyes. The discussion of her son's birth thus reiterates and recontextualizes a central theme of the memoir—the need to retrospectively exonerate herself in the face of a nation that sees her as always-already to blame, from the recent example of the "Old Clothes" scandal to the trials of her girlhood, where she was plagued by a master and mistress who contended that she would never be "worth her salt," to the aforementioned round of persecutions by her new mistress and master and their neighbors, and beyond.

Fleischner reads Keckley's tone in the passage about her son as one of "reproach and blame" toward him, a mode she adapts as a defense against the belief that he, or her reader, would hold a similar attitude toward her.[101] Yet Keckley's assertion that she never wanted "to give [her son] life" resonates as an expression of *care* that turns the sentimental understanding of maternal "nature" back on itself: her "unnatural" desire to refuse the joys of motherhood becomes the strongest expression of maternal "care" she can articulate from her position. Her resistance to childbearing becomes at once a negation and an affirmation of sentimental family values, extending the middle-class familial mandate that we saw in chapter 1, where even dead children continued to require maternal care, to the nonchild, the child that was never born, as well. She represents her inclination to refuse a later proposal of marriage from a free black man along similar lines of affectionate negation: "for a long time I refused to consider his proposal, for I could not bear the thought of bringing children into slavery—of adding one single recruit to the millions bound to hopeless servitude, fettered and shackled with chains stronger and heavier than manacles of iron" (29). Keckley's resistance to further childbearing counterbalances middle-class sentimental-domestic investment in the deep future—the desire to perpetuate the family across time—by weighing down the burden of the flesh that the child inherits; countering the "love" that launches the middle-class child onward, Keckley insists that love, which persists despite the chaining of the bloodline—of her already-born child, she remarks, "He came into the world through no will of mine, and yet, God only knows how I loved him" (29–30)—might be better served by forswearing such perpetuation. Her suggestive deployment of the word "recruit" here, moreover, blurs the distinction between voluntary conscription and compulsion, mimicking the legal mystification that underlies the slave-child's "recruitment" through the mother's body without the "consent" of either.

This reflection, however, initiates a discussion of Keckley's desire to make a change in the course of the future that it is too late to forswear—or rather, to ensure that there will be, for George, a future that registers as such, instead of the perpetuation of "generations of despair" (30). Keckley's initial attempts to buy herself and her son out of slavery are delayed by her inability to save enough money, hindered by a husband who proved "a burden instead of a helpmate" and by her master's family, who lived almost entirely off her labor (32). Her plan to go north to raise money for the purchase is later hindered by a white man who insists that she will be seduced by the rhetoric of the abolitionists and will run away instead. At this point, Keckley falls into despair, prompting the most extensive consideration of her own sorrow that she offers in the narrative:

> I had dreamed such a happy dream, in imagination had drunk of the water, the pure, sweet crystal water of life, but now—now—the flowers had withered before my eyes; darkness had settled down upon me like a pall, and I was left alone with cruel mocking shadows. (34–35)

Keckley's lament for the apparent death of her dream of freedom—which is, significantly, rendered in terms far more dramatic than her restrained report of the loss of her son later in the memoir—also reiterates the broken repetition that attended the reporting of that earlier sorrowful event, the involuntary birth of her child. The repetition of the "now" emphasizes the break between past and present, a suspension with a mournful present tense, further underscored by her description of the scene as a "paroxysm of grief"— a term that will be used later to describe Mary Todd Lincoln's hysterical mourning (35). But her stuttering "now" recalls, as well, a continuity between this moment and the last event to produce that effect: in both cases, white men take away from Keckley a kind of freedom by presuming her always-already worthy of blame. Consolation appears, however, in the form of Mrs. LeBourgois, a neighboring white woman who develops a plan to help Keckley raise the money at home for her purchase, since "it would be a shame to allow you to go north to beg for what we should give you" (35). LeBourgois's offer reads alternately as expressing the "human" kinship of sympathy, responding generously to another's display of grief, or, less sentimentally, as expressing a kind of genteel feminine modesty on behalf of Southern custom, since she notes that Keckley would "shame" the neighborhood by going north and exposing to hostile eyes their lack of generosity. From the latter perspective, LeBourgois, by deciding to raise the money among the white women of the city, in effect seeks to keep the story of Keckley and her son "private" by keeping it a secret from Northerners. The difficulty in determining Mrs. LeBourgois's motives here highlights the ambivalence of bourgeois constructions of sentimentality in the memoir, as they both "work" to support reformist faith in the power of sympathy and *unwork* that account by exposing its complicity with the occlusion of certain aspects of "intimate" life in the very location of others as the "foundation" of social harmony. Thus, Keckley's paroxysm of grief functions at once to support a sentimental account of a nation moved to action through a responsive recognition of the suffering of the oppressed and to expose the hypocrisy of that account as it continues to deliberately misrecognize the complex "nature" of the sexual body.

Insofar as Keckley's moments of mourning over the hopelessness of her condition act to directly provide further means of hope—her regret over her son's birth inspires her to work for freedom, and her sorrow over the delayed arrival of that freedom inspires others to help out—her grief functions not as a time apart from but as a time *within* the ongoing work of progress, both individual and national (for, as she points out in the introduction, her self-emancipation both contributed to and allowed her to work within the larger movement against slavery). Yet this conciliatory revision of affective nationality cannot wholly resolve the intimate violence that Keckley experiences as an effect of the slave system—the violence linked to the birth of the very son whose violent death takes on national significance later on. In this sense, *Behind the Scenes* exposes the melancholic erasure of the sexualized body by the rhetoric of sentimentality—an erasure that, as I argued earlier, remains complicit in the repeated violations of that body that are peculiarly, though not only, visible within slavery. The story of Keckley's years in slavery thus remains at once indissoluble from and radically inassimilable to the later story of her years in the White House because the sentimental rhetoric that structures the preserved image of the mourner-president, through which Keckley confirms her own synchronous nationalism, has literally nothing to say to the question of sex; accordingly, it cannot address directly the history of sexual violence that does not just accompany but *constitutes* the slave system. This history escapes the monumental time that, as I have shown, inheres in the sacralization of figures like Lincoln: for the emphasis on the regenerativity of national sentiment, with its tender embrace of the nation's wounding moments as reminders of the timeless ideals to which it remains devoted despite their inconsistent manifestation in time, remains keyed to the register of a familialized model of feeling that negates the temporally uncertain sexualized body in order to confirm pure feeling as foundational. Though Keckley may both feel with Lincoln, in their mutual love of the (dead) child that confirms the tenderly nationalistic significance of their most intimate passions, and *for* him in her sorrow over his death, his grief over the death of his child and her grief over the birth of her own suggest distinct and unreconciled modes of significant feeling.

Keckley's ambivalent account of her son's birth and of her reluctance to use her body to add other bodies to the condition into which she herself was born underscores that slavery is not simply a system in which sexual violence is tolerated but, rather, that it is itself a systematic perpetuation of sexual violence, the material and economic alienation of the body from its "effects"—effects that are, crucially, not limited to what we conventionally understand as "biological" reproduction. For although the fate of her son is central to Keckley's sustained attempt to win freedom, and becomes the narrative's primary justification for that labor, Keckley's desire for intellectual and corporeal self-control is also visible throughout her memoir, beginning with the preface's insistence that "a wrong was inflicted upon me; a cruel custom deprived me of my liberty, and since I was robbed of my dearest right, I would not have been human had I not rebelled against the robbery" (4). Keckley's insistence on her rebellion against slavery as bound up with the humanity that the slave system seeks to negate is not, here, effaced within a maternalist desire to secure the future of the child; it remains, rather, a desire directed toward the self, echoed in her later mourning over the withered "flower" of her hopes for freedom, which also makes no reference to her son. In this sense, her desire to win freedom begins and ends with the self, encompassing her son as an extension of that self in a manner distinct from the conventional sentimental insistence on the affective incompleteness of the maternal. Her love for him is not, finally, a question of the "natural" and foundational inclination of woman's affection toward the child but a supplementary extension of her auto-affection, as expressed in the syntax of her assertion, "He came into the world through no will of mine, *and yet,* God only knows how I loved him."

We might, then, comprehend Keckley's work to free her son not as an example of maternal "self-sacrifice" but within a framework that considers care for the child as an extension of care for the self, part of the "self-reliance" that she ironically cites as the most important and earliest lesson of her life in slavery, a framework that would refigure both the emotional and the historical logic of reproductive generationality. For just as Keckley challenges the distinction between material and economic labor that sustains the fictive division of public from private, she also resists, in her recounting of her early history, either subsuming herself into her son, making him into the figure of the future, or turning her affections entirely "inward" in a manner that might be cited as a hysterical abandonment of the child. The difference of Keckley's relation to her son is that, finally, he signifies not as a future-directed extension but a resonant augmentation of her "I"—an augmentation whose temporality suggests not the linear/cyclical progress of the generational nation but the charged and uncertain time of the "now."

Yet Keckley's story also differs from her son's in its unfolding: at its "end" —that is, at the present moment stressed in the preface—he is dead, while she finds herself to no insignificant degree in the same place she began: bearing the burden of blame for someone else's transgressions and being forced to defend herself against allegations of indecency. The hostility directed toward Keckley as Mary Todd Lincoln's collaborator in the sale of her old clothes thus appears, despite the memoir's insistence on her own advancement, as a *lack of discontinuity* between her condition as a slave and as a freedwoman; in place of the respect she might expect to have earned from a nation that conventionally lauds the accomplishments of the self-made individual, she finds only a continuation of the perpetual suspicion of wrongdoing directed against her in her youth. But the impossibility of speaking "decently" in response to the temporal collapse enacted by this perpetuated charge ordains the melancholy undertelling that characterizes this aspect of her tale. In this light, what is most "telling" about *Behind the Scenes* is not Keckley's inability to "work through" her grief for her son—a grief she effectively articulates through her deployment of the Lincoln-image's representative mournfulness—but the failure of conventional forms of sentimental and/or monumental nationality to finally resolve, or even to provide a means of coherently addressing, the continual grief she receives for being a black woman in America.

Conclusion: Serial and Sentimental Lincolns

The Lincoln selected in 1922 for "permanent" enshrinement in the Washington, D.C., memorial was not the loving mourner, nor even the rugged, self-reliant actor, but the superior statesman, the lawyer who implicitly understood the need for rational self-abstraction as central to the just exercise of democratic power. This image, as Barry Schwartz observes, emerged from the particular needs of American nationalism during and after World War I —the same period in which the Gettysburg Address's canonicity was consolidated, and the one in which the abstracted "serial" model of nationalist monumentality emphasized in Benedict Anderson's analysis came to dominate war memorials.[102] From time to time, however, the melancholy motherly lover peers out from behind the statesman, as the site of the tribute to American justice is appropriated to testify to the continuing incompleteness of this idea in practice. Marian Anderson's open-air concert on Easter 1939, after she had been barred from performing in both Constitution Hall and the District of Columbia public schools, was one such event. Martin Luther King's 1963 address to the March for Jobs and Freedom, which alluded to both Anderson's concert, in its play on the anthem "America (My Country 'Tis of Thee)" with which she opened, and to Lincoln's Gettysburg Address, was another. In his 1994 memoir *Last Watch of the Night,* the gay poet Paul Monette reflects on his visit, during the 1993 Gay and Lesbian Rights March on Washington, to the Lincoln Memorial, where, standing in tearful awe before the statue of Lincoln—its gaze "melancholy, but also rock-solid sure that the nation's wounds would heal"—and between the two plaques bearing Lincoln's canonized speeches, he recollects both earlier events in the context of the present one.[103] Monette, thinking through Lincoln's rumored homosexuality, muses, "I didn't think the Lincoln of my understanding would have any trouble equating the Civil Rights struggle of people of color with the latter-day dreams of the gay and lesbian movement. There's too much compelling evidence in his own life . . . of the 'dear love of comrades'

. . . And oh, how we needed a Lincoln to stand for equal justice and bind us all together again."[104] Monette's reflection, bringing together Anderson, King, himself, and Whitman (whom he cites to invoke Lincoln's homoerotic attachments), develops a personal version ("the Lincoln of my understanding") of the President that we have already seen, the one whose affective inclinations guided and gave force to his passion for justice. This reflection, in turn, effectively accomplishes on its own, as Charles Morris observes, what Monette wishes for in the dream of Lincoln's second coming: binding together movements for full citizenship through the power of an inclusive vision.[105] I would note, however, that the form of national history that Monette adapts in his recitation of successive struggles (a succession that has become central to the contemporary gay-rights movement's self-understanding) is predicated on a temporality that limits the way that movement can be thought.[106] Monette's reliance on a politics of sequential recognition, using the "earlier" struggles to make visible the "latter-day" claims, risks the temporal double-bind that Lisa Duggan's critique of recognition makes clear: the belief that recognition alone, in the form of the "rights" that serve as signs of the nation's affirmation, will suffice to overcome the damage of the past tends both to leave the forms of the nation unchanged and, as a consequence, to efface its particularized histories of sexual marginalization —an effacement that itself creates the conditions for further perpetuation of those histories.[107] Moreover, its tendency to view the horizon of "equality" in terms of a linear march of movements, wherein distinct disenfranchised populations in turn arrive to demand and receive "equal justice," embraces the liberal-sentimental account of justice itself as a timeless truth successively being extended in time to those overlooked in the past, a formulation that limits the potentialities of justice by assuming that it is a form the nation has already perfected and now needs only to "apply" to everyone equally. I suggest that Keckley's memoir might serve as a reminder of the consequences of a sentimentalizing affective nationality that renders the politics of sex unspeakable—and remind us, as well, of the need to trace such effaced effects back and forth through time. And consequently, among the queer versions of the Lincoln-image that condense and conserve the national significance of this figure, I would propose not the embrace of the sentimental lover but Whitman's other Lincoln, the one he cruised, as we saw at the opening of this chapter, on the streets of Washington, D.C.: resonant, vital, and *perpetually unfinished*—a Lincoln that we do not yet fully know how to know; one that we must invent new strategies for approaching, strategies that might require us to look farther—and differently—into the past, instead of simply embracing the idea of steady "progress" forward; one that we might, finally, understand in relation to another form of time, by positing "justice" not as the redemptive promise held out by a perpetually mournful nationality but as the always-provisional effect of working through it.

Coda

Everyday Grief

> I know better than to claim any completeness for my picture. I am a
> fragment, and this is a fragment of me.
>
> —Ralph Waldo Emerson, "Experience"

Talking with others about this project over the past few years, I have been
struck by the persistent repetition of one particular question: whether I
planned to include any discussion of the events of September 11, 2001. The
query in itself was not what stood out for me; cultural critics, after all, ordi-
narily feel a certain obligation to analyze such events, an obligation experienced as all the more pressing in periods when, as today, the pursuit of critical thought is depicted not merely as unnecessary luxury but as unpatriotic
dissent.[1] What *did* eventually surprise me about the question, however—
and I am abashed at how long it took me even to notice—was that no one
ever argued for, or even inquired after, my inclusion in this study of any
other contemporary grief-marked event: not, say, the December 2004 Indian
Ocean tsunami, not the Iraq war, not even (to keep the space of the event
within a geographically narrow "American" frame) the catastrophic 2005
flooding of the Gulf Coast. In terms of the politics of grief, 9/11 was evidently *the* event of our times. I do not think this selectivity means that
my interlocutors were simply indifferent to the devastation of those other
events. Instead, it suggests something more specific about the conceptual
landscape of the present, and about the way 9/11 has come to signify as the
gold standard of contemporary affective eventfulness, the way it has become what Jacques Derrida identifies as a *fait date,* a date marked but also
felt, marked *as* felt.[2] The feelings linked with 9/11 are, moreover, universalized: "everyone" is invited to participate in its trauma, everyone is addressed
as co-participant, fellow-sufferer, witness, survivor, mourner. One does not
need to be "American" to feel the mingled awe and reverent sorrow that

emerged as the appropriate affective response to the event—but anyone who responds with a different feeling, who feels, say, indifferent or unsympathetic, is open to the charge of inhumanity. The flooding of the Gulf Coast, in contrast, was followed by an interposition of *distance* between Katrina's victims and the witnesses: the witnesses were invited to feel compassion and horror at the events, but not, I think, in a way that marked the date as *universally* felt. The bulk of the U.S. media coverage, orienting itself toward a generically "national" viewer, was always intensely aware of and shaped around the disproportionate poverty and blackness of Katrina's victims, limiting the amount of sympathy required via the projection of a Gothicized disorder in place of 9/11's transcendent trauma.[3] At this point in time, then, among the events that I have mentioned (and others that might also have been), 9/11 alone has been singled out to speak of and for the nation-before-the-world, to retain the charge that bears perpetual witness to a sense of sublime significance, and to be, through the endless citation of its neofoundational status, its unchallenged ushering in of a new era, made sacred.

The nationalist invocation of 9/11 works through a condensation of its meaning in a resonantly typical commemorative language: on the "public" side, there is the resolve to defy grief by constructing a massive, monumental tower, 1,776 feet tall, commemorating "Freedom," footnoted by a contemplative parklike setting that will house the (literally) reflective memorial for the dead; and on the "intimate" side, there remains the desire to sacralize the trauma of the day, maintaining its pain across time in a manner similar to the mediated preservation of the public's grief over Lincoln, a mode of preservation visible in the insistent recirculation of official images and stories containing that trauma which now distinguishes anniversaries of the date. Markers of one's participation in the great national mourning can be secured in everything from T-shirts to commemorative license plates insisting, "We Will Never Forget."[4] The permanence of the remembering affirmed in this slogan effectively communicates the sense that 9/11 exists outside ordinary time: as trauma recollected and recirculated, it rapidly claimed what James Der Derian terms a sense of "exceptional ahistoricity," a sense of being "beyond experience, outside of history and between war."[5] The maintenance of such exceptional times within the story of the nation is predicated, as I argued in chapter 5, upon the possibility of ritual return: a ritualization that confirms the continuity of national narrative in and through the very trauma of its disruption. Abraham Lincoln's assassination marked one such moment; 9/11 has come to stand as another date distinguished by its inassimilability into the flow of ordinary time. Indeed, it is remarkable how common, and how necessary, such disruptions have become to the nation's own account of itself. Endowed with sacred significance, these gaps in the flow of time create new foundations for the American story, sites that mask the ongoing revision of the very truths they affirm as timeless, that can, for instance, render seemingly incontrovertible a definition of "freedom" that celebrates the free market but negates civil liberties. (So, too, have such less violent disruptions as the specter of same-sex marriage, the legalization of abortion, and the election of Latin American leaders resistant to U.S. hemispheric hegemony all furnished occasions for the rhetorical affirmation of a uniform and timeless "heritage" suddenly imperiled by these disturbing new developments.) The periodic intercession of traumatic suspensions of national narratives serves to generate occasion for their perpetual reiteration and renovation, in the invention of "traditions" to uphold, consistencies to maintain, futures to defend.

Yet if 9/11 itself exists in the sacred time of exception, the time of its witnessing does not appear, generally, as extra- but as *super*historical, transforming what would otherwise be ordinary survival into something achieved. The scene of public mourning, Laurent Berlant observes, "is a scene of sentimental education; for, like sex, death must be meaningful, engendering knowledge that in moving us beyond the finality of another ending performs and confirms a future in which we are not abandoned to the beyond or the beneath of history."[6] The consolidation of sublime meaning around 9/11 not only creates a sense of national belonging—an assurance that there is after all a "we" to do the work of never-forgetting—but constructs, as well, an imprecise yet affirmative narrative in which that witnessing is projected across time. In this light, the citizenry's embrace of an appropriately reverent attitude toward the events of 9/11 reads not as the performance of dead citizenship, the passivity of a populace too bamboozled to do anything but shop obediently for commemorative artifacts while its government wages endless war; instead, it signals a displacement, the maintenance of sorrowful attachments to the cut-short lives of strangers standing in for the work of imagining ways of living otherwise, of inventing new futures.

Seeking strategies to enliven the sentimental vagueness of the popular response and to resist the conservative arrest of meaning around 9/11, Left cultural critics frequently posit a lingering and contemplative grief as a means of *slowing down* the process of meaning-making, refusing closure and leaving it, instead, deliberately fragmentary and provisional, along the lines of the countermonumentalism I discussed in chapter 4. For instance, David Simpson, in a recently published study of the politics of 9/11 commemoration, maintains the "imperative for the taking of time," even as the possibility of constructive intervention into the meaning of the event may seem to be foreclosed as time passes.[7] Likewise, Judith Butler affirms the value of "tarrying with grief," seeking, in an essay responding directly to 9/11, to extend the duration of grief around the event against those who would have done with it in order to convert its remainder into a drive for war.[8] Insisting, instead, on the need to "make grief itself into a resource for politics," Butler points to the potential gain that emerges from comprehending grief as a recollection of intersubjective origins, of the subject's capacity to be "undone" by the other.[9] If this is a humanism, she contends, then it is one distinguished by a speculative temporality, since the embrace of a common, foundational vulnerability that generates this humanist ethic is presumably altered when one concedes both the necessity and the contingency and mutability of those norms (or narratives) that govern the recognizability of the human. Never simply given, the human, for Butler, "comes into being, again and again, as that which we have yet to know."[10] Butler's speculative pedagogy of mourning nevertheless remains affiliated with the scene of sentimental education that Berlant identifies—unsurprisingly, since it is understandably difficult to tell a politically attractive story about grief that does not have some version of a happy, or at least compensatory, ending. Notably, Butler's revision of the human into an iterative immanence shares with sentimental mourning culture not only a common story of the subject's affectionate origin but also an optimistic orientation toward the future, revealed in the persistence of the conviction that grief properly engaged, worked through in the *right* way (she insists, for instance, that grief must overcome the narcissism of melancholia in order to create this new understanding) will make one *better*—not, here, a better earner or a better Christian but rather a better person, better neighbor, better thinker.[11] Yet Butler's post-9/11 revision of mourning abandons the putative continuities of "tradition" and identity in favor of a speculative expansion of the human, rendered legible as a mode of continuity only by the positing of an affective connection, a connection that, she affirms, repeatedly undoes the subject rather than securing its time. In this light, her account recalls our discussion, in chapter 1, of "The Little Shroud's" dual depiction, through grief, of the potential of "love"—at once disciplinary and limitless, calling the subject back to a timeless truth about familial relations and yet remaining open to whatever the future marked by love may become.

Butler's account thus stands as one effort to deploy grief, in the wake of 9/11, to affirm not only new relations but also new temporalities in which relatedness might be imagined, intervening in and partly redirecting the histories of sentimental and psychological mourning even as she inherits from nineteenth-century condolence culture a certain faith in the instructive value of grief. That faith, however, is forcefully challenged by an essay written contemporaneously with the culture that engenders it, one that runs counter to Butler's embrace of grief as a political resource and that, accordingly, I want to examine here—the resolutely antisentimental and ostensibly apolitical engagement with grief in Ralph Waldo Emerson's 1844 essay "Experience" (whose working title was "Life"). Countering the insistence of nineteenth-century mourning culture on the centrality of affective bonds to the subject (an insistence later taken up by Butler in the register of desire), Emerson instead proclaims their ultimate irrelevance. Asserting the theatrical falseness of any putative truth produced within those "moods in which we court suffering," Emerson considers, in an oft-cited passage, his own response to the death of his child, and the absence of change it produces in him.[12] He laments the inability to bring this feeling near enough to touch and transform him; it feels, instead, like the loss of property, a long-lasting inconvenience that leaves him

> neither better nor worse. So is it with this calamity: it does not touch me: something which I fancied was a part of me, which could not be torn away without tearing me, nor enlarged without enriching me, falls off from me, and leaves no scar. It was caducous. I grieve that grief can teach me nothing, nor carry me one step into real nature.[13]

This passage, identified by a number of critics as central to the logic of the essay, effectively retains as negated—or rather, as *lamented*—the compelling cultural fantasy that grief can make one better. Yet the abandonment of this fantasy, in the end, generates its own forms of compensation. Grief fails to create an authentic experience insofar as it fails to modify the mourner over time, leaving him essentially unchanged. But it is here, in the collapse of a cherished cultural narrative, the sundering of a posited continuity, that the essay locates both the possibility of another way of thinking community and, consequently, the basis of a radical politics of futurity. Though Emerson's inability to engage in mourning has provoked several critics to describe the aforementioned passage as melancholic, his depiction of his son as "caducous," Pamela Schirmeister argues, belies this description; melancholia, as she notes, is bound up with a disordered identification, whereas the passage in question affirms the absolute loss of the son, the dissevering of all points of identification.[14] In this sense, Schirmeister proposes, the essay centers on the question of what happens to the notion of community when even the seemingly natural and instinctual primary bond between a parent and a child turns out to have been propped upon fantasy. By mourning not the child but the fantasy of familial mourning, the essay moves toward "a groundlessness that might allow the future to arrive"—a future that has no necessary continuity with the present, that is unknown and unpredictable.[15] This community is not a sentimental community based on the sharing of loss but a community *of* loss: "not a community of similar identities, of anything rooted in the idea of *oikos*: it is not familial, natural, given, present, accounted for in any way, but precisely the loss of those things. In fact, we can go so far as to say that this loss *is* community, an impossible possible community, a community without community."[16]

Just as, for Schirmeister, the failure of recognized forms of continuity constitutes another kind of community, the traumatized discontinuity of the time of life that opens the essay—a series of moments lacking the security of any clear beginning or certain end, the condition of finding oneself "on a stair"[17]—takes on a more optimistic cast, coming to promise a capaciousness and malleability, a depth and flexibility that an insistence on homogeneous, sequential time would negate. Warning the reader to "be very suspicious of the deceptions of the element of time," Emerson undermines the time-orientation of his world in favor of an inspirational task-orientation, commenting that "[i]t takes a good deal of time to eat or to sleep, or to earn a hundred dollars, and a very little time to entertain a hope and an insight which becomes the light of our life."[18] The potential of this nonhomogeneous momentous time emerges, in the essay, in the wake of a shift from mortal time to what Emerson identifies as a "deep and secular" time, a time beyond ordinary timeframes, though not timeless, nor beyond nature as Emerson conceives it.[19] This capacious and worldly temporality may be understood to develop both from Emerson's reading of scientific texts and, as Wai Chee Dimock has recently observed, from his immersion in global religions—and that worldly temporality, in turn, furnishes time for the making of other possible worlds.[20]

At the outset of this book, I asserted that grief might work most productively when it was arranged not to conserve or consolidate but to proliferate possibilities for the experience of time. This does not mean, I would add, that all such times are necessarily good times or that the capacity for proliferation and variability, itself a key feature of capitalism's timescape, must be incessantly celebrated or embraced. Responding, in different affective registers, to the desire for other ways in which to think grief, Butler's and Emerson's essays propose temporalities more mobile than the monumental, more effectively engaged than traumatized time. But the point of such proposals is not the presentation of yet more temporal "choices" in an age already saturated with time; it is, finally, the dissolution of the fictive impossibility that life might proceed otherwise, by encountering time and engaging the past in ways that open possibilities for historical experience. We might consider, as one such engagement, Art Spiegelman's book *In the Shadow of No Towers* (2004), a mélange of comics and found text spanning over a century, from Spiegelman's renowned black *New Yorker* cover bearing the faint afterimage of the World Trade Center towers to the ten monthly full-page comic spreads he produced between 2002 and 2003, pages that were rejected by several U.S. mainstream media organs for their overtly political content, to a collection of newspaper comics from the early twentieth century, which stand as a record of the long history of engagement with political and psychological issues in the "funny pages" of the daily papers as well as their official "news" sections.[21] (An astonishingly ironic fragment of the latter is also incorporated, in the book's reproduction of the front page of the September 11, 1901, *New York World,* whose banner headline, following up on the shooting of President McKinley that would, three days later, prove fatal, reads, "President's Wound Reopened: Slight Change for Worse.") Spiegelman's drawings dwell extensively on his own traumatized response to the attacks, at once hysterical and realistic. Accordingly, they deliberately disarrange space and disorder time, following on and expanding the dead-serious transgenerational temporal play of his renowned Holocaust narrative *Maus.*[22] *In the Shadow's* first panel begins with a synopsis observing, "In our last episode, as you might recall, the world ended . . . ," yet it centers around the unbearable suspense that New Yorkers experience as, presumably in the wake of the end of time, they at once attempt, not very successfully, to "move on" and anxiously wait around for "that other shoe to drop." A faux archival strip, "Etymological Vaudeville," offers a lesson on the origin of this expression of suspense, under a header that proclaims, "Revealed: 19th century source for 21st century's dominant metaphor!" The tracing of this mock genealogy, the elaboration of meaning across time, is provocatively juxtaposed to the strip's insistence that both meaning and time have been evacuated by the attacks. Despite the artist's insistence that time hangs suspended around the events, the movements of history permeate the strip; and rather than remaining outside history, 9/11 becomes the occasion for a proliferation of histories of disaster and violence, a proliferation that expands into another register as, in the second half of the book, Spiegelman's artwork gives way to an archive of historical comic strips. Crucially, the artist comments, in a text balloon in his final strip, that in the aftermath of the 9/11 attacks, "many found comfort in poetry," while "others searched for solace in old newspaper comics." The archive of early-twentieth-century strips illustrates a significant historical continuity—the political engagement of comics—denied by the insistently "depoliticized" atmosphere after 9/11; it serves, as well, to mime and transpose the mourner's books popular in the nineteenth century, which incorporated consolatory texts brought together from a number of points in time and space. As postmodern mourner's handbook, *In the Shadow of No Towers* threatens, in its insistent, near-manic polychrony, to overwhelm the reader with a traumatizing time-saturation, to simply reproduce rather than interrogate the pace of its times, to affirm, along with its artist, that "right under the surface, we're all still just a bunch of stunned pigeons." Yet because this polychronous compendium reckons grief in times and registers beyond the melotraumatic—because it engages the ongoingness of life as well as the structuring (or destruction) of recognized life-stories, addressing not only the sublimity and suspension of suffering but also its banality, its ordinariness, even its predictability, the book challenges any clear distinction between a historically eventful time and the ostensibly unhistorical time of everyday life.[23] That challenge, in turn, permits *In the Shadow of No Towers* to sketch new connections across temporalities and between times, remapping relations between past and present so that—despite the artist's anxious insistence that the future has already terminated—another one, unexpected at present, may yet arrive. And if grief, in itself, can teach us nothing, its interminable insufficiency, in these times and others, may still be arranged in the service of this possibility.

Notes

Notes to the Introduction

1. Laura M. Stevens cites this commercial as exemplifying the persistent association of the Indian with death in the American cultural imaginary. I am arguing, however, that the PSA's staging of what is, in effect, an act of auto-mourning deserves consideration through the lens of affect, rather than mortality alone. See Stevens, "The Christian Origins of the Vanishing Indian," in Nancy Isenberg and Andrew Burstein, eds., *Mortal Remains: Death in Early America* (Philadelphia: University of Pennsylvania Press, 2002).

2. On the history of time in this period, see Jerome Hamilton Buckley, *The Triumph of Time: A Study of the Victorian Concepts of Time, History, Progress and Decadence* (Cambridge, MA: Harvard University Press, 1966); Robin Gilmour, *The Victorian Period: The Intellectual and Cultural Context of English Literature, 1830–1930* (New York: Longman, 1994); Raymond Chapman, *The Sense of the Past in Victorian Literature* (London: Croon Helm, 1986); Peter J. Bowler, *The Invention of Progress: The Victorians and the Past* (Oxford, UK: Blackwell, 1989). For a critique of the way these studies fail to take sufficient account of the gendered politics of time, see Patricia Murphy, *Time Is of the Essence: Temporality, Gender, and the New Woman* (Albany: State University of New York Press, 2001). See also J. T. Fraser, ed., *The Voices of Time: A Cooperative Survey of Man's Views of Time as Expressed by the Sciences and by the Humanities* (Amherst: University of Massachusetts Press, 1981).

3. See Buckley, *The Triumph of Time*. Both Bowler and Gilmour point out that this dominant linear historiography coexisted with what Bowler calls "cyclical" and Gilmour calls "apocalyptic" approaches. See Bowler, *The Invention of Progress*; Gilmour, *The Victorian Period*.

4. Gilmour, *The Victorian Period*, p. 25.

5. See Michel Foucault, *The History of Sexuality, Volume 1: An Introduction*, trans. Robert Hurley (New York: Vintage, 1990), esp. pp. 135–49.

6. Phillipe Ariès, *Western Attitudes toward Death: From the Middle Ages to the Present*, trans. Patricia M. Ranum (Baltimore: Johns Hopkins University Press, 1974), pp. 67–

68. See also Phillipe Ariès, *The Hour of Our Death*, trans. Helen Weaver (New York: Oxford University Press, 1991), esp. part 4, pp. 407–556.

7. In their important adaptations of Ariès's framework to the North American context, David Stannard and James J. Farrell both echo Ariès's insistence that the focus on mourning amounts to a repression of death's finality. Stannard, for instance, asserts that the "self-indulgence, sentimentalization, and ostentation of the nineteenth-century approach to death" reveals "a world that had lost a meaningful and functioning sense of community," and Farrell describes the period as the core of what he designates the "dying of death" in America, the concealment of the reality of death within a framework of "liberal optimism" that negated its status as an individual rite of passage. See David E. Stannard, *The Puritan Way of Death: A Study in Religion, Culture, and Social Change* (New York: Oxford University Press, 1977), p. 185; James J. Farrell, *Inventing the American Way of Death, 1830–1920* (Philadelphia: Temple University Press, 1980).

8. Foucault, *The History of Sexuality, Volume 1*, p. 5. By pointing to this similarity, I am not suggesting that death has not been repressed or denied in the West during this period; the point of Foucault's critique of the repressive hypothesis is not that repression does not exist but that repression should be understood as simply one among a range of strategies characterizing a particularly modern mode of production.

9. Charles O. Jackson, for instance, admits that in order to arrange the essays in his volume *Passing: The Vision of Death in America* in accordance with an argument derived from Ariès's framework, he was required to omit work dealing with regional and ethnic variations in the culture of death and dying. Charles O. Jackson, ed., *Passing: The Vision of Death in America* (Westport, CT: Greenwood, 1977), p. x. Recent cross-cultural studies such as Joseph Roach's seminal *Cities of the Dead: Circum-Atlantic Performance* (New York: Columbia University Press, 1996) have helped to correct this omission.

10. Indeed, some scholars dismiss this body of work as itself an act of melancholy worship; Joachim Whaley, for example, asserts that Ariès's writing is "not a work of scholarship but a piece of nostalgic devotional literature." Joachim Whaley, ed., *Mirrors of Mortality: Studies in the Social History of Death* (London: Europa, 1981), p. 8, quoted in Neil Small, "Death and Difference," in David Field, Jenny Hockey, and Neil Small, eds., *Death, Gender and Ethnicity* (London: Routledge, 1997), p. 208. In an intriguing psychobiographical account of the politics of longing in Ariès's work, Patrick Hutton argues that the nostalgic mournfulness shaping Ariès's histories of death results from his own disappointment, in youth, that the return to traditional values touted by the Vichy regime resulted not in cultural renewal but in repression. According to Hutton, "History became Ariès's consolation for a politics that was no longer viable and a way of life that was passing. His historical writing became his means of reconciling himself with the eclipse of a traditional culture that he had loved." Patrick H. Hutton, "Of Death and Destiny: The Ariès-Vovelle Debate about the History of Mourning," in Peter Homans, ed., *Symbolic Loss: The Ambiguity of Mourning and Mem-*

ory at Century's End (Charlottesville: University Press of Virginia, 2000), p. 148. Yet Ariès's conservatism cannot alone account for the popularity of an account that has, until quite recently, dominated the field of Western thanatohistory, particularly since the dying-of-death narrative by no means originated with him; it was already well established in the work of scholars like Geoffrey Gorer, whose 1955 essay "The Pornography of Death" asserts that death had replaced sex as the great taboo of the twentieth century. See Geoffrey Gorer, "The Pornography of Death," in *Death, Grief and Mourning in Contemporary Britain* (London: Cresset, 1965), pp. 169–75.

11. Karen Halttunen, "Mourning the Dead: A Study in Sentimental Ritual," in *Confidence Men and Painted Women: A Study of Middle-Class Culture in America, 1830–1870* (New Haven, CT: Yale University Press, 1982). For an example of the New Historicist account of grief's disciplinarity, see Richard Brodhead's "Sparing the Rod," in *Cultures of Letters: Scenes of Reading and Writing in Nineteenth-Century America* (Chicago: University of Chicago Press, 1993), p. 34. I discuss Brodhead's argument more extensively in chapter 3 of this book. Other examples of this approach include Shirley Samuels, ed., *The Culture of Sentiment: Race, Gender and Sentimentality in Nineteenth-Century America* (New York: Oxford University Press, 1993); Gillian Brown, *Domestic Individualism: Imagining Self in Nineteenth-Century America* (Berkeley: University of California Press, 1992); and Lora Romero, *Home Fronts: Domesticity and Its Critics in the Antebellum United States* (Durham, NC: Duke University Press, 1997).

12. Cf. Max Weber, *The Protestant Ethic and the "Spirit" of Capitalism and Other Writings,* trans. Peter Baehr and Gordon C. Wells (New York: Penguin, 2002).

13. Edgar Allan Poe, "Al Araaf," in *Collected Poetry and Tales* (New York: Library of America, 1984), p. 49, quoted in Candace Vogler, "Much of Madness and More of Sin: Compassion, for Ligeia," in Lauren Berlant, ed., *Compassion: The Culture and Politics of an Emotion* (New York: Routledge, 2004), p. 33. Vogler emphasizes the aggressiveness of the pleasure taken by women in displaying this kind of sorrow, underlining what I will later discuss as a distinctively sentimental combination of mixed feeling and altered temporality.

14. Mitchell Breitwieser, *American Puritanism and the Defense of Mourning: Religion, Grief and Ethnology in Mary White Rowlandson's Captivity Narrative* (Madison: University of Wisconsin Press, 1990), p. 59.

15. Andreas Hyperias, *The Practice of Preaching* (London, 1577), quoted in Breitwieser, *American Puritanism and the Defense of Mourning,* p. 65.

16. See, for example, David Landes, *Revolution in Time: Clocks and the Making of the Modern World* (New York: Belknap, 1983); Gerhard Dohrn-van Rossum, *History of the Hour: Clocks and Modern Temporal Orders,* trans. Thomas Dunlap (Chicago: University of Chicago Press, 1996). Two fine local accounts of the authority of the clock are Stuart Sherman, *Telling Time: Clocks, Diaries and English Diurnal Form, 1660–1785* (Chicago: University of Chicago Press, 1996), and Mark M. Smith, *Mastered by the Clock: Time, Slavery and Freedom in the American South* (Chapel Hill: University of North Carolina Press, 1997).

17. On the modernization of time under capitalism, see E. P. Thompson, "Time, Work-Discipline and Industrial Capitalism," in *Customs in Common* (New York: New Press, 1991), pp. 352–403.

18. This assessment dominates Marxist accounts of the modernization of time as an effect of industrialization; for a key instance, see Thompson, "Time, Work-Discipline and Industrial Capitalism."

19. Michael O'Malley, *Keeping Watch: A History of American Time* (New York: Viking, 1990), p. 48. For a history of the nineteenth-century American movement toward time standardization, see Ian Bartky, *Selling the True Time: Nineteenth-Century Timekeeping in America* (Stanford, CA: Stanford University Press, 2000).

20. Akos Ostor notes the repeated reinvention, across the history of industrialization, of idealized preindustrial notions of time with each successive generation. See Ostor, *Vessels of Time: An Essay on Temporal Change and Social Transformation* (Delhi: Oxford University Press, 1993), p. 38.

21. The account of sacred time I present here draws upon Mircea Eliade's analysis in *The Sacred and the Profane: The Nature of Religion* (New York: Harcourt, 1987). Although Eliade's approach, as a number of anthropologists and historians have asserted, is ahistorical and overly simplified (particularly in his general opposition of "religious" and "modern" man), the notion of sacred time he outlines is useful, I believe, precisely because it articulates a fantasy that effectively corresponds to (and presumably draws upon and contributes to) the cultural temporal imaginary with which I am concerned in this study.

22. Talal Asad, *Formations of the Secular: Christianity, Islam, Modernity* (Stanford, CA: Stanford University Press, 2003), p. 25.

23. Ibid., p. 31.

24. Mitchell Meltzer, *Secular Revelations: The Constitution of the United States and Classic American Literature* (Cambridge, MA: Harvard University Press, 2005), pp. 12–13.

25. Michel Foucault, "Of Other Spaces," trans. Jay Miskowiec, *Diacritics* 16.1 (spring 1986): p. 23.

26. Tracy Fessenden, "Gendering Religion," *Journal of Women's History* 14, no. 1 (spring 2002): p. 165.

27. For a denominationally and theologically attentive discussion of antihierarchical deployments of Protestant faiths in the nineteenth century, see Carolyn A. Haynes, *Divine Destiny: Gender and Race in Nineteenth-Century Protestantism* (Jackson: University of Mississippi Press, 1998).

28. Asad notes that "*sacredness* in the modern secular state is attributed not to real living persons but precisely to 'the human' conceptualized abstractly, or imagined in a state of nature." Asad, *Formations of the Secular,* p. 143 (emphasis in original).

29. Giorgio Agamben, *Homo Sacer: Sovereign Power and Bare Life,* trans. Daniel Heller-Roazen (Stanford, CA: Stanford University Press, 1998).

30. Ibid., pp. 9, 124.

31. My thinking about Agamben's assessment of the sacred owes a great deal to conversations with Lauren Berlant.

32. Foucault, *The History of Sexuality, Volume 1*, p. 139.

33. Cf. ibid., p. 114. See also the discussion of time in *Discipline and Punish*, in which Foucault outlines linkages between the uses of the body and time. Foucault, *Discipline and Punish: The Birth of the Prison*, trans. Alan Sheridan (New York: Vintage, 1979), esp. pp. 135–39.

34. On modernity articulated as a regional development in European temporal thought, see Rene Kosseleck, *Futures Past: On the Semantics of Historical Time*, trans. Keith Tribe (New York: Columbia University Press, 2004).

35. Foucault, *The History of Sexuality, Volume 1*, p. 155. Bruce Burgett cites this observation in his call for the construction of a "queer history of sexuality," a history that refuses to assume that the content of sexuality is determined by an *a priori* agreement on what constitutes "sex." Burgett, "Between Speculation and Population: The Problem of 'Sex' in Our Long Eighteenth Century," *Early American Literature* 37, no. 1 (2002): pp. 119–53.

36. Foucault, *The History of Sexuality, Volume 1*, p. 125.

37. Ann Laura Stoler, *Race and the Education of Desire: Foucault's History of Sexuality and the Colonial Order of Things* (Durham, NC: Duke University Press, 1995).

38. Julie Ellison, *Cato's Tears and the Making of Anglo-American Emotion* (Chicago: University of Chicago Press, 1999).

39. Here I have in mind, especially, Homi Bhabha's pointed critique, in *The Location of Culture*, of Foucault's "disallowing" of the "temporal disjunction that the modern question of race would introduce" into biopolitics. Noting Foucault's insistence that "we must conceptualize the deployment of sexuality on the basis of the techniques of power that are contemporary with it," Bhabha argues that Foucault repeats the tendency of the European world to represent the raced "other" as out of sync with modernity. This critique rightly describes the Eurocentric terrain of *The History of Sexuality*'s first volume, where Foucault alternately undercites (as in this hasty gloss on dynamic racism) and hypostatizes (in his later insistence that racism ultimately corresponds to the deployment of alliance rather than sexuality) modern logics of race. See Homi Bhabha, *The Location of Culture* (London: Routledge, 1994). Nevertheless, I hold that the possibilities of a Foucauldian analysis animated by a nuanced understanding of the temporalities of the body, or chronobiopolitics, can effectively address the raced and sexed imbrications of time-spaces across modernity—but only if that understanding remedies Foucault's chronically limited understanding of culture, gender, and race. My thinking here is particularly indebted to the work of Ann Laura Stoler. See Stoler, *Race and the Education of Desire*, and Stoler, *Carnal Knowledge and Imperial Power: Race and the Intimate in Colonial Rule* (Berkeley: University of California Press, 2002).

40. Philip Fisher, *The Vehement Passions* (Princeton, NJ: Princeton University Press, 2002), p. 78.

41. Ibid., p. 79.

42. Ibid., p. 90.

43. For instance, Mary Louise Kete, whose work I discuss later in this chapter, observes that the "individualist" framework of Freudian mourning is out of step with what she terms the "collaborative" model of the subject embraced by midcentury sentimentalists. Similarly, in *Bearing the Dead,* Esther Schor notes that contemporary attention to the Freudian psychological model of mourning tends to overshadow the social rituals that constituted mourning in the nineteenth century. See Kete, *Sentimental Collaborations: Mourning and Middle-Class Identity in Nineteenth-Century America* (Durham, NC: Duke University Press, 2000); Schor, *Bearing the Dead: The British Culture of Mourning from the Enlightenment to Victoria* (Princeton, NJ: Princeton University Press, 1995).

44. Michael Moon, "Memorial Rags," in George E. Haggerty and Bonnie Zimmerman, eds., *Professions of Desire: Lesbian and Gay Studies in Literature* (New York: Modern Language Association, 1995), pp. 233–40.

45. See Tammy Clewell, "Mourning beyond Melancholia: Freud's Psychoanalysis of Loss," *Journal of the American Psychoanalytic Association* 52, no. 1 (2004): p. 47.

46. For instance, Julia Kristeva's account of the atemporality of the unconscious assesses neurosis and perversion alike as linked to the subject's play with "outside time." Kristeva, *Time and Sense: Proust and the Experience of Literature,* trans. R. Guberman (New York: Columbia University Press, 1996).

47. Sigmund Freud, "On Transience," in *Character and Culture,* ed. Philip Rieff (New York: Macmillan, 1963), p. 149 [148–51].

48. Ibid.

49. Ibid., p. 150.

50. For an analysis of this shift in Freud's thinking, see Judith Butler, *The Psychic Life of Power: Theories in Subjection* (Stanford, CA: Stanford University Press, 1997).

51. Sigmund Freud, letter to Ludwig Binswanger (1929), in Ernst L. Freud, ed., *Letters of Sigmund Freud* (New York: Basic Books, 1960), p. 386, quoted in Clewell, "Mourning beyond Melancholia," pp. 61–62 (emphasis added).

52. See Clewell, "Mourning beyond Melancholia," p. 57; for an account of modern poetry that repeats the tenets of this assessment of Victorian and modern thought on loss, see Jahan Ramazani, *Poetry of Mourning: The Modern Elegy from Hardy to Heaney* (Chicago: University of Chicago Press, 1994).

53. Breitwieser, *American Puritanism and the Defense of Mourning,* p. 5. I read this passage *not* as mapping a sentimental-domestic championing of "private" values against a heartless "public" but, rather, as positioning an idiosyncratic process of psychic change against the projected stasis of official history.

54. On the links between sentimental and Freudian subjects, see also Julia Stern, *The Plight of Feeling: Sympathy and Dissent in the Early American Novel* (Chicago: University of Chicago Press, 1997); Glenn Hendler, *Public Sentiments: Structures of Feeling in Nineteenth-Century American Literature* (Chapel Hill: University of North Carolina Press, 2001); and Marianne Noble, *The Masochistic Pleasures of Sentimental Literature* (Princeton, NJ: Princeton University Press, 2000). On Rowlandson's anachronistic moments, see Breitwieser, *American Puritanism and the Defense of Mourning,* pp. 142, 158.

55. Anne McClintock, *Imperial Leather: Race, Gender and Sexuality in the Colonial Contest* (New York: Routledge, 1995).

56. Wai Chee Dimock, *Through Other Continents: American Literature across Deep Time* (Princeton, NJ: Princeton University Press, 2006).

57. See also Jeffrey Insko's consideration of the way anachronism presents history as a "negotiation," a conceptualization that is, as he stresses, central to a "nonteleological democratic project" in which the national and cultural identities informed by the past remain open forms because that past remains a work in progress; Insko, "Anachronistic Imaginings: *Hope Leslie*'s Challenge to Historicism," *American Literary History* 16, no. 2 (2004): pp. 179–207. I discuss this essay further in chapter 2.

58. Peter Osborne, *The Politics of Time: Modernity and Avant-Garde* (London: Verso, 1995), p. 200.

59. For important recent correctives to this history of neglect, see Christopher Nealon, *Foundlings: Gay and Lesbian Historical Emotion before Stonewall* (Durham, NC: Duke University Press, 2001); Judith Halberstam, *In a Queer Time and Place: Transgender Bodies, Subcultural Lives* (Durham, NC: Duke University Press, 2005); and Elizabeth Freeman, "Packing History, Count(er)ing Generations," *New Literary History* 31, no. 4 (autumn 2000): pp. 727–44.

60. Roland Barthes, *Camera Lucida: Reflections on Photography* (New York: Hill and Wang, 1981), p. 21, quoted in Noble, *The Masochistic Pleasures of Sentimental Literature*, p. 77.

61. Barthes, *Camera Lucida*, p. 59.

62. On the evolution of this connotation of "sentimental," see Raymond Williams, *Keywords: A Vocabulary of Culture and Society* (New York: Oxford University Press, 1976), pp. 281–82.

63. For an overview of the way this approach responds to and corrects the polemical oppositions of the Douglas-Tompkins debate, see Shirley Samuels, introduction to Samuels, ed., *The Culture of Sentiment*, pp. 4–6. See also Romero, *Home Fronts*.

64. Kete, *Sentimental Collaborations*, pp. 17 (emphasis in original), 45. Kete's intriguing description of the sentimental as a transgeneric impulse, characterized by a mixing of "narrative" and "lyric" temporalities, provides a nuanced description of sentimental form. Her characterization of temporal modes in terms of *genre* alone, however, avoids any extensive discussion of nineteenth-century cultural frameworks for the politics of time. As a consequence, Kete's highly suggestive study is less effective at connecting its formal insights to the timeworlds in which they operate.

65. Noble, *The Masochistic Pleasures of Sentimental Literature*, pp. 137, 138.

66. Lauren Berlant, *The Queen of America Goes to Washington City: Essays on Sex and Citizenship* (Durham, NC: Duke University Press, 1997), p. 72.

67. Lauren Berlant, "Poor Eliza," *American Literature* 70, no. 3 (September 1988): p. 646 [635–88].

68. Dillon outlines the dependence of liberalism on a developmental narrative that renders corporeal difference mute facts of the natural world; I discuss these claims more extensively in subsequent chapters.

69. See Jacques Derrida's understanding of the (interminable) work of mourning in *Specters of Marx: The State of the Debt, the Work of Mourning and the New International,* trans. Peggy Kamuf (New York: Routledge, 1994). Derrida's argument in this book strikes me as a version of what the sentimental critique of the market might have put forth had it transformed its understanding of historical time by moving away from its insistence on the priority of origins and on eternity as telos.

70. Elizabeth Grosz, "The Nature of Culture," in *Time Travels: Feminism, Nature, Power* (Durham, NC: Duke University Press, 2005), p. 52. See also Grosz, *The Nick of Time: Politics, Evolution, and the Untimely* (Durham, NC: Duke University Press, 2004).

71. On the establishment of capitalist consciousness in this period, see Charles Sellers, *The Market Revolution: Jacksonian America, 1815–1846* (New York: Oxford University Press, 1991).

72. On the need to reenergize the languages of the aesthetic in contemporary literary and cultural studies, see Christopher Castiglia and Russ Castronovo, eds., "Aesthetics and the End(s) of Cultural Studies," special issue of *American Literature* 76, no. 3 (September 2004).

73. These observations are drawn from my reading of Walter Benjamin. See especially Benjamin, *The Origin of German Tragic Drama,* trans. John Osborne (London: NLB, 1977), and "Theses on the Philosophy of History," in *Illuminations,* trans. Harry Zohn (New York: Schocken Books, 1969).

74. On queer theory's status as a world-making project, see especially Michael Warner and Lauren Berlant, "What Does Queer Theory Teach Us about X?" *PMLA* 110, no. 3 (fall 1995): pp. 343–49. For more recent studies that exemplify the critical potentiality of queer theory in relation to historiographic and temporal practice, see José Muñoz, *Disidentifications: Queers of Color and the Performance of Politics* (Minneapolis: University of Minnesota Press, 1999), and Carolyn Dinshaw, *Getting Medieval: Sexualities and Communities, Pre- and Post-Modern* (Durham, NC: Duke University Press, 1999).

Notes to Chapter 1

1. John Adams to Thomas Jefferson, March 2, 1816, in Lester J. Capon, ed., *The Adams-Jefferson Letters: The Complete Correspondence between Thomas Jefferson and Abigail and John Adams, vol. 2, 1812–1826* (Chapel Hill: University of North Carolina Press, 1959), p. 464.

2. Jefferson to Adams, April 8, 1816, in *The Adams-Jefferson Letters,* p. 467.

3. Ibid.

4. Ibid.

5. Adams to Jefferson, May 6, 1816, in *The Adams-Jefferson Letters,* p. 472.

6. Ibid., p. 472.

7. Ibid., p. 473.

8. Ibid.

9. Ibid.

10. On contemporary conceptions of melancholia, see Stanley W. Jackson, *Melancholia and Depression: From Hippocratic Times to Modern Times* (New Haven, CT: Yale University Press, 1986).

11. Thomas Jefferson to Thomas Law (June 13, 1824), quoted in Jan Lewis, " 'Those Scenes for Which My Heart Alone Was Made': Affection and Politics in the Age of Jefferson and Hamilton," in Peter N. Stearns and Jan Lewis, eds., *An Emotional History of the United States* (New York: NYU Press, 1998), p. 5.

12. Thomas Jefferson to Angelica Church (August 17, 1788), quoted in Lewis, " 'Those Scenes for Which My Heart Alone Was Made,' " p. 58.

13. Ernst Cassirer, *The Philosophy of the Enlightenment* (Princeton, NJ: Princeton University Press, 1951), p. 242, quoted in Helen Carr, *Inventing the American Primitive: Politics, Gender and the Representation of Native American Literary Traditions, 1789–1936* (New York: NYU Press, 1996), p. 31.

14. Thomas Jefferson to Thomas Law (June 13, 1824), quoted in Lewis, " 'Those Scenes for Which My Heart Alone Was Made,' " p. 57.

15. On the temporality of the modern nation, see Benedict Anderson, *Imagined Communities: Reflections on the Origin and Spread of Nationalism* (London: Verso, 1991); Homi Bhabha, "DissemiNation: Time, Narrative and the Margins of the Modern Nation," in Bhabha, ed., *Nation and Narration* (New York: Routledge, 1990), pp. 291–322.

16. Karen Sánchez-Eppler, "Then When We Clutch Hardest: On the Death of a Child and the Replication of an Image," in Mary Chapman and Glenn Hendler, eds., *Sentimental Men: Masculinity and the Politics of Affect in American Culture* (Berkeley: University of California Press, 1999), p. 65 [64–85]. A later version of this essay appears in Sánchez-Eppler, *Dependent States: The Child's Part in Nineteenth-Century American Culture* (Chicago: University of Chicago Press, 2005).

17. "A Lady" [pseud.], "On Seeing a Deceased Infant," in *The Mourner's Book* (1836; repr., Boston: Benjamin B. Mussey, 1850), p. 139.

18. David E. Stannard, *The Puritan Way of Death: A Study in Religion, Culture, and Social Change* (New York: Oxford University Press, 1977).

19. The phrases are drawn from the poem "On Seeing a Deceased Infant," cited in note 17: "I wonder not that parents' eyes / In gazing thus grow cold and dim / That burning tears and aching sighs / Are blended with the funeral hymn; / The spirit hath an earthly part / That weeps when earthly pleasure flies, / And heaven would scorn the frozen heart / That melts not when the infant dies."

20. Jacob Scales, *Weeping: A Funeral Sermon Delivered at Henniker, New Hampshire, November 30, 1828, the Sabbath Following the Death of Mrs. Abel Connar* (Concord, NH: George Hough, 1829), p. 4.

21. See Ann Douglas, *The Feminization of American Culture* (New York: Anchor Books, 1988); Mark Noll, *America's God: From Jonathan Edwards to Abraham Lincoln* (New York: Oxford University Press, 2002).

22. P. H. Fowler, *The Voice of the Dead: A Sermon, on the Occasion of the Death of Mrs. Catherine Huntington Williams, Preached September 21, 1856* (Utica, NY: Curtiss and White, 1856), p. 6.

23. Mourning conventions indicated both the degree of kinship to the deceased and the period elapsed since the moment of death, ameliorating the interior dislocation of the grieving subject through the use of exterior symbols that connected the spatial and temporal dislocation of the mourner to an event in historical time. For instance, the length of a widow's veil shortened over time, and the black borders of mourning stationery, meant to be used for two years after the death of a spouse, diminished from one-fourth to one-eighth of an inch after the first year and to one-sixteenth of an inch after eighteen months.

24. Washington Irving, "Rural Funerals," in *The Sketch-Book of Geoffrey Crayon* (Reading, PA: Spencer, 1936), p. 153 [144–57].

25. For a history of the rural cemetery movement, see David Charles Sloan, *The Last Great Necessity: Cemeteries in American History* (Baltimore: Johns Hopkins University Press, 1991).

26. See, e.g., James J. Farrell, "The Development of the Modern Cemetery," in *Inventing the American Way of Death, 1830–1920* (Philadelphia: Temple University Press, 1980), pp. 99–145.

27. Jacob Bigelow, *A History of the Cemetery of Mount Auburn* (Boston: James Munroe, 1860), n.p.

28. Jacob Bigelow, "Interment of the Dead," in Cornelia Walker, *Mt. Auburn Illustrated* (New York: R. Martin, 1847), pp. 29, 34–35, quoted in Gary Laderman, *The Sacred Remains: American Attitudes toward Death* (New Haven, CT: Yale University Press, 1996), pp. 71–72.

29. The memorial space of the rural cemetery itself took on some of the outlines of middle-class domesticity. More space could be allotted to individual burial sites than had been possible in church burial yards, and individualized variation in the design of monuments also became possible. Families that could afford it were allowed to purchase lots for their own members to be buried, thus gaining distance from neighboring plots. Indeed, the more affluent the bereaved, the better they could mimic the privacy of the nineteenth-century middle-class household in the space that held their dead.

30. Thomas Baldwin Thayer, *Over the River; or, Pleasant Walks into the Valley of Shadows and Beyond* (Boston: Tompkins, 1864), p. 249, quoted in Karen Halttunen, "Mourning the Dead: A Study in Sentimental Ritual," in *Confidence Men and Painted Women: A Study of Middle-Class Culture in America, 1830–1870* (New Haven, CT: Yale University Press, 1982), p. 133.

31. For an overview of nineteenth-century memorial artifacts, see Martha V. Pike and Janice Gray Armstrong, eds., *A Time to Mourn: Expressions of Grief in Nineteenth Century America* (Stony Brook, NY: Museums at Stony Brook, 1980).

32. See Robin Gilmour, *The Victorian Period: The Intellectual and Cultural Context of English Literature, 1830–1930* (London: Longman, 1994), p. 25.

33. For a perceptive overview of the interrelation of linear and cyclical temporal logics in Western culture, see Stephen Jay Gould, *Time's Arrow, Time's Cycle: Myth and Met-*

aphor in the Discovery of Geological Time (Cambridge, MA: Harvard University Press, 1987).

34. For an account of duration, see John Locke, *An Essay Concerning Human Understanding*, ed. Peter H. Nidditch (New York: Oxford University Press, 1979). Originally published 1690.

35. Nehemiah Adams, *Catharine* (Boston: J. E. Tilton, 1859), pp. 25–26.

36. Ibid., pp. 29–30.

37. Henri Bergson uses music to express the idea of duration; see Bergson, *Time and Free Will: An Essay on the Immediate Data of Consciousness*, trans. F. L. Pogson (New York: Harper and Brothers, 1960), p. 100. Originally published 1889.

38. Nehemiah Adams, *Catharine*, p. 112.

39. Ibid., pp. 112, 115.

40. In addition to the collections cited elsewhere in this chapter, see Mary A. Patrick, ed., *The Mourner's Gift* (New York: Van Nostrand and Dwight, 1837); James Abercrombie, *The Mourner Comforted* (Philadelphia: S. Potter, 1821); Mrs. H. Dwight Williams, *Voices from the Silent Land; or, Leaves of Consolation for the Afflicted* (Boston: John P. Jewett, 1853); S. Iranaeus Prime et al., *The Smitten Household; or, Thoughts for the Afflicted* (New York: Anson D. F. Randolph, 1856); "A Village Pastor" [pseud.], *The Comforter; or, Extracts Selected for the Consolation of Mourners, under the Bereavement of Friends and Relations* (New York: J & J Harper, 1832). For a still widely read example of the earlier model, see John Flavel, *A Token for Mourners* (1674; repr., Brattleboro, VT: William Fessenden, 1813).

41. See, e.g., Hannah More, "Active Duty a Relief to Sorrow," in Rufus Griswold, ed., *The Cypress Wreath: A Book of Consolation for Those Who Mourn* (Boston: Gould, Kendall, and Lincoln, 1844), p. 54.

42. The common injunction against "the appearance of repining" appears, for instance, in Scales, *Weeping*, p. 11.

43. Orville Dewey, *On the Duties of Consolation, and the Rites and Customs Appropriate to Mourning* (New Bedford, MA: Book Tract Association, 1825), p. 6.

44. *North American Review* (October 1836), quoted in N. Cleaveland, *Greenwood in 1846, Illustrated in a Series of Views Taken Especially for This Work by James Smillie* (New York: R. Martin, 1847), p. 53.

45. The nineteenth-century fashion of human-hair memorial tokens—the weaving of pieces of hair of the departed into lockets, mourning samplers, bracelets, et cetera—is the noteworthy exception that proves this rule, since hair was the only form of human remains easily available to the mourner that did not change over the course of time. See Laderman, *The Sacred Remains*.

46. Michel Foucault, *The History of Sexuality, Volume 1*, trans. Robert Hurley (New York: Pantheon, 1978), sec. 5.

47. *The Mourner's Book*, pp. iii–iv.

48. Thomas Jefferson to Thomas Law (June 13, 1824), quoted in Lewis, " 'Those Scenes for Which My Heart Alone Was Made,' " p. 57.

49. Willis Giest, "The Tear of Sympathy," in J. B. Syme, ed., *The Mourner's Friend; or, Sighs of Sympathy for Those Who Sorrow* (Worcester, MA: William Allen, 1852), p. 12.

50. Halttunen, "Mourning the Dead," p. 138; Timothy Taylor, *The Solace; or, Afflictions Lightened*, p. 82, quoted in Halttunen, "Mourning the Dead," p. 138.

51. Nehemiah Adams, *Agnes and the Key of Her Little Coffin* (Boston: S. K. Whipple, 1857), p. 102.

52. Ibid., p. 103.

53. Halttunen, "Mourning the Dead," p. 136.

54. Adams, *Agnes,* p. 123.

55. See Michael O'Malley, *Keeping Watch: A History of American Time* (New York: Viking, 1990), for a discussion of the part played by this perspective in nineteenth-century American attitudes toward time.

56. See Patricia Murphy, *Time Is of the Essence: Temporality, Gender, and the New Woman* (Albany: State University of New York Press, 2001), esp. pp. 16–18.

57. Julie Ellison, *Cato's Tears and the Making of Anglo-American Emotion* (Chicago: University of Chicago Press, 1999).

58. Roger Williams, *A Key into the Language of America; or, An Help to the Language of the Natives in That Part of America, Called New-England* (1643; repr., New York: Russell and Russell, 1973), p. 202, p. 5.

59. Thomas Jefferson, *Notes on the State of Virginia* (Chapel Hill: University of North Carolina Press, 1955), p. 60. Originally published 1787.

60. Jonathan Carver, *Three Years' Travel through the Interior of North America* (Philadelphia: Cruikshank and Bell, 1784), p. 166.

61. Ibid.

62. Ibid., pp. 166–67.

63. For an overview of these arguments, see Lucy Maddox, *Removals: Nineteenth-Century American Literature and the Politics of Indian Affairs* (New York: Oxford University Press, 1991), chap. 1.

64. See Helen Carr, *Inventing the American Primitive: Politics, Gender, and the Representation of Native American Literary Traditions* (New York: NYU Press, 1996).

65. Henry Schoolcraft, *Western Scenes and Reminisces: Together with Thrilling Legends and Traditions of the Red Men of the Forest* (Buffalo, NY: Derby, Orton & Mulligan, 1853), p. 103.

66. Schoolcraft's assessment of Native American timeways will be further examined in chapter 2 of this book.

67. See Ellison, *Cato's Tears,* for a consideration of the eighteenth-century embrace of the dying Indian as a figure for Anglo-American sensibility.

68. This case illustrates the framing of the sacralizing exception as it constitutes the construction of expendable populations, and it underscores my contention, in the introduction to this book, that Giorgio Agamben's suggestive description of this "state of exception" is in need of greater temporal precision. See Agamben, *Homo Sacer: Sovereign Power and Bare Life* (Stanford, CA: Stanford University Press, 1998).

69. Rev. John Sharpe, "Proposal for Erecting a School, Library and Chapel at New

York" (1712), quoted in Albert J. Raboteau, *Slave Religion: The "Invisible Institution" in the Antebellum South* (Oxford: Oxford University Press, 1978), p. 66.

70. Eighteenth-century slave traders complained of the peculiar vulnerability of enslaved Africans to an often-fatal condition they called "fixed melancholy," a terminal unresponsiveness to external stimulation; this condition resonated as a bodily imbalance, an excess of black bile that prevented the slave from adapting to new conditions. See Peter Kolchin, *American Slavery 1619–1877* (New York: Hill and Wang, 1995), p. 21.

71. Jefferson, *Notes on the State of Virginia*, p. 139. For a discussion of this passage in the context of that construction of citizenship that relies upon the affective capacities of the subject, see Peter Coviello, "Agonizing Affection: Affect and Nation in Early America," *Early American Literature* 37, no. 3 (2002): pp. 447–48.

72. Elizabeth Maddock Dillon, *The Gender of Freedom: Fictions of Liberalism and the Literary Public Sphere* (Stanford, CA: Stanford University Press, 2004), p. 19.

73. Ibid., p. 18–19.

74. Ibid., p. 17 (emphasis added).

75. On the similarity of this internal suspension of the racial "other" to the Freudian model of melancholia, see Anne Anlin Cheng, *The Melancholy of Race: Psychoanalysis, Assimilation and Hidden Grief* (New York: Oxford University Press, 2001).

76. "[C]an the liberties of a nation be thought secure when we have removed their only firm basis, a conviction in the minds of the people that these liberties are the gift of God?" Jefferson, *Notes on the State of Virginia*, p. 163.

77. Sánchez-Eppler, *Dependent States*, p. 109.

78. Harriet Beecher Stowe, *Uncle Tom's Cabin* (New York: Penguin, 1981). Further references to this edition will be cited parenthetically within the text.

79. See especially Lauren Berlant's reading of the traumatized temporality of sentimental spectacle, focusing on the afterlives of *Uncle Tom's Cabin* in commodity culture, "Poor Eliza," *American Literature* 70, no. 3 (September 1998): pp. 635–68. Marianne Noble's assessment of the function of ecstatic wounding in the novel also decries the paralyzing narcissism that accompanies the politics of sympathy, though she stops short of condemning the form of Stowe's appeal entirely. See Noble, *The Masochistic Pleasures of Sentimental Literature* (Princeton, NJ: Princeton University Press, 2000), pp. 145–46.

80. Glenn Hendler, *Public Sentiments: Structures of Feeling in Nineteenth-Century American Literature* (Chapel Hill: University of North Carolina Press, 2001), p. 8.

81. William Apess, "Eulogy on King Philip, as Pronounced at the Odeon, on Federal Street, Boston," in *On Our Own Ground: The Complete Writings of William Apess, a Pequot*, ed. Barry O'Connell (Amherst: University of Massachusetts Press, 1992), pp. 275–310. For an analysis that connects Apess's use of strategies of reversal in the *Eulogy* to his earlier works, see Renee Bergland, *The National Uncanny: Indian Ghosts and American Subjects* (Hanover, NH: University Press of New England, 2000), pp. 120–44.

82. See Cheryl Walker, *Indian Nation: Native American Literature and Nineteenth-Century Nationalisms* (Durham, NC: Duke University Press, 1997), chap. 8; Anne Marie Dannenberg, " 'Where, Then, Shall We Place the Hero of the Wilderness?': William Apess' *Eulogy on King Philip* and the Doctrines of Racial Destiny," in Helen Jaskoski, ed., *Early Native American Writing: New Critical Essays* (New York: Cambridge University Press, 1996), pp. 66–82. For an overview of contemporary Anglo-American revisions of Philip's legacy, see Philip Gould, "Remembering Metacom: Historical Writing and the Cultures of Masculinity in Early Republican America," in Chapman and Hendler, eds., *Sentimental Men*, pp. 112–24.

83. Apess, "Eulogy on King Philip," p. 277.

84. Ibid., p. 280.

85. Ibid., p. 281.

86. Ibid., p. 286.

87. Shame's temporality is underscored in Eve Kosofsky Sedgwick's consideration, by way of Silvan Tompkins, of the suddenness that marks the interruption of a self-confirming circuit. In this way, it might be understood to function affectively in much the same way that Paul de Man has described irony to function rhetorically: as a present-tense temporal doubling signaling the suspension of "the innocence or authenticity of our sense of being in the world." See Eve Kosofsky Sedgwick, "Shame, Theatricality, and Queer Performativity: Henry James's *The Art of the Novel*," in *Touching Feeling: Affect, Pedagogy, Performativity* (Durham, NC: Duke University Press, 2003), pp. 35–65; Paul de Man, "The Rhetoric of Temporality," in *Blindness and Insight: Essays in the Rhetoric of Contemporary Criticism* (Minneapolis: University of Minnesota Press, 1983), pp. 187–228. I return to the temporality of irony in chapter 4 of this study.

88. Apess, "Eulogy on King Philip," p. 301.

89. Ibid., p. 310.

90. Barry O'Connell, introduction to O'Connell, ed., *On Our Own Ground*, p. lxxii.

91. Dillon, *The Gender of Freedom*, pp. 15–16.

92. See Ellison, *Cato's Tears*.

93. *The Mourner's Book*, pp. iii–iv.

94. See Dillon, *The Gender of Freedom*, pp. 18–19. I discuss the protonational function of the mother more extensively in chapter 3.

95. Julia Kristeva, "Women's Time," in *The Kristeva Reader*, ed. Toril Moi (New York: Columbia University Press, 1986), pp. 187–213.

96. Ibid., p. 191. As I noted in the preceding section, the gradual absorption of Christianity into privileged forms of Western historical identity signaled a gradual transformation of the principle of static time from the pure timelessness of eternity to what Kristeva calls the "massive" temporality of the monumental. But although eternity and monumentality are so closely aligned in Kristeva's writing as to appear interchangeable, the monumental should properly be understood as a *historical* form of temporal stasis; it is, as Nietzsche reminds us, a mode of viewing the past that establishes an essential identity between past and present, making time stand still in the service of "truth." See Friedrich Nietzsche, *On the Advantage and Disadvantage of History for Life*, trans. Peter Prauss (Indianapolis: Hackett, 1980).

97. Kristeva, "Women's Time," p. 192.

98. Hortense J. Spillers, "Momma's Baby, Poppa's Maybe: An American Grammar Book," in *Black, White and in Color: Essays on American Literature and Culture* (Chicago: University of Chicago Press, 2003), pp. 203–29.

99. The conventional assumption that mourning was "women's work" in nineteenth-century America has been challenged by recent scholarship that looks beyond the "separate spheres" ideology informing early studies of sentimental culture. See especially Mary Chapman and Glenn Hendler, eds., *Sentimental Men: Masculinity and the Politics of Affect in American Culture* (Berkeley: University of California Press, 1999); Milette Shamir and Jennifer Travis, eds., *Boys Don't Cry? Rethinking Narratives of Masculinity and Emotion in the U.S.* (New York: Columbia University Press, 2002). Nevertheless, the centrality of both the allegorical female figure of the mourner and, especially, the figure of the mother in nineteenth-century mourning culture foregrounds a persistent association of grief with femininity—an association that is, as I will argue, typified as the radical openness of the female body. On the figure of the mother in nineteenth-century mourning culture, see especially Mary Ryan, *Empire of the Mother: American Writing about Domesticity, 1830–1860* (New York: Harrington Park, 1985), and Carolyn Dever, *Death and the Mother from Dickens to Freud: Victorian Fiction and the Anxiety of Origins* (New York: Oxford University Press, 1998).

100. Indeed, the excessively mournful mother might well be viewed as a quasi-Gothic figure, shadowing the nurture of the sentimental mother and threatening to undo her temporal labor.

101. As a vehicle for temporal stability, the vulnerable child also regulated the compatibility of the public and private spheres; the iterative space of the home could be mapped along the linear time of collective national life insofar as both articulated themselves as temporal constructs concerned with the future of the child, as both an idealized figure of collective temporal progression and as actualized fragments of individual developmental time. The sacralization of the child, then, stabilized both the linear time of the public and the cyclical time of the household. Lee Edelman has described this deployment of the child as the principle of "reproductive futurity." What I am outlining here is, to a certain extent, the cultural prehistory of the psychoanalytic framework upon which Edelman's polemic draws. See Edelman, *No Future: Queer Theory and the Death Drive* (Durham, NC: Duke University Press, 2004). See also Lauren Berlant's discussion of infantile citizenship in her *The Queen of America Goes to Washington City: Essays on Sex and Citizenship* (Durham, NC: Duke University Press, 1997).

102. Letitia Elizabeth Landon, "The Little Shroud," in *Poems from the Literary Gazette*, ed. F. J. Snyder (Ann Arbor, MI: Scholar's Facsimiles and Reprints, 2003), pp. 428–30. Also reprinted in *The Mourner's Book*, pp. 136–37.

103. For an analysis of nineteenth-century elegy that emphasizes its structural compatibility with the Freudian account of the mourning process, see Peter Sacks, *The English Elegy: Studies in the Genre from Spenser to Yeats* (Baltimore: Johns Hopkins University Press, 1985).

104. Sigmund Freud, "Mourning and Melancholia," in *The Standard Edition of the*

Complete Psychoanalytic Works of Sigmund Freud, vol. 14, trans. James Strachey (London: Hogarth Press, 1957).

105. Sigmund Freud, letter to Ludwig Binswanger (1929), in Ernst L. Freud, ed., *Letters of Sigmund Freud* (New York: Basic Books, 1960), p. 386.

106. This aspect of the poem points to a significant difficulty in the argument posed by Mary Louise Kete on the centrality of mourning to sentimental culture. That culture functions in Kete's view as a gift economy, circulating tokens of remembrance not only of the dead but also of mutual affection and sympathy among the living to create networks of obligation. Sentimental culture's idealization of continuity leads to its insistence on the fundamentally collaborative nature of subjectivity, an insistence that, for Kete, places it at odds with other nineteenth-century aesthetic and economic structures—Romanticism, the market, Freudian psychoanalysis—all of which are founded upon versions of the self-possessed, autonomous individual. I emphasize, in contrast, the interdependence of these modes of conceiving the temporality of the subject. This moment in Landon's poem may serve to exemplify that distinction. Kete challenges the formal reading of (Romantic) apostrophe as a disruptive "turning away" in and of language by insisting that sentimental apostrophe is essentially reparative, insofar as it "bridges the gap between temporality and eternity." See Mary Louise Kete, *Sentimental Collaborations: Mourning and Middle-Class Identity in Nineteenth-Century America* (Durham, NC: Duke University Press, 2000), p. 45. I would argue, however, that the diffusive movement of the apostrophe makes the choice between "disruption" and "reparation" finally impossible, an impossibility that gestures toward the difficulty of establishing distinct boundaries between Romanticism as an "individualist" and sentimentality as a "collaborative" genre.

107. The transformation of the mother's melancholy into ordinary maternal mournfulness in this poem recalls Juliana Schiesari's contention that the philosophical insight accorded to melancholy in the modern era was reserved for men and that this insight required a simultaneous projection onto women (and, I would add, onto people of color) of a naturalized and consequently mute melancholia. See Juliana Schiesari, *The Gendering of Melancholia: Feminism, Psychoanalysis, and the Symbolics of Loss in Renaissance Literature* (Ithaca, NY: Cornell University Press, 1992). My argument that readers could not "see" but could "sense" the wounds of time in poetry such as Landon's might seem uncritically to reproduce a version of this very distinction by suggesting that these (women) readers' melancholy operated "mutely," as opposed to the "insight" reserved for the privileged critic. I would insist, however, that such "sensory" reading practices were, first of all, not limited to female readers but were, as the "universalizing" appeal of grief in texts such as Adams's posits, adopted by a range of nineteenth-century readers and, second and much more important for my purposes, that "sensory" reading is *not* inherently opposed to critical thought as such. Rather, as queer theory has most usefully shown, the corporeal knowledges engaged in what I am here calling "sensory reading" are not only not inherently opposed to critical contemplation but should in fact be understood as central to it.

108. Esther Schor, *Bearing the Dead: The British Culture of Mourning from the Enlightenment to Victoria* (Princeton, NJ: Princeton University Press, 1995), p. 3. For analyses of the American side of this market phenomenon, see Douglas, *The Feminization of American Culture,* and Halttunen, "Mourning the Dead."

Notes to Chapter 2

1. James Fenimore Cooper, *The Pioneers* (New York: Penguin, 1988), p. 450. Originally published 1823.

2. Ibid., p. 452.

3. Ibid.. Though Natty appears to accede, in his approbation of the "truth" of Effingham's speech, to the stone's distinction between Indian flaws and (white) men's virtue, the reminiscence with which he follows this melancholy reflection undermines that very distinction; Natty confirms Chingachgook's manly valor by recalling the number of scalps he secured in a long-ago battle, exclaiming, "He did lay about him like a man! I met him as I was coming home from the trail, with eleven Mingo scalps on his pole" (452). Natty's memory thus locates the Mohican's manly virtue not in opposition to his Indianness, as did the stone, but *within* its frames of reference. In response to the "civilized" womanly sensibilities of Oliver's new bride Elizabeth, he defends Chingachgook by pointing out that he followed tribal law: "You needn't shudder, Madam Effingham, for they was all shaved heads and warriors" (452). In the second novel of the series, *The Last of the Mohicans,* Natty maintains this temporal distinction in masculine norms, insisting that scalping, which appears savage to civilized whites, is normal for Indians. See *The Last of the Mohicans: A Narrative of the Year 1757* (1826; repr., New York: Penguin, 1986), p. 114. Further references to this novel will be cited parenthetically within the text.

4. I am drawing here on Friedrich Nietzsche's description of monumental history as a strategy of "approximation" that entails forgetting. See Friedrich Nietzsche, *On the Advantage and Disadvantage of History for Life,* trans. Peter Prauss (1874; repr., Indianapolis: Hackett, 1980). I discuss Nietzsche's writing on monumental history more extensively in chapter 4 of this book.

5. Cooper, *The Pioneers,* p. 452.

6. Cooper's discussion of Indian languages in the preface to *The Last of the Mohicans,* the second novel in the Leatherstocking series, highlights the meaningfulness of sound in those languages, noting, "they will even convey different significations by the simplest inflexions of the voice." See *The Last of the Mohicans,* p. 5.

7. My argument here owes much to Renee Bergland's account of the "ghosting" of the Indian in *The National Uncanny: Indian Ghosts and American Subjects* (Hanover, NH: University Press of New England, 2000). Bergland sees ghosting as suggesting at once the Anglo-American drive to render the Indian past and an inability to fully maintain that pastness. By focusing on voice, however, I supplement the register of the visual in Bergland's analysis with a consideration of the sonic and its accrued temporal meanings.

8. John Smith, *Map of Virginia* (1612), quoted in Bruce R. Smith, *The Acoustic World of Early Modern England* (Chicago: University of Chicago Press, 1999), p. 324.

9. I am thus extending the New Historicist intervention in the analysis of the "Vanishing American" narrative. New Historicist work in this area locates itself in opposition to the depoliticizing readings of mythopoetic and psychoanalytic critics, which, they argue, reiterate the naturalization of the historical erasure of Native American populations by turning the Indian into the timeless sign of primal humanity. I seek to articulate the fundamentally temporal logic that made this transposition possible in both centuries by analyzing the ambivalent attitude toward time that underlies the nineteenth-century embrace of historical order. In this sense, I am interested in the historicity of time itself, an area that most New Historicism has not yet ventured into. For fine examples of the New Historicist critique of the Vanishing American, see Shirley Samuels, *Romances of the Republic: Women, the Family, and Violence in the Literature of the Early American Nation* (New York: Oxford University Press, 1996), and Dana Nelson, *The Word in Black and White: Reading "Race" in American Literature, 1638–1867* (New York: Oxford University Press, 1993).

10. I avoid, in this chapter, citing the by-now-familiar poststructuralist account of being-in-language as an inescapably melancholic condition, choosing instead to focus on the historical citation of voice as an anterior exception to language. Indeed, as the writing of Paul de Man, frequently cited as exemplifying this position, itself suggests, this view of language should be understood as marking not language per se but the account of language developed in Romanticism. For a critique of the (historically charged) dehistoricizing of melancholia in de Man, see Eric Santner, *Stranded Objects: Mourning, Memory and Film in Postwar Germany* (Ithaca, NY: Cornell University Press, 1990).

11. On the refusal of "coevalness" as foundational to the discipline of anthropology, see Johannes Fabian, *Time and the Other: How Anthropology Makes Its Object* (New York: Columbia University Press, 2002).

12. This is a location that Natty both consents to and resists by leaving the settlements to go West at the end of the novel. His travel toward the next frontier supplements the linear accumulation of progress with the cyclical movement of repetition: in one location, Natty's life may be "over," but by moving West he is able to re-create his pioneer status.

13. Giorgio Agamben, *Homo Sacer: Sovereign Power and Bare Life,* trans. Daniel Heller-Roazen (Stanford, CA: Stanford University Press, 1998), pp. 7–8.

14. As I noted in the introduction, I am skeptical about the historicity of Agamben's "correction or completion" of Foucault. (Agamben, *Homo Sacer,* p. 9); my concern in this study remains with the emergence of a modern chronobiopolitics.

15. Margot Bouman, "Introduction: The Loop as a Temporal Form," *Invisible Culture: An Electronic Journal for Visual Culture* 8 (2004), http://www.rochester.edu/in_visible_culture/Issue_8/issue8intro.html (accessed November 1, 2005).

16. Walter J. Ong, *The Presence of the Word: Some Prolegomena for Cultural and Religious History* (New Haven, CT: Yale University Press, 1967), p. 74.

17. Ibid., pp. 74, 168.

18. Ibid., pp. 302, 288. Leigh Eric Schmidt has recently criticized Ong's historiographic frame, charging that his equation of modernity's hearing loss with the absence of God overlooks numerous debates about the embodied status of faith from the eighteenth century to the present. See Leigh Eric Schmidt, *Hearing Things: Religion, Illusion and the American Enlightenment* (Cambridge, MA: Harvard University Press, 2000).

19. See Sterne's critique of Ong in *The Audible Past: Cultural Origins of Sound Reproduction* (Durham, NC: Duke University Press, 2003), pp. 16–18.

20. Ong, *The Presence of the Word*, p. 302.

21. Sterne, *The Audible Past*, p. 18.

22. Indeed, Rousseau argues that the physical needs of the body can be sufficiently communicated through movement: "if the only needs we ever experienced were physical, we should most likely never have been able to speak; we would fully express our meanings by the language of gesture alone." Jean-Jacques Rousseau, "Essay on the Origin of Language," in Rousseau and Johann Gottfried Herder, *On the Origin of Language*, trans. John H. Moran and Alexander Gode (New York: Frederick Ungar, 1966), p. 9.

23. Ibid., pp. 14, 12.

24. See Jacques Derrida, *Of Grammatology*, trans. Gayatri Chakravorty Spivak (Baltimore: Johns Hopkins University Press, 1976).

25. Kaja Silverman, *The Acoustic Mirror: The Female Voice in Psychoanalysis and Cinema* (Bloomington: Indiana University Press, l988), p. 75.

26. Christopher Looby, *Voicing America: Language, Literary Form, and the Origins of the United States* (Chicago: University of Chicago Press, 1996), pp. 4, 5. For another account of the centrality of the voice in Revolutionary and post-Revolutionary culture, see Jay Fliegelman, *Declaring Independence: Jefferson, Natural Language and the Culture of Performance* (Stanford, CA: Stanford University Press, 1993).

27. Paul Downes critiques the recent critical tendency to posit analyses of the authority of language in early America in terms of an "opposition between print anonymity and vocal utterance," insofar as the two constitute "mutually determining investments." See Downes, *Democracy, Revolution and Monarchism in Early American Literature* (New York: Cambridge University Press, 2002), pp. 130, 131.

28. Michael Warner, "The Public Sphere and the Cultural Mediation of Print," in William S. Solomon and Robert W. McChesney, eds., *Ruthless Criticism: New Perspectives in U.S. Communication History* (Minneapolis: University of Minnesota Press, 1993), p. 21 [7–37].

29. Richard Cullen Rath, *How Early America Sounded* (Ithaca, NY: Cornell University Press, 2003), pp. 174–75.

30. Diane Krumrey comments, along these lines, that nineteenth-century Anglo-Americans indulged in the fantasy that Indian language represented the "ideal illocutionary act," a kind of speech that could make things happen. See Krumrey, "'Your Ear Shall Drink No Lie': Articulating the American Voice in *The Last of the Mohicans*," *Language and Literature* 22 (1997): pp. 45–61.

31. John Heckewelder, a Moravian missionary whose chronicles of life with the Lenni Lenape were an important source for Fenimore Cooper, declared, for instance, that "[t]he eloquence of the Indians is natural and simple; they speak what their feelings dictate without art and without rule; their speeches are forcible and impressive, their arguments few and pointed, and when they mean to persuade as well as convince, they take the shortest way to reach the heart." John Heckewelder, *History, Manners and Customs of the Indian Nations Who Once Inhabited Pennsylvania and the Neighbouring States* (1819; repr., Philadelphia: Historical Society of Pennsylvania, 1876), p. 132.

32. Peter Duponceau, quoted in Heckewelder, *History, Manners and Customs of the Indian Nations*, pp. 405–6.

33. Duponceau's praise of the sonorous enchantment of the Delaware language is all the more striking because he studied that language through written correspondence with Heckewelder; his praise of its "magic sounds" thus demonstrates an investment in the sonic materiality of Indian speech that imaginatively resounded even within writing.

34. See Michael Warner, *The Letters of the Republic: Publication and the Public Sphere in Eighteenth-Century America* (Cambridge, MA: Harvard University Press, 1992), pp. 151, 152.

35. Philip J. Deloria, *Playing Indian* (New Haven, CT: Yale University Press, 1998).

36. This seemingly impossible preservation of sound in writing suggests the way in which, as Mark M. Smith has argued, writing itself, before the advent of the phonograph and other devices for sound collection, functioned as a recording technology. The preservation of sound in print in colonial and antebellum America very much shaped how listeners understood the heard world and, in turn, how they described and responded to those sounds both in writing and in speech. The writing of sound, that is, was understood not as an impossibly melancholic attachment to absence but, rather, as a form of transmission of sonic experience. See Mark M. Smith, *Listening to Nineteenth-Century America* (Chapel Hill: University of North Carolina Press, 2001), p. 8.

37. Roger Williams, *A Key into the Language of America* (London, 1643), p. 202.

38. *Journals of Samuel Kirkland,* ed. Walter Pilkington (Clinton, NY: Hamilton College, 1980), p. 11. Entry is dated 1764.

39. Julie Ellison, *Cato's Tears and the Making of Anglo-American Emotion* (Chicago: University of Chicago Press, 1999), p. 123.

40. Schoolcraft held that Christianization would *eradicate* the Indian, insofar as Indian religion constituted the "basis of Indian character," which he identified as "barbarian" and "pagan." Henry Rowe Schoolcraft, "Character of the Red Man of America," in *Western Scenes and Reminisces: Together with Thrilling Legends and Traditions of the Red Men of the Forest* (Buffalo, NY: Derby, Orton & Mulligan, 1853), p. 67.

41. Henry Rowe Schoolcraft, *Algic Researches, Comprising Inquiries Respecting the Mental*

Characteristics of the North American Indians (New York: Harper and Brothers, 1839), pp. 50–51.

42. Schoolcraft, *Algic Researches*, p. 52.

43. Juliana Schiesari, *The Gendering of Melancholia: Feminism, Psychoanalysis, and the Symbolics of Loss in Renaissance Literature* (Ithaca, NY: Cornell University Press, 1992).

44. See Lucy Maddox, *Removals: Nineteenth-Century American Literature and the Politics of Indian Affairs* (New York: Oxford University Press, 1991), esp. pp. 30–32.

45. Joseph Story, "Discourse Pronounced at the Request of the Essex Historical Society, September 18, 1828, in Commemoration of the First Settlement of Salem, Mass.," quoted in Deloria, *Playing Indian*, p. 64.

46. For an overview of the (incomplete) transition from patriarchy to modern heterosexuality in this historical period, see Michael Warner, "Irving's Posterity," *ELH* 67 (2000): pp. 773–99.

47. Cooper, too, was both inspired and troubled by the rapid pace of progress on the American scene; as Robert Clark has shown, he understood his own writing as a means of resolving that temporal dilemma. In his introduction to the 1831 edition of the novel, Cooper specifically defends the character of Natty against critics who highlight the implausibility of his career; these critics, Cooper argues, misunderstand Natty's function as a figure for the American past, who works "poetically to furnish a witness to the truth of those wonderful alterations which distinguish the progress of the American nation, to a degree that has been hitherto unknown, and to which hundreds of living men might equally speak" (7). See Robert Clark, " 'The Last of the Iroquois': Myth and History in *The Last of the Mohicans*," *Poetics Today* 3 (1982): pp. 115–34.

48. See Eric Cheyfitz, "Literally White, Figuratively Red: The Frontier of Translation in *The Pioneers*," in Robert Clark, ed., *James Fenimore Cooper: New Critical Essays* (London: Vision Press, 1985), pp. 55–95; Diane Krumrey, " 'Your Ear Shall Drink No Lie': Articulating the American Voice in *The Last of the Mohicans*," *Language and Literature* 22 (1997): pp. 45–61; and Lawrence Rosenwald, "*The Last of the Mohicans* and the Languages of America," *College English* 60, no. 1 (January 1998): pp. 9–30.

49. My thinking on questions of family and gender in Cooper's writing is indebted to feminist analyses by Shirley Samuels and, especially, Lora Romero. See Samuels, *Romances of the Republic: Women, the Family, and Violence in the Literature of the Early American Nation* (New York: Oxford University Press, 1996); Romero, *Home Fronts: Domesticity and Its Critics in the Antebellum United States* (Durham, NC: Duke University Press, 1997).

50. The clearest example of this is the eagerly awaited letter sent by the leader of the British forces, General Webb, which disappoints when it arrives by acknowledging his inability to defend Fort William Henry and advising its surrender to the French—the very surrender that precedes the mass carnage of the massacre. The authority of writing is also, ironically, insisted upon by the Puritan psalmodist David Gamut, who supports his doctrinal arguments by demanding that Natty quote Bible passages "chapter and verse." Indeed, Gamut carries with him in the forest not a Bible but a seventeenth-century psalmody, whose archaicness seems to emphasize the irrelevance of writing—although, as I will later demonstrate, Gamut's textual archaism is given a significantly queer twist by his musical sonocentrism.

51. On the chronotope, see Mikhail Bakhtin, "Forms of Time and of the Chronotope in the Novel: Notes towards a Historical Poetics," in *The Dialogic Imagination: Four Essays*, ed. Michael Holquist, trans. Caryl Emerson and Michael Holquist (Austin: University of Texas Press, 1981), pp. 84–258.

52. See Thomas Philbrick, "*The Last of the Mohicans* and the Sounds of Discord," *American Literature* 43, no. 1 (March 1971): pp. 25–41. Philbrick insists that Gamut's singing represents a healing power, the harmonious antithesis to the violent world of the novel, but that this power is impotent in that world and he is eventually reduced to lament. As will be seen, I read the figure of Gamut differently.

53. Indeed, the narrator describes them as listening "with an attention that seem[s] to turn them into stone" (59). The same sounds that soften the scout toward the human affections of the family harden the Indians into an inhuman form of durability, foreshadowing the monumental status they will be assigned by the end of the novel.

54. An adopted Mohawk, Magua takes advantage of the Six Nations alliance with the English to serve as a runner to their army, but he eventually leaves this cover to revert to the (French-allied) Huron, his tribe of origin.

55. Tamenund's temporal confusion is explained by the auditory resemblance of the young Mohican to the ancestral Uncas, whom the sage knew when a child (310).

56. This melancholy turn of events also occasions the final breakage of Chingachgook's voice, which fails him as his turn comes to take part in the tribe's ritual lament for the young sachem.

57. As Patricia Murphy observes, the recognition of a cyclical model of time did not in itself disrupt the fundamentally linear model of the historical perspective; indeed, she notes that nineteenth-century historians themselves tended to understand history in terms of large-scale cycles—the rise and fall of great civilizations—a comprehension that confirmed their own sense of greatness by incorporating a sense of relativity that, they believed, marked their own perspective as an improvement on the past. See Patricia Murphy, *Time Is of the Essence: Temporality, Gender, and the New Woman* (Albany: State University of New York Press, 2001).

58. Mladen Dolar, "The Object-Voice," in Renate Saleci and Slavoj Zizek, eds., *Gaze and Voice as Love Objects* (Durham, NC: Duke University Press, 1996), p. 17 [7–31].

59. Ibid., p. 21.

60. Romero, *Home Fronts*, p. 48.

61. The speech comes in the wake of Magua's "wounding" proposal to Cora, which includes a promise to free Alice if Cora consents; Cora, reporting the proposal to Alice, extends to her sister the option to decide both their fates, an act that Alice recognizes as an essentially maternal willingness to forgo her happiness on behalf of the younger woman's return to the settlements.

62. This phrase is used to characterize her grateful response to a chivalrous speech of Heyward's during the proposal scene.

63. Natty comments after a particularly brave speech of Cora's that if the English army possessed "a thousand men . . . who feared death as little as [she]," they could win the war within a week (142). Even Magua, in a way, identifies Cora with masculinity when he fixes on the eldest of Munro's offspring as the likeliest means of revenge; mistakenly assuming that Munro's first-born daughter would be the one he most values, he extends to Cora a logic more suitable for sons.

64. As Cora tells Heyward, "That I cannot see the sunny side of the picture of life, like [Alice] . . . is the penalty of experience, and, perhaps, the misfortune of my nature" (150).

65. This sense of "shame," significantly, references *at once* the multiple chronologies that resound through Cora's figuration in the narrative insofar as shame, which Eve Sedgwick identifies as announcing an *immediate* gap in the self-confirming circuits of identity, transposes the temporal self-division that characterizes the mournful subject into the present tense. See Eve Kosofsky Sedgwick, *Touching Feeling: Affect, Pedagogy, Performativity* (Durham, NC: Duke University Press, 2003), esp. chap. 3 (pp. 93–122).

66. The argument that follows this tradition-bound submission to the "stern customs" of the Delaware itself permits an intriguing perspective on the novel's negotiation of savage against civilized time. Tamenund attempts to persuade Cora that marrying a warrior will be an honor, consoling her with the promise of children: "your race will not end"; yet for Cora, this promise constitutes a "degradation" too great to be borne. Tamenund then attempts to dissuade Magua from marrying a woman whose mind is so clearly "in the tents of her fathers," an ambiguous phrase that at once lauds Cora for her attachment to her own family and chides her for sharing their prejudices. Magua, however, replies, "she speaks with the tongue of her people, . . . a race of traders . . . [who] will bargain for a bright look" (313). Magua derides whites as a race whose modes of economic accumulation are supported in time through the exchange of women as a means of generational reproduction. As if bent on actualizing this account, Heyward and Natty immediately begin bargaining with Magua for Cora. Though tempted by the offer of Natty's life in trade for Cora, a look at Cora redoubles Magua's purpose, and he refuses.

67. Mark Twain, "Fenimore Cooper's Literary Offenses," in *Literary Essays* (New York: P. F. Collier and Son, 1918), pp. 60–77.

68. Uncas's arrival momentarily diverts Magua's attention, enabling one of his assistants to stab Cora to death, and the distracted Mohican is then, in turn, overpowered and killed by the Huron.

69. Cooper used this method of closure in *The Pioneers* as well. For a discussion of how this ending contradicts the critical conviction of Cooper's lack of interest in the reproductive/generational narrative, see Janet Dean, "The Marriage Plot and National Myth in *The Pioneers,*" *Arizona Quarterly* 52, no. 4 (1997): 1–29.

70. Many contemporary critics complain that the elegance of the funeral chapter smoothes over the frantic violence of the preceding pages and, by extension, the genocidal violence of the novel as a whole. This complaint, which is, from the historical perspective, fully realist, nevertheless misrecognizes the inverted time of the novel's narrative drive. That is to say, it positions mourning as an aftereffect of murderousness, when for the novel the reverse is true: the narrative, in all its expressed and repressed violence, has been constructed entirely for the purpose of getting to the funeral scene. That is to say, in *The Last of the Mohicans*, the death of Uncas (along with that of Cora) in the penultimate chapter ironically becomes the secondary effect of a primary intention to mourn; these two characters are not mourned because they have died, but rather, they die so that mourning can restore the time of civilization. This necessity underscores the dual structural necessity of mourning to the narrative: as a narrative mode enabling historical transition and as an affective mode whose attention to the temporality of voice models for the reader the kind of *feeling* necessary to the proper American subject.

71. Cooper models the Delaware burial ceremony loosely on the chapter on funerals in John Heckewelder's 1819 *History*, which extensively details the bereavement rituals among the Delaware. Heckewelder's account stresses the frenzied nature of the chanted lament, emphasizing "the shrillness of their cries and the frantic expression of their sorrow" and the violence of the ritual: "They even took hold of her [the corpse's] arms and legs; at first it seemed as if they were caressing her, afterwards they appeared to pull with more violence, as if they intended to run away with the body, crying out all the while, 'Arise, arise! Come with us! Don't leave us! Don't abandon us!' At last they retired, plucking at their garments, pulling their hair, and uttering loud cries and lamentations, with all the appearance of frantic despair." Cooper's Romantic revision of this ritual, however, substitutes melodious song and mild melancholy for the more unrestrained behavior detailed by Heckewelder. See Heckewelder, *History, Manners and Customs of the Indian Nations*, pp. 269–74.

72. The timing of the scene itself emphasizes the ambiguity of his rejection, as the narrator is careful to report the song's entire content *before* alluding to Natty's rejection, which occurs early on. For Natty's ambivalent relation to the Indian afterlife, see *The Pioneers*, p. 422.

73. I want to emphasize that I emphatically do *not* mean simply to reproduce the uncritical homophobic resonance that resounds through Leslie Fiedler's well-known characterization of such bonds as the story of the "[white] man on the run" from civilization and the "mature" life-trajectory of marriage and reproduction (Fiedler, *Love and Death in the American Novel* [New York: Criterion, 1960], p. xx). Rather, I am interested in the way that an embrace of an authorizing tradition that motivates the abjection (rather than, as Fiedler sees it, the rejection) of the feminine lies at the heart of such masculine bonds as they are lauded in male adventure fiction—an abjection that, as David Greven points out, directs itself toward the "queer potentiality" of the feminized male as well as the female. See David Greven, "Troubling Our Heads about Ichabod: 'The Legend of Sleepy Hollow,' Classic American Literature, and the Sexual Politics of Homosocial Brotherhood," *American Quarterly* 56, no. 1 (March 2004): pp. 83–110.

74. Here, Gamut's singing doubles Magua's simultaneously menacing and protecting appearance; just as the Huron's captivation of the women saves them from random death in the massacre, Gamut's song at once helps Magua locate them and preserves his own and the women's lives, as he repels more than one Indian attack by virtue of the mingled "astonishment" and "admiration" that his singing under such circumstances provokes (177).

75. Natty insists, for instance, that Gamut "has fallen into the hands of some silly woman, when he should have been gathering his education under a blue sky, and among the beauties of the forest" (224). Natty does, however, concede to Gamut's habit of "musickating" a limited usefulness; significantly, he invites the psalmodist, in the cavern scene, to sing the women to sleep.

76. Earlier in the novel, Natty also tries to convince Gamut that the existence of the Christian god is confirmed in the book of nature, countering Gamut's text-bound doctrinal convictions; Gamut, however, simply waits for Natty to finish speaking and then breaks into another Puritan hymn. In this respect, then, the Delaware women succeed where Natty has failed.

77. David Greven's description of Gamut as "a non-normative male rendered starkly isolate from the province of male friendship, to say nothing of heterosexual desire" is thus both accurate and somewhat misleading, insofar as Gamut's ambiguous attachment to Cora, which does not quite fall within the bounds of normative heterosexuality, nevertheless briefly redeems him from his feminized isolation, as it inspires him to join the other men in the final battle against Magua. See Greven, "Troubling Our Heads about Ichabod," p. 98.

78. The narrator remarks that it is "impossible to say" what the "short and silent" communication exchanged between "two such singular men" might have inspired Gamut to say, had he not been distracted by the appearance of the whites (18).

79. Gamut's Puritan mindset, however, leads him to label himself as always-already an offender, a self-characterization that emerges, most notably, in his vision of having "united with two comely maidens, in lifting up our voices" during the cavern scene, after which he imagines himself "visited with a heavy judgment for [his] sins"—the discord that makes him believe the end of days is at hand (82).

80. Sedgwick's novel, set in the mid-seventeenth century, returns to the very time period that generated the hymns Gamut so relishes. And indeed, a minor character in Sedgwick's novel, the schoolmaster Craddock seems deliberately to echo the mixture of comic relief and generosity located in Gamut. Craddock, like Gamut, is a distinctly archaic figure strangely attached to dusty antiquarian books, supplemented by a peculiarly animating attachment to Hope, which seems hopelessly romantic but which he finally rearticulates as dotingly parental. This attachment enables Hope to press him into service at a crucial moment by standing in for Magawisca, in order to help her escape from prison, just as Gamut, in *The Last of the Mohicans,* enables Uncas's escape from captivity by standing in for him. One important aspect of Gamut escapes Craddock, however: the musicality of Gamut's voice, which Sedgwick, crucially, reserves for Magawisca. On connections between Cooper and Sedgwick, see Susanne Opfermann, "Lydia Maria Child, James Fenimore Cooper, and Catharine Maria Sedgwick: A Dialogue on Race, Culture, and Gender," in Karen L. Kilcup, ed., *Soft Canons: American*

Women Writers and Masculine Tradition (Iowa City: University of Iowa Press, 1999); Margaret R. Higonnet, "Comparative Reading: Catharine M. Sedgwick's Hope Leslie," *Legacy* 15, no. 1 (1998): pp. 17–22; and Patricia Kalayjian, "Cooper and Sedgwick: Rivalry or Respect?" in *James Fenimore Cooper Society Miscellany* 4 (September 1993): pp. 9–19.

81. Catharine Maria Sedgwick, *Hope Leslie; or, Early Times in the Massachusetts,* ed. Mary Kelley (New Brunswick, NJ: Rutgers University Press, 1993), p. 5 (emphasis added). Further references to this novel will be cited parenthetically within the text.

82. In his preface to the 1831 edition, Cooper states, "It would, perhaps, have been more observant of reality to have drawn him of less moral elevation, but it would also have been less attractive; and the business of a writer of fiction is to approach, as near as his powers will allow, to poetry." Cooper, *The Last of the Mohicans,* p. 7.

83. Jeffrey Insko, "Anachronistic Imaginings: *Hope Leslie's* Challenge to Historicism," *American Literary History* 16, no. 2 (2004): p. 188.

84. The novel's concentration of the power of voice in this one individual links Magawisca's auratic talents to the form of explosive public pedagogy that Lauren Berlant has described as "Diva Citizenship." In the Diva Citizen form, Berlant argues, a performance of lament projected through the body of the minoritized woman is imaginatively endowed with the ability to suspend national narratives in order to expose sexual and other corporeal abuses, interposing alternative histories of sexuality through the disruptive sound of the voice. See Lauren Berlant, *The Queen of America Goes to Washington City: Essays on Sex and Citizenship* (Durham, NC: Duke University Press, 1997), esp. pp. 221–46. Gustavus Stadler also makes a brief, speculative connection between Magawisca and the Diva Citizen. See Stadler, "Magawisca's Body of Knowledge: Nation Building in *Hope Leslie,*" *Yale Journal of Criticism* 12 (1999): p. 46n. 28.

85. This account is discussed in Robert D. Madison, "Wish-ton-Wish: Muck or Melancholy?" *James Fenimore Cooper Society Miscellaneous Papers* 4 (September 1993): pp. 1–29. Sedgwick alludes to this myth more than once in the pages of *Hope Leslie,* indicating that she is consciously playing upon the doubled significance of Magawisca's name.

86. This, too, is consistent with Diva Citizen performance, which, as Berlant notes, has historically failed to generate new social forms within the space of possibility it seems to open; rather, it tends to collapse into nostalgia, becoming complicit with the forces working to turn citizenship into a fundamentally private form. For a reading of *Hope Leslie* along similar lines, see Maddox, *Removals.*

87. This episode marks the narrative's second demonstration of the power of Magawisca's voice to turn narrative time back on itself: in this case, her summoning of Hope to a meeting in the burial ground at the end of the novel's first volume must be explained at the beginning of its second by a series of chapters that move successively backward, rather than forward, in story time.

88. The allusion is, of course, to Patrick Henry's famous speech, which Sandra Gustafson discusses as the very archetype of Revolutionary models of uncontainable oratory.

See Sandra M. Gustafson, *Eloquence Is Power: Oratory and Performance in Early America* (Chapel Hill: University of North Carolina Press, 2000), pp. 164–65.

89. Insko identifies this act of "ventriloquy" as typical of the novel's revolutionary deployment of anachrony, but his reading omits the maternal dimension that grounds this speech in sentimental time. See Insko, "Anachronistic Imaginings," p. 179.

90. Gustavus Stadler and Michelle Burnham both point to Esther's productive spinsterhood—on which the narrative closes—as the novel's most radical mode of resistance, casting it in opposition to the romance of marital/heterosexual "union" that overtakes Hope. I am arguing, however, that insofar as both Hope and Everell's marriage and Esther's refusal of marriage are both innovations that resist the patriarchal model of reproduction, they are more alike than different, constituting new formations within the affective deployment of sexuality. See Stadler, "Magawisca's Body of Knowledge," and Michelle Burnham, *Captivity and Sentiment: Cultural Exchange in American Literature, 1682–1861* (Hanover, NH: University Press of New England, 1997), p. 117.

91. Contemporary critics, indeed, tend to fault Sedgwick for her conservative "embrace" of the Vanishing narrative in an otherwise "progressive" novel. Although they differ on the cause of this apparent contradiction between Sedgwick's ostensibly progressive vision and her regression to the Vanishing cliché at the end of the novel, they tend to agree that it results from contradictions in Sedgwick's own historical moment. Accordingly, it is caused, according to Phillip Gould, by the novel's incomplete attempt to regender the postrevolutionary understanding of virtue; according to Dana Nelson, by the ambivalent nineteenth-century politics of sympathy; and according to Judith Fetterley, by the historically palpable possibility that excess radicalism might end in persecution. These readings all share a sense that the fate Sedgwick assigns to the Pequots was determined by the dominant politics of the novel's own historical moment. Insko, in contrast, argues that Sedgwick's sense of history is *not* fundamentally progressive and accordingly assigns this conclusion to the "formal constraints of the novel itself," which, unlike history, "has to end" (Insko, "Anachronistic Imaginings," p. 199). I am arguing, however, that this neat formal resolution of a fundamentally temporal dilemma undervalues the ambivalent resonance of "melancholy" in the novel's deployment of the politics of voice as a possible challenge to this enddetermination. See Phillip Gould, "Catharine Sedgwick's 'Recital' of the Pequot War," *American Literature* 66, no. 4 (December 1994): pp. 641–62; Dana Nelson, *The Word in Black and White: Reading "Race" in American Literature, 1638–1867* (New York: Oxford University Press, 1992), pp. 65–89; and Judith Fetterley, " 'My Sister! My Sister!': The Rhetoric of Catharine Sedgwick's *Hope Leslie*," *American Literature* 70, no. 3 (September 1998): pp. 491–516.

92. Susan Sniader Lanser, *Fictions of Authority: Women Writers and Narrative Voice* (Ithaca, NY: Cornell University Press, 1992) p. 3.

93. On voice as an index of value, see Susan Gal, "Between Speech and Silence: The Problematics of Research on Language and Gender," in Micaela di Leonardo, ed., *Gender at the Crossroads of Knowledge: Feminist Anthropology in the Postmodern Era* (Berkeley:

University of California Press, 1991), pp. 175–203. For a feminist critique of the sentimental romance of voice in feminist thought, see Berlant, *The Queen of America Goes to Washington City.*

Notes to Chapter 3

1. James Fenimore Cooper, *The Last of the Mohicans: A Narrative of the Year 1757* (1826; repr., New York: Penguin, 1986), p. 159.

2. Alexis de Tocqueville, *Democracy in America*, vol. 2 (1840; repr., New York: Random House, 1990), pp. 98–99.

3. See Michael Warner, "Irving's Posterity," *ELH* 67, no. 3 (fall 2000): p. 781 [773–99].

4. Tocqueville, *Democracy in America*, vol. 2, p. 99.

5. Warner, "Irving's Posterity," p. 781. Warner's essay analyzes, in Washington Irving's "Rip Van Winkle," the way that generational continuity masters temporal isolation in Rip's story precisely when a mother appears to set the story straight.

6. Tocqueville, *Democracy in America*, vol. 2, p. 214. For a critique of Tocqueville's limited perspective, along with its subsequent distorting effect on twentieth-century historiography, see Linda Kerber, "Separate Spheres, Female Worlds, Women's Place: The Rhetoric of Women's History," in *Toward an Intellectual History of Women* (Chapel Hill: University of North Carolina Press, 1997), pp. 159–99.

7. See, e.g., William A. Alcott, *The Young Wife; or, Duties of Woman in the Marriage Relation* (Boston: George W. Light, 1837), esp. p. 37; also Catharine Beecher, *A Treatise on Domestic Economy*, ed. Kathryn Kish Sklar (1841; repr., New York: Schocken Books, 1977), p. 14.

8. Mitchell Meltzer, *Secular Revelations: The Constitution of the United States and Classic American Literature* (Cambridge, MA: Harvard University Press, 2005), p. 11.

9. Lydia H. Sigourney, *Letters to Mothers* (Hartford, CT: Hudson and Skinner, 1838), p. 81, quoted in Richard Brodhead, *Cultures of Letters: Scenes of Reading and Writing in Nineteenth-Century America* (Chicago: University of Chicago Press, 1993), p. 23.

10. Lori Merish, *Sentimental Materialism: Gender, Commodity Culture, and Nineteenth-Century American Literature* (Durham, NC: Duke University Press, 2000), pp. 140–44.

11. Karen Sánchez-Eppler, *Dependent States: The Child's Part in Nineteenth-Century American Culture* (Chicago: University of Chicago Press, 2005), p. xviii.

12. Sigourney, for instance, maintains that the mother's duty to the child outweighed the wife's responsibility to the husband; though a wife should support the husband's labor outside the home by practicing "consistent economy" within it, Sigourney insists that it is not truly economical if the mother neglects the duties to her child in order to save the expense of hiring domestic help, as the moral damage done to the future will far outweigh the pecuniary savings in the present. Sigourney, *Letters to Mothers*, p. 81.

13. Carolyn Dever, *Death and the Mother from Dickens to Freud: Victorian Fiction and the*

Anxiety of Origins (New York: Cambridge University Press, 1998), p. 19 (emphasis in original). On the nineteenth-century cult of the dead white mother, see also Eva Cherniavsky, *That Pale Mother Rising: Sentimental Discourses and the Imitation of Motherhood in 19th-Century America* (Bloomington: Indiana University Press, 1995).

14. Julia Kristeva, "Women's Time," in *The Kristeva Reader,* ed. Toril Moi (New York: Columbia University Press, 1986), p. 187–213.

15. This configuration does not, of course, exhaust the multiplicity of either sentimentalities or domesticities in operation in this period. For some important works that think through other domestic/sentimental forms, see Lora Romero, *Home Fronts: Domesticity and Its Critics in the Antebellum United States* (Durham, NC: Duke University Press, 1997); Mary Chapman and Glenn Hendler, eds., *Sentimental Men: Masculinity and the Politics of Affect in American Culture* (Berkeley: University of California Press, 1999); Robert Reid-Pharr, *Conjugal Union: The Body, the House and the Black American* (New York: Oxford University Press, 1999); Bruce Burgett, *Sentimental Bodies: Sex, Gender, and Citizenship in the Early Republic* (Princeton, NJ: Princeton University Press, 1998); Glenn Hendler, *Public Sentiments: Structures of Feeling in Nineteenth-Century American Literature* (Chapel Hill: University of North Carolina Press, 2001).

16. Lydia Maria Child, *The American Frugal Housewife,* ed. Alice M. Geffen (1835; repr., New York: Harper and Row, 1972).

17. Kathleen McHugh, *American Domesticity from How-To Manual to Hollywood Melodrama* (New York: Oxford University Press, 1999), pp. 22–23.

18. Child, *The American Frugal Housewife,* pp. 3–4.

19. Ibid., p. 4.

20. Child's own maternal manual, *The Mother's Book,* also endorses the value of a sentimental education, which she defines as an education in "feeling right." Although she too occasionally waxes sentimental over the pleasures of motherhood, her emphasis on "plain practical good sense" continues to value regular, productive development of the child above affective timelessness. See Lydia Maria Child, *The Mother's Book,* 2d ed. (1831; repr., New York: Arno, 1977), p. 22.

21. See McHugh, *American Domesticity,* p. 33. Hale quoted in Carolyn Karcher, *The First Woman in the Republic: A Cultural Biography of Lydia Maria Child* (Durham, NC: Duke University Press, 1994), p. 133.

22. Amy Dru Stanley observes that this logic was also projected, from the market side of the equation, as a means of keeping domestic dependencies from "contaminating" the marketplace. See Stanley, "Home Life and the Morality of the Market," in Melvyn Stokes and Steven Conway, eds., *The Market Revolution in America: Social, Political and Religious Expressions, 1800–1880* (Charlottesville: University Press of Virginia, 1996), p. 86 [74–96].

23. Sigourney, *Letters to Mothers,* p. 21.

24. Ibid., pp. 55, viii.

25. See, e.g., McHugh, *American Domesticity,* pp. 43–44.

26. Beecher, *A Treatise on Domestic Economy,* p. 14. On Beecher's participation in the modernization of time, see also Thomas Allen, "Clockwork Nation: Modern Time, Moral Perfection and American Identity in Catharine Beecher and Henry Thoreau," *Journal of American Studies* 39, no. 1 (2006): pp. 65–86.

27. Beecher, *A Treatise on Domestic Economy*, p. 137. The postbellum revision of this manual, *The American Woman's Home*, which Beecher coauthored with her sister Harriet Beecher Stowe, deepened the scope of the future in its reproduction of this passage by changing "hundreds" to "thousands." See Catharine Beecher and Harriet Beecher Stowe, *The American Woman's Home*, ed. Nicole Tonkovich (1869; repr., New Brunswick, NJ: Rutgers University Press, 2002), p. 163.

28. Sigourney, *Letters to Mothers*, p. 11.

29. E. P. Thompson, "Time, Work-Discipline and Industrial Capitalism," in *Customs in Common* (New York: New Press, 1991), pp. 381–82 [352–403]. Thompson places scare quotes around the term "pre-industrial" to indicate that he is not talking about a seamlessly sequential transition.

30. Sigourney, *Letters to Mothers*, pp. 32, 29, 21.

31. Ibid., p. 30.

32. Ibid., p. 21.

33. Mary Collier, "The Woman's Labour," quoted in Thompson, "Time, Work-Discipline and Industrial Capitalism," p. 381 (emphasis in original).

34. Sigourney, *Letters to Mothers*, p. 36.

35. Mary Ryan, *The Empire of the Mother: American Writing about Domesticity, 1830–1860* (New York: Harrington Park, 1985), pp. 67–69.

36. Sigourney, *Letters to Mothers*, pp. 50–55.

37. Brodhead, *Cultures of Letters*, p. 20. Brodhead's substitution of "parent" for "mother" and the neuter "child" for the "son" specifically addressed in the Sigourney passage that he cites is presumably intended to emphasize the way that, as he shows, men too were drawn into antebellum schemes of sentimental education, and they were applied to children of both sexes. However, as I will argue later, the generalized model of intimacy that Brodhead employs tends toward obscuring the temporal particularities of sentimental-domestic gender arrangements.

38. Sigourney, *Letters to Mothers*, p. 30.

39. Ibid., p. 20.

40. Michel Foucault, *The History of Sexuality, Vol. 1*, trans. Robert Hurley (New York: Pantheon, 1978), p. 45.

41. Brodhead, *Cultures of Letters*, p. 34.

42. Sánchez-Eppler, *Dependent States*, p. xxvi.

43. Ibid., pp. xxvi–xxvii

44. See Harriet Appleton, "To a Picture of My Mother," reprinted in Sánchez-Eppler, *Dependent States*, p. xxvi.

45. Kaja Silverman, *The Acoustic Mirror: The Female Voice in Psychoanalysis and Cinema* (Bloomington: Indiana University Press, 1988), p. 75.

46. George W. Bethune, "To My Mother," in *Lays of Love and Faith, with Other Fugitive Poems* (Philadelphia: Lindsay and Blakiston, 1848).

47. Ibid.

48. Since, as Hortense J. Spillers points out, it makes sense to speak of gender only in relation to a gendered subject, these norms themselves remain bound to the specificity of the audience that Sigourney addresses, despite her essentialized assumption that they derive from nature. See Spillers, "Momma's Baby, Poppa's Maybe: An American Grammar Book," in *Black, White and in Color: Essays on American Literature and Culture* (Chicago: University of Chicago Press, 2003), pp. 203–29.

49. Cherniavsky, *That Pale Mother Rising*, p. 50.

50. Sigourney, *Letters to Mothers*, p. 120.

51. Beecher and Stowe, *The American Woman's Home*, p. 25.

52. In addition to Brodhead's reading of *The Wide, Wide World* in *Cultures of Letters*, see, e.g., Barbara McGuire, "The Orphan's Grief: Transformational Tears and the Maternal Fetish in Mary Jane Holmes's *Dora Deane; or, The East-India Uncle*," *Legacy: A Journal of American Women Writers* 15, no. 2 (1998): pp. 171–87.

53. On the connections between fallen women and lost mothers, see Elizabeth Barnes, *States of Sympathy: Seduction and Democracy in the American Novel* (New York: Columbia University Press, 1997); on the anachronism of True Womanhood, see Nina Baym, *Women's Fiction: A Guide to Novels by and about Women in America, 1820–70,* 2nd ed. (Urbana: University of Illinois Press, 1993), pp. xxxix, 39.

54. On Warner's career, see Mary Ryan, *Private Woman, Public Stage: Literary Domesticity in Nineteenth-Century America* (New York: Oxford University Press, 1984).

55. Jane Tompkins, *Sensational Designs: The Cultural Work of American Fiction, 1790– 1860* (New York: Oxford University Press, 1985), p. 173.

56. Ibid., p. 170.

57. In addition to Brodhead's aforementioned insistence on the coincidence of tender affection and disciplinary power, which takes Warner's novel as a central example, Marianne Noble's more recent assessment of sentimental masochism reads the novel as setting a maternalized True Womanhood alongside male religious authority to induce both protagonist and reader to sacrifice corporeal pleasure for obedience. See Marianne Noble, *The Masochistic Pleasures of Sentimental Literature* (Princeton, NJ: Princeton University Press, 2000), pp. 94–125. For a reading that understands Warner's novel as conflicted in its representation of the erotics of suffering, see Catherine O'Connell, " 'We Must Sorrow': Silence, Suffering and Sentimentality in Susan Warner's *The Wide, Wide World*," *Studies in American Fiction* 25, no. 1 (spring 1997): pp. 21–39.

58. Susan Warner, *The Wide, Wide World*, ed. Jane Tompkins (New York: Feminist Press, 1987). Further references will be cited parenthetically within the text.

59. Brodhead, *Cultures of Letters*, p. 32.

60. The collapse of time surfaces even in the conversation about conversion; when Ellen asks her mother, "what shall I do without you?" the narrator remarks, "Alas, Mrs. Montgomery's heart echoed the question; it had no answer" (38). It is impossible to tell, here, whether Mrs. Montgomery's heart-echo inverts or maintains the subject/ object relation of the question—whether she too wonders what Ellen will do without her, or what she will do without her daughter. Either way, however, the affective response—lament—remains.

61. Barnes, *States of Sympathy,* pp. 100–101.

62. Cindy Weinstein argues that the novel is far more critical of blind obedience, which it links to a compulsion that finds its limit-case in slavery, than most recent readings recognize. See Weinstein, "Love American Style: *The Wide, Wide World,*" in *Family, Kinship and Sympathy in Nineteenth-Century American Literature* (Cambridge: Cambridge University Press, 2004), pp. 130–58.

63. The shopping trip does, however, have an afterlife that emphasizes the dangerous sexual undertones of the market; a store clerk who tries to cheat Ellen when she attempts to shop alone, but who is found out by an older male customer and subsequently fired, later runs across Ellen, again alone, in the country and terrifies her by seizing her horse's reins and whipping it.

64. The sequence is implicitly confirmed by the *order* of the gifts: the maternal love embodied in the ring's sacrifice, followed by the Bible, writing desk, sewing box, and clothes—precisely the order in which sentimental domesticity organized the child's development, moving from maternal love to early religious instruction to intellectual growth and the establishment of productive habits of self-arrangement.

65. Veronica Stewart argues that Warner *intentionally* represents this inability precisely to critique patriarchal theology by drawing attention to its indifference to a mother-love that it presents as universally appealing. I see the critique posited by this juxtaposition of the two principles, however, in less unidirectional terms. See Stewart, "Mothering a Female Saint: Susan Warner's Dialogic Role in *The Wide, Wide World,*" *Essays in Literature* 22, no. 1 (spring 1995): pp. 59–74.

66. Hendler, *Public Sentiments,* p. 125.

67. For Noble, this sensuality appears as a pretext for disciplining the female body; here, however, I suggest a more capacious biopolitical function. Noble, *The Masochistic Pleasures of Sentimental Literature,* p. 98. For a reading of Ellen and Alice's relationship as manifesting an intensely homoerotic attachment that nevertheless fails to contest conventional forms of family, see Kathryn R. Kent, *Making Girls into Women: American Women's Writing and the Rise of Lesbian Identity* (Durham, NC: Duke University Press, 2003), pp. 12–14.

68. See, e.g., Stanley Fish, "Progress in *The Pilgrim's Progress,*" in *Self-Consuming Artifacts: The Experience of Seventeenth Century Literature* (Berkeley: University of California Press, 1972), pp. 224–64. On the Americanization of Calvinism in the Whig era, see Mark Noll, *America's God: From Jonathan Edwards to Abraham Lincoln* (New York: Oxford University Press, 2002), pp. 312–19.

69. Barnes, *States of Sympathy,* p. 105.

70. Tompkins suggests, along these lines, that Mrs. Montgomery's second textual inscription locates "the effective force of divinity in this world in women." Tompkins, *Sensational Designs,* pp. 164–65.

71. John too holds to the doctrine of celestial reunion among loved ones and professes the domestic affections the closest thing to perfection on earth; yet he also insists that "[w]e must wait till we join the ranks of the just made perfect, before we see society that will be all we wish for," and never embraces the ministrations of spirits other than God (281). John's denomination is never specified, though his convictions and preaching style support the critical contention that it is a revivalist Presbyterianism similar to that of the Mercer Street church that Warner attended in her youth.

72. Warner, "A Note on the Text," *The Wide, Wide World,* p. 8; Tompkins, afterword to *The Wide, Wide World,* p. 603.

73. Susan S. Williams, "Widening the World: Susan Warner, Her Readers, and the Assumption of Authorship," *American Quarterly* 42, no. 4 (December 1990): pp. 577–78 [565–86]; Jana Argersinger, "Family Embraces: The Unholy Kiss and Authorial Relations in *The Wide, Wide World,*" *American Literature* 74, no. 1 (June 2002): p. 277–79 [251–85].

74. Argersinger, "Family Embraces," p. 270.

75. Though the type of story indicated by the term "novel"—which contemporary readers interpreted as a sexual/romantic one—comes in for the most consistent condemnation here, all stories (with the apparent exception of exegetic allegory) appear as potential wastes of time, or worse.

76. The narrator identifies this painting only as a copy of "Correggio's recumbent Magdalen" (578). It is clear from the adjective and Ellen's subsequent description, however, that the image meant is the celebrated painting known as the *Reading Magdalen.*

77. This "older" view emerged, in America, roughly contemporaneously with the seduction novels discussed earlier—which themselves frequently linked their protagonists' downfalls to overindulgence in novels. See Cathy Davidson, *Revolution and the Word: The Rise of the Novel in America* (Oxford: Oxford University Press, 1986).

78. Brodhead, *Cultures of Letters,* p. 46.

79. Wai Chee Dimock, *Through Other Continents: American Literature across Deep Time* (Princeton, NJ: Princeton University Press, 2006).

80. Both the book's history and the biography of its author have since been substantially restored. A new edition of Wilson's novel contains the most thorough overview of this work, including newly discovered information about Wilson's life subsequent to the publication of the novel. See Harriet Wilson, *Our Nig; or, Sketches from the Life of a Free Black,* ed. P. Gabrielle Forman and Reginald Pitts (New York: Penguin, 2005). In addition to the work by Gates and Ellis cited later in the chapter, see also Barbara A. White, "*Our Nig* and the She-Devil: New Information about Harriet Wilson and the 'Bellmont' Family," *American Literature* 65, no. 1 (March 1993): pp. 19–52; Eric Gardner, " 'This Attempt of Their Sister': Harriet Wilson's *Our Nig* from Printer to Readers," *New England Quarterly* 66, no. 2 (June 1993): pp. 226–46.

81. Henry Louis Gates Jr., introduction to Harriet Wilson, *Our Nig,* 3rd ed., ed. Henry Louis Gates Jr. (New York: Vintage, 2002), p. xlvii, pp. xlvi–xlvii. References to the novel itself will be cited parenthetically within the text.

82. The response to Gates's evaluation of the novel's negative portrayal of Mag as "irresponsible" (Gates, introduction to *Our Nig,* p. xlvii) has ranged from an insistence that it is too harsh, overlooking the novel's deep sympathy for Mag, to a suggestion that it is not harsh enough, insofar as it fails to register the way that a destructive maternality cannibalizes *Our Nig*'s relation to the sentimental. For an example of the former position, see Claudia Tate, *Domestic Allegories of Political Desire: The Black Heroine's Text at the Turn of the Century* (New York: Oxford University Press, 1992), pp. 32–50; for the latter, see Julia Stern, "Excavating Genre in *Our Nig*," *American Literature* 67, no. 2 (September 1995): p. 458 [439–66].

83. Gates, "Notes to the Text," in Wilson, *Our Nig*, pp. lv–lxvii.

84. R. J. Ellis, *Harriet Wilson's* Our Nig: *A Cultural Biography* (Amsterdam: Rodopi, 2003), pp. 173–81.

85. Gillian Brown argues that color, as "the telltale sign of the market," is deployed narratively to label sexually "damaged goods" in this novel and other sentimental fiction. Brown, *Domestic Individualism: Imagining Self in Nineteenth-Century America* (Berkeley: University of California Press, 1990), pp. 57–58.

86. Stern, "Excavating Genre in *Our Nig*," p. 440.

87. Ibid., p. 447.

88. Ibid., p. 445.

89. Karen Sánchez-Eppler's innovative recent rereading of this novel juxtaposes the model of sentimental childhood that I outline here with an emergent model of autonomous childhood imagined in and through an ateleological emphasis on *play*; the figure of Frado, she argues, oscillates between both models. See Sánchez-Eppler, *Dependent States*, pp. 40–51.

90. Giorgio Agamben, *Homo Sacer: Sovereign Power and Bare Life*, trans. Daniel Heller-Roazen (Stanford, CA: Stanford University Press, 1998).

91. See Reid-Pharr, *Conjugal Union*, p. 101; Xiomara Santamarina, *Belabored Professions: Narratives of African American Working Womanhood* (Chapel Hill: University of North Carolina Press, 2006), p. 72.

92. Here, I am drawing upon Robert Reid-Pharr's observation that it is the *household*, rather than the family as such, that should be understood as the locus of production of embodied subjects in the private sphere. See Reid-Pharr, *Conjugal Union*.

93. Lois Leveen, "Dwelling in the House of Oppression: The Spatial, Racial and Textual Dynamics of Harriet Wilson's *Our Nig*," *African American Review* 35, no. 4 (2001): p. 566 [561–80].

94. Stern observes, similarly, that the intimate mother-daughter bond valorized in sentimental fiction is also engaged in the Bellmont house specifically at Frado's expense, as Mrs. Bellmont conspires with her favorite daughter, Mary, in mistreating Frado. Stern, "Excavating Genre in *Our Nig*," p. 452.

95. Santamarina, *Belabored Professions*, p. 90.

96. Ibid., p. 95.

97. Ibid., pp. 88, 99.

98. Reid-Pharr, *Conjugal Union*, p. 109.

99. Peter Coviello reads the sentimentality of Phyllis Wheatley's poetry through the lens of this cultural denial of affective significance. See Coviello, "Agonizing Affection: Affect and Nation in Early America," *Early American Literature* 37, no. 3 (September 2002): pp. 439–68.

100. Lauren Berlant, "Slow Death (Sovereignty, Obesity, Lateral Agency)," *Critical Inquiry* 33.4 (summer 2007).

101. Gates, introduction to *Our Nig*, p. xlvii.

Notes to Chapter 4

1. Frederick Douglass, "What to the Slave Is the Fourth of July? An Address Delivered in Rochester, New York, on 5 July 1852," in *The Frederick Douglass Papers, Series One: Speeches, Debates and Interviews, Vol. 2: 1847–54,* ed. John Blassingame (New Haven, CT: Yale University Press, 1982), p. 368 [359–88]. Further references to this speech will be cited parenthetically within the text.

2. Michel Foucault, "Nietzsche, Genealogy, History," in *Language, Counter-Memory, Practice: Selected Essays and Interviews,* ed. Donald F. Bouchard, trans. Donald F. Bouchard and Sherry Simon (Ithaca, NY: Cornell University Press, 1977), p. 160 [139–64].

3. Castronovo's reading of Frederick Douglass and Herman Melville's "ironic" resistance to monumentalism has strongly influenced my own thinking in this chapter; I build on Castronovo's analytic framework by emphasizing countermonumental, rather than antimonumental perspectives, which complicate the temporality of irony, as I will show, by coupling it with allegory in an attempt to make possible an engagement in reparative critical history. See Russ Castronovo, *Fathering the Nation: American Genealogies of Slavery and Freedom* (Berkeley: University of California Press, 1995), p. 183. On monumentalism and antislavery pedagogy, see also Kirk Savage, *Standing Soldiers, Kneeling Slaves: Race, War, and Monument in Nineteenth-Century America* (Princeton, NJ: Princeton University Press, 1997). For another recent analysis of Herman Melville's challenge to the pedagogy of the monument, see Edgar Dryden, *Monumental Melville: The Formation of a Literary Career* (Stanford, CA: Stanford University Press, 2004).

4. Daniel Webster, *Daniel Webster's First Bunker Hill Oration, Together with Other Addresses Relating to the Revolution,* ed. Fred Newton Scott (New York: Longmans, Green, 1895), p. 6.

5. Castronovo points out that one of the effects of this incursion of divinity into the time of the nation was to "guard against prodigal sons," in effect regularizing the time of the nation by discouraging American waywardness. Castronovo, *Fathering the Nation,* p. 148.

6. The mode of simultaneity that I am invoking here differs from the modern "meanwhile" that Benedict Anderson identifies as the temporality from which modern national identity springs. This temporality, which, drawing on Benjamin, he aligns with the " 'homogenous, empty time' . . . measured by clock and calendar" that emerges as the sign of the modern is developed against the older, cosmological simultaneity that operates against a notion of the temporal as vertically linked to the eternal. In effect, both the simultaneity evoked by the national monument and the one I will describe as characteristic of sentimental culture draw on and adapt this "earlier" mode of simultaneity, in which fragments of time are collected in relation to a timeless truth. See Benedict Anderson, *Imagined Communities: Reflections on the Origin and Spread of Nationalism* (London: Verso, 1991), pp. 24–25.

7. William Hoppin, *Transactions of the American Art-Union, III* (1846), quoted in Neil Harris, *The Artist in American Society: The Formative Years, 1790–1860* (New York: George Braziller, 1966), p. 194.

8. Harris, *The Artist in American Society,* pp. 189–94.

9. Alexis de Tocqueville, *Democracy in America,* vol. 2 (1840; repr., New York: Random House, 1990), p. 53.

10. Friedrich Nietzsche, *On the Advantage and Disadvantage of History for Life,* trans. Peter Prauss (Indianapolis: Hackett, 1980) p. 17.

11. Nietzsche, *On the Advantage and Disadvantage of History for Life,* p. 17.

12. Elizabeth Maddock Dillon, *The Gender of Freedom: Fictions of Liberalism and the Literary Public Sphere* (Stanford, CA: Stanford University Press, 2004). On the gendered temporal imaginary of the nation, see also Anne McClintock, *Imperial Leather* (New York: Routledge, 1995).

13. Harris, *The Artist in American Society,* pp. 191, 192. As Harris points out, a few commentators hoped to have the nation depicted as a loving mother, but this aesthetic did not prevail.

14. See Savage, *Standing Soldiers, Kneeling Slaves,* esp. pp. 21–23.

15. Lauren Berlant, "Poor Eliza," *American Literature* 70, no. 3 (September 1998): pp. 635–68.

16. Philip Fisher, "Democratic Social Space: Whitman, Melville, and the Promise of American Transparency," *Representations* 24 (fall 1988): p. 76 [60–101].

17. Harriet Beecher Stowe, preface to *Uncle Tom's Cabin; or, Life among the Lowly* (Boston: Jewett, 1852).

18. Jane Tompkins, *Sensational Designs: The Cultural Work of American Fiction, 1790–1860* (New York: Oxford University Press, 1985), p. 124.

19. Harriet Beecher Stowe, *Uncle Tom's Cabin* (New York: Penguin, 1981). Further references to this edition will be cited parenthetically within the text.

20. Jane Tompkins, *Sensational Designs,* pp. 135–36. Tompkins identifies this typological mode as typical of allegory; however, it is important to note here that the model of allegory that Tompkins describes is specific to the premodern form of exegetic allegory, in which all earthly experience is but the exemplification of Biblical principles. Stowe's messianic perspective views this mode of exemplification as the privileged form of temporal completeness insofar as it understands all human activity in relation to eternity. In chapter 5, I discuss the emergence of modernized forms of national allegory in relation to the temporal perspective of Christian exegesis.

21. Herman Melville, *Pierre; or, The Ambiguities* (Evanston, IL: Northwestern University Press, 1971), p. 197. Originally published 1852.

22. Lewis Mumford, *The Culture of Cities* (New York: Harcourt and Brace, 1938), p. 438.

23. Mumford's echoing of Melville's *Pierre* is an effect of affinity, not coincidence; nine years before *The Culture of Cities* appeared, Mumford had published a book-length study of Melville in which he lauded the writer as a proto-modernist visionary and which analyzed *Pierre* as a meditation on transience. See Mumford, *Herman Melville* (New York: Harcourt and Brace, 1929).

24. James E. Young, *The Texture of Memory: Holocaust Memorials and Meaning* (New Haven, CT: Yale University Press, 1993), p. 27.

25. Jochen Gerz, quoted in James E. Young, *At Memory's Edge: After-Images of the Holocaust in Contemporary Art and Architecture* (New Haven, CT: Yale University Press, 2000), p. 130.

26. Andreas Huyssen remarks that given the traditional monument's effort to present history as positive, any monument to the Holocaust is a countermonument of sorts. My use of the term "countermonument" here designates monumental efforts that revise both the content and the form of historical memory. Though monumental structures such as those built by the Gerzes and others are sometimes designated "anti-monuments," particularly in the European press, here I reserve that term to describe the attempt to refuse to give commemoration *any* form, as distinct from the radically revisionist forms favored by countermonumental projects. See Andreas Huyssen, *Twilight Memories: Marking Time in a Culture of Amnesia* (New York: Routledge, 1995), p. 258; for further considerations of Holocaust countermonuments, see also James E. Young, ed., *The Art of Memory: Holocaust Memorials in History* (New York: Jewish Museum with Prestel-Verlag, 1994), and Caroline Alice Wiedmer, *The Claims of Memory: Representations of the Holocaust in Contemporary Germany and France* (Ithaca, NY: Cornell University Press, 1999).

27. Displacement can be seen, for example, in Jochen Gerz's "hidden" monument, the Square of the Vanished, where the names of the dead were inscribed on the unseen undersides of paving stones; in Horst Hoheisel's negative-form monument in Kassel, which "restored" a fountain destroyed by the Nazis by inverting it into the ground; and in Renata Stih and Frieder Schnock's proposal for a "nonmonument," a bus that would transport people out of downtown Berlin to the sites of the concentration camps. Evanescence, in contrast, is evoked by Gerz and Shalev-Gerz's Vanishing Monument against Fascism, a graffitied obelisk gradually sunk into the ground over time until nothing remained but a plaque marking the site of its burial; by Shimon Attie's photographic projections of vanished Jewish sites onto the still-extant buildings that used to house them; and by Hoheisel's infamous proposal to blow up the Brandenburg Gate. For fuller discussions of these countermonuments, see Young, *The Texture of Memory* and *At Memory's Edge,* and Young, ed., *The Art of Memory.*

28. It is this that sets the countermonument apart from the (also untraditional) Minimalist monument. Although Minimalist forms—the best known of which in this country is perhaps Maya Lin's Vietnam Veteran's Memorial—also resist assigning a singular meaning to loss, they rely heavily on symbolism rather than allegory in this resistance. For a thoughtful discussion of the complex relationship between form and function in the Vietnam Veteran's Memorial, see Marita Sturcken, *Tangled Memories: The Vietnam War, the AIDS Epidemic, and the Politics of Remembering* (Berkeley: University of California Press, 1997).

29. See Bainard Cowan, *Exiled Waters: Moby-Dick and the Crisis of Allegory* (Baton Rouge: Louisiana State University Press, 1982).

30. Walter Benjamin, *The Origin of German Tragic Drama*, trans. John Osborne (London: NLB, 1977), p. 177.

31. Nancy Fraser, "Rethinking the Public Sphere: A Contribution to the Critique of Actually Existing Democracy," in Craig Calhoun, ed., *Habermas and the Public Sphere* (Cambridge, MA: MIT Press, 1992), pp. 109–42. Fraser's more recent work assesses the problems with this elaboration of counterpublics and calls for closer analysis of the structural function of multiple publics. See Fraser, "Transnationalizing the Public Sphere," manuscript, March 2005, available online at http://eipcp.net/transversal/0605/fraser/en (accessed December 12, 2006).

32. Notably, Douglass insists that labor, not blood, should be understood as that which constructs ties across time. Reminding the audience of the responsibility to act, he asserts, "You have no right to enjoy a child's share in the labor of your fathers, unless your children are to be blest by your labors. You have no right to wear out and waste the hard-earned fame of your fathers to cover your indolence" (366). Even as he figures the child-future to chastise the present, Douglass also uses that figure to denaturalize the structure of generational inheritance; neither family ties nor national "heritage," he argues, can create a "right" to anything that one has not earned, including the freedoms that Americans celebrate on this date. Having begun by implying his own distance from the Revolutionary fathers, Douglass now works to open that distance between his audience and those fathers—the fathers they claim as the nation's, and therefore as their, *own*—as well; replacing the logic of kinship with a standard of labor, Douglass insists that Americans have no right to possession of a past that they have not *worked for.*

33. See Walter Benjamin, "Theses on the Philosophy of History," in *Illuminations*, trans. Harry Zohn (New York: Schocken Books, 1969), pp. 253–64.

34. See Paul de Man, "The Rhetoric of Temporality," in *Blindness and Insight: Essays in the Rhetoric of Contemporary Criticism* (Minneapolis: University of Minnesota Press, 1983), p. 226. De Man's understanding of allegory, in "The Rhetoric of Temporality" and elsewhere, is clearly indebted to Benjamin's, but the extent to which the two are compatible is a matter of some debate. Although most critics read de Man's comments on allegory as if they were continuous with Benjamin's, this tendency, Doris Sommer argues, obscures the extent to which one finds in de Man's work "a polemic against the values de Man had guarded, namely time and the dialectic time makes possible." In this sense, de Man's dehistoricizing of the dialectic, Sommer insists, moves the contemporary analysis of allegory away from the historical materialism for which Benjamin meant to retrieve it—even though, as she acknowledges, Benjamin's ultimate success in that project is itself a matter of some dispute. See Doris Sommer, "Allegory and Dialectics: A Match Made in Romance," *Boundary 2* 18, no. 1 (spring 1991): p. 61 [60–82]. Other critics contend, however, that de Man's rejection of history has been overestimated.

35. See Glenn Hendler, *Public Sentiments: Structures of Feeling in Nineteenth-Century American Literature* (Chapel Hill: University of North Carolina Press, 2001), p. 7.

36. Sharon Cameron, *Lyric Time: Dickinson and the Limits of Genre* (Baltimore: Johns Hopkins University Press, 1979), pp. 70–71.

37. Ibid., p. 71.

38. Mary Louise Kete, *Sentimental Collaborations: Mourning and Middle-Class Identity in Nineteenth-Century America* (Durham, NC: Duke University Press, 2000), p. 82.

39. Wai Chee Dimock, *Through Other Continents: American Literature across Deep Time* (Princeton, NJ: Princeton University Press, 2006).

40. Virginia Jackson, *Dickinson's Misery: A Theory of Lyric Reading* (Princeton, NJ: Princeton University Press, 2005), pp. 41–42.

41. In addition to the aforementioned studies by Kete and Jackson, see Max Cavitch, "The Man That Was Used Up: Poetry, Particularity, and the Politics of Remembering George Washington," *American Literature* 75, no. 2 (June 2003): pp. 247–74.

42. Frances E. W. Harper, "The Slave Auction," in *A Brighter Coming Day: A Frances Ellen Watkins Harper Reader,* ed. Frances Smith Foster (New York: Feminist Press, 1990), pp. 64–65. Originally published in Harper, *Poems on Miscellaneous Subjects* (Boston: J. B. Yerrinton and Son, 1854).

43. See Bruce Burgett's comparable assessment of Harriet Jacobs's sentimental strategies in *Sentimental Bodies: Sex, Gender, and Citizenship in the Early Republic* (Princeton, NJ: Princeton University Press, 1998).

44. Hendler, *Public Sentiments,* p. 7.

45. Maurice Jackson stresses that references to death in slave culture read largely as secular, expressing not an otherworldly desire for heaven but a demand for improvements on earth. Jackson, "The Black Experience with Death: A Brief Analysis through Black Writings," in Richard A. Kalish, ed., *Death and Dying: Views from Many Cultures* (Farmingdale, NY: Baywood, 1980), pp. 92–98.

46. Harper's antislavery lectures proposed economic boycotts of slave-produced goods as one manifestation of this interruptive action. See Frances Smith Foster, introduction to *A Brighter Coming Day,* p. 15.

47. See Wendy Brown's discussion of political time in *Edgework: Critical Essays on Knowledge and Politics* (Princeton, NJ: Princeton University Press, 2005), esp. pp. 7–14. See also Samuel A. Chambers, *Untimely Politics* (New York: NYU Press, 2003).

48. Herman Melville, "Benito Cereno," in Dan McCall, ed., *Melville's Short Novels* (New York: Norton, 2002), pp. 34–102. Originally published 1855/1856. Further references will be cited parenthetically within the text.

49. For instance, F. O. Matthiessen, who interpreted the narrative as symbolizing an abstract and dehistoricized conflict between good and evil, faulted Melville for failing to realize that slavery itself constituted a history of evil. See F. O. Matthiessen, *Ameri-*

can Renaissance: Art and Expression in the Age of Emerson and Whitman (New York: Oxford University Press, 1941), p. 508.

50. For perceptive discussions of Melville's political pessimism as manifested in "Benito Cereno," see Michael Paul Rogin, *Subversive Genealogy: The Politics and Art of Herman Melville* (Berkeley: University of California Press, 1979); Peter Coviello, "The American in Charity: 'Benito Cereno' and Gothic Anti-Sentimentality," *Studies in American Fiction* 30.2 (fall 2002): pp. 155–80; and Maurice S. Lee, "Melville's Subversive Political Philosophy: 'Benito Cereno' and the Fate of Speech," *American Literature* 72, no. 3 (2000): pp. 495–519.

51. James H. Kavanagh, for example, sums up the central question posed in "Benito Cereno" as "how a man like Delano . . . can think of himself as liberal, progressive, and charitable while staring in the face of his own racism." Kavanagh, " 'That Hive of Subtlety': 'Benito Cereno' as Critique of Ideology," *Bucknell Review* 29, no. 1 (1984): p. 137.

52. Coviello, "The American in Charity," p. 158.

53. Alois Riegl, "The Modern Cult of Monuments: Its Character and Its Origin" (1903), trans. Kurt W. Foster and Diane Ghirardo, in K. Michael Hays, ed., *The Oppositions Reader* (New York: Princeton Architectural Press, 1998), pp. 621–51. For Walter Benjamin's exploration of the Baroque significance of the ruin, see *The Origin of German Tragic Drama,* trans. John Osborne (London: NLB, 1977).

54. Philip Fisher, "Democratic Social Space: Whitman, Melville, and the Promise of American Transparency," *Representations* 24 (1988): p. 97.

55. Fredric Jameson, *The Political Unconscious* (Ithaca, NY: Cornell University Press, 1981), p. 102.

56. Hershel Parker, *Herman Melville: A Biography, Vol. 2, 1851–1891* (Baltimore: Johns Hopkins University Press, 2002), p. 250.

57. Amasa Delano, *A Narrative of Voyages and Travels in the Northern and Southern Hemispheres: Comprising Three Voyages Round the World; Together with a Voyage of Survey and Discovery, in the Pacific Ocean and Oriental Islands* (1817; repr., New York: Praeger Reprints, 1970), p. 311.

58. See Susan Weiner, " 'Benito Cereno' and the Failure of Law," *American Quarterly* 47, no. 2 (1991): pp. 1–28. Though Melville apparently intended, originally, to reveal his historical source for the narrative upon its publication in book form, as he did in the preface to his earlier novel *Israel Potter,* he later wrote to his publishers asking them to delete the revelatory headnote.

59. Geoffrey Sanborn, *The Sign of the Cannibal: Melville and the Making of a Post-Colonial Reader* (Durham, NC: Duke University Press, 1998), p. 195.

60. For a discussion of American Puritan mortuary iconography, see David E. Stannard, *The Puritan Way of Death: A Study in Religion, Culture, and Social Change* (New York: Oxford University Press, 1977). On the *danse macabre,* see also Ariès, *The Hour of Our Death,* trans. Helen Weaver (New York: Oxford University Press, 1991).

61. Indeed, the long tradition of reading "Benito Cereno" as a story about the struggle between good and evil, eliding its historical context, demonstrates the ease with

which gestures toward "death" in the abstract can be stripped of all historical relevance and attached, instead, to other abstract ideas.

62. de Man, "The Rhetoric of Temporality," pp. 222, 225.

63. In Delano's narrative, Babo is not among these rebels because he did not survive long enough to be convicted and executed; he and Atufal were killed by the Americans as they boarded the *Tryal*.

64. Aranda's recovered bones would likely have been interred before Babo's execution, yet his postmortem gaze appears to foresee them; similarly, the head, which remained in place "for many days," would not have been in position three months later to witness Cereno's burial, as the sentence suggests it does.

65. Benjamin, "Theses on the Philosophy of History," p. 261.

66. C. L. R. James, *Mariners, Renegades and Castaways: The Story of Herman Melville and the World We Live In* (New York: Author, 1953), p. 134.

67. Arnold Rampersad, "Shadow and Veil: Melville and Modern Black Consciousness," in John Bryant and Robert Milder, eds., *Melville's Evermoving Dawn: Centennial Essays* (Kent, OH: Kent State University Press, 1997), pp. 168–69.

68. James's critique of Melville may recall to us Adorno's criticism of Benjamin during the latter's engagement in the Arcades project; Adorno repeatedly cautioned Benjamin that his mosaic methodology risked omitting theory from the project and hence creating a mere re-presentation of the past that omitted dialectical critique. See Max Pensky, *Melancholy Dialectics: Walter Benjamin and the Play of Mourning* (Amherst: University of Massachusetts Press, 1993), esp. pp. 225–27 and 276n. 32.

69. Lee, "Melville's Subversive Political Philosophy," p. 513. Contemporary engagements with the "now" of Melville do not inevitably fall into this tendency; indeed, despite my own critique of James, I would nevertheless question the extent to which James's critique of the "shallowness" of modern aestheticism corresponds to Lee's on-target wariness of Marvin Fisher's and H. Bruce Franklin's insistence that the readers of "today" understand the story better than Melville's contemporaries could have. Lindsay Waters's recent eloquent essay employing "Benito Cereno" to work through the global politics of American "innocence" and amnesia around the events of 9/11 is a recent example of the way a critical "now" can be engaged without privileging the superiority of present over past. See Lindsay Waters, "Life against Death," *Boundary 2* 29, no. 1 (2002): pp. 272–88.

70. The title of this section echoes, of course, Walter Benjamin's well-known insistence that "[t]o articulate the past historically does not mean to recognize it 'the way it really was' . . . [but] to seize hold of a memory as it flashes up at a moment of danger." I suggest in this section, however, that the melodramatic tone implicit in this invocation tends to mask Benjamin's critical insight that the state of emergency is also what we know as "everyday life." In this sense, I would emphasize, Benjamin's own work remains marked by what I characterize as an inclination to heroic melancholy that is at once conventionally masculinist and highly sentimental, and I would, accordingly, warn against fetishizing his tendency to imply that the critical gesture must be explosive to be truly "revolutionary." Benjamin, "Theses on the Philosophy of History," p. 255. For a suggestive discussion of the sentimentality of Benjamin's method, see Pensky, *Melancholy Dialectics*.

71. See Young, *At Memory's Edge*.

72. My use of the term "reparative" is both indebted to and distinct from Eve Kosofsky Sedgwick's use of the term in her essay "Paranoid Reading and Reparative Reading." Sedgwick derives her understanding of "reparative reading," as distinct from the "hermeneutics of suspicion" that she argues characterizes much of contemporary literary criticism, from affect theory. As Sedgwick frames it, "reparative reading" constitutes an interpretive strategy associated with the depressive position that makes possible the growth, often in unpredictable ways, of the subject. Reparative reading, as Sedgwick, following Klein, frames it, is "additive and accretive. . . . it wants to assemble and confer plenitude on an object that will then have resources to offer an inchoate self." See Sedgwick, "Paranoid Reading and Reparative Reading; or, You're So Paranoid, You Probably Think This Introduction Is About You," in Sedgwick, ed., *Novel Gazing: Queer Readings in Fiction* (Durham, NC: Duke University Press, 1997), pp. 27–28 [1–37]. That said, I remain skeptical about this ostensibly reparative move in contemporary public memorial since it does not offer a *dialogic* space for interpretation of its "additive and accretive" responses.

73. Douglass refrained from criticizing the monument directly on this occasion but did remark explicitly on the historic newness of the event, noting that "no such demonstration would have been tolerated here twenty years ago," and, as I note in the next chapter, implicitly critiqued the rhetoric of the monument by observing that Lincoln, when "viewed from the genuine abolition ground," seemed "tardy, cold, dull, and indifferent," though "measuring him by the sentiment of his country, a sentiment he was bound as a statesman to consult, he was swift, zealous, radical, and determined." Frederick Douglass, "The Freedmen's Monument to Abraham Lincoln: An Address Delivered in Washington, D.C. on April 14th, 1876," *The Frederick Douglass Papers, Series One: Speeches, Debates and Interviews, Vol. 4: 1864–80*, ed. John W. Blassingame and John R. McKivigan (New Haven, CT: Yale University Press, 1991), p. 436.

74. The older monument was turned around so that it faced the new statue, and the *Washington Post* reported in 1978 that members of the neighboring black community had begun to refer to the site as "Bethune Park" rather than "Lincoln Park."

75. This sort of revision is richly engaged in work on queer pedagogy. See, for instance, Kathryn Bond Stockton's lovely reading of Henry James's "The Pupil" in "Eve's Queer Child," in Stephen M. Barber and David L. Clark, eds., *Regarding Sedgwick: Essays on Queer Culture and Critical Theory* (New York: Routledge, 2002), pp. 181–200.

76. The full text of the inscription reads, "I leave you love. I leave you hope. I leave you the challenge of developing confidence in one another. I leave you a thirst for education. I leave you a respect for the use of power. I leave you faith. I leave you racial dignity. I leave you a desire to live harmoniously with your fellow men. I leave you, finally, a responsibility to our young people."

77. See Elizabeth Freeman, "Packing History, Count(er)ing Generations," *New Literary*

History 31, no. 4 (2000): pp. 727–44. For a discussion of the politics of (queer) pedagogy to which my thinking here is indebted, see Freeman's response to contemporary discussions of humanities pedagogies, *"Monsters, Inc.*: Notes on the Neoliberal Arts Education," *New Literary History* 36, no. 1 (2005): pp. 83–95.

78. Samuel Delany, *Times Square Red, Times Square Blue* (New York: NYU Press, 1999).

Notes to Chapter 5

1. Walt Whitman, "Death of President Lincoln," in *Memoranda during the War and Death of President Lincoln,* ed. Roy P. Basler (Westport, CT: Greenwood, 1972), p. 11.

2. Ibid., p. 12.

3. Ralph Waldo Emerson, *Representative Men,* ed. Pamela Schirmeister (New York: Marsilio, 1995), p. 5.

4. Ralph Waldo Emerson, "A Plain Man of the People," in Waldo W. Braden, ed., *Building the Myth: Selected Speeches Memorializing Abraham Lincoln* (Urbana: University of Illinois Press, 1990), p. 33.

5. Ibid. (emphasis added).

6. C. M. Butler, *Funeral Address on the Death of Abraham Lincoln, Delivered in the Church of the Covenant, April 19, 1865* (Philadelphia: Henry B. Ashmead, 1865), p. 11.

7. For an analysis of the poetics of fellow-feeling in the poetry eulogizing Washington, see Max Cavitch, "The Man That Was Used Up: Poetry, Particularity, and the Politics of Remembering George Washington," *American Literature* 73, no. 2 (June 2003): pp. 257–74.

8. Whitman, *Memoranda during the War,* in *Memoranda during the War and Death of President Lincoln,* ed. Roy P. Basler (Westport, CT: Greenwood, 1972), p. 23.

9. Ibid., p. 24.

10. Frederick Douglass, "The Freedmen's Monument to Abraham Lincoln: An Address Delivered in Washington, D.C. on April 14th, 1876," *The Frederick Douglass Papers, Series One: Speeches, Debates and Interviews, Vol. 4: 1864–80,* ed. John W. Blassingame and John R. McKivigan (New Haven, CT: Yale University Press, 1991), pp. 427–43.

11. Giorgio Agamben, *Stanzas: Word and Phantasm in Western Culture* (Minneapolis: University of Minnesota Press, 1993), p. 20.

12. Ibid. Agamben's essay critiques this strategy, noting, "it is what the ancient humoral theorists rightly identified in the will to transform into an object of amorous embrace what should have remained only an object of contemplation" (ibid.). Although, as I observed in chapter 3, I resist the hierarchical mind/body distinction uncritically reiterated in Agamben's opposition of the pathological "embrace" to transformative "contemplation," the two temporalities of melancholy expressed in these two modes of approaching the unreal are central to the kind of insufficiently critical sentimental nationalism that I investigate here, as it develops a purely emotional response to the question of injustice that tends to disable rather than empower contemplation.

13. On the centrality of mournfulness to contemporary nationalism, see Lauren Berlant, "Uncle Sam Needs a Wife: Citizenship and Denegation," in Russ Castronovo and Dana D. Nelson, eds., *Materializing Democracy: Toward a Revitalized Cultural Politics* (Durham, NC: Duke University Press, 2002), pp. 144–74; and Peter Coviello, "Epilogue: Nation Mourns," in *Intimacy in America: Dreams of Affiliation in Antebellum Culture* (Minneapolis: University of Minnesota Press, 2005), pp. 157–75.

14. Berlant, "Uncle Sam Needs a Wife," p. 161.

15. Whitman, "Death of President Lincoln," p. 12.

16. Benedict Anderson, *Imagined Communities: Reflections on the Origin and Spread of Nationalism* (London: Verso, 1991). In a later essay addressing the Lincoln Memorial in Washington, D.C., Anderson points out that the "ghostly and indefinitely replicable" memories enshrined in the monuments of official nationalism point toward a "forever" that is "visibly coterminous with this nation, this people, rather than pointing toward Judgment Day." See Anderson, "Replica, Aura, and Late Nationalist Imaginings," in *The Spectre of Comparisons: Nationalism, Southeast Asia, and the World* (London: Verso, 1998), p. 48.

17. Anderson, *Imagined Communities*, p. 205.

18. Ibid., p. 206.

19. Anderson, "Replica, Aura, and Late Nationalist Imaginings," p. 51.

20. A well-known orator, Everett had, in helping to found Cambridge's Mount Auburn Cemetery, already demonstrated his commitment to the pedagogical possibilities of the burial ground. For a discussion of Everett's speech, see Gary Wills, *Lincoln at Gettysburg: The Words That Remade America* (New York: Simon and Schuster, 1992).

21. Abraham Lincoln, "Address at Gettysburg, November 19, 1863," in *Abraham Lincoln: Speeches and Writings, Vol. 2, 1859–65* (New York: Library of America, 1989), p. 536.

22. Ibid.

23. Priscilla Wald, *Constituting Americans: Cultural Anxiety and Narrative Form* (Durham, NC: Duke University Press, 1995), p. 66.

24. Lincoln, "Address at Gettysburg," p. 536.

25. Ibid.

26. See Anderson, "Replica, Aura, and Late Nationalist Imaginings," p. 52; also see Anderson, "Nationalism, Identity, and the Logic of Seriality," in *The Spectre of Comparisons*, pp. 29–45.

27. Although Lincoln's speech found admirers throughout the latter part of the nineteenth century, it was, as Barry Schwartz has shown, the commemorative discourse of World War I—the historical event whose memorials first inaugurate the notion of the statistical citizen outlined by Anderson—that enshrined the Gettysburg Address at the heart of American nationalist commemoration. Like Lincoln himself at Gettysburg, commemorators located a text from the past that seemed congenial to their own purposes and then worked to convince their audience that this truth had been at the core of its values, unchanged, all along. Hence, the idealization of the Gettysburg Address in the twentieth century replicates its own retrospective construction of a nation brought into being by the notion of equality, moving backward/forward in serial time toward the gradual realization of its own timeless ideals. See Barry Schwartz, *Abraham Lincoln and the Forge of National Memory* (Chicago: University of Chicago Press, 2000).

28. The political attachments of the dead Confederate soldiers buried at Gettysburg, for instance, linked them to a national future quite different from the one Lincoln wished to depict, in the address, as the one to which all Americans were devoted. See Michael Davis, *The Image of Lincoln in the South* (Knoxville: University of Tennessee Press, 1971).

29. Marc Redfield, "Imagi-Nation: The Imagined Community and the Aesthetics of Mourning," *Diacritics* 29, no. 4 (winter 1999): p. 68.

30. Ibid., p. 71.

31. Redfield recognizes that Anderson's conceptual elision of this dimension of nationalism in his emphasis on the abstracted serial citizen, even as he implicitly recognizes it in his allusions to the role of the mother, demonstrates, finally, that "part of the achievement of *Imagined Communities* [is] to have shown how poorly grounded, yet also how insistent, that patriarchal fantasy is" (ibid.). Similarly, Sharon Patricia Holland's critique of *Imagined Communities* identifies Anderson's articulation of the role of death in modern nationalism as exemplifying the same modern anxiety about the status of the dead that it seeks to elucidate—an anxiety that, as she shows, contributes to the uneven racialization of the dead in America. See Holland, *Raising the Dead: Readings of Death and (Black) Subjectivity* (Durham, NC: Duke University Press, 2000), pp. 22–23.

32. Lincoln, "Address at Gettysburg," p. 536.

33. Abraham Lincoln, "Second Inaugural Address, March 4, 1865," in *Abraham Lincoln: Speeches and Writings, Vol. 2*, p. 687.

34. Ibid.

35. Ibid.

36. Ibid.

37. See especially David B. Chesebrough, *No Sorrow Like Our Sorrow: Northern Protestant Ministers and the Assassination of Lincoln* (Kent, OH: Kent State University Press, 1994); also Thomas Reed Turner, *Beware the People Weeping: Public Opinion and the Assassination of President Lincoln* (Baton Rouge: Louisiana State University Press, 1982).

38. Schwartz, *Abraham Lincoln and the Forge of National Memory*, p. 30.

39. Richard Morris observes that one of the key issues at play in the memorial discourse about Lincoln is an ambivalence about the role of emotion. However, in his analytic division of the eulogistic discourse into three separate "cultures," Religionists, Romanticists, and Heroists, Morris neglects to consider the ambivalence about emotion that permeated even the most romanticized and/or sentimentalized approaches to grief in the nineteenth century. See Richard Morris, *Sinners, Lovers and Heroes: An Essay on Memorializing in Three American Cultures* (Albany: State University of New York Press, 1997).

40. See Harold Holzer, *Lincoln Seen and Heard* (Lawrence: University Press of Kansas, 2000), pp. 107–8.

41. Joseph William Fifer, "Speech to the Bar Association of Illinois" (1880); quoted in Michael Burlingame, *The Inner World of Abraham Lincoln* (Urbana: University of Illinois Press, 1994), p. 93.

42. William H. Herndon and Jesse W. Weik, *Herndon's Life of Lincoln,* ed. Paul M. Angle (Cleveland: World Publishing Company, 1949), p. 273.

43. Ibid.; Joshua Shenk, *Lincoln's Melancholy: How Depression Challenged a President and Fueled His Greatness* (Boston: Houghton Mifflin, 2005).

44. Charles Carroll Everett, *A Sermon in Commemoration of the Death of Abraham Lincoln, Late President of the United States, Bangor ME, 1865* (Bangor, ME: Benjamin Burr, 1865), p. 18.

45. Henry Ward Beecher, in *Our Martyr President, Abraham Lincoln: Voices from the Pulpit of New York and Brooklyn* (New York: Tibbals and Whiting, 1865), p. 40 [33–48].

46. Gilbert Haven, *The Uniter and Liberator of America: A Memorial Discourse on the Character and Career of Abraham Lincoln* (Boston: James P. Magee, 1865), p. 12.

47. J. G. Holland, "Eulogy," in *The Nation Weeping for Its Dead: Observances at Springfield, Massachusetts, on President Lincoln's Funeral Day, Wednesday, April 19, 1865, Including Dr. Holland's Eulogy; From the Springfield Republican's Report* (Springfield, MA: Samuel Bowles; L. J. Powers, 1865), p. 19.

48. Rev. John McClintock, in *Our Martyr President,* p. 135.

49. Haven, *Uniter and Liberator,* p. 13.

50. Charles S. Robinson, in *Our Martyr President,* p. 90

51. Beecher, in *Our Martyr President,* pp. 37–38.

52. Schwartz, *Abraham Lincoln and the Forge of National Memory,* p. 23.

53. Haven, *Uniter and Liberator,* p. 12.

54. Beecher, in *Our Martyr President,* p. 38.

55. Preface to *Our Martyr President,* p. viii.

56. Henry Lyman Morehouse, "Evil Its Own Destroyer" (East Saginaw, MI: Enterprise Print, 1865), pp. 6–7; quoted in Chesebrough, *No Sorrow Like Our Sorrow,* p. 3.

57. Holland, "Eulogy," pp. 15–16.

58. Beecher, in *Our Martyr President,* p. 40.

59. Ibid., p. 46.

60. George Bancroft, "How Shall the Nation Show Its Sorrow?" in Braden, ed., *Building the Myth,* p. 71, p. 66.

61. On the conventional obligation to limit indulgence in grief, see Karen Halttunen, "Mourning the Dead: A Study in Sentimental Ritual," in *Confidence Men and Painted Women: A Study of Middle-Class Culture in America, 1830–1870* (New Haven, CT: Yale University Press, 1982).

62. On the development of the heroic Lincoln-image, see Schwartz, *Abraham Lincoln and the Forge of National Memory,* esp. pp. 257–64; and Morris, *Sinners, Lovers and Heroes,* pp. 115–52.

63. This tradition has continued through the twentieth century, visible, for example, in Bill Maudlin's 1963 cartoon commemorating the Kennedy assassination by showing the Lincoln Memorial statue in Washington, D.C., hiding its face mournfully in its hands. For a discussion of this cartoon, see Roger A. Fischer, "The 'Monumental' Lincoln as an American Cartoon Convention," *Inks: Cartoon and Comic Art Studies* 2, no. 1 (February 1995): pp. 12–25.

64. On the feminine image of Christ in the nineteenth century, see Ann Douglas, *The Feminization of American Culture* (New York: Anchor Books, 1988).

65. Haven, *Uniter and Liberator,* p. 13; Emerson, "A Plain Man of the People."

66. Emma Hardinge, *The Great Funeral Oration on Abraham Lincoln, Delivered Sunday, April 16, 1865 at Cooper Institute* (New York: American News Company, 1865), p. 17.

67. Reverend E. B. Webb, in *Sermons Preached in Boston on the Death of Abraham Lincoln* (Boston: J. E. Tilton, 1865), p. 151.

68. Holland, "Eulogy," p. 24.

69. Ibid., pp. 25–26.

70. Beecher, in *Our Martyr President,* pp. 46–47.

71. Robinson, in *Our Martyr President,* pp. 91–92.

72. T. L. Cuyler, in *Our Martyr President,* p. 170.

73. Ibid., p. 171.

74. Holland, again, provides a partial exception; he asserts that Lincoln's name will be "embalmed in the memory of an enfranchised people, and associated with every blessing they may enjoy and every good they may achieve." The prospect of these future achievements—envisioned here for the sake of Lincoln's glory, a "better fame than the proudest conquerors can boast"—carries African Americans forward in lived time, something that many other white eulogists failed to imagine. Holland, "Eulogy," p. 25.

75. Jacob Thomas, "Sermon Preached in the African Methodist Episcopal Zion Church," in *A Tribute of Respect by the Citizens of Troy to the Memory of Abraham Lincoln* (Troy, NY: Young and Benson, 1865), p. 44 [43–47].

76. Ibid., p. 47.

77. J. Sella Martin, "Letter to the Editor of the *New York Evening Post,* 24 April 1865," in C. Peter Ripley, ed., *The Black Abolitionist Papers, Vol. 5: The United States, 1859–65* (Chapel Hill: University of North Carolina Press, 1992), p. 319 [317–20]. After a telegram from the War Department, New York City officials allowed black mourners to participate in the procession; the *Evening Post,* however, did not print Sella's letter.

78. Schwartz, *Abraham Lincoln and the Forge of National Memory,* p. 52.

79. Ibid., p. 58.

80. Reverend Joseph A. Prime, "Sermon Preached in the Liberty Street Presbyterian Church," in *A Tribute of Respect by the Citizens of Troy,* pp. 154, 156 [151–57].

81. Thomas, "Sermon Preached in the African Methodist Episcopal Zion Church," pp. 44–45.

82. Elizabeth Keckley, *Behind the Scenes: Thirty Years a Slave and Four Years in the White House,* ed. Frances Smith Foster (Urbana: University of Illinois Press, 2001), p. 6. Further references to this edition will be cited parenthetically within the text.

83. Keckley's complex relationship with Mary Todd Lincoln has been the subject of much debate, beginning with the negative critical response that the memoir received on publication and continuing through present-day readings of the text. Some contemporary critics read Keckley's "defense" of the First Widow's behavior as a direct but pragmatically veiled attack exposing Mrs. Lincoln's complicity with the structures that negated black female agency, and others see a good deal of ambivalence in her representation of her relations with Mary Todd, noting that despite Mary's egregious behavior, Keckley seems to maintain a strong personal affection for the woman as a result of their years of intimacy. For examples of the former position, see Rafia Zafar, "Dressing Up and Dressing Down: Elizabeth Keckley's *Behind the Scenes at the White House* and Eliza Potter's *A Hairdresser's Experience in High Life*," in *We Wear the Mask: African Americans Write American Literature* (New York: Columbia University Press, 1997), and Elizabeth Young, "Black Woman, White House: Race and Redress in Elizabeth Keckley's *Behind the Scenes*," in *Disarming the Nation: Women's Writing and the American Civil War* (Chicago: University of Chicago Press, 1999); for an example of the latter position, see Katherine Adams, "Freedom and Ballgowns: Elizabeth Keckley and the Work of Domesticity," *Arizona Quarterly* 57 (winter 2001): pp. 45–87. See also Jennifer Fleischner's recent dual biography, *Mrs. Lincoln and Mrs. Keckly: The True Story of the Remarkable Friendship between a First Lady and a Former Slave* (New York: Broadway Books, 2003).

84. James Olney, introduction to Elizabeth Keckley, *Behind the Scenes; or, Thirty Years a Slave and Four Years in the White House* (New York: Oxford University Press, 1988), p. xxxiv.

85. Rafia Zafar, *We Wear the Mask: African Americans Write American Literature, 1760–1870* (New York: Columbia University Press, 1997), p. 180.

86. Ibid., p. 178.

87. Zafar, Jennifer Fleischner, and Carolyn Sorisio offer similar readings of this contrast. Yet whereas Fleischner's reading views Keckley's reticence psychologically, as a symptomatic resurfacing that indexes the depths of slavery's traumatic effects, Zafar and Sorisio both place a stronger emphasis on Keckley's indirection as central to a consciously chosen narrative strategy that Zafar frames within a history of African American "undertelling" and Sorisio sees as a canny appropriation of the gentility of the middle-class woman. See Zafar, *We Wear the Mask*, p. 175; Jennifer Fleischner, *Mastering Slavery: Memory, Family and Identity in Women's Slave Narratives* (New York: NYU Press, 1996), p. 130; Carolyn Sorisio, "Unmasking the Genteel Performer: Elizabeth Keckley's *Behind the Scenes* and the Politics of Public Wrath," *African American Review* 34 (spring 2000): pp. 19–38.

88. Most recent critical considerations of the narrative tend to privilege the gender politics of Keckley's relationship to Mary Todd Lincoln over her depiction of the President. Two exceptions to this tendency are Lynn Domina, "I Was Re-elected President: Elizabeth Keckley as Quintessential Patriot," in Lynn Coleman, ed., *Women's Life Writing: Finding Voice/Building Community* (Bowling Green, OH: Bowling Green University Press, 1997); and Shirley Samuels, "Lincoln's Body," in *Facing America: Iconography and the Civil War* (New York: Oxford University Press, 2004).

89. Holland, "Eulogy," p. 19.

90. Xiomara Santamarina argues, along similar lines, that Keckley's reporting of her intimate view of Mary Todd Lincoln's grief constitutes a kind of "emotional labor" that, rather than exploiting black women, "admit[s] them into a recognized form of participation in political affect." See Santamarina, *Belabored Professions: Narratives of African American Working Womanhood* (Chapel Hill: University of North Carolina Press, 2006), p. 155. I would stress, however, that Mrs. Lincoln's extended "paroxysms" (141) were generally understood as politically *destructive* affect—a fact of which Keckley herself, whatever her own feelings about the First Lady, was well aware, as her defense of her harshly judged employer in the introduction reveals. Her own depiction of her less violent, protoproductive and nationally typical moment of grief operates, in contrast, as positive participation in positive political affect.

91. Fleischner, *Mastering Slavery*, p. 101.

92. Frances Smith Foster, "Historical Introduction," in Keckley, *Behind the Scenes*, pp. lvi, lvii.

93. Ibid., p. lviii.

94. Ibid., pp. lviii, lix.

95. *Columbus Sun*, quoted in Foster, "Historical Introduction," p. xliv.

96. *New York Citizen*, quoted in Foster, "Historical Introduction," pp. lvii–lviii.

97. "Indecent Publications," *New York Citizen*, April 18, 1868, p. 4, quoted in Santamarina, *Belabored Professions*, p. 156.

98. Fleischner, *Mastering Slavery*, p. 121.

99. Gilles Deleuze, *The Logic of Sense*, trans. Constantine Boundas (New York: Columbia University Press, 1990), p. 4.

100. On the structure of phantomatic transmission and its relation to melancholia, see Nicholas Abraham and Maria Torok, *The Shell and the Kernel: Renewals of Psychoanalysis*, trans. Nicholas T. Rand (Chicago: University of Chicago Press, 1994).

101. Fleischner, *Mastering Slavery*, p. 97.

102. Schwartz, *Abraham Lincoln and the Forge of National Memory*, chap. 7.

103. Paul Monette, *Last Watch of the Night: Essays Too Personal and Otherwise* (New York: Harcourt Brace Jovanovich, 1994), p. 147.

104. Ibid., pp. 148–49.

105. Charles E. Morris III, "My Old Kentucky Homo: Lincoln and the Politics of Queer Public Memory," in Kendall R. Phillips, ed., *Framing Public Memory* (Tuscaloosa: University of Alabama Press, 2004), p. 90.

106. For a sustained interrogation of the tendency to posit racial oppression as the analogous antecedent to gay oppression, see Steven Seidman, "Identity and Politics in a 'Postmodern' Gay Culture: Some Historical and Conceptual Notes," in Michael Warner, ed., *Fear of a Queer Planet* (Minneapolis: University of Minnesota Press, 1993), pp. 105–42.

107. Lisa Duggan, *The Twilight of Equality: Neoliberalism, Cultural Politics and the Attack on Democracy* (Boston: Beacon, 2003).

Notes to the Coda

1. Cf. Austin Sarat, ed., *Dissent in Dangerous Times* (Ann Arbor: University of Michigan Press, 2005).

2. Jacques Derrida, quoted in Giovanna Borradori, *Philosophy in a Time of Terror: Dialogues with Jürgen Habermas and Jacques Derrida* (Chicago: University of Chicago Press, 2003).

3. See Glenda Dicker/sun's reading of mediated blackness in "Katrina: Acting Black/ Playing Blackness," *Theatre Journal* 57, no. 4 (December 2005): pp. 614–16.

4. For critiques of the commercialization of 9/11, see Dana Heller, ed., *The Selling of 9/11: How a National Tragedy Became a Commodity* (New York: Palgrave, 2005).

5. James Der Derian, "*In Terrorem*: Before and After 9/11," in Ken Booth and Timothy Dunne, eds., *Worlds in Collision: Terror and the Future of Global Order* (New York: Palgrave Macmillan, 2002), pp. 102–3, quoted in James Trimarco and Molly Hurley Depret, "Wounded Nation, Broken Time," in Heller, ed., The *Selling of 9/11*, p. 37 [27–53].

6. Lauren Berlant, "Uncle Sam Needs a Wife: Citizenship and Denegation," in Russ Castronovo and Dana C. Nelson, eds., *Materializing Democracy: Towards a Revitalized Cultural Politics* (Durham, NC: Duke University Press), p. 161. See also Berlant, "The Epistemology of State Emotion," in Sarat, ed., *Dissent in Dangerous Times*, pp. 46–74.

7. David Simpson, *9/11: The Culture of Commemoration* (Chicago: University of Chicago Press, 2006), p. 9.

8. Judith Butler, "Violence, Mourning, Politics," in *Precarious Life: The Powers of Mourning and Violence* (London: Verso, 2004), p. 30. The phrase "tarrying with grief" adapts Hegel's description of the necessity of negation in *The Phenomenology of Spirit*. See also David Eng, who argues that the maintenance of nationalist melancholia works to support war insofar as melancholia can be converted, as Freud observes, into an aggressive mania compatible with the war drive. Eng, "The Value of Silence," *Theatre Journal* 54, no. 1 (2002): pp. 85–94.

9. Butler, "Violence, Mourning, Politics," pp. 30, 23.

10. Ibid., p. 49.

11. The essay's Hegelian inflection of the bereavement work-ethic coexists rather uneasily with its Freudian framework; the Freudian assessment of mourning also contains a conviction that mourning will make us "better," but in the sense of resuming a posited normative state, the basic level of psychic health that Freud insists is necessary for the subject to regain the possibility of making new attachments—not the progressive generation and display of one's own moral superiority, in other words, but a return to a state marked at once by sameness and alterity. Notably, while Butler's understanding of the psyche incorporates a careful attention to Freud's later attention to melancholia, her argument here is inflected in the more optimistic tone that characterizes the earlier Freud, the Freud of "Mourning and Melancholia." In contrast, Derrida's assessment of the interminability of mourning, with which Butler's shares a strong conceptual overlap, remains closer in tone to the melancholy suggested in the language of the later Freud. See Pascal-Anne Brault and Michael Naas, "To Reckon with the Dead: Jacques Derrida's Politics of Mourning," in Jacques Derrida, *The Work of Mourning* (Chicago: University of Chicago Press, 2001), pp. 1–30.

12. Ralph Waldo Emerson, "Experience," in *The Collected Works of Ralph Waldo Emerson, Vol. 3* (Cambridge, MA: Harvard University Press, 1983), p. 29 [25–49].

13. Ibid.

14. Pamela Schirmeister, *Less Legible Meanings: Between Poetry and Philosophy in the Work of Emerson* (Stanford, CA: Stanford University Press, 1999), pp. 123–24. Sharon Cameron's well-known reading of "Experience" is one example of an interpretation that posits the author's melancholia. See Cameron, "Representing Grief: Emerson's 'Experience,'" *Representations* 15 (summer 1986): pp. 15–41. Mary Chapman enumerates the many meanings of the unusual word "caducous"—which connotes at once a placeholder (the *e caduque*), a purely transitory body part (such as baby teeth or the scabbing over a wound), and, in Roman law, "the refusal or *failure* to accept an inheritance"—and demonstrates the relevance of each meaning in the essay. Chapman, "The Economics of Loss: Emerson's 'Threnody,'" *American Transatlantic Quarterly* (June 2002): p. 77.

15. Schirmeister, *Less Legible Meanings*, p. 133.

16. Ibid., p. 140.

17. Emerson, "Experience," p. 27.

18. Ibid., p. 49.

19. Ibid., p. 48. "Secular" here signifies in the scientific sense, meaning "of profound duration." Emerson refers to nature as "secular" in the essay "Circles." See *The Collected Works of Ralph Waldo Emerson, Vol. 3*, p. 191n. 48.2.

20. On Emerson's interest in contemporary scientific discoveries about time, see James R. Guthrie, *Above Time: Emerson's and Thoreau's Temporal Revolutions* (Columbia: University of Missouri Press, 2001). On his reading of world religions, see Wai Chee Dimock, *Through Other Continents: American Literature across Deep Time* (Princeton, NJ: Princeton University Press, 2006), pp. 34–49.

21. Art Spiegelman, *In the Shadow of No Towers* (New York: Pantheon, 2004).

22. For a reading of *Maus's* temporal multivalence, see Erin McGlothlin, "No Time Like the Present: Narrative and Time in Art Spiegelman's *Maus*," *Narrative* 11, no. 2 (May 2003): pp. 177–98.

23. Lauren Berlant discusses the need to develop a language of agency within "a zone of temporality we can gesture toward as that of ongoingness, getting by, and living on," an *uneventful* time. Berlant, "Slow Death (Sovereignty, Obesity, Lateral Agency)," *Critical Inquiry* 33.4 (summer 2007). See also Thomas L. Dunn, *A Politics of the Ordinary* (New York: NYU Press, 1999).

Selected Bibliography

Abercrombie, James. *The Mourner Comforted*. Philadelphia: S. Potter, 1821.

Abraham, Nicolas, and Maria Torok. *The Shell and the Kernel: Renewals of Psychoanalysis*. Trans. Nicholas T. Rand. Chicago: University of Chicago Press, 1994.

Adams, Katherine. "Freedom and Ballgowns: Elizabeth Keckley and the Work of Domesticity." *Arizona Quarterly* 57 (winter 2001): 45–87.

Adams, Nehemiah. *Agnes and the Key of Her Little Coffin*. Boston: S. K. Whipple, 1857.

———. *Catharine*. Boston: J. E. Tilton, 1859.

Agamben, Giorgio. *Homo Sacer: Sovereign Power and Bare Life*. Trans. Daniel Heller-Roazen. Stanford, CA: Stanford University Press, 1998.

———. *Stanzas: Word and Phantasm in Western Culture*. Minneapolis: University of Minnesota Press, 1993.

Alcott, William A. *The Young Wife; or, Duties of Woman in the Marriage Relation*. Boston: George W. Light, 1837.

Allen, Thomas. "Clockwork Nation: Modern Time, Moral Perfection and American Identity in Catharine Beecher and Henry Thoreau." *Journal of American Studies* 39, no. 1 (2006): 65–86.

Anderson, Benedict. *Imagined Communities: Reflections on the Origin and Spread of Nationalism*. London: Verso, 1991.

———. *The Spectre of Comparisons: Nationalism, Southeast Asia, and the World*. London: Verso, 1998.

Apess, William. *On Our Own Ground: The Complete Writings of William Apess, a Pequot*. Ed. Barry O'Connell. Amherst: University of Massachusetts Press, 1992.

Argersinger, Jana. "Family Embraces: The Unholy Kiss and Authorial Relations in *The Wide, Wide World*." *American Literature* 74, no. 1 (June 2002): 251–85.

Ariès, Phillipe. *The Hour of Our Death*. Trans. Helen Weaver. New York: Knopf, 1981.

———. *Western Attitudes toward Death: From the Middle Ages to the Present*. Trans. Patricia M. Ranum. Baltimore: Johns Hopkins University Press, 1974.

Asad, Talal. *Formations of the Secular: Christianity, Islam, Modernity*. Stanford, CA: Stanford University Press, 2003.

Bakhtin, Mikhail. "Forms of Time and of the Chronotope in the Novel: Notes towards a Historical Poetics." In *The Dialogic Imagination: Four Essays*. Ed. Michael Holquist. Trans. Caryl Emerson and Michael Holquist. Austin: University of Texas Press, 1981: 84–258.

Barnes, Elizabeth. *States of Sympathy: Seduction and Democracy in the American Novel*. New York: Columbia University Press, 1997.

Barthes, Roland. *Camera Lucida: Reflections on Photography*. New York: Hill and Wang, 1981.

Barthold, Bonnie J. *Black Time: Fictions of Africa, the Caribbean, and the United States*. New Haven, CT: Yale University Press, 1981.

Bartky, Ian. *Selling the True Time: Nineteenth-Century Timekeeping in America*. Stanford, CA: Stanford University Press, 2000.

Baym, Nina. *Woman's Fiction: A Guide to Novels by and about Women in America, 1820–70*. 2nd ed. Urbana: University of Illinois Press, 1993.

Beecher, Catharine. *A Treatise on Domestic Economy*. Ed. Kathryn Kish Sklar. New York: Schocken Books, 1977.

Beecher, Catharine, and Harriet Beecher Stowe. *The American Woman's Home*. Ed. Nicole Tonkovich. New Brunswick, NJ: Rutgers University Press, 2002.

Bender, John, and David E. Wellbery, eds. *Chronotypes: The Construction of Time*. Stanford, CA: Stanford University Press, 1991.

Benjamin, Walter. *Illuminations*. Trans. Harry Zohn. New York: Schocken Books, 1969.

———. *The Origin of German Tragic Drama*. Trans. John Osborne. London: NLB, 1977.

Bergland, Renee. *The National Uncanny: Indian Ghosts and American Subjects*. Hanover, NH: University Press of New England, 2000.

Bergson, Henri. *Time and Free Will: An Essay on the Immediate Data of Consciousness*. Trans. F. L. Pogson. New York: Harper and Brothers, 1960.

Berlant, Lauren. "Poor Eliza," *American Literature* 70, no. 3 (September 1988): 635–88.

———. *The Queen of America Goes to Washington City: Essays on Sex and Citizenship*. Durham, NC: Duke University Press, 1997.

———. "Slow Death (Sovereignty, Obesity, Lateral Agency)." *Critical Inquiry* 33.4 (summer 2007).

———. "Uncle Sam Needs a Wife: Citizenship and Denegation." In Russ Castronovo and Dana D. Nelson, eds., *Materializing Democracy: Toward a Revitalized Cultural Politics*. Durham, NC: Duke University Press, 2002: 144–74.

Bethune, George W. *Lays of Love and Faith, with Other Fugitive Poems*. Philadelphia: Lindsay and Blakiston, 1848.

———. *Memoirs of Mrs. Joanna Bethune, by Her Son*. New York: Harper and Brothers, 1863.

Bhabha, Homi. *The Location of Culture*. London: Routledge, 1994.

Bigelow, Jacob. *A History of the Cemetery of Mount Auburn*. Boston: James Munroe, 1860.

Blight, David. *Race and Reunion: The Civil War in American Memory*. Cambridge, MA: Harvard University Press, 2001.

Bouman, Margot. "Introduction: The Loop as a Temporal Form." *Invisible Culture: An Electronic Journal for Visual Culture* 8 (2004), http://www.rochester.edu/in_visible_culture/Issue_8/issue8intro.html (accessed November 1, 2005).

Borradori, Giovanna. *Philosophy in a Time of Terror: Dialogues with Jürgen Habermas and Jacques Derrida.* Chicago: University of Chicago Press, 2003.

Bowler, Peter J. *The Invention of Progress: The Victorians and the Past.* Oxford, UK: Blackwell, 1989.

Braden, Waldo W., ed. *Building the Myth: Selected Speeches Memorializing Abraham Lincoln.* Urbana: University of Illinois Press, 1990.

Breitwieser, Mitchell. *American Puritanism and the Defense of Mourning: Religion, Grief and Ethnology in Mary White Rowlandson's Captivity Narrative.* Madison: University of Wisconsin Press, 1990.

Brodhead, Richard. *Cultures of Letters: Scenes of Reading and Writing in Nineteenth-Century America.* Chicago: University of Chicago Press, 1993.

Brown, Gillian. *Domestic Individualism: Imagining Self in Nineteenth-Century America.* Berkeley: University of California Press, 1992.

Brown, Wendy. *Edgework: Critical Essays on Knowledge and Politics.* Princeton, NJ: Princeton University Press, 2005.

Buckley, Jerome Hamilton. *The Triumph of Time: A Study of the Victorian Concepts of Time, History, Progress and Decadence.* Cambridge, MA: Harvard University Press, 1966.

Burgett, Bruce. "Between Speculation and Population: The Problem of 'Sex' in Our Long Eighteenth Century." *Early American Literature* 37, no. 1 (2002): 119–53.

———. *Sentimental Bodies: Sex, Gender and Citizenship in the Early Republic.* Princeton, NJ: Princeton University Press, 1998.

Burlingame, Michael. *The Inner World of Abraham Lincoln.* Urbana: University of Illinois Press, 1994.

Burnham, Michelle. *Captivity and Sentiment: Cultural Exchange in American Literature, 1682–1861.* Hanover, NH: University Press of New England, 1997.

Butler, C. M. *Funeral Address on the Death of Abraham Lincoln, Delivered in the Church of the Covenant, April 19, 1865.* Philadelphia: Henry B. Ashmead, 1865.

Butler, Judith. *Precarious Life: The Powers of Mourning and Violence.* London: Verso, 2004.

———. *The Psychic Life of Power: Theories in Subjection.* Stanford, CA: Stanford University Press, 1997.

Cameron, Sharon. *Lyric Time: Dickinson and the Limits of Genre.* Baltimore: Johns Hopkins University Press, 1979.

———. "Representing Grief: Emerson's 'Experience.'" *Representations* 15 (summer 1986): 15–41.

Capon, Lester J., ed. *The Adams-Jefferson Letters: The Complete Correspondence between Thomas Jefferson and Abigail and John Adams, Vol. 2, 1812–1826.* Chapel Hill: University of North Carolina Press, 1959.

Carr, Helen. *Inventing the American Primitive: Politics, Gender and the Representation of Native American Literary Traditions, 1789–1936.* New York: NYU Press, 1996.

Carver, Jonathan. *Three Years' Travel through the Interior of North America*. Philadelphia: Cruikshank and Bell, 1784.

Castiglia, Christopher, and Russ Castronovo, eds. "Aesthetics and the End(s) of Cultural Studies," special issue of *American Literature* 76, no. 3 (September 2004).

Castronovo, Russ. *Fathering the Nation: American Genealogies of Slavery and Freedom*. Berkeley: University of California Press, 1995.

Cavitch, Max. "The Man That Was Used Up: Poetry, Particularity, and the Politics of Remembering George Washington." *American Literature* 75, no. 2 (June 2003): 247–74.

Chakrabarty, Dipesh. *Provincializing Europe: Postcolonial Thought and Historical Difference*. Princeton, NJ: Princeton University Press, 2000.

Chambers, Samuel A. *Untimely Politics*. New York: NYU Press, 2003.

Chapman, Mary. "The Economics of Loss: Emerson's 'Threnody.'" *American Transatlantic Quarterly* (June 2002): 73–87.

Chapman, Mary, and Glenn Hendler, eds. *Sentimental Men: Masculinity and the Politics of Affect in American Culture*. Berkeley: University of California Press, 1999.

Chapman, Raymond. *The Sense of the Past in Victorian Literature*. London: Croon Helm, 1986.

Cheng, Anne Anlin. *The Melancholy of Race: Psychoanalysis, Assimilation and Hidden Grief*. New York: Oxford University Press, 2001.

Cherniavsky, Eva. *That Pale Mother Rising: Sentimental Discourses and the Imitation of Motherhood in 19th-Century America*. Bloomington: Indiana University Press, 1995.

Chesebrough, David B. *No Sorrow Like Our Sorrow: Northern Protestant Ministers and the Assassination of Lincoln*. Kent, OH: Kent State University Press, 1994.

Cheyfitz, Eric. "Literally White, Figuratively Red: The Frontier of Translation in *The Pioneers*." In Robert Clark, ed., *James Fenimore Cooper: New Critical Essays*. London: Vision Press, 1985.

Child, Lydia Maria. *The American Frugal Housewife*. Ed. Alice M. Geffen. New York: Harper and Row, 1972.

———. *The Mother's Book*. 2nd ed. New York: Arno Press, 1977. Originally published Boston: Carter and Hendee, 1831.

Clark, Robert. "'The Last of the Iroquois': Myth and History in *The Last of the Mohicans*." *Poetics Today* 3 (1982): 115–34.

Cleaveland, N. *Greenwood in 1846, Illustrated in a Series of Views Taken Especially for This Work by James Smillie*. New York: R. Martin, 1847.

Clewell, Tammy. "A Mourning beyond Melancholia: Freud's Psychoanalysis of Loss." *Journal of the American Psychoanalytic Association* 52, no. 1 (2004): 43–67.

Cooper, James Fenimore. *The Last of the Mohicans: A Narrative of the Year 1757*. 1826; repr., New York: Penguin, 1986.

———. *The Pioneers*. 1823; repr., New York: Penguin, 1988.

Coviello, Peter. "The American in Charity: 'Benito Cereno' and Gothic Anti-Sentimentality." *Studies in American Fiction* (fall 2002): 155–80.

———. *Intimacy in America: Dreams of Affiliation in Antebellum Literature*. Minneapolis: University of Minnesota Press, 2005.

Cowan, Bainard. *Exiled Waters: Moby-Dick and the Crisis of Allegory*. Baton Rouge: Louisiana State University Press, 1982.

Cutler, Edward S. *Recovering The New: Transatlantic Roots of Modernism*. Hanover, NH: University Press of New England, 2003.

Dannenberg, Anne Marie. "'Where, Then, Shall We Place the Hero of the Wilderness?' William Apess' *Eulogy on King Philip* and the Doctrines of Racial Destiny." In Helen Jaskoski, ed., *Early Native American Writing: New Critical Essays*. New York: Cambridge University Press, 1996: 66–82.

Davis, Michael. *The Image of Lincoln in the South*. Knoxville: University of Tennessee Press, 1971.

Dean, Janet. "The Marriage Plot and National Myth in *The Pioneers*." *Arizona Quarterly* 52, no. 4 (1997): 1–29.

Delany, Samuel. *Times Square Red, Times Square Blue*. New York: NYU Press, 1999.

Deleuze, Gilles. *The Logic of Sense*. Trans. Constantine Boundas. New York: Columbia University Press, 1990.

Deloria, Philip J. *Playing Indian*. New Haven, CT: Yale University Press, 1998.

de Man, Paul. "The Rhetoric of Temporality." In *Blindness and Insight: Essays in the Rhetoric of Contemporary Criticism*. Minneapolis: University of Minnesota Press, 1983: 187–228.

Derrida, Jacques. *Of Grammatology*. Trans. Gayatri Chakravorty Spivak. Baltimore: Johns Hopkins University Press, 1976.

———. *Specters of Marx: The State of the Debt, the Work of Mourning and the New International*. Trans. Peggy Kamuf. New York: Routledge, 1994.

de Tocqueville, Alexis. *Democracy in America*. New York: Random House, 1990.

Dever, Carolyn. *Death and the Mother from Dickens to Freud: Victorian Fiction and the Anxiety of Origins*. Cambridge: Cambridge University Press, 1998.

Dewey, Orville. *On the Duties of Consolation, and the Rites and Customs Appropriate to Mourning*. New Bedford, MA: Book Tract Association, 1825.

Dicker/sun, Glenda. "Katrina: Acting Black/Playing Blackness." *Theatre Journal* 57, no. 4 (December 2005): 614–16.

di Leonardo, Micaela, ed. *Gender at the Crossroads of Knowledge: Feminist Anthropology in the Postmodern Era*. Berkeley: University of California Press, 1991.

Dillon, Elizabeth Maddock. *The Gender of Freedom: Fictions of Liberalism and the Literary Public Sphere*. Stanford, CA: Stanford University Press, 2004.

Dimock, Wai Chee. *Through Other Continents: American Literature across Deep Time*. Princeton, NJ: Princeton University Press, 2006.

Dinshaw, Carolyn. *Getting Medieval: Sexualities and Communities, Pre- and Post-Modern*. Durham, NC: Duke University Press, 1999.

Dohrn-van Rossum, Gerhard. *History of the Hour: Clocks and Modern Temporal Orders*. Trans. Thomas Dunlap. Chicago: University of Chicago Press, 1996.

Dolar, Mladen. "The Object-Voice." In Renate Saleci and Slavoj Zizek, eds., *Gaze and Voice as Love Objects*. Durham, NC: Duke University Press, 1996: 7–31.

Domina, Lynn. "I Was Re-elected President: Elizabeth Keckley as Quintessential Patriot." In Lynn Coleman, ed., *Women's Life Writing: Finding Voice/Building Community*. Bowling Green, OH: Bowling Green University Press, 1997.

Douglas, Ann. *The Feminization of American Culture*. New York: Anchor Books, 1988.

Douglass, Frederick. "The Freedmen's Monument to Abraham Lincoln: An Address Delivered in Washington, D.C. on April 14th, 1876," *The Frederick Douglass Papers, Series One: Speeches, Debates and Interviews, Vol. 4: 1864–80*. Ed. John W. Blassingame and John R. McKivigan. New Haven, CT: Yale University Press, 1991: 427–43.

———. "What to the Slave Is the Fourth of July? An Address Delivered in Rochester, New York, on 5 July 1852," in *The Frederick Douglass Papers, Series One: Speeches, Debates and Interviews, Vol. 2: 1847–54*. Ed. John Blassingame. New Haven, CT: Yale University Press, 1982: 359–88.

Downes, Paul. *Democracy, Revolution and Monarchism in Early American Literature*. New York: Cambridge University Press, 2002.

Dryden, Edgar. *Monumental Melville: The Formation of a Literary Career*. Stanford, CA: Stanford University Press, 2004.

Duggan, Lisa. *The Twilight of Equality: Neoliberalism, Cultural Politics and the Attack on Democracy*. Boston: Beacon, 2003.

Edelman, Lee. *No Future: Queer Theory and the Death Drive*. Durham, NC: Duke University Press, 2004.

Ellis, R. J. *Harriet Wilson's* Our Nig: *A Cultural Biography*. Amsterdam: Rodopi, 2003.

Ellison, Julie. *Cato's Tears and the Making of Anglo-American Emotion*. Chicago: University of Chicago Press, 1999.

Emerson, Ralph Waldo. "Experience." In *The Collected Works of Ralph Waldo Emerson, Vol. 3*. Cambridge, MA: Harvard University Press, 1983: 25–49.

———. *Representative Men*. Ed. Pamela Schirmeister. New York: Marsilio, 1995.

Eng, David. "The Value of Silence." *Theatre Journal* 54, no. 1 (2002): 85–94.

Eng, David, and David Kazanjian, eds. *Loss: The Psychic and Social Contexts of Melancholia*. Berkeley: University of California Press, 2003.

Everett, Charles Carroll. *A Sermon in Commemoration of the Death of Abraham Lincoln, Late President of the United States, Bangor ME, 1865*. Bangor, ME: Benjamin Burr, 1865.

Fabian, Johannes. *Time and the Other: How Anthropology Makes Its Object*. New York: Columbia University Press, 2002.

Farrell, James J. *Inventing the American Way of Death, 1830–1920*. Philadelphia: Temple University Press, 1980.

Fessenden, Tracy. "Gendering Religion." *Journal of Women's History* 14, no. 1 (spring 2002): 163–69.

Fetterley, Judith. " 'My Sister! My Sister!': The Rhetoric of Catharine Sedgwick's *Hope Leslie*." *American Literature* 70, no. 3 (September 1998): 491–516.

Fiedler, Leslie. *Love and Death in the American Novel*. New York: Criterion, 1960.

Field, David, Jenny Hockey, and Neil Small, eds. *Death, Gender and Ethnicity*. London: Routledge, 1997.

Fischer, Roger A. "The 'Monumental' Lincoln as an American Cartoon Convention." *Inks: Cartoon and Comic Art Studies* 2, no. 1 (February 1995): 12–25.

Fish, Stanley. "Progress in *The Pilgrim's Progress*." In *Self-Consuming Artifacts: The Experience of Seventeenth Century Literature*. Berkeley: University of California Press, 1972: 224–64.

Fisher, Philip. "Democratic Social Space: Whitman, Melville, and the Promise of American Transparency." *Representations* 24 (fall 1988): 60–101.

———. *The Vehement Passions*. Princeton, NJ: Princeton University Press, 2002.

Flavel, John. *A Token for Mourners*. Brattleboro, VT: William Fessenden, 1813.

Fleischner, Jennifer. *Mastering Slavery: Memory, Family and Identity in Women's Slave Narratives*. New York: NYU Press, 1996.

———. *Mrs. Lincoln and Mrs. Keckly: The True Story of the Remarkable Friendship between a First Lady and a Former Slave*. New York: Broadway Books, 2003.

Fliegelman, Jay. *Declaring Independence: Jefferson, Natural Language and the Culture of Performance*. Stanford, CA: Stanford University Press, 1993.

Foucault, Michel. *Discipline and Punish: The Birth of the Prison*. New York: Vintage, 1979.

———. *The History of Sexuality, Vol. 1: An Introduction*. Trans. Robert Hurley. New York: Vintage, 1990.

———. "Nietzsche, Genealogy, History." In *Language, Counter-Memory, Practice: Selected Essays and Interviews*. Ed. Donald F. Bouchard. Trans. Donald F. Bouchard and Sherry Simon. Ithaca, NY: Cornell University Press, 1977: 139–64.

Fowler, P. H. *The Voice of the Dead: A Sermon, on the Occasion of the Death of Mrs. Catherine Huntington Williams, Preached September 21, 1856*. Utica, NY: Curtiss and White, 1856.

Fraser, J. T., ed. *The Voices of Time: A Cooperative Survey of Man's Views of Time as Expressed by the Sciences and by the Humanities*. Amherst: University of Massachusetts Press, 1981.

Fraser, Nancy. "Rethinking the Public Sphere: A Contribution to the Critique of Actually Existing Democracy." In Craig Calhoun, ed., *Habermas and the Public Sphere*. Cambridge, MA: MIT Press, 1992.

Freeman, Elizabeth. "*Monsters, Inc.*: Notes on the Neoliberal Arts Education," *New Literary History* 36, no. 1 (2005): 83–95.

———. "Packing History, Count(er)ing Generations." *New Literary History* 31, no. 4 (autumn 2000): 727–44.

Freud, Ernst L., ed. *Letters of Sigmund Freud*. New York: Basic Books, 1960.

Freud, Sigmund, "Mourning and Melancholia." In *The Standard Edition of the Complete Psychoanalytic Works of Sigmund Freud*. Vol. 14. Trans. James Strachey. London: Hogarth, 1957.

———. "On Transience." In *Character and Culture*. Ed. Philip Rieff. New York: Macmillan, 1963: 148–51.

Gardner, Eric. " 'This Attempt of Their Sister': Harriet Wilson's *Our Nig* from Printer to Readers." *New England Quarterly* 66, no. 2 (June 1993): 226–46.

Gilmour, Robin. *The Victorian Period: The Intellectual and Cultural Context of English Literature, 1830–1930.* New York: Longman, 1994.

Gorer, Geoffrey. *Death, Grief and Mourning in Contemporary Britain.* London: Cresset, 1965.

Gould, Phillip. "Catharine Sedgwick's 'Recital' of the Pequot War." *American Literature* 66, no. 4 (December 1994): 641–62.

Gould, Stephen Jay. *Time's Arrow, Time's Cycle: Myth and Metaphor in the Discovery of Geological Time.* Cambridge, MA: Harvard University Press, 1987.

Greven, David. "Troubling Our Heads about Ichabod: 'The Legend of Sleepy Hollow,' Classic American Literature, and the Sexual Politics of Homosocial Brotherhood." *American Quarterly* 56, no. 1 (March 2004): 83–110.

Griswold, Rufus, ed. *The Cypress Wreath: A Book of Consolation for Those Who Mourn.* Boston: Gould, Kendall, and Lincoln, 1844.

Grosz, Elizabeth. *The Nick of Time: Politics, Evolution, and the Untimely.* Durham, NC: Duke University Press, 2004.

———. *Time Travels: Feminism, Nature, Power.* Durham, NC: Duke University Press, 2005.

Guthrie, James R. *Above Time: Emerson's and Thoreau's Temporal Revolutions.* Columbia: University of Missouri Press, 2001.

Halberstam, Judith. *In a Queer Time and Place: Transgender Bodies, Subcultural Lives.* Durham, NC: Duke University Press, 2005.

Halttunen, Karen. "Mourning the Dead: A Study in Sentimental Ritual." In *Confidence Men and Painted Women: A Study of Middle-Class Culture in America, 1830–1870.* New Haven, CT: Yale University Press, 1982.

Hardinge, Emma. *The Great Funeral Oration on Abraham Lincoln, Delivered Sunday, April 16, 1865 at Cooper Institute.* New York: American News Company, 1865.

Harper, Frances E. W. "The Slave Auction." In *A Brighter Coming Day: A Frances Ellen Watkins Harper Reader.* Ed. Frances Smith Foster. New York: Feminist Press, 1990: 64–65.

Harris, Neil. *The Artist in American Society: The Formative Years, 1790–1860.* New York: George Braziller, 1966.

Haven, Gilbert. *The Uniter and Liberator of America: A Memorial Discourse on the Character and Career of Abraham Lincoln.* Boston: James P. Magee, 1865.

Haynes, Carolyn A. *Divine Destiny: Gender and Race in Nineteenth-Century Protestantism.* Jackson: University of Mississippi Press, 1998.

Heckewelder, John. *History, Manners and Customs of the Indian Nations Who Once Inhabited Pennsylvania and the Neighbouring States.* 1819; repr., Philadelphia: Historical Society of Pennsylvania, 1876.

Hendler, Glenn. *Public Sentiments: Structures of Feeling in Nineteenth-Century American Literature.* Chapel Hill: University of North Carolina Press, 2001.

Herndon, William H., and Jesse W. Weik. *Herndon's Life of Lincoln*. Ed. Paul M. Angle. Cleveland: World Publishing Company, 1949.

Higonnet, Margaret R. "Comparative Reading: Catharine M. Sedgwick's *Hope Leslie*." *Legacy* 15, no. 1 (1998): 17–22.

Holland, Sharon. *Raising the Dead: Readings of Death and (Black) Subjectivity*. Durham, NC: Duke University Press, 2000.

Holzer, Harold. *Lincoln Seen and Heard*. Lawrence: University Press of Kansas, 2000.

Homans, Peter, ed. *Symbolic Loss: The Ambiguity of Mourning and Memory at Century's End*. Charlottesville: University Press of Virginia, 2000.

Hurt, James. "All the Living and the Dead: Lincoln's Imagery," *American Literature* 52, no. 3 (November 1980): 351–80.

Huyssen, Andreas. *Twilight Memories: Marking Time in a Culture of Amnesia*. New York: Routledge, 1995.

Insko, Jeffrey. "Anachronistic Imaginings: *Hope Leslie*'s Challenge to Historicism." *American Literary History* 16, no. 2 (2004): 179–207.

Irving, Washington. *The Sketch-Book of Geoffrey Crayon*. Reading, PA: Spencer, 1936.

Isenberg, Nancy, and Andrew Burstein, eds. *Mortal Remains: Death in Early America*. Philadelphia: University of Pennsylvania Press, 2002.

Jackson, Charles O., ed. *Passing: The Vision of Death in America*. Westport, CT: Greenwood, 1977.

Jackson, Stanley W. *Melancholia and Depression from Hippocratic Times to the Present*. New Haven, CT: Yale University Press, 1986.

Jackson, Virginia. *Dickinson's Misery: A Theory of Lyric Reading*. Princeton, NJ: Princeton University Press, 2005.

James, C. L. R. *Mariners, Renegades and Castaways: The Story of Herman Melville and the World We Live In*. New York: Author, 1953.

Jameson, Fredric. *The Political Unconscious*. Ithaca, NY: Cornell University Press, 1981.

Jefferson, Thomas. *Notes on the State of Virginia*. Chapel Hill: University of North Carolina Press, 1955.

Kalayjian, Patricia. "Cooper and Sedgwick: Rivalry or Respect?" *James Fenimore Cooper Society Miscellany* 4 (September 1993): 9–19.

Kalish, Richard A., ed. *Death and Dying: Views from Many Cultures*. Farmingdale, NY: Baywood, 1980.

Karcher, Carolyn. *The First Woman in the Republic: A Cultural Biography of Lydia Maria Child*. Durham, NC: Duke University Press, 1994.

Kavanagh, James H. " 'That Hive of Subtlety': 'Benito Cereno' as Critique of Ideology." *Bucknell Review* 29, no. 1 (1984): 127–57.

Keckley, Elizabeth. *Behind the Scenes: Thirty Years a Slave and Four Years in the White House*. Ed. Frances Smith Foster. Urbana: University of Illinois Press, 2001.

Kent, Kathryn R. *Making Girls into Women: American Women's Writing and the Rise of Lesbian Identity*. Durham, NC: Duke University Press, 2003.

Kerber, Linda. "Separate Spheres, Female Worlds, Women's Place: The Rhetoric of

Women's History." In *Toward an Intellectual History of Women*. Chapel Hill: University of North Carolina Press, 1997: 159–99.

Kete, Mary Louise. *Sentimental Collaborations: Mourning and Middle-Class Identity in Nineteenth-Century America*. Durham, NC: Duke University Press, 2000.

Kilcup, Karen L., ed. *Soft Canons: American Women Writers and Masculine Tradition*. Iowa City: University of Iowa Press, 1999.

Kirkland, Samuel. *Journals of Samuel Kirkland*. Ed. Walter Pilkington. Clinton, NY: Hamilton College, 1980.

Kolchin, Peter. *American Slavery 1619–1877*. New York: Hill and Wang, 1995.

Kosseleck, Rene. *Futures Past: On the Semantics of Historical Time*. Trans. Keith Tribe. New York: Columbia University Press, 2004.

Kristeva, Julia. *Black Sun: Depression and Melancholia*. New York: Columbia University Press, 1989.

———. *Time and Sense: Proust and the Experience of Literature*. Trans. R. Guberman. New York: Columbia University Press, 1996.

———. "Women's Time." In *The Kristeva Reader*. Ed. Toril Moi. New York: Columbia University Press, 1986: 187–213.

Krumrey, Diane. " 'Your Ear Shall Drink No Lie': Articulating the American Voice in *The Last of the Mohicans*," *Language and Literature* 22 (1997): 45–61.

Laderman, Gary. *The Sacred Remains: American Attitudes toward Death*. New Haven, CT: Yale University Press, 1996.

Landes, David. *Revolution in Time: Clocks and the Making of the Modern World*. New York: Belknap, 1983.

Landon, Letitia Elizabeth. *Poems from the Literary Gazette*. Ed. F. J. Snyder. Ann Arbor, MI: Scholar's Facsimiles and Reprints, 2003.

Lanser, Susan Sniader. *Fictions of Authority: Women Writers and Narrative Voice*. Ithaca, NY: Cornell University Press, 1992.

Lee, Maurice S. "Melville's Subversive Political Philosophy: 'Benito Cereno' and the Fate of Speech." *American Literature* 72, no. 3 (2000): 495–519.

Lerner, Laurence. *Angels and Absences: Child Deaths in the Nineteenth Century*. Nashville, TN: Vanderbilt University Press, 1997.

Leveen, Lois. "Dwelling in the House of Oppression: The Spatial, Racial and Textual Dynamics of Harriet Wilson's *Our Nig*," *African American Review* 35, no. 4 (2001): 561–80.

Levine, Lawrence W. *Black Culture and Black Consciousness: Afro-American Folk Thought from Slavery to Freedom*. Oxford: Oxford University Press, 1977.

Lincoln, Abraham. "Address at Gettysburg, November 19, 1863." In *Abraham Lincoln: Speeches and Writings, Vol. 2, 1859–65*. New York: Library of America, 1989: 536.

———. "Second Inaugural Address, March 4, 1865." In *Abraham Lincoln: Speeches and Writings, Vol. 2, 1859–65*. New York: Library of America, 1989: 686–87.

Looby, Christopher. *Voicing America: Language, Literary Form, and the Origins of the United States*. Chicago: University of Chicago Press, 1996.

Mack, Arien, ed. *Death in American Experience*. New York: Schocken Books, 1973.

Maddox, Lucy. *Removals: Nineteenth-Century American Literature and the Politics of Indian Affairs*. New York: Oxford University Press, 1991.

Madison, Robert D. "Wish-ton-Wish: Muck or Melancholy?" *James Fenimore Cooper Society Miscellaneous Papers* 4 (September 1993): 1–29.

Martin, J. Sella. "Letter to the Editor of the *New York Evening Post*, 24 April 1865." In C. Peter Ripley, ed., *The Black Abolitionist Papers, Vol. 5: The United States, 1859–65*. Chapel Hill: University of North Carolina Press, 1992: 317–20.

McClintock, Anne. *Imperial Leather: Race, Gender and Sexuality in the Colonial Contest*. New York: Routledge, 1995.

McGlothlin, Erin. "No Time Like the Present: Narrative and Time in Art Spiegelman's *Maus*." *Narrative* 11, no. 2 (May 2003): 177–98.

McGuire, Barbara. "The Orphan's Grief: Transformational Tears and the Maternal Fetish in Mary Jane Holmes's *Dora Deane; or, The East-India Uncle*." *Legacy: A Journal of American Women Writers* 15, no. 2 (1998): 171–87.

McHugh, Kathleen. *American Domesticity from How-To Manual to Hollywood Melodrama*. New York: Oxford University Press, 1999.

Meltzer, Mitchell. *Secular Revelations: The Constitution of the United States and Classic American Literature*. Cambridge, MA: Harvard University Press, 2005.

Merish, Lori. *Sentimental Materialism: Gender, Commodity Culture, and Nineteenth-Century American Literature*. Durham, NC: Duke University Press, 2000.

Monette, Paul. *Last Watch of the Night: Essays Too Personal and Otherwise*. New York: Harcourt Brace Jovanovich, 1994.

Moon, Michael. "Memorial Rags." In George E. Haggerty and Bonnie Zimmerman, eds., *Professions of Desire: Lesbian and Gay Studies in Literature*. New York: Modern Language Association, 1995: 233–40.

Morris, Charles E., III. "My Old Kentucky Homo: Lincoln and the Politics of Queer Public Memory." In Kendall R. Phillips, ed., *Framing Public Memory*. Tuscaloosa: University of Alabama Press, 2004: 89–114.

Morris, Richard. *Sinners, Lovers and Heroes: An Essay on Memorializing in Three American Cultures*. Albany: State University of New York Press, 1997.

The Mourner's Book. Boston: Benjamin B. Mussey, 1850.

Mumford, Lewis. *The Culture of Cities*. New York: Harcourt and Brace, 1938.

———. *Herman Melville*. New York: Harcourt and Brace, 1929.

Muñoz, José Esteban. *Disidentifications: Queers of Color and the Performance of Politics*. Minneapolis: University of Minnesota Press, 1999.

Murphy, Patricia. *Time Is of the Essence: Temporality, Gender, and the New Woman*. Albany: State University of New York Press, 2001.

The Nation Weeping for Its Dead: Observances at Springfield, Massachusetts, on President Lincoln's Funeral Day, Wednesday, April 19, 1865, Including Dr. Holland's Eulogy; From the Springfield Republican's Report. Springfield, MA: Samuel Bowles; L. J. Powers, 1865.

Nealon, Christopher. *Foundlings: Gay and Lesbian Historical Emotion before Stonewall*. Durham, NC: Duke University Press, 2001.

Nelson, Dana. *The Word in Black and White: Reading "Race" in American Literature, 1638–1867*. New York: Oxford University Press, 1993.

Nietzsche, Friedrich. *On the Advantage and Disadvantage of History for Life*. Trans. Peter Prauss. Indianapolis: Hackett, 1980.

Noble, Marianne. *The Masochistic Pleasures of Sentimental Literature*. Princeton, NJ: Princeton University Press, 2000.

Noll, Mark. *America's God: From Jonathan Edwards to Abraham Lincoln*. New York: Oxford University Press, 2002.

O'Connell, Catherine. " 'We Must Sorrow': Silence, Suffering and Sentimentality in Susan Warner's *The Wide, Wide World*." *Studies in American Fiction* 25, no. 1 (spring 997): 21–39.

O'Malley, Michael. *Keeping Watch: A History of American Time*. New York: Viking, 1990.

Ong, Walter J. *The Presence of the Word: Some Prolegomena for Cultural and Religious History*. New Haven, CT: Yale University Press, 1967.

Osborne, Peter. *The Politics of Time: Modernity and Avant-Garde*. London: Verso, 1995.

Oster, Akos. *Vessels of Time: An Essay on Temporal Change and Social Transformation*. Delhi: Oxford University Press, 1993.

Our Martyr President, Abraham Lincoln: Voices from the Pulpit of New York and Brooklyn. New York: Tibbals and Whiting, 1865.

Parker, Hershel. *Herman Melville: A Biography, Vol. 2, 1851–1891*. Baltimore: Johns Hopkins University Press, 2002.

Patrick, Mary A., ed. *The Mourner's Gift*. New York: Van Nostrand and Dwight, 1837.

Pensky, Max. *Melancholy Dialectics: Walter Benjamin and the Play of Mourning*. Amherst: University of Massachusetts Press, 1993.

Pfister, Joel, and Nancy Schnog, eds. *Inventing the Psychological: Toward a Cultural History of Emotional Life in America*. New Haven, CT: Yale University Press, 1997.

Philbrick, Thomas. "*The Last of the Mohicans* and the Sounds of Discord." *American Literature* 43, no. 1 (March 1971): 25–41.

Phillips, Adam. *Terrors and Experts*. Cambridge, MA: Harvard University Press, 1997.

Pike, Martha V., and Janice Gray Armstrong, eds. *A Time to Mourn: Expressions of Grief in Nineteenth Century America*. Stony Brook, NY: Museums at Stony Brook, 1980.

Prime, S. Iranaeus, William B. Sprague, George W. Bethune, J. B. Waterbury, and Clement M. Butler. *The Smitten Household; or, Thoughts for the Afflicted*. New York: Anson D. F. Randolph, 1856.

Raboteau, Albert J. *Slave Religion: The "Invisible Institution" in the Antebellum South*. New York: Oxford University Press, 1978.

Ramazani, Jahan. *Poetry of Mourning: The Modern Elegy from Hardy to Heaney*. Chicago: University of Chicago Press, 1994.

Rath, Richard Cullen. *How Early America Sounded*. Ithaca, NY: Cornell University Press, 2003.

Redfield, Marc. "Imagi-Nation: The Imagined Community and the Aesthetics of Mourning." *Diacritics* 29, no. 4 (winter 1999): 58–83.

Reid-Pharr, Robert. *Conjugal Union: The Body, the House and the Black American*. New York: Oxford University Press, 1999.

Riegl, Alois. "The Modern Cult of Monuments: Its Character and Its Origin." Trans. Kurt W. Foster and Diane Ghirardo. In K. Michael Hays, ed., *The Oppositions Reader*. New York: Princeton Architectural Press, 1998: 621–51.

Roach, Joseph. *Cities of the Dead: Circum-Atlantic Performance*. New York: Columbia University Press, 1996.

Rogin, Michael Paul. *Subversive Genealogy: The Politics and Art of Herman Melville*. Berkeley: University of California Press, 1979.

Romero, Lora. *Home Fronts: Domesticity and Its Critics in the Antebellum United States*. Durham, NC: Duke University Press, 1997.

Rosenwald, Lawrence. "*The Last of the Mohicans* and the Languages of America." *College English* 60, no. 1 (January 1998): 9–30.

Rousseau, Jean-Jacques. "Essay on the Origin of Language." In Jean-Jacques Rousseau and Johann Gottfried Herder, *On the Origin of Language*. Trans. John H. Moran and Alexander Gode. New York: Frederick Ungar, 1966.

Ryan, Mary. *Empire of the Mother: American Writing about Domesticity 1830–1860*. New York: Harrington Park, 1985.

———. *Private Woman, Public Stage: Literary Domesticity in Nineteenth-Century America*. New York: Oxford University Press, 1984.

Sacks, Peter. *The English Elegy: Studies in the Genre from Spenser to Yeats*. Baltimore: Johns Hopkins University Press, 1985.

Samuels, Shirley. *Facing America: Iconography and the Civil War*. New York: Oxford University Press, 2004.

———. *Romances of the Republic: Women, the Family, and Violence in the Literature of the Early American Nation*. New York: Oxford University Press, 1996.

Samuels, Shirley, ed. *The Culture of Sentiment: Race, Gender and Sentimentality in Nineteenth-Century America*. New York: Oxford University Press, 1992.

Sanborn, Geoffrey. *The Sign of the Cannibal: Melville and the Making of a Post-Colonial Reader*. Durham, NC: Duke University Press, 1998.

Sánchez-Eppler, Karen. *Dependent States: The Child's Part in Nineteenth-Century American Culture*. Chicago: University of Chicago Press, 2005.

Santamarina, Xiomara. *Belabored Professions: Narratives of African American Working Womanhood*. Chapel Hill: University of North Carolina Press, 2006.

Santner, Eric. *Stranded Objects: Mourning, Memory and Film in Postwar Germany*. Ithaca, NY: Cornell University Press, 1990.

Sarat, Austin, ed. *Dissent in Dangerous Times*. Ann Arbor: University of Michigan Press, 2005.

Savage, Kirk. *Standing Soldiers, Kneeling Slaves: Race, War, and Monument in Nineteenth-Century America*. Princeton, NJ: Princeton University Press, 1997.

Scales, Jacob. *Weeping: A Funeral Sermon Delivered at Henniker, New Hampshire, November 30, 1828, the Sabbath Following the Death of Mrs. Abel Connar*. Concord, NH: George Hough, 1829.

Schiesari, Juliana. *The Gendering of Melancholia: Feminism, Psychoanalysis and the Symbolics of Loss in Renaissance Literature*. Ithaca, NY: Cornell University Press, 1992.

Schirmeister, Pamela. *Less Legible Meanings: Between Poetry and Philosophy in the Work of Emerson*. Stanford, CA: Stanford University Press, 1999.

Schoolcraft, Henry Rowe. *Algic Researches, Comprising Inquiries Respecting the Mental Characteristics of the North American Indians*. New York: Harper and Brothers, 1839.

———. *Western Scenes and Reminisces: Together with Thrilling Legends and Traditions of the Red Men of the Forest*. Buffalo, NY: Derby, Orton & Mulligan, 1853.

Schor, Esther. *Bearing the Dead: The British Culture of Mourning from the Enlightenment to Victoria*. Princeton, NJ: Princeton University Press, 1995.

Schwartz, Barry. *Abraham Lincoln and the Forge of National Memory*. Chicago: University of Chicago Press, 2000.

Sedgwick, Catharine Maria. *Hope Leslie; or, Early Times in the Massachusetts*. Ed. Mary Kelley. New Brunswick, NJ: Rutgers University Press, 1993.

Sedgwick, Eve Kosofsky. *Touching Feeling: Affect, Pedagogy, Performativity*. Durham, NC: Duke University Press, 2003.

Seidman, Steven. "Identity and Politics in a 'Postmodern' Gay Culture: Some Historical and Conceptual Notes." In Michael Warner, ed., *Fear of a Queer Planet*. Minneapolis: University of Minnesota Press, 1993.

Sellers, Charles. *The Market Revolution: Jacksonian America, 1815–1846*. New York: Oxford University Press, 1991.

Sermons Preached in Boston on the Death of Abraham Lincoln. Boston: J. E. Tilton, 1865.

Shamir, Milette, and Jennifer Travis, eds. *Boys Don't Cry? Rethinking Narratives of Masculinity and Emotion in the U.S.* New York: Columbia University Press, 2002.

Shenk, Joshua. *Lincoln's Melancholy: How Depression Challenged a President and Fueled His Greatness*. Boston: Houghton Mifflin, 2005.

Sherman, Stuart. *Telling Time: Clocks, Diaries and English Diurnal Form, 1660–1785*. Chicago: University of Chicago Press, 1996.

Sigourney, Lydia H. *Letters to Mothers*. Hartford, CT: Hudson and Skinner, 1838.

Silverman, Kaja. *The Acoustic Mirror: The Female Voice in Psychoanalysis and Cinema*. Bloomington: Indiana University Press, 1988.

Simpson, David. *9/11: The Culture of Commemoration*. Chicago: University of Chicago Press, 2006.

Sloan, David Charles. *The Last Great Necessity: Cemeteries in American History*. Baltimore: Johns Hopkins University Press, 1991.

Smith, Bruce R. *The Acoustic World of Early Modern England*. Chicago: University of Chicago Press, 1999.

Smith, Mark M. *Listening to Nineteenth-Century America*. Chapel Hill: University of North Carolina Press, 2001.

———. *Mastered by the Clock: Time, Slavery and Freedom in the American South*. Chapel Hill: University of North Carolina Press, 1997.

Sommer, Doris. "Allegory and Dialectics: A Match Made in Romance." *Boundary 2* 18, no. 1 (spring 1991): 60–82.

Sorisio, Carolyn. "Unmasking the Genteel Performer: Elizabeth Keckley's *Behind the Scenes* and the Politics of Public Wrath." *African American Review* 34 (spring 2000): 19–38.

Spiegelman, Art. *In the Shadow of No Towers*. New York: Pantheon, 2004.

Spillers, Hortense J. *Black, White and in Color: Essays on American Literature and Culture*. Chicago: University of Chicago Press, 2003.

Stadler, Gustavus. "Magawisca's Body of Knowledge: Nation Building in *Hope Leslie*." *Yale Journal of Criticism* 12 (1999): 41–56.

Stanley, Amy Dru. "Home Life and the Morality of the Market." In Melvyn Stokes and Steven Conway, eds., *The Market Revolution in America: Social, Political and Religious Expressions, 1800–1880*. Charlottesville: University Press of Virginia, 1996: 74–96.

Stannard, David E. *The Puritan Way of Death: A Study in Religion, Culture, and Social Change*. New York: Oxford University Press, 1977.

Stearns, Peter N., and Jan Lewis, eds. *An Emotional History of the Unites States*. New York: NYU Press, 1998.

Stern, Julia. "Excavating Genre in *Our Nig*." *American Literature* 67, no. 3 (fall 1995): 439–66.

———. *The Plight of Feeling: Sympathy and Dissent in the Early American Novel*. Chicago: University of Chicago Press, 1997.

Sterne, Jonathan. *The Audible Past: Cultural Origins of Sound Reproduction*. Durham, NC: Duke University Press, 2003.

Stewart, Veronica. "Mothering a Female Saint: Susan Warner's Dialogic Role in *The Wide, Wide World*." *Essays in Literature* 22, no. 1 (spring 1995): 59–74.

Stockton, Kathryn Bond, "Eve's Queer Child." In Stephen M. Barber and David L. Clark, eds., *Regarding Sedgwick: Essays on Queer Culture and Critical Theory*. New York: Routledge, 2002: 181–200.

Stoler, Ann Laura. *Carnal Knowledge and Imperial Power: Race and the Intimate in Colonial Rule*. Berkeley: University of California Press, 2002.

———. *Race and the Education of Desire: Foucault's History of Sexuality and the Colonial Order of Things*. Durham, NC: Duke University Press, 1995.

Stowe, Harriet Beecher. *Uncle Tom's Cabin*. 1852; repr., New York: Penguin, 1981.

Sturcken, Marita. *Tangled Memories: The Vietnam War, the AIDS Epidemic, and the Politics of Remembering*. Berkeley: University of California Press, 1997.

Syme, J. B., ed. *The Mourner's Friend; or, Sighs of Sympathy for Those Who Sorrow*. Worcester, MA: William Allen, 1852.

Tate, Claudia. *Domestic Allegories of Political Desire: The Black Heroine's Text at the Turn of the Century*. New York: Oxford University Press, 1992.

Taylor, Charles. *Modern Social Imaginaries*. Durham, NC: Duke University Press, 2004.

Thayer, Thomas Baldwin. *Over the River; or, Pleasant Walks into the Valley of Shadows and Beyond: A Book of Consolations for the Sick, the Dying, and the Bereaved*. Boston: Tompkins, 1864.

Thompson, E. P. "Time, Work-Discipline and Industrial Capitalism." In *Customs in Common*. New York: New Press, 1991: 352–403.

Tompkins, Jane. *Sensational Designs: The Cultural Work of American Fiction, 1790–1860*. New York: Oxford University Press, 1985.

A Tribute of Respect by the Citizens of Troy to the Memory of Abraham Lincoln. Troy, NY: Young and Benson, 1865.

Turner, Thomas Reed. *Beware the People Weeping: Public Opinion and the Assassination of President Lincoln*. Baton Rouge: Louisiana State University Press, 1982.

Twain, Mark. "Fenimore Cooper's Literary Offenses." In *Literary Essays*. New York: P. F. Collier and Son, 1918: 60–77.

Vernon, Glenn M. *Sociology of Death: An Analysis of Death-Related Behavior*. New York: Ronald Press Company, 1970.

"A Village Pastor" [pseud.]. *The Comforter; or, Extracts Selected for the Consolation of Mourners, under the Bereavement of Friends and Relations*. New York: J & J Harper, 1832.

Vogler, Candace. "Much of Madness and More of Sin: Compassion, for Ligeia." In Lauren Berlant, ed., *Compassion: The Culture and Politics of an Emotion*. New York: Routledge, 2004.

Wald, Priscilla. *Constituting Americans: Cultural Anxiety and Narrative Form*. Durham, NC: Duke University Press, 1995.

Walker, Cheryl. *Indian Nation: Native American Literature and Nineteenth-Century Nationalisms*. Durham, NC: Duke University Press, 1997.

Warner, Michael. "Irving's Posterity." *ELH* 67, no. 3 (fall 2000): 773–99.

———. *The Letters of the Republic: Publication and the Public Sphere in Eighteenth-Century America*. Cambridge, MA: Harvard University Press, 1990.

———. "The Public Sphere and the Cultural Mediation of Print." In William S. Solomon and Robert W. McChesney, eds., *Ruthless Criticism: New Perspectives in U.S. Communication History*. Minneapolis: University of Minnesota Press, 1993: 7–37.

Warner, Michael, and Lauren Berlant, "What Does Queer Theory Teach Us about X?" *PMLA* 110, no. 3 (fall 1995): 343–49.

Warner, Susan. *The Wide, Wide World*. Ed. Jane Tompkins. New York: Feminist Press, 1987.

Waters, Lindsay. "Life against Death." *Boundary 2* 29, no. 1 (2002): 272–88.

Weber, Max. *The Protestant Ethic and the "Spirit" of Capitalism and Other Writings*. Trans. Peter Baehr and Gordon C. Wells. New York: Penguin, 2002.

Webster, Daniel. *Daniel Webster's First Bunker Hill Oration, Together with Other Addresses Relating to the Revolution*. Ed. Fred Newton Scott. New York: Longmans, Green, 1895.

Weiner, Susan. " 'Benito Cereno' and the Failure of Law." *American Quarterly* 47, no. 2 (1991): 1–28.

Weinstein, Cindy. *Family, Kinship and Sympathy in Nineteenth-Century American Literature*. Cambridge: Cambridge University Press, 2004.

White, Barbara A. "*Our Nig* and the She-Devil: New Information about Harriet Wilson and the 'Bellmont' Family." *American Literature* 65, no. 1 (March 1993): 19–52.

Whitman, Walt. *Memoranda during the War and Death of President Lincoln*. Ed. Roy P. Basler. Westport, CT: Greenwood, 1972.

Wiedmer, Caroline Alice. *The Claims of Memory: Representations of the Holocaust in Contemporary Germany and France*. Ithaca, NY: Cornell University Press, 1999.

Williams, Mrs. H. Dwight. *Voices from the Silent Land; or, Leaves of Consolation for the Afflicted*. Boston: John P. Jewett, 1853.

Williams, Raymond. *Keywords: A Vocabulary of Culture and Society*. New York: Oxford University Press, 1976.

Williams, Roger. *A Key into the Language of America; or, An Help to the Language of the Natives in that Part of America, Called New-England*. 1643; repr., New York: Russell and Russell, 1973.

Williams, Susan S. "Widening the World: Susan Warner, Her Readers, and the Assumption of Authorship." *American Quarterly* 42, no. 4 (December 1990): 565–86.

Wills, Garry. *Lincoln at Gettysburg: The Words That Remade America*. New York: Simon and Schuster, 1992.

Wilson, Harriet. *Our Nig; or, Sketches from the Life of a Free Black*. 3rd ed. Ed. Henry Louis Gates Jr. New York: Vintage, 2002.

———. *Our Nig; or, Sketches from the Life of a Free Black*. Ed. P. Gabrielle Forman and Reginald Pitts. New York: Penguin, 2005.

Woodward, Kathleen. "Freud and Barthes: Theorizing Mourning, Sustaining Grief." *Discourse: Berkeley Journal for Theoretical Studies in Media and Culture* 13, no. 1 (1990): 93–110.

Young, Elizabeth. *Disarming the Nation: Women's Writing and the American Civil War*. Chicago: University of Chicago Press, 1999.

Young, James E. *The Texture of Memory: Holocaust Memorials and Meaning*. New Haven, CT: Yale University Press, 1993.

———. *At Memory's Edge: After-Images of the Holocaust in Contemporary Art and Architecture*. New Haven, CT: Yale University Press, 2000.

Young, James E., ed. *The Art of Memory: Holocaust Memorials in History*. New York: Jewish Museum with Prestel-Verlag, 1994.

Zafar, Rafia. *We Wear the Mask: African Americans Write American Literature, 1760–1870*. New York: Columbia University Press, 1997.

Zerubavel, Eviatar. *Time Maps: Collective Memory and the Social Shape of the Past*. Chicago: University of Chicago Press, 2003.

Index

ABOUT THE AUTHOR

Dana Luciano is an assistant professor teaching sexuality and gender studies and nineteenth-century American literature in the English department at Georgetown University. She received her Ph.D. from Cornell University in 1999. She has taught previously at Hamilton College and held a Tanner Humanities Center Fellowship at the University of Utah in 2003–2004.